Fighting for Rights

A volume in the series

Cornell Studies in Security Affairs

edited by Robert J. Art
Robert Jervis
Stephen M. Walt

A list of titles in this series is available at www.cornellpress.cornell.edu

Fighting for Rights

Military Service and the Politics of Citizenship

Ronald R. Krebs

Cornell University Press
Ithaca and London

First published 2006 by Cornell University Press

Printed in the United States of America

Library of Congress Cataloging-in-Publication Data

Krebs, Ronald R., 1974–
  Fighting for rights : military service and the politics of citizenship / Ronald R. Krebs.
      p. cm. — (Cornell studies in security affairs)
  Includes bibliographical references and index.
  ISBN-13: 978-0-8014-4465-4 (cloth : alk. paper)
  ISBN-10: 0-8014-4465-9 (cloth : alk. paper)
    1. United States—Armed Forces—Minorities. 2. Israel. Tseva haganah le-Yiśra'el—Minorities. 3. Sociology, Military—United States. 4. Sociology, Military—Israel. 5. Civil-military relations—United States. 6. Civil-military relations—Israel. 7. Citizenship—United States. 8. Citizenship—Israel. I. Title. II. Series.
UB417.K74   2006
306.2'70973—dc22   2006006525

Cornell University Press strives to use environmentally responsible suppliers and materials to the fullest extent possible in the publishing of its books. Such materials include vegetable-based, low-VOC inks and acid-free papers that are recycled, totally chlorine-free, or partly composed of nonwood fibers. For further information, visit our website at www.cornellpress.cornell.edu.

Cloth printing   10 9 8 7 6 5 4 3 2 1

For Shira

רעייתי יפתי

Contents

Acknowledgments

This book is about militaries and about minorities, but ultimately it is about communities. Political communities often establish high barriers to entry, to nurture the mutual trust that sustains exchange and to ensure that membership remains valuable and desirable. Intellectual communities, however, require a different mix. They thrive only when the barriers to entry are low and when diffuse reciprocity is widely practiced—that is, when a broad spectrum of people hawk their wares in the marketplace and when generosity is extended without certainty that the favor will be returned. Given this peculiar combination, it is a wonder that intellectual communities exist at all. Yet thankfully, somehow, they do. Scholarly research is often solitary, but it would be impossible without community.

Healthy communities require good citizens. During this project I have been fortunate to have encountered many of them. The end product is far better as a consequence, and I have accumulated many a debt that cannot possibly be repaid. I met my first model of good citizenship early on in my academic career, at Princeton University. A man who could never say no, Dick Ullman soon became my mentor and eventually a friend, and his copious comments on drafts of my senior thesis set the standard to which I aspire as a teacher myself. Dick paved the way for me to obtain a one-year position as an assistant editor at *Foreign Affairs*, and there I met Fareed Zakaria, who (wisely?) advised me to abandon law school and give graduate study in political science a try.

At Columbia University, I was blessed with advisers who cared about me and my research. Bob Jervis and Jack Snyder's catholic approach to the discipline, combined with their habitual constructive skepticism, gave me just enough rope to hang myself. In the years since the dissertation, I have been grateful for their continued mentorship. Ira Katznelson always drew me back to the big picture, asking probing questions I would have avoided if left to my own devices. For whatever contribution this book makes, all three deserve much credit.

Numerous individuals read portions of this book in its various incarnations and sought, at times unsuccessfully, to save me from the error of my ways. For their (usually) gentle criticism and (always) useful comments, I am grateful to Deborah Avant, Michael Barnett, Gabi Ben Dor, Dick Betts, Henry Bienen, Bill Boettcher, Bill Childs, Consuelo Cruz, Mike Desch, Alex Downes, Amitabh Dubey, Amitai Etzioni, Sam Fitch, Eric Foner, Hillel Frisch, Hein Goemans, Arman Grigorian, Jim Guyot, Chris Howard, Jacques Hymans, Bob Jervis, Ben Judkins, Aaron Lobel, Ira Katznelson, Beth Kier, Phil Klinkner, Margot Krebs, Shira Krebs, Mark Leff, Jack Levy, Kim Marten, Joel Migdal, Dan Nexon, David Pion-Berlin, Steve Rosen, Robert Saxe, Shy Shankar, Allan Silver, Jack Snyder, Chuck Tilly, Monica Duffy Toft, Leslie Vinjamuri, Ken Waltz, and Naomi Weinberger. Particular thanks are due to Patrick Jackson with whom, in the course of writing a coauthored article, I rethought many of this book's theoretical claims; to Jim Burk and Steve Walt, who carefully reviewed the manuscript for Cornell University Press and made extraordinarily helpful suggestions; and especially to Dave Edelstein and Stacie Goddard, who went far above and beyond the call of duty in reading the entire manuscript and helping me shape it in the final excruciating stages. For any flaws that remain, I have only myself to blame.

In recent years, I have enjoyed the collegiality of the University of Minnesota's Department of Political Science. I have been surrounded by models of good citizenship, and many colleagues—too many to enumerate—have given me valuable advice on this project.

Fellowships from Harvard's John M. Olin Institute for Strategic Studies, the University of Virginia's Miller Center of Public Affairs, the United States Institute of Peace, and the Eisenhower World Affairs Institute freed me from teaching and allowed me to write. Funding from the Institute for the Study of World Politics, the Dwight D. Eisenhower Presidential Library, and Columbia's Institute for War and Peace Studies made possible extended research trips to archives in Israel and the United States. The Olin Institute, Columbia's Institute for Social and Economic Research and Policy, and Harvard's Belfer Center for Science and International Affairs provided me with office space and, more important, a nurturing intellectual environment. Thanks are also due to the many archivists in Israel and the United States who aided my research and to the many current and former government officials in Israel who consented to be interviewed on and off the record.

The final stages of this project were made far more pleasant by the staff at Cornell University Press. Roger Haydon was throughout immensely honest but also encouraging, and the book's more spare published form is a consequence of his well-considered interventions. Karen Laun expertly shepherded the book through the process of publication, and Katy Meigs caught many mistakes and skillfully pared my prose still further. Thanks as well to Barbara Stroup for compiling the index.

Part of chapter 1 appeared, in expanded form, as "A School for the Nation? How Military Service Does Not Build Nations, and How It Might," in *International Security* 28, no. 4 (Spring 2004): 85–124. Small portions of the empirical material presented in chapters 5 and 7 appeared in "One Nation under Arms? Military Participation Policy and the Politics of Identity," *Security Studies* 14, no. 3 (Spring 2005): 529–64. Thanks to the publishers for granting permission to use the material here.

Finally, some more personal words. I entered Columbia with Amitabh Dubey and Stacie Goddard; without them I could not have survived the stresses of graduate school. During my years at Harvard, I was fortunate to have office mates who became valued friends and advisers: Leslie Vinjamuri, Dave Edelstein, and Aaron Lobel. My parents, Margot and Leon Krebs, have always inspired and supported me, even when their innocent questions about the progress of my research prompted brusque replies.

My daughter Yonit became a wonderful, if distracting, addition to my life just as I was completing my doctorate, and her younger sister Dahlia arrived not long before I sent the manuscript of this book off for review. Both are partly at fault for delaying the book's completion, but they have also helped make the process tolerable.

This book is dedicated to my wife Shira. Living with me is trying enough. Living with me while I suffer research-induced mood swings is more than most could bear. More often than not, Shira endured those difficult moments with a smile, and she has, even while pursuing her own demanding career, facilitated mine. Equally important, she knew just when I needed a kick in the pants. Thank you.

Archival Sources and Abbreviations

Israel
Abba Ḥushi Archive (University of Ḥaifa, Ḥaifa)   **(AHA)**
Committee of the Directors-General Files (Papers of Salman Falaḥ,
   Ministry of Education, Jerusalem)   **(CDG)**
Druze Archive (University of Ḥaifa, Ḥaifa)   **(DA)**
Israel Defence Forces Archive (Giv'atayim)   **(IDFA)**
Sarah and Ya'akov Eshel Peace Library, Giv'at Ḥaviva Institute   **(GH)**
State Archive (Jerusalem)   **(SA)**
   • Foreign Ministry Files   **(FM)**
   • Interior Ministry Files   **(IM)**
   • Office of the Prime Minister Files   **(PM)**

United States
Harry S. Truman Presidential Library (Independence, Mo.)   **(HSTL)**
   • Papers of Harry S. Truman, Presidential Papers   **(Truman Papers)**
      —White House Central Files   **(WHCF)**
         Official File   **(OF)**
         President's Personal File   **(PPF)**
      —President's Secretary's File   **(PSF)**
      —Staff Member and Office Files   **(SMOF)**
         Clark M. Clifford Files   **(Clifford Files)**
         George M. Elsey Files   **(Elsey Files)**
         Philleo Nash Files   **(Nash Files)**
   • Clark M. Clifford Papers   **(Clifford Papers)**
   • George M. Elsey Papers   **(Elsey Papers)**
   • Charles S. Fahy Papers   **(Fahy Papers)**
   • J. Howard McGrath Papers   **(McGrath Papers)**

- Philleo Nash Papers **(Nash Papers)**
- David K. Niles Papers **(Niles Papers)**
- Stephen J. Spingarn Papers **(Spingarn Papers)**

Records of the President's Committee on Equality of Treatment
and Opportunity in the Armed Services, Record Group 220–Records
of Temporary Committees, Commissions, and Boards **(Fahy Committee Records RG 220)**

Dwight D. Eisenhower Library (Abilene, Kan.) **(DDEL)**
    Papers of Dwight D. Eisenhower as President **(Eisenhower Papers)**
    See also HSTL designations

Papers of the Congress of Racial Equality, 1941–1967 (microfilm ed.)
    (CORE Papers)
Papers of the NAACP (microfilm ed.) **(NAACP Papers)**
Papers of the President's Committee on Civil Rights (microfilm ed.)
    (PCCR Papers)
Morris J. MacGregor and Bernard C. Nalty, eds., *Blacks in the United
States Armed Forces: Basic Documents* (Wilmington, Del.): Scholarly
Resources, 1977), 13 vol. **(*BUSAF*)**

CHAPTER 1

A School for the Nation?

An ideological world and over half a century apart, Theodore Roosevelt and Leonid Brezhnev had little in common, but both proclaimed the social virtues of military service. Roosevelt and his fellow Progressives hoped that military training would "Americanize" the mass of newcomers who had recently landed on their country's shores.[1] Brezhnev similarly believed that service in the Red Army would forge a unified Soviet citizenry committed to the Socialist Motherland, internationalism, and "the friendship of the peoples."[2] Like many leaders before and after them, they turned to the armed forces to create a cohesive national identity and more broadly to mold a political community.

Implicit was a belief, whose roots stretch back to ancient Greece, that the military was a key institution for the labeling and transmission of social values.[3] Thus Machiavelli sought to banish foreign mercenaries, believing that regular military training would rekindle the virtues of republican Rome in his degenerate contemporaries.[4] Max Weber too saw in military discipline a means of transforming ordinary citizens into members of a heroic society.[5] Particularly in Europe in the latter half of the nineteenth century, leaders hailed the military as a "school for the nation" that would transform multiethnic chaos into a cohesive national order. This European faith in the armed forces found adherents among nation-building elites the world over: from czarist Russia to Meiji Japan and even to Brazil, statesmen embraced universal conscription both to bolster their country's military power and to inculcate national values.[6]

If decision makers in the twentieth century suspected that the military would not be able to live up to this billing, they gave few indications of it: countries across the ideological spectrum and at all levels of development turned to the armed forces in the quest for national cohesion. The Soviet

Union assigned the Red Army the mission of creating "the New Socialist Man"; China burdened its People's Liberation Army with a comparable task. In the 1950s and 1960s, in the optimistic heyday of decolonization, militaries were widely saluted, by practitioners and scholars alike, as "modernizing" and "nationalizing" forces that would help new countries overcome communal rifts. Early in his reign, King Hussein looked to the Jordanian military to unite the fractious society it served,[7] and, after years of civil war, Lebanon turned to its army to wipe away traditional animosities and forge a new Lebanese identity.[8] The Israel Defense Forces (IDF) was early on—and still is—a key institution charged with assimilating Jews from around the world and propagating Zionist orthodoxy. Even in the United States, where mistrust of concentrated power has long held sway, the merits of universal military training were debated after each of the century's major confrontations, less because the threats from abroad were so intense than precisely because they no longer were: in the absence of an overwhelming menace and a unifying experience, many feared that ethnic, racial, religious, class, and even sectional divisions would again rear their ugly heads and threaten the nation's cohesion.[9]

Debates over who serves continue to arouse passion today in part because the military's manpower policies are widely viewed as having important implications for citizenship and national identity—arguably a polity's most central questions.[10] With the cold war waning, and then in its wake, calls in the United States for the draft, or at least national service, resurfaced. Advocates have argued variously that it would dispel the supposed perils of multiculturalism and large-scale immigration, reinvigorate the civic-mindedness that they believe characterized earlier generations, foster equality, and reinstill the sense of shared mission and community that is allegedly absent. It would, in short, remake the American nation.[11]

But how and under what conditions do the participation policies of armed forces transform political communities, especially democratic ones? More specifically, how and when do these military patterns contribute to redrawing the nation's outlines, to assigning membership in the nation? Surprisingly little scholarly literature directly addresses these questions. Few sociologists, historians, and political scientists have doubted that the armed forces would dramatically reshape society, for good or for ill. Even fewer have unpacked the underlying causal logic and evaluated these claims in light of available evidence. This book takes these underexplored questions as its central concern.[12]

The Argument in Brief

Scholars and statesmen alike have generally shared a faith in the military as a nation builder, but critically evaluating that belief's theoretical coherence and empirical foundation requires that the very abstract notion of national identity be made more concrete. Following a venerable tradition in political sociology, I associate nationhood with membership in the political community, as reflected in the formal rules, and especially the effective practices, of citizenship. Through continual contestation over the nature and extent of citizenship, political communities define themselves and identify their boundaries. The most revealing struggles are those of minorities as they negotiate and clarify their relationship with the political community. This yields the central research question: Under what conditions and how does military service shape the nature and outcome of minorities' struggles for effective citizenship?

In answering this question, this book focuses on two complementary causal pathways. First, especially after war, groups seeking first-class citizenship may deploy their military record as a rhetorical device, framing their demands as the just reward for their people's sacrifice. This effort to exploit a widely recognized norm has at times cornered state leaders, leaving them without room for rhetorical maneuver. Though a weapon of the weak, "mere" rhetoric thus has on more than one occasion proved powerful. Even a cursory glance through the historical record, however, indicates that minorities have often put forward such claims to no good effect. In many instances, the reason is obvious: material resources, not rhetorical choices, determine the success of claims making. How claimants frame their appeals can be crucial to the outcome, compensating for a dearth of standard influence assets.

Why does a minority's invocation of its military sacrifice prove successful in some cases but not others? Why does it sometimes compel leaders to acknowledge the justice of minority claims, and on other occasions draw no response or lead to rejection? The key lies in the interaction between the minority's rhetorical choices and the prevailing citizenship discourse and in the resulting possibilities for continued rhetorical play. When only republican themes are socially sustainable—that is, when the dominant discourse idealizes citizens who exemplify civic virtue—state leaders will be unable to craft acceptable rebuttals to the minority's demands, and a good part of the battle will have been won thanks to such "rhetorical coercion." Minorities excluded from military service, however, must frame their demands in other terms, and their claims-making may consequently prove less effective.

Second, in times of war but particularly in times of peace, the military's participation (or manpower) policies may constitute a strong signal of how the state would respond to minority citizenship claims, and they may thus shape the process of political contestation. These policies determine who serves in the armed forces and in what capacity. Accused of disloyalty or incompetence, communal minorities (ethnic, racial, and religious) have often faced discrimination in military institutions. They have been segregated. They have been limited to support units because it was believed that there they could do the least damage to national security or were best suited by virtue of their intellectual and physical capacities. They have been sent into battle as cannon fodder, with minimal training and shoddy equipment. Hemmed in by promotion ceilings, they have been underrepresented in the officer corps. They have, in other words, often occupied positions on the exclusionary half of the manpower policy scale—when they have not been barred from service altogether.[13] At times, in contrast, militaries have pursued more inclusive policies. They have not simply permitted minorities to serve but have integrated them into mainstream units, opened the full range of career tracks, provided opportunities for all assignments, and ensured qualified members access to officer training and appointments. Between these poles lie many positions, and armed forces have historically occupied all of them.

States rarely grant excluded minorities the full rights of citizenship without a fight, and the success of the sacrifice frame is predicated on the minority's willingness to engage in political activity. Because normally minorities are relatively weak, states comparatively strong, and the political contest to wrest rights costly, minorities must base their decision in part on whether authorities will respond to their demands with equanimity or repression. But the uncertainty endemic to social life prevents the minority from estimating these probabilities with great confidence, and it will consequently often refrain from forceful claims-making. However, shifts in the military's participation policy can, under conditions explored in chapter 2, serve as a potent signal of the state's intentions. When the signal is strong, it may shape the objectives, tactics, and timing of the minority's challenge. These, in turn, have implications for the form and degree of effective citizenship the minority may attain.

Underlying both mechanisms is Western culture's traditional intertwining of military service and citizenship.[14] As the historian Michael Geyer suggests, citizenship, nationhood, and military service were all of a piece in nineteenth-century Europe, where "state and society were yoked together by a mutual bond of violence, expressed through conscription and redeemed in the rights of citizenship," and where "to be German or to be French always also meant to be militarily prepared and, that is, to be conscripted."[15] In the absence of this long-standing relationship, the military sacrifice frame would not resonate, and military performance would not sustain the claim to civic virtue and citizenship. In its absence, the manpower policy signal would be incomprehensible, for the minority would infer nothing regarding its struggle for citizenship from the armed forces' policies.

Soldiers into Countrymen?

In the early 1960s, in the wake of decolonization, the armed forces were widely portrayed as the critical institutions that would help the newly formed states of Africa and Asia overcome parochial kinship structures and loyalties that rendered populations largely indifferent to national politics, created incentives for leaders to craft narrow political programs, and prevented the emergence of stable national parties. Through this supremely modern organization, it was hoped, a national culture might emerge to bind diverse peoples into a homogeneous mass.[16] Scholars differed over whether military service would remake recruits into modern men above sectional and ethnic politics, or whether the army might more practically serve as a model for emulation by society at large.[17] But they shared the belief that the military would, in part through its manpower policy, build nations.

As many newly independent states suffered military regimes that slowed economic growth, retarded political development, and stifled democracy, disillusionment replaced optimism. The next wave of research demonstrated that military rulers were often corrupt, played ethnic and sectional politics, and exhibited more traditional than modern characteristics.[18] Some maintained that military service normally highlights and reinforces communal cleavages and is, therefore, more a nation destroyer than a nation builder.[19] These divergent views of the armed forces share something more fundamental, however: both affirm that the military's participation policies are of critical importance to patterns of communal and national politics. Some find the prospect of military norms spreading throughout society alluring, others find it frightening—but they agree that the prospect is very real.

A third tradition suggests that the military's capacity to shape society is limited, since it is more likely to reflect existing social cleavages.[20] The military is a mirror of the nation, reflecting its warts as well as its beauty. The roots of the French defeat in the Franco-Prussian War went beyond poor organization and leadership to the corruption of the Second Empire, and seventy years later, the French were again decisively routed in part because the army "was so genuinely the French people in arms, . . . embod[ying] at every level the uncertainties, the divisions and the pessimism of French society as a whole."[21] While this literature has persuasively documented the cases in which militaries have paralleled their societies, it has underestimated the state's ability to act autonomously of social forces. History furnishes examples of armed forces that have accorded minority groups more equal treatment than the latter received from society at large. The contemporary U.S. military—acclaimed as "an organization unmatched in its level of racial integration . . . unmatched in its broad record of black achievement . . . [and] the only place in American life where whites are routinely bossed around by blacks"[22]—is the best known, but hardly the only, instance.

While the competing views of the military as nation destroyer and as national mirror have at times held sway over the conceptual terrain, statesmen and scholars alike have, time and again, turned to the military as a nation builder. But how would the military exert such effects? Implicit has been an intuitive image: individual change wrought by military service, especially during times of war. Deeply shaped by their time in the armed forces, individuals would reconsider their sense of selves and their attachments, bringing these into line with their personal experiences and hence with manpower policy. As veterans, they would diffuse this definition of the nation through-out civilian society.[23] Shortly after the U.S. Civil War, the *Army and Navy Journal* observed this process: "It is easy to see that the great body of citizen-soldiers have melted back into the great body of the people, their leaven has 'leavened the whole lump.'"[24] This conventional wisdom—that the military transforms soldiers and officers' basic habits, their aspirations and friend-ships, even their deepest identity commitments—runs through military mem-oirs, war fiction, and public opinion surveys. A German World War I veteran vividly depicted the war as "a gash [that] goes through all our lives. . . . With a brutal hand, it has torn our lives in two." Across Europe, notes the historian Eric Leed, arguments raged "over whether the veteran had been brutalized or ennobled, infantilized or matured by his war experience; but there was no debate over whether a deep and profound alteration of identity had taken place."[25]

Variations on this basic story are embedded in three seemingly plausible mechanisms: socialization of the masses to military norms, the operation of the contact hypothesis within a military context, and the military-induced transformation of influential elites.[26]

Socialization

The armed forces may socialize the rank and file and officers to national norms reflected in the military's manpower policy. Because the military is (of-ten presumed to be) a "total institution" and because soldiers generally serve during their "impressionable years," inductees may be nearly blank slates on which the military can inscribe values, both great and small.[27] While military socialization penetrates more deeply the longer one serves, the more one's long-term fortunes depend on one's performance, and the closer one comes to actual combat, even the relatively brief periods of service typical of mass recruitment systems may be sufficiently long to shape conscripts' basic atti-tudes and allegiances. Nearly a century ago, a Brazilian proponent of the draft put it well, albeit in terms offensive to modern ears: "The cities are full of unshod vagrants and ragamuffins. . . . For these dregs of society, the barracks would be a salvation. The barracks are an admirable filter in which men cleanse and purify themselves: they emerge conscientious and dignified Brazilians."[28]

In line with this view, governments have often sought to employ their mil-itaries to indoctrinate the populace. The imperial German mass army, like many of its counterparts in the age of nationalism, was designed to serve as "a great national school in which the officer would be an educator in the grand style, a shaper of the people's mind."[29] During the twentieth century, all manner of regimes pinned their hopes for national cohesion on military edu-cational programs, as they called their indoctrination efforts. From the Red

Army to the Yugoslav People's Army to even the U.S. armed forces, militaries unleashed ideological projects on their soldiers.[30] Through extensive *hasbara* (literally, "explanation"), the IDF still seeks to instill in its soldiers a Zionist fervor on the grounds that Zionism constitutes the "unequivocal national consensus."[31]

Contact

The armed forces may bring together individuals of various backgrounds in common cause and in a collaborative spirit, providing a setting seemingly well-suited to breaking down dividing lines based on race, ethnicity, religion, or class, as the "contact hypothesis" would suggest.[32] Required to perform common tasks in a highly structured environment and in close quarters, they would not just interact but would learn how truly to communicate with one another. With these tasks of vital importance to national security, one could count on a supportive normative milieu, enforced by orders down the chain of command. Through military service, individuals would escape the strictures of parochial commitments, and they would emerge cognizant that they were constitutive pieces of a larger project.[33]

This logic underpins the contention that the military can serve (and has served) as a national melting pot. When immigrants and native born rub "elbows in a common service to a common Fatherland," Assistant Secretary of War Henry Breckinridge maintained in 1916, "out comes the hyphen—up goes the Stars and Stripes.... Universal military service will be the elder brother of the public school in fusing this American race."[34] Although these dreams inspired but ultimately frustrated U.S. military planners during World War I, World War II has been widely acclaimed as having brought them to fruition.[35] Americans were not alone in finding this militarized version of the contact hypothesis attractive. From Italy to Brazil, military reformers broke with the Prussian model of territorial recruitment in the belief that only national recruitment could overcome their countries' deep divides. The historian John Keegan has even sought to explain the post–World War I transformation in British middle-class attitudes toward the impoverished (and the eventual creation of the modern welfare state) by observing middle-class amateur officers' "discovery" during the war of their working-class charges.[36]

Elite Formation and Transformation

The military experience may shape the communal orientations of future political leaders, who are particularly well positioned to set the boundaries of nationality. Through legislation, the creation and alteration of institutions, political agitation, and rhetorical appeals, these elites, majority and minority alike, work to shape the social categories through which the populace apprehends their national world. Time spent in uniform may "politicize" veterans, increasing their motivation to engage in political activity. French veterans of the American Revolution were in the vanguard of their own revolution a decade later, and African veterans of World War II were allegedly central to their countries' anticolonialist struggles.[37] Minority veterans in particular may be more sensitive to the political milieu, more fluent in the dominant political rhetoric, and more likely to demand the redress of inequity.[38] Thus black American veterans of World War II, infuriated by their ill-treatment stateside, supposedly took the lead in pressing for voting and employment rights in the immediate postwar period.[39]

At the same time, veterans may also enjoy access to unusual resources in the political arena. By making possible social networks that undergird political associations of national scope, military service may help veterans overcome collective action problems.[40] Military service, especially when distinguished, has also been viewed as a useful asset in political campaigns. Senior officers may retire with well-honed skills—from expertise in crafting rousing speeches to ease with public displays to unflappability during crisis—that serve them well in the political arena. Veteran status may also suggest a candidate's devotion to civic duty and may thus reassure the public as to her incorruptibility. Cognizant of this, veterans aspiring to political office have exploited their military records, sometimes to good effect.[41] From their positions of influence, veterans spread the military's image of the national community.

Theoretical and Empirical Critique

Military service, particularly in wartime, has undeniably changed individuals: it has exposed soldiers to new technologies, political tactics, and forms of social and economic organization, and it has exerted profound effects on veterans' employment prospects, psychological well-being, and personal relationships. But it is unclear whether one may safely extrapolate to national identification. Although reports that veterans were "never the same afterward" cannot be casually dismissed, self-evaluation is a notoriously poor guide: individuals routinely overstate the extent to which experiences change their beliefs and behavior.[42] A healthy skepticism is thus warranted.

Both the socialization and contact mechanisms suffer from a number of flaws, logical and conceptual as well as empirical. First, the socialization model—and, to an extent, the contact hypothesis—problematically conceive of soldiers as passive receivers, but cultural systems always contain enough contradictory material so that individuals can challenge hegemonic projects.[43] Not surprisingly, soldiers have rarely learned the lessons the military would have liked,[44] and "much of what appears to be the product of the training environment," military sociologists have concluded, "is . . . a function of what the trainee himself brought into that environment."[45] Thus the U.S. Army found during World War II that, despite measurable effects on factual knowledge, its various informational programs had minimal impact on soldiers' attitudes toward the war, their personal stake in it, and their more general opinions.[46]

Second, even if the military were an effective inculcator of values, the messages absorbed are not necessarily portable to other social contexts. In modern societies, individuals have multiple identities, and they may well behave as the military desires as long as they are subject to the strictures of military life—as long as they are members of the armed forces, are in uniform, and are on base. But identity is highly contextual, and one should not be surprised to see soldiers adopting regional, class, gendered, religious, or ethnic perspectives when they are off base or out of uniform or when they have returned to civilian life.

The American experience with the racial desegregation of the armed forces, often portrayed as an unadulterated success story, illustrates this point. Social learning certainly took place, as black soldiers earned their white counterparts' respect and admiration for their battlefield bravery. But such learning was of a highly bounded nature, for social barriers remained intact.[47] The U.S. military has justifiably been acclaimed for its efforts, and it is today arguably the least racist institution in American society. But its achievements have largely been limited to the workplace. "As a rule of thumb," two observers conclude, "the more military the environment, the more complete the integration."[48] After hours blacks and whites have generally returned to civilian norms of association.[49]

Third, even if military service could powerfully influence individuals' fundamental identity commitments across social contexts, that influence need not prove long-lasting—even though soldiers typically serve during their "impressionable" years.[50] To the extent that attitudes persist, they do so not because human beings are biologically programmed against attitudinal change beyond early adulthood but because most individuals (at least in the past) have settled down, geographically but more crucially socially, by their mid-thirties. When social networks are stable, attitudes are stable, but when social networks are disrupted, change is likely as beliefs are exposed to challenge.[51] The implication is that the attitudinal impact of military service depends on a social environment consistent with those military norms. But veterans are not surrounded exclusively, or even mostly, by their own kind after discharge. Reentering largely nonveteran social networks, they face strong pressures to leave their military past behind and adapt to civilian ways. Some veterans, both the highly self-assured and the highly alienated, will cling stubbornly to military norms and networks, but they are the exception rather than the rule.

This logic is consistent with empirical studies of veterans.[52] Among U.S. soldiers who had experienced combat—that is, among those for whom the military experience would presumably have been most salient—views on numerous matters, from attitudes toward adversaries and allies to the possibility of interracial camaraderie, reverted after discharge toward the preservice norm.[53] A similar dynamic has been observed among African veterans of both world wars as well.[54] These effects of reintegration are reinforced by the fact that military service is often an unwelcome intrusion, at least for conscripts. Even in the "good war" of World War II, U.S. soldiers generally perceived their service as "a vast detour made from the main course of life in order to get back to that main (civilian) course again."[55] This generation was later hailed for its unparalleled civic engagement, but that generation of civic joiners and doers was a product not of widespread military service per se, but of an unprecedented concomitant: the GI Bill.[56]

Fourth, even sophisticated versions of the contact hypothesis are theoretically indeterminate.[57] True understanding of others may just as easily contribute to deadlock and the recognition of incompatibility as to commonality. The prospect of extensive contact may even promote anxiety and suspicion, and thereby lower the likelihood of intergroup cooperation and good feeling.[58] The contact hypothesis assumes that intergroup conflict is rooted in prejudice and that prejudice is fundamentally a problem of ignorance, but intergroup hostility is often caused by factors other than a lack of knowledge or inaccurate perceptions.[59] As social identity theory suggests, group membership itself has prejudicial implications that additional knowledge, even if acquired during cooperative episodes, cannot overcome. Moreover, despite an active research program that has flourished for decades, the causal claim of the contact hypothesis remains unverified. Numerous studies have reported a positive correlation between interaction with out-group members and friendly attitudes toward that group, but it remains possible that these positive views are the reason for high levels of interaction rather than the consequence.[60]

Finally, and perhaps most important, these mechanisms' shared conception of nation building is problematic. Both suggest that the boundaries of nationality are drawn and redrawn as individuals' attitudes change in the military crucible. The definition of the nation, they imply, can be apprehended by aggregating individual beliefs. From this perspective, identity is cognitive and subjective: it is a matter of individual consciousness and, in the case of the nation, numerous individual consciousnesses added together. However, identity is necessarily social, not the property of given agents; it is intersubjective, not subjective.[61] Conceiving of large-scale social outcomes as the aggregate of individual responses, these mechanisms suffer from insufficient attention to the political contest through which nations are constructed.[62] Acutely aware of what is at stake in different national configurations, actors passionately defend their preferred position. Any satisfying account of the relationship between military institutions and nationhood must bring the politics of nation building, more than its psychology, front and center.

As for the final mechanism, which claims that military service shapes the capacities and national orientations of political elites, there are reasons for skepticism here as well. It has a number of virtues. It presumes that the armed forces can broadly and permanently rework individuals' identities, but it is agnostic as to whether this transformation is driven by socialization or contact. It does not depend on a historically rare military recruitment system: near-universal service. It explains how those who do not serve in the armed forces acquire a definition of the nation in line with military norms. And, although it relies on a subjective and cognitive conceptualization of identity, its vision of nation building is laced with politics and bargaining. However, a hypothesis is only as strong as its weakest link, and this one depends implicitly on claims regarding the capacity of the military to reshape basic allegiances that have already been shown to be suspect. Moreover, its plausibility turns on questionable empirical assertions. Is military service in fact a common, if not ubiquitous, feature of the politician's résumé? Does the military experience spark political and social activism? Evidence suggests that military service is neither necessary nor sufficient for electoral victory or political activity, though it may be of causal import in particular cases.

Rethinking the Nation

Over two decades ago Benedict Anderson felicitously described the nation as an "imagined community." This formulation gave voice to the intuition that, unlike small communities grounded in face-to-face contact, the commonality of nationhood is necessarily a creature of the imagination.[63] Nationality is assuredly an imagined construct, but that does not imply that the mechanisms by which its boundaries are drawn and redrawn are best grasped through models emphasizing cognition and mental creativity.

Any adequate account of military manpower policy's impact must begin by situating this potentially critical variable within a larger process of contention over the boundaries of nationhood. Political communities, as sociologists have long noted, regulate membership through the rules of citizenship.[64] Focused on the post–cold war paroxysm of violent hypernationalism, we tend to forget that in citizenship dwells the everyday, taken-for-granted nationalism that modern nation-states regularly exercise. Citizenship establishes a permanent home for some, declares some probationary residents, and fully excludes still others, and citizens alone are entitled to particular rights and subject to particular duties. Debates over formal definitions of citizenship often run hot because they are wrapped up as much with the politics of identity as the politics of interest. To challenge another's citizenship is to challenge his or her place in the community.

However, the most consequential battles normally occur in a realm far removed from formal categories, as populations and authorities negotiate over their *effective* mutual rights and obligations, over how those mutual claims are enforced in practice.[65] To cast nationality as citizenship is to bring politics to the fore, for the boundaries of effective citizenship have been the sites of intense political struggle: as Charles Tilly notes, modern citizenship reflects "the historical accumulation of continual negotiation."[66] This move makes possible a more social and more concrete conceptualization of identity, as a particular configuration of social ties.[67] For those interested in the nexus of armies and nations, associating nationhood with citizenship may be particularly productive, for the history of citizenship in the West has been intertwined with military service. It suggests a potentially rich set of research questions regarding the relationship between the policies of militaries and the struggle of social groups for citizenship.

The citizenship campaigns of communal minorities in particular may be most consequential for national identity. Definitions, whether of nations or any other corporate group, are carved at their outer limits, and it is there that minorities reside. These groups are liminal, both like and unlike the national core, and "their likeness permits contemplation and recognition, their difference the abstraction of those ideal traits that will henceforth define the nation."[68] Minorities are signposts indicating the nation's frontiers, and it is their struggles for effective citizenship that we must examine most closely. As these groups plead for first-class citizenship, protest for equal treatment and equal rights, demand autonomy, and even rise up in rebellion, they necessarily give shape to the larger community with which they are in dialogue and with which their relationship is ambiguous and perhaps ambivalent.[69]

To interrogate the relationship between military service and nation building is not to consider how the military experience might directly shape and reshape individuals' mental horizons. This book's central research question is more concrete and more tractable: Under what conditions and how do the military's manpower policies shape the struggles of communal minorities for first-class citizenship?

What Is at Stake

Specialists on military affairs are not the only ones attentive to the origins and ramifications of military recruitment systems. The nature of the military's participation policy is often bitterly contested, most obviously (but not only) in developing countries, where who serves is frequently who rules. In recent years, the question of whether gays should be permitted to serve openly in the U.S. armed forces has featured prominently in presidential contests, thanks to the larger "culture wars" in which this debate has been situated. In the wake of the cold war, Europeans struggled over whether to abandon their mass armies and build smaller professional forces—not because they worried that reforms would undermine effectiveness (just the opposite!), but because universal service was widely seen as underpinning national cohesion and democratic government. These debates have proceeded on the premise that militaries are social institutions, shaped by but often also shaping social structures and values. And they have pivoted on claims about the social and political consequences of military reform. Would more liberal treatment of gays in the U.S. armed forces usher in an era in which, as supporters might put it, discrimination on the basis of sexual orientation is nearly unknown? Would it result in societal approval of the "homosexual lifestyle," as opponents might claim? Or would it have nearly no impact, reflecting rather than giving rise to broader social forces? Those who answer these kinds of questions generally do so on the basis of faith more than fact, of inspired passion more than reasoned analysis. In this book I hope to rectify that imbalance.

The ramifications of military service have also featured in contemporary debates about the nature of citizenship in the United States. Communitarians blame the all-volunteer force, which replaced the Selective Service System in 1973, for many social ills. In the absence of the draft, American youth had no shared experience, no understanding of sacrifice for the common good, no comprehension of the national community.[70] Although I am sympathetic to the notion that a renewed emphasis on civic duty would reinvigorate American democracy, I question the communitarian agenda, especially in its more militarized form. Militarized republican discourse undoubtedly created opportunities for some, but it constrained others, particularly women. Republicanism has, in *practice*, often had a dark side.[71]

In this book I also speak to larger disciplinary concerns. I take issue with approaches that treat rhetoric as epiphenomenal, and I suggest instead that political analysis would be richer and more realistic if rhetoric were central to the study of politics. Building on the recent rhetorical turn, I elaborate in chapter 2 a generalizable mechanism of *rhetorical coercion* that shows how political contestants can rhetorically box their opponents into a corner, leaving the latter without the rhetorical resources with which to deny the former's claims. Political scientists have of late devoted much attention to mechanisms of persuasion, but persuasion is relatively rare in the political arena. Even in rhetorical interplay's more pedestrian moments, however—even when the targets of claims-making are not persuaded of the moral rectitude or practical advisability of the claimant's preferred policies—it may critically affect outcomes.

More broadly, in this book I seek to break down the often-false divide between rationalist and culturalist modes of analysis. Many political scientists may look askance at ascribing causal power to both rational signaling dynamics and cultural framing effects. They may argue that culture and rationality cannot be so conjoined, for the latter suggests the logic of instrumentalism and the former the logic of appropriateness.[72] Others may link them serially, treating culture as the source of inputs such as preferences and beliefs, and still others may invoke culture when multiple equilibria prevent any rational resolution of the game.[73] Both approaches are misguided, however. Rationalist and culturalist causal logics are not mutually exclusive, nor are they merely complementary. A complete explanation necessarily depends on a deep intertwining of these two touchstones of social and political analysis.

Political scientists cannot accord either rationality or culture analytical priority, for politics is incomprehensible without attention to both strategic choice and cultural materials.[74] Although individuals or groups sometimes engage in purely expressive behavior, political action is usually designed to achieve some preferred end. Moreover, the complexity of social situations would stump the unreflective servant of norms. Those who highlight the power of culture rightly make little effort to deny the strategic component of politics.[75]

Although political actors are not "cultural dopes," they are nonetheless deeply cultural creatures. The meaning-making practices that constitute culture render social and political action intelligible even as the context of action "help[s] determine the range of significations that are possible and pertinent."[76] Culture makes political activity possible, enabling the almost dizzying exercise of creativity, and it is the stuff out of which actors construct "strategies of action." But culture also limits actors' opportunities for invention, presenting them with a restricted set of symbols, narratives, and modes of protest. Cultural "tool kits," to borrow Ann Swidler's image, are—at least in the short to medium run—relatively narrow and fixed.[77] Over time, certainly, their contents are not static: new tools emerge or become affordable, old ones grow rusty or are even lost. But in any given episode, political actors must work with the tool kits at their disposal.

My argument knits together these two elemental threads of political and social life: interwoven and inseparable, they are neither incompatible nor merely complementary. It is possible that both minorities and state elites arrive at their respective frames through something approaching a rational calculation of the costs and benefits of the rhetorical alternatives. At the same time, only certain arguments are socially sustainable, thus constraining choice. While I develop an informal rationalist signaling model to explain the objectives, timing, and form of the minority's mobilization for first-class citizenship, culture is equally the game's essential glue. The coherence and content of the signal hinge on cultural elements, notably the longstanding link between military service and citizenship. Without it, the manpower policy signal would make little sense.[78] In short, like all political and social stories worth telling, this story cannot be told properly without embracing culture and rationality in equal measure.

The book is divided into three main sections. Chapters 1 and 2 together introduce the theoretical framework that will guide the empirical discussions. As described briefly above, chapter 2 delineates two causal mechanisms linking the military's participation policies to the struggles of communal minorities for effective citizenship and explores the conditions under which these mechanisms are operative.

The next three chapters, proceeding chronologically and thematically, explore the role of the IDF in the making of Israel. More specifically, they seek to understand why the Druze, a small Arabic-speaking minority, have succeeded in acquiring an intermediate place in the Jewish state—well above other Arabs and well below Jews. At least part of the answer lies in the policies of the IDF. Chapter 3, reviewing the history of Jews and Arabs in Palestine and Israel from the First Aliyah through the state's early years, establishes a critical baseline. Contrary to the received historical wisdom, it shows that Druze behavior did not differ markedly from that of other rural Arabs and that the young state, in its first decade, rarely drew meaningful distinctions among Arabs when it came to substantive policy. Chapter 4 argues that the conscription of the Druze in 1956 and the pointed exclusion of other Arabs constituted a strong signal of how the state would respond to their respective demands. Consistent with theoretical expectations, the Druze engaged in political activity earlier than other Arabs, played within the rules of the Israeli political game (while their fellow Arabs embraced contentious politics), and pursued integration (while other Arabs sought separation). Chapter 5 seeks to explain why the Druze were surprisingly successful, especially compared to their Christian and Muslim brethren, in making headway toward the first-class citizenship they desired. In republican Israel, the Druze's service in the IDF bequeathed a rhetorical advantage, which other Arabs, excluded from the IDF, lacked.

The next two chapters focus on the effects of the U.S. military's racial policies on African Americans' quest for civil and political rights in the twentieth century. Throughout U.S. history, African Americans have perceived a tight bond between military service and civil rights. When war beckoned, they flocked to the armed forces, despite segregation and limited opportunities for promotion. During the conflict and afterward, they contended that their collective sacrifice must be repaid, that the country was compelled to grant them first-class citizenship. Chapter 6 explores the effect of military service on African American politics in the context of World War I. In conjunction with postwar racial violence, African Americans' encounter with a deeply discriminatory armed forces rendered Marcus Garvey's vision of black autonomy attractive and, at the same time, suppressed intense mobilization for civil rights. The chapter also seeks to understand why white politicians could safely ignore black Americans' efforts to turn their military service to their political advantage. Chapter 7 takes the story forward to World War II and the early cold war, when African Americans proved far more politically effective. This greater efficacy can be attributed in part to the reshaping of discursive fields thanks to the Great Depression, wartime rhetoric, and the anticommunist crusade and the consequent rhetorical possibilities. African Americans' appeals to the country's liberal heritage played well, but their abandonment of the traditional republican rights frame came at a cost.

The book's conclusion, chapter 8, revisits some older themes and takes up some new ones. It summarizes the book's theoretical logic and empirical findings, but it also demonstrates their continued relevance for contemporary political debates—notably that surrounding gays in the U.S. armed forces. It then rebuts two arguments suggesting that this study is of historical relevance alone.

CHAPTER 2

The Power of Military Service

Statesmen and scholars alike have long asserted that the military exerts a powerful impact on the surrounding political community—not only through its intervention in domestic politics or its performance in war but also by virtue of its internal design, specifically its manpower or participation policy. This claim has often been treated as an article of faith, rather than as a proposition worthy of examination and explanation. The previous chapter suggested that the politics of nationality might be effectively captured by exploring struggles over the meaning and extent of effective citizenship, especially those of minorities who figuratively reside at the border of the nation. This draws attention to the place of military service in two sets of causal processes: framing and signaling.

These two avenues of inquiry suggest a host of questions. First, if military service does indeed make available a categorical claim on the state, when does this way of framing the claim prove effective, and how might the invocation of supreme sacrifice lead recalcitrant state leaders to acknowledge the justice of minorities' demands? Second, if change in the military's policies can serve as a potent signal of how the state would respond to appeals for citizenship rights, when does such a policy shift constitute a strong signal? And what specific consequences would such a signal have for the political activity of communal minorities? This chapter is devoted to unpacking the causal relationship between military service and the political processes through which citizenship is continually renegotiated and thereby to developing a theory of military institutions as shapers of nations.

Blood and Belonging

Militaries are more than war-fighting machines: they are important sites of social and cultural power and contestation. More specifically, military institutions and military service have, in the popular imagination, long been linked with citizenship and nationhood.[1] Militaries thus occupy a relatively distinctive place among state institutions as central national symbols, repositories of mythical constructions of the past and embodiments of the nation's aspirations. Few other institutions can as credibly claim to promote the interests not of a particular few or of a given class but of the nation as a whole.[2]

The place of the armed forces in the sociocultural complex is undoubtedly rooted in their association with war. For those whose lives are touched by it, their political or ideological stance aside, war is at times a source of immense energy, even a thrill.[3] Wars may be deeply divisive, but they also possess an unparalleled capacity to unify: William James analogized war to "the gory nurse that trained societies to cohesiveness," and he therefore saw "martial values" as "the enduring cement."[4] War, and consequently the armed forces, are central to the stories peoples tell about themselves, to tales of national origins and of struggles for independence.[5] It is no accident that the symbols and rituals surrounding festivals of national independence and unification have traditionally been interwoven with martial imagery.[6]

The link between military service and citizenship can be traced back to the republican city-states of ancient Greece and to ancient Rome.[7] It was preserved in medieval European militias, and while the salience of this tradition has at times waned, it has been continually reborn over the centuries. Machiavelli drew on it when he discovered in military *virtù* the highest form of civic virtue, in military discipline the training ground for the citizen attentive to the common good, and in the willingness and ability to bear arms the test of individual autonomy.[8] Hegel too saw military service as the "ultimate expression of the individual's recognition of his membership [in] the ethical community of the state."[9] Nearly thirty years after the United States abandoned the draft, "the ideal that citizens should bear arms in their country's defense . . . remains an essential ingredient of citizenship."[10]

Participation in the armed forces has, at least in the nation-state system, been depicted as a sign of one's full membership in the political community as well as evidence of one's worthiness for membership. As Otto Hintze put it, "Whoever puts himself in the service of the state must logically and fairly be granted the regular rights of citizenship."[11] And it is still viewed that way. In July 2002, as President George W. Bush announced that the thousands of noncitizens serving in the U.S. armed forces would immediately be eligible for naturalization, he proclaimed military service "the highest form of citizenship."[12]

Not surprisingly, veterans have exploited the rhetoric of sacrifice in advancing their claims for benefits. The Republic and every subsequent regime acknowledged the "sacred debt" owed veterans of France's Revolutionary and Napoleonic Wars, who were "by far the state's most favored ward[s]."[13] Across early nineteenth-century America, property requirements for suffrage gave way before the onslaught of propertyless veterans demanding the vote.[14] Europe's former soldiers were, after World War I, key figures in the "economy of social guilt," and, after World War II, Australian veterans campaigned effectively for benefits by stressing "duty, obligation, sacrifice, and debt."[15] For veterans, the rhetoric of sacrifice has come seemingly naturally, and it has been a regular feature of their claims-making.

Even those who have not themselves donned a uniform have invoked these themes when making claims on behalf of a collective whose ranks include veterans. The leaders of communal groups relegated to second-class citizenship have time and again contrasted the reality of entrenched political and social inequity to their people's unassailable record of loyalty and sacrifice—at times to good effect. So strong has been their faith in the power of this argument that they have counseled strongly against draft evasion during times of war and have even urged their followers to enlist. African Americans came forward in droves for the Union Army in the U.S. Civil War and wrapped their postwar demands in the bloody flag: as Frederick Douglass complained, "If [the black man] knows enough to shoulder a musket and to fight for the flag, fight for the government, he knows enough to vote. . . . Shall we be citizens in war, and aliens in peace?"[16] In independent India, opposition to the demand for Punjabi Suba—a separate state dominated by speakers of Punjabi and perceived by the center as effectively a Sikh entity—broke down in 1966 in large part because the Sikhs had fought valiantly on India's behalf in the 1965 victory over Pakistan.[17] Similarly, the bloody War of the Triple Alliance (1864–1870) reportedly accelerated slavery's demise in Brazil, as the valor of the largely black, mulatto, and mestizo forces "called attention to the country's archaic social and political system."[18]

By invoking their collective military record, groups have sought to exploit a widely recognized norm, raise consciousness among both the aggrieved and their oppressors, draw attention to an imbalance in the equation of rights and obligations, and ultimately trap leaders in their own rhetorical commitments.[19] When such claims framed around military sacrifice have been granted, the reason has not been an epiphany on the part of the authorities. Concessions have instead come when the authorities have found themselves without access to suitable rhetorical materials for crafting a sustainable rebuttal—when they have fallen victim to "rhetorical coercion." The point here, however, is that such claims-making draws on a long-standing Western tradition linking national citizenship and military sacrifice.

Among the reasons state authorities have imposed discriminatory manpower policies and resisted liberalizing reforms is that they too have recognized the strength of the discursive link between the rights and obligations of citizenship, between full participation in the political community and service in the armed forces. For leaders who are committed to and profit from the existing social and political order, subjecting groups at present excluded from the political system to military service is unattractive because it may bolster their claim for inclusion in the polity. For advocates of liberalization, the prospect of inclusion is a virtue, not a vice. Bestowing on a group the tools with which it could effect its emancipation might ensure its allegiance. The British adviser to the Hashemites argued in vain after 1948 for the induction of Palestinians, from both the East and the West Banks, into the Jordanian military: "We must make them feel trusted, and the first sign of trust was to arm them."[20]

Service, Sacrifice, and Rhetorical Coercion

In the wake of war, minorities eager to receive their just deserts and those (inside and outside government) equally eager to deny them commonly engage in intense disputes over the former's recent performance under fire. As they seek respectively to establish and to discredit the group's military record, they struggle to impose meaning on the past, for the present and the future are at stake: who wins this competition over memory may determine whether the minority can effectively turn its sacrifice on the field of battle to its political advantage. While service in segregated or minority-dominated support units does not preclude framing a claim in terms of the preeminent obligation of citizenship, the frame will seem more apropos the more heavily—even the more disproportionately—the group is represented in the armed forces, especially in combat units, and the more impressive its record.

But why would those in control of the state cower before mere words, before rights claims framed around military sacrifice? For those who see rhetoric as a way of cloaking the material power resources that really matter or of communicating the ideas that move agents to action, this outcome is mystifying. Those who view rhetoric as possibly persuasive are on the right track in according it causal status, but true persuasion is rare, particularly in the political arena. I suggest that we might more productively think of rhetoric in this case, and perhaps more generally, as potentially *coercive*. Much of politics involves neither powering nor puzzling,[21] but framing—that is, strategic efforts to force debate onto favorable rhetorical terrain. Such maneuvering aims to deprive opponents of rhetorical options, of materials out of which they might construct a socially sustainable rebuttal. Consequently, how claimants craft their demands must be added to the list of potentially consequential political resources.

Rethinking Rhetoric

Many, if not most, political scientists disparage rhetoric as epiphenomenal. The very phrase "mere rhetoric" captures this view: what counts is not the language people use or even the ideas they espouse but the material power resources on which they can draw. How claimants frame their appeals matters hardly at all to the outcome of political contest, for, more often than not, they have framed their agenda in a misleading fashion, and others know it. In short, talk is cheap. This perspective is shared by realist writers on politics, and it accords with a well-established understanding of political power.

Political scientists disenchanted with strictly materialist approaches have sought to harness the power of ideas. Many have invoked beliefs and culture to supply inputs (preferences, beliefs, and information) and to serve as focal points in games with multiple equilibria.[22] Political psychologists have long argued that belief structures, cognitive maps, scripts, and schemata influence how actors interpret evidence and sift through information. Students of collective action have suggested that principled commitment can motivate participants in social movements and render them unusually insensitive to the costs of protest.[23] But even scholars with an ideational bent have typically relegated talk to the margins. For them, rhetorical deployments matter only insofar as they reveal actors' true motives. Statements made behind closed doors are thus more informative than public pronouncements, but they have no independent causal power. Public rhetoric is at most of consequence only from the top down, as leaders deploy resonant rhetorics to mobilize mass support.[24] While devotees of "interests" and "ideas" vigorously debate the relative power of their favored variables, both traditions have little use for public rhetorical contestation. As Michel Foucault lamented, albeit with regard to a different but related object, they generally have sought to "ensure that discourse should occupy the smallest possible space between thought and action" and appear as no more than "a thought dressed in signs and made visible by means of words."[25]

However, the struggles of actual political actors, weak and strong alike, suggest that their rhetorical formulations are not merely fat surrounding the meat of politics.[26] The universal human need for meaning and narrative order renders political activity impossible in the absence of an interpretive context. Political contestants "frame" their stances and actions, explaining the purposes to which material power is put: they advance "a central organizing idea or story line that provides meaning to an unfolding strip of events, weaving a connection among them."[27] Those holding the reins of power recognize that the acquisition and maintenance of rule ultimately hinge as much on legitimacy as on physical coercion and that such legitimacy can be established only through rhetorical action. Those without a hold on the reins would agree with the leader of the Zapatista rebellion that "the word is the weapon."[28] Thus in the United States, marginal groups have routinely employed "rights talk" out of the unshakeable conviction in the normative but also the strategic value of devoting resources to constitutional struggles.[29] Proponents of intervention in cases of genocide have believed that "Holocaustizing" works, at least in raising awareness.[30] More germane to our substantive concerns, minorities have repeatedly braved the bullets so that they might credibly craft a more powerful claim for first-class citizenship rights. These actors clearly believe that talk matters: it is troubling that so many social scientists do not.[31] Their rhetorical contests should be at the center of the study of politics.

Rationalists and political psychologists might both protest that they have done precisely this. The former have pointed out that talk is not *always* cheap and that leaders who renege on their public rhetorical commitments may bear substantial domestic and international costs.[32] The latter have demonstrated that how an issue is framed is critical to both elite decision making and mass opinion.[33] While the rationalist insight informs the model of rhetorical coercion developed below, rationalist accounts have facilitated the formal modeling of public rhetoric by flattening rhetoric into a purely informational tool, a way of efficiently revealing whether one is a high-cost or low-cost actor. While political psychologists have usefully drawn attention to the power of framing, nearly all framing experiments have abstracted far from the reality of politics and have exposed subjects to just a single issue frame.[34] Recent exceptions exploring the consequences of frame competition have concluded that the framing effect disappears when targets are exposed to competing frames from equally credible sources.[35] Both rationalist and even sophisticated psychological accounts have thus rendered the intense rhetorical contests familiar to all observers of politics both peripheral and baffling. They yield only limited insight into the framing battles that often accompany minorities' struggles for citizenship and into minorities' abiding faith in military sacrifice. Powerful frames can and do emerge, however, and the rhetorical interplay itself is as much a part of the story as the target's predispositions or the speaker's credibility.[36]

A third approach, rooted in the constructivist literature in international and comparative politics, has productively brought rhetoric back in. Among the universe of mechanisms through which political actors develop "shared understandings" and embrace new norms, and arguably occupying pride of place, is persuasion.[37] The targets of persuasive rhetorical moves do not grudgingly comply but, rather, sincerely internalize new beliefs and consequently adopt new identities and preferences. Through persuasion, "agent action becomes social structure, ideas become norms, and the subjective becomes the intersubjective."[38] Persuasion—and consequently rhetoric—has emerged as the coin of the constructivist realm.[39]

How and under what conditions does persuasion occur? Some have drawn on well-grounded psychological findings to generate hypotheses.[40] Yet these frameworks typically emphasize how characteristics of the source, the recipient, and the setting can strengthen or undermine a message's persuasive power. Even "message variables" normally boil down to attributes of the recipient rather than of the message itself.[41] In short, such approaches to persuasion have much to offer, but rhetoric itself receives scant attention, for the causal work is done elsewhere.

Others have turned to Jürgen Habermas's model of communicative action to explain the persuasive potential of rhetoric.[42] These scholars acknowledge that actors often engage in narrowly goal-directed (teleological) action, but they also affirm the prevalence of rational dialogue—in which actors leave power and rank at the door and embark on open-minded deliberation in the quest for truth. They seek to persuade others and, perhaps most crucially, are themselves open to persuasion as they strive for mutual agreement. For Habermas, politics (at least in its ideal form) is less about contest than consensus, less about powering than puzzling, and argumentation consequently takes center stage.[43]

This emphasis on the dynamics of public deliberation is welcome, but it does not do sufficient justice to the realities of power. Habermas's "ideal speech situation," which encapsulates the conditions necessary for rational deliberation, is, as the term implies, an ideal type. In reality, power and rank are omnipresent in the political realm: actors do not speak from behind the veil of ignorance, and they do not use language unadulterated by earlier rounds of teleological political contest. As Foucault has stressed, discourse is never wholly free but is always structured: rules of exclusion and employment dictate what arguments can be proffered, under what conditions, and by whom.[44] Insofar as constructivists invoke "communicative action" to explain real-world processes, it is fair to ask whether rational deliberation characterizes actual political debate, for only when it does can Habermasian discourse ethics yield empirical insight into political contestation. But the higher the stakes, presumably, the less political interaction approximates that "ideal speech situation." The politics of citizenship are often so intense precisely because the stakes are so high—for both the distribution of material resources and the identity of the political community. As political theorist Mary Dietz concludes, "Those who rely upon the consensuality of communicative rationality must necessarily come to grief among so many who are not communicative or, more accurately, always and inevitably strategically communicative and communicatively strategic."[45]

True persuasion undoubtedly takes place in the political realm, but it remains relatively rare. Cognitive structures are stubborn, and those of political elites are more rigid, precisely because this stratum tends to be better informed, more self-consciously reflective, more beholden to well-developed and complex beliefs, and therefore more adept at reconciling discrepant information.[46] Cognitive psychologists have argued that people abandon deeply held views only when the external pressure is great and the contrary evidence overwhelming and clear[47]—which it rarely is in matters of politics. Democratic politics is better characterized by irresolvable contest and unbridgeable chasms than by collaboration and consensus. The "logic of argumentation" or the psychology of persuasion may help explain those exceptional times when political actors embrace new values and beliefs, but rhetoric can exert substantial causal effects even in more mundane moments.

In contrast to materialist and ideational accounts, I argue that language has a real impact on political processes. In contrast to deliberative (or liberal) constructivists, I am skeptical that actors can regularly transcend the workings of power. Actors' rhetorical moves can nevertheless affect political outcomes, even when all are cynical political operators with little interest in genuine deliberation. It often does not matter whether actors believe what they say, whether they are motivated by crass material interests or inspired by sincere commitment. What is important is that they can be rhetorically "hemmed in and left without a move," as Adeimantus complained to Socrates.[48] When state authorities accede to minorities' demands for citizenship rights, it is not necessarily because they have turned over a new leaf—though that is possible. Such concessions often have less to do with persuasion than with coercion, for governments may see themselves as having little alternative given prior commitments and attentive audiences.[49] Rhetorical coercion is a political strategy that seeks to twist arms by twisting tongues.

Rhetorical coercion captures a process alluded to by scholars rooted in a range of intellectual traditions. Students of norms and transnational activism have drawn attention to the "mobilization of shame."[50] Others have introduced such terms as "argumentative self-entrapment,"[51] "heresthetics,"[52] and "rhetorical action."[53] Similar processes have been highlighted by scholars informed by sociological role theory, social network approaches, Jean-Francois Lyotard's narrative analysis, and the later Wittgenstein's language games.[54] Drawing on and extending these diverse perspectives, I explore how rhetorical coercion works in general and examine how it would operate within the particular context of the struggle of minorities for first-class citizenship rights.

How Rhetorical Coercion Works

Rhetorical coercion is possible because of two key facts of social life. First, political actors cannot typically advance policy positions without justifying their stances and behaviors—in short, without framing. Politics may entail coercion or distribution, but at the same time it involves the struggle over meanings. Meanings, however, cannot be imposed unilaterally or through the exercise of material power alone: they are, by their very nature, intersubjective. The effort to forge shared meaning necessarily implicates some public audience in the process, and thus all parties continually strive to legitimate their positions in the eyes of the public.[55] Framing is "strategic dramaturgy"—performed before an audience with a political objective in mind.[56]

Second, and related, rhetoric is not infinitely elastic: speakers may not say just anything they would like in the public arena. The "civilizing force of hypocrisy" ensures that even egoistic actors must couch their claims in the language of the public good rather than that of self-interest.[57] But the constraints on speakers do not end at interest's edge. Every community of discourse shares a number of rhetorical forms that enable and constrain rhetorical possibilities.[58] Although speakers are free to weave these together in creative, and consequently somewhat unpredictable, ways, they are not free to deploy utterly novel formulations in the course of contestation. In any particular bounded episode, the existing rhetorical arrays constitute the "boundary condition" of political contest, forming "the limits within which cultural action occurs."[59] While such public semiotic codes reflect relations of power, they do not shut off the spigot of change, for the existing order's defenders and challengers must both draw on them.[60] No social actor, no matter how powerful, can stand outside the web of culture.

Political rhetoric is sometimes characterized as so stylized and predictable as to be banal, and while this claim is hyperbolic, it does contain at least a grain of truth.[61] The Federalists, in arguing for centralized power and the U.S. Constitution, "had to reach back into the sources of the received tradition, . . . take these ideas and apprehensions apart and where necessary rephrase them, reinterpret them—not reject them in favor of a new paradigm, a new structure of thought, but reapply them and bring them up to date."[62] Students of national and transnational activism have likewise concluded that ways of framing claims cannot be fabricated out of whole cloth but must at least draw on existing themes and "graft" them on to new concerns.[63] Public semiotic codes constrain social actors regardless of whether they truly "believe" in these codes' content.[64]

Rhetorical innovation, while possible and even inevitable in the long run, is far less likely in the short run for two reasons. First, while rhetorical universes are continually being reworked, coherent political action would be impossible if they were in a state of continuous flux. Relative rhetorical stabilities constitute a language game within whose rules strategic maneuver is possible.[65] Second, imagining, formulating, and disseminating a new rhetorical form requires an unusual level of commitment on the part of a claimant—in terms of material resources, time, and effort. Deploying existing forms is obviously far less costly. Campaigns to reconfigure the rhetorical terrain, to transform that which is fresh and unusual into that which seems commonplace, are of necessity lengthy and uncertain.[66] Actors engaged in political contest, who normally possess shorter time horizons, will generally refrain from such innovative action.

Rhetorical contestation consists of parties attempting to maneuver each other onto more favorable terrain and thereby to close off routes of acceptable rebuttal. Rhetorical coercion is successful when one deprives one's opponent of materials out of which to craft a reply that falls within the bounds of what the public will accept. This audience patrols the temporarily stable boundaries of sustainable rhetoric, privileging some formulations and placing others beyond the pale, and it thus limits the policy stances that can be legitimated. Sentences, as Wittgenstein argued, are not logical pictures of facts but are socially sustained.[67] Political actors are naturally free to say anything they would like, but they run the risk either of not being understood or of being

punished for a breach of the rules of argumentation.[68] "Someone who proph-
esies without troubling himself with the reactions of those who hear him,"
Chaim Perelman colorfully suggests, "is quickly regarded as a fanatic, the
prey of interior demons, rather than as a reasonable person seeking to share
his convictions."[69] Thus interpreters of the law "are constrained by their tacit
awareness of what is possible and not possible to do, what is and is not a reasonable thing to say, what will and will not be heard as evidence, in a given
enterprise."[70]

Opponents may end up endorsing (or at least acquiescing in) one's stance
regardless of whether they believed the words they uttered. The alternatives—enduring punishment for stepping beyond the existing contours
of rhetorical contestation or investing resources in creating new commonplaces—may be prohibitively costly and time consuming, and actors consequently have incentives to play the game of politics within such limits.[71] One
of the most effective means of rhetorical coercion, therefore, involves drawing attention to inconsistencies between the existing state of affairs and previously articulated commitments.[72] When done skillfully, "opponents are left
vulnerably speechless: their words have been taken out of their mouths and
return to mock them."[73] These considerations are most apparent when
claims-making is public, but they can influence even private negotiations—
as long as the claimant can credibly threaten to bring the audience into the
conversation. In short, persuasion is not necessary to command rhetorical
assent.[74]

When a communal minority approaches government authorities, charges
them with discrimination, and demands first-class citizenship, several avenues of response are possible. The government may issue a *denial* that any
offense has occurred. It may submit a *justification:* claim that the act or its consequences are not as negative as the minority suggests while admitting responsibility. It may offer an *excuse:* admit a negative outcome but deny full or
partial responsibility for the act or its consequences.[75] Finally, it may grant a
concession: acknowledge that the offense has occurred, assume responsibility
for the transgression, and perhaps even express regret or apologize.[76] Which
of these avenues is available and attractive cannot be analyzed outside of a
given episode of contestation.[77]

Nevertheless, the logic of rhetorical coercion suggests that two key variables explain when it has causal impact. First, is the public a party to the
claims-making? As long as the claimant can credibly threaten, implicitly or
explicitly, to bring the audience in on its side, its opponent is compelled to acknowledge and respond to its demands. However, if such a threat cannot be
credibly made, then the target can safely ignore these appeals, no matter how
they are framed. We can readily imagine circumstances under which the
public would not be relevant. Perhaps the public simply cannot hear the
claimant—because the latter is being repressed or because it lacks sufficient
material resources to publicize its message. Perhaps the claims regard mis-

deeds that transpired far from the public eye, as when the target is a government whose decisions are implemented by a large, complex, and secretive bureaucracy. Finally, in some social contexts, explanations are not required. Superiors often do not explain their logic to subordinates, and exasperated parents often tell children, "Just do as I say!"[78] If audiences capable of imposing substantial costs are not engaged, targets often need not respond at all and certainly need not be consistent. The prevalence of justificatory behavior in the political arena suggests, however, that audiences are, more often than not, listening intently—or at least so the actors believe.

Second, how constrained is the universe of rhetorical commonplaces? A skeptic might argue that it is nearly always expansive, especially in the political realm: verbal appeals are multivocal, and those on both sides can normally express themselves in the same terms.[79] Thus French elites have often couched conservative stances in the language of the Left: critics of gay marriage have accused gays of displaying bourgeois tendencies, and defenders of the ban on the Islamic head scarf in public schools have justified it on feminist, not nationalist or religious, grounds.[80] One legal scholar has similarly concluded, "Americans of all political stripes have . . . used the language of rights to support their various causes, and all of the greatest political conflicts in American history have involved, and been spoken about as, conflicts of rights."[81] If the skeptics are correct, striving for rhetorical coercion is a fool's errand.

This position, however, overstates the flexibility inherent in language. Even a rhetoric as capacious as that of rights in the American context has rendered some arguments unsustainable. The individualistic terms of certain constitutional amendments have undermined the legal efforts of those seeking to protect the rights of collectives such as families. "Using the inherited categories of rights talk as a way of articulating grievances, wants, and hopes," one historian has noted, "disciplines the speaker. Not all wants can be posed as rights."[82] Rhetorical universes are never so narrow as to shut down political debate, and the meaning attached to signifiers is the subject of continual play. But as long as some conceivable arguments are excluded from the permissible realm, rhetorical coercion remains possible. Keith Sawyer's study of improvisational theater is suggestive in its conclusion that the space for coherent and consistent moves shrinks as the dialogue proceeds.[83] On those occasions when the target is backed into a rhetorical corner, it is driven forward "by the imperatives of the argument, almost regardless of [its] desires, character, or convictions."[84]

Even skilled rhetoricians, however, cannot always succeed in rhetorical coercion, for the degree of slack is variable. When such structures are loose, numerous rhetorical strands are available, ensuring that the target can almost always put forward a meaningful rebuttal. In such circumstances, the terms of debate are hardly constraining. When these structures are relatively restricted, rhetorical coercion is more easily achieved, as the target has less rhetorical "wiggle room"—that is, fewer socially plausible ways of rebutting the claimant.

No matter how plausible, this theoretical analysis seems somewhat empty in its current form. Students of conversation and argumentation from the disciplines of anthropology, communications, sociology, philosophy, and psychology have vigorously argued that context is unusually crucial to their field of study.[85] To generate more powerful hypotheses, the context of claims-making must be entered into the equation, and it is, therefore, time to return to military sacrifice, civic virtue, and claims to citizenship.

Talking about Citizenship

Communal minorities have often demanded first-class citizenship on the basis of their performance of military obligations. Even if a broad audience is party to the discussion, authorities do not necessarily buckle before such claims-making. The nature of the prevailing citizenship discourse—that is, the principal ways of speaking about the qualifications for citizenship and the origins of rights—is equally important. Successful claims-making connects the cause with these idioms and plumbs the disjunctures between social and political ideals and reality. Appeals to broaden the political community are destined for failure when the political system is explicitly justified on the basis of inequity, for then the major rhetorical practices provide little room for expansion. The lower classes would make little headway in an environment dominated by the doctrine of the elect. Strictly ethno-national definitions of the community similarly would offer little room for minority progress. In such circumstances, appeals premised on just rewards for public service fall flat.

At the same time, arguments invoking military sacrifice will have little effect when liberal talk about citizenship is the norm. Liberalism, devoted to maximizing individual liberty, conceives of such liberty as freedom from interference.[86] From the liberal perspective, all law, all state action, necessarily infringes on liberty, except when it corresponds to citizens' freely chosen preferences, and liberals imagine the state largely as a neutral forum in which rights-bearing actors bargain. Liberal citizenship thus consists of a bundle of rights, and it consequently lacks a persuasive basis for civic obligation. Liberal citizens may of course perform civic functions and actively engage in politics, but they would not accede to binding commitments that would limit their freedom of action.[87] Liberalism thus envisions the citizen primarily as the holder of a status, and while liberal theorists have disagreed over who counts as a subject, all ground citizenship in who an individual is, not in what an individual does.[88] Thus liberalism "carries within it not the seeds of its destruction, but the seeds of its expansion," for leaders cannot easily harmonize its individualist language with group inequality.[89] In the postwar era, African Americans invoked the liberal discourse of universal human rights to bolster their citizenship claims, and white American politicians increasingly had difficulty rebuffing those demands, in part because the racist tropes on which they had so often relied in the past were decreasingly available. A liberal milieu may prove receptive to claims that seek to rectify inequities, but appeals crafted around military service as evidence of civic commitment will carry no special weight.[90]

The frame of "military sacrifice and its just rewards" proves most effective when only republican ways of speaking about citizenship are socially sustainable. Republicans share with liberals a focus on individual liberty, but they conceive of such liberty as the absence of domination—that is, the lack of the capacity to intentionally interfere in an arbitrary fashion in the choices of others. Republicans are consequently more tolerant than liberals of (nonarbitrary) state interference "provided it is properly constrained," but they are less tolerant of both relations and structures of domination, even when acts of domination are infrequent.[91] Although republicans, like liberals, believe that the state must remain neutral with respect to conceptions of the good, they are more open to civic obligation.[92] Moreover, the republican tradition has long emphasized the critical importance of civic virtue in sustaining republican institutions by fostering identification with the larger polity. Republicans thus see great value in active participation in democratic politics not because—as in the Aristotelian "positive liberty" or Rousseauian populist republican tradition—it is an end in itself, but because it fosters the public-spiritedness that promotes a political culture hostile to domination and protective of liberty.[93]

Republican citizens prove their virtue through their contributions to the common good, and the community's "test of full membership, . . . by which the individual becomes a citizen, is performance of the duties of the practice of citizenship."[94] The republican tradition has historically treated military service as the preeminent civic obligation and identified the good citizen as one willing to die on the battlefield for the political community.[95] The military sacrifice frame thus embodies the republican logic of rights. When state authorities are bound to a civic republican citizenship discourse, when ascriptive justifications for citizenship practices are not available, wrapping one's rights claims in the bloody flag may leave the powers that be without an acceptable way to justify exclusionary policies. This frame was the centerpiece of the Druze's political strategy in Israel, and, as a consequence, they proved surprisingly successful in achieving their aims. Faced with two unattractive options—broadening membership in the political community or opening themselves to potential punishment—state elites may find the former to be the lesser of two evils.

State leaders may accede to a minority's demands for first-class citizenship because the latter possesses some conventional political resource they desire or fear. But, when a minority invokes the equation of military service and citizenship, they may also yield because they lack the rhetorical means with

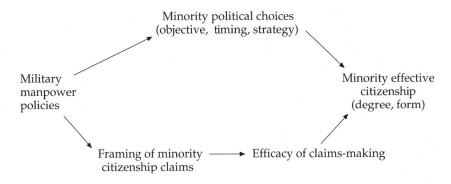

Figure 1. The argument

which to deny the minority's claim. When republican forms of citizenship talk are dominant, the prospects for rhetorical coercion based on the military sacrifice frame are brightest (represented in the bottom half of figure 1).

Mobilizing Manpower, Mobilizing Politics

States face difficult choices with regard to minority military service, but minorities confront equally severe dilemmas. Rights are rarely granted without struggle with central authorities, and claims-making, particularly when aggressive, may bring repression. Although actors in "identity-driven" social movements are often willing to endure high expected costs, even they typically engage in loose calculation and wait for an opening in the political opportunity structure.[96] Writing in his journal in 1964, in the wake of the disappearance and suspected murder of three civil rights workers in Mississippi, voter-registration volunteer Stuart Rawlings projected the chances of his death at one in fifty.[97] Rawlings and many others stayed the course that Freedom Summer, but they were aware of the possible costs and drew up back-of-the-envelope estimates, implicitly weighing these against the gains to civil rights if they persevered. An activated identity may shape the calculations that underlie action, but it does not supplant them or render them otiose. Presumably, had Rawlings placed the risk at one in two, he might have had second thoughts. As Donald Horowitz puts it in his study of communal riots, "Angry or aroused people are not necessarily heedless of risk. . . . Passion has its calculus."[98]

The minority's predicament can be captured in a simple incomplete-information "trust game."[99] The minority must decide whether to mobilize or remain quiescent,[100] and the costs of each strategy depend on how likely the state is to grant citizenship rights and how likely it is to crush the movement. In other words, as in any trust game, the behavior of player 1 (in this case, the minority) is in large part a function of its estimate of player 2's (the state's) "type." Two further calculations are also in principle critical: (1) the costs if the state were to opt for repression in the case of minority mobilization (the size of the "sucker's payoff"); and (2) the benefits if the minority were to achieve first-class citizenship (the size of the reward for mutual cooperation). In this context, both costs and benefits are likely to be quite high, presenting the minority with substantial incentives as well as disincentives for mobilization.

In short, this problem is rooted in the uncertainty that inheres in social life. If the minority could be sure of the state's response, its dilemma would disappear, but in real politics actors very rarely can be positive as to others' types, because key pieces of information are both private and valuable. Actors, however, are not entirely without recourse, for strong signals can provide at least rickety bridges over these informational chasms. By revealing actors' likely behavior in a variety of settings, they can reduce uncertainty and render mutual cooperation more probable.

Because of their historical association with citizenship, the military's manpower policies can serve as such a strong signal. There are at least three reasons states may liberalize the conditions of military service: to resolve a pressing manpower need, to respond to domestic or international political pressure, or to secure the minority's loyalty.[101] Since the minority is not privy to confidential policy discussions and can observe only the change in policy, it will often not know the reason for reform. For the minority, however, this is crucial, as it may indicate how the authorities would respond to citizenship demands. Two questions follow. First, what features of the shift in manpower policy allow the minority to infer the reason for the policy change, and what are the key components of signal strength? Second, presuming that the signal is strong, what are the consequences for the minority's political behavior and for the ensuing bargaining?

The Components of Signal Strength

Strong signals are *credible, clear,* and *available.* The first hurdle over which any signal must jump is *credibility*. Actors of one type at times have incentives to pretend to be the opposite, and they consequently design signals to yield that impression. Targets, suspicious of deception, are highly sensitive to "cheap talk" and therefore interrogate the sincerity of the signal. Perhaps, minority leaders may fear, state elites have revised the manpower policy to tempt them into protesting their group's subordinate status and thereby giving the authorities an excuse to clamp down. Perhaps government decision makers are merely courting international audiences, pretending to a liberalism that resonates abroad but that they have no intention of implementing at home. Perhaps state leaders are responding to domestic political pressure but would prefer not to reform the larger society. Wary of decision makers' motives, the leaders of minority groups seek to separate the credible signals from the cheap talk. The credibility of a signal is a function of its costliness, its reversibility, and the likelihood of involuntary defection.

Costly signals distinguish true actors from pretenders. In a sense, costs inhere in whatever manpower policy states put in place. At one extreme, potentially rebellious minorities may be allowed to serve in the most sensitive units and positions, imposing substantial expected costs.[102] Discriminatory policies imply their own costs, however, for they lead to the suboptimal allocation of resources. Assigning ethnic troops, regardless of their individual talents, to menial and support duties deprives intelligence and combat units of valuable members. After World War II, civil rights activists highlighted the demonstrated inefficiency of racial segregation in the U.S. armed forces. Widely dispersing armies, so as to avoid concentrations of troops of any single ethnicity, seems like a reasonable precaution, but it significantly slowed Russia's mobilization before World War I and bolstered Germany's belief that the Schlieffen Plan was feasible. Finally, fully excluding minorities from military service obviously limits mobilizable manpower. However, not all manpower decisions are equally costly. The inclusion of minorities that have incentives to betray the state—such as those whose hostile ethnic or coreligionist fellows live just across the border—entails higher expected costs than the inclusion of minorities with few options.[103]

Policies of minority exclusion from military service are typically relatively low in cost, but they are also less likely to lack credibility. The inclusion of antagonistic minorities could in theory sharply undermine military effectiveness: if the traitors were to turn their guns on their countrymen or provide the enemy with classified information, they might supply the crucial difference. In contrast, exclusion generally nibbles at the margins. With forces employed in suboptimal ways, the distribution of power would have to be tight for the outcome to hang in the balance. The complete exclusion of minorities would prove decisive only when prevailing doctrines and technologies rendered additional increments of manpower critical and when minorities were present in sufficiently large numbers to compensate for manpower shortfalls. Establishing the credibility of exclusionary policies is nonetheless not difficult, for one is hard pressed to conceive of what the state would stand to gain from a deceptive exclusionary signal.

Aside from such *strategic* costs, reform of the military's participation policies can also entail high *political* costs, and thus civilian-initiated reform is more revealing.[104] Military leaders care most deeply about preserving their autonomy,[105] and they would intensely resist any civilian interference with internal policies, especially standards for who can be soldiers and officers. Militaries may be particularly effective in parrying pressure because they enjoy an expertise their civilian masters do not possess and they can exploit a rhetorical trump card: national security. The armed forces may also mobilize their civilian protectors to hound the executive into abandoning reform. Given such daunting potential costs, civilians who nevertheless expend substantial political resources in liberalizing manpower policy credibly signal their willingness to widen the boundaries of the political community. Such costs are of course absent when the military transforms itself, unprompted by civilians.[106]

A signal's credibility hinges not only on its cost but on the likelihood of "involuntary defection"—that is, the probability that the state or its agents will fail to uphold their end of the military service bargain, even if their sincerity is not in question. Two hypotheses follow. First, a costly shift in manpower policy would be less credible in a political system with a high rate of leadership turnover. Current leaders can only with great difficulty credibly bind their successors and prevent future defection. Second, the more centralized the state, the less likely involuntary defection is to occur. While the central state presumably controls manpower policy, other actors in a decentralized political system retain coercive resources that may be brought to bear should the minority mobilize. Because minorities are uncertain about the views of these other powerful and germane actors, even costly manpower signals will typically have but weak effects when the state is organized along federal lines or when the central government itself is divided.

Finally, a signal's credibility also depends on its reversibility: the more easily inclusion can be converted back into exclusion, the weaker the signal. Two hypotheses again follow. First, shifts in manpower policy during crisis are less credible than those undertaken in peacetime. On the one hand, the expected costs of signaling inclusion are higher during war, for the very survival of the state may be at stake. Moreover, war typically brings about an expansion of the central state, lowering the likelihood of involuntary defection.[107] On the other hand, if the state is in dire straits, the military may readily accede to liberalizing service, reducing the costliness of the signal. Most important, wartime institutions are typically fragile. While the capacity of the postwar state has typically exceeded that of the prewar state, it does not begin to approach that of the wartime state.[108] In fact, minorities have often been called upon during times of national emergency only to find themselves unwanted at the conflict's conclusion. When policy is transparently driven by the exigencies of the moment, the signal has little impact.

Second, such signals will prove less easily reversed when state elites find that their hands have been tied by the expected costs of reversing course, even though they might prefer to renege. Domestic or international audiences may, for principled or instrumental reasons, threaten to punish the state should it fail to follow through on its pledges. Powerful bureaucratic interests may have arisen that, for their own parochial purposes, oppose a return to the past. From the minority's perspective, these are third-party enforcers ensuring a credible commitment. The minority then no longer fears that it is subject simply to the whim of state elites, and its concerns about the reversibility of the policy fall away.

Beyond credibility, a strong signal must exhibit *clarity*, for credibility provides no guarantee that the signal and its meaning are apparent.[109] Three factors contribute to the clarity of the manpower-policy signal. First, the more highly centralized the state, the clearer the signal. In decentralized political systems, multiple actors wield coercive power, and targets must consequently be attuned to numerous senders. Faced with a babel of voices, often speaking at cross-purposes, the observer comes away with no distinct impression except that of noise. Second, a military-led reform is also far less clear than a civilian-driven shift, for a move initiated by the military leadership need not reflect broader political currents. When, however, the overlap between military and civilian elites is so great as to render the spheres indistinguishable, decisions justified on military grounds alone, although not necessarily costly, may nonetheless indicate the receptivity of national elites as a whole. Third, recruitment systems marked by high levels of conscription are somewhat clearer signals than are highly selective or all-volunteer forces. Militaries' policies toward minorities are often not explicitly stated but must be inferred through observation. While the pattern of minority representation is clear under a relatively nonselective draft, the signal is more muddy under other circumstances, in that an evolving applicant pool or shifting entry standards could plausibly account for the change. The recruitment system is, however, only of limited import for signal strength, as politically relevant shifts in group representation will often coincide with, and be highlighted by, episodes of civil-military strife.

Finally, credibility and clarity are insufficient and must be joined to content: any signal must be culturally *available* if it is to have an impact.[110] As Robert Jervis has pointed out, "while behavior may reveal something important about the actor, often it is not clear exactly what is being revealed, what is intended to be revealed, and what others will think is being revealed. . . . Knowing that the behavior is costly, then, tells us little about what inferences observers will draw."[111] Thomas Schelling playfully suggested, for example, that kidnapping another country's ballerinas would not prove effective retaliation for espionage.[112] If the signal made any impression, it would likely violate an intuitive sense of appropriateness. One could well imagine other societies, however, in which a tighter interconnectedness reigned and in which ballerinas were consequently fair game. Not all signals will resonate with their targets, at least not as the sender intends. Thus we must explore the conditions under which a shift in the military's manpower policy will be an available signal—that is, one that targets will notice, respond to, and associate with the political opportunity structure and citizenship.

Manpower-policy signals are available under three conditions. First, and most important, in societies in which republican rights talk is prevalent, the link between military service and citizenship will be particularly salient. Sec-

TABLE 1
The components of signal strength: Hypotheses

---

1. *Credibility—manpower signaling is more credible when:*
   - minorities are perceived as more likely to defect (costliness)
   - the policy change originates with civilian leaders (costliness)
   - rates of leadership turnover are lower (involuntary defection)
   - the state is more highly centralized (involuntary defection)
   - reform occurs during peacetime (reversibility)
   - the authorities' hands are tied by opposed bureaucratic or other interests (reversibility)

2. *Clarity—manpower signaling is more clear when:*
   - the state is more highly centralized
   - the policy reform originates with civilians
   - the basis for military recruitment approaches universal service

3. *Availability—manpower signaling is more available when:*
   - the prevailing citizenship discourse is republican
   - the surrounding society is relatively militaristic
   - the polity recently concluded fighting a major war

---

ond, militaristic societies—that is, those in which the armed forces are "essential to the social experience and collective identity, . . . [and] rank as one of the collectivity's central symbols"[113]—will be more sensitive to such signals. When the policies and place of the armed forces constitute a central reference point, we are dealing with a militaristic political culture.[114] Third, for citizens who have recently taken part in a major war, even from the relative safety of the home front, military manpower signals will also have special meaning. Societies that have recently emerged from a brutal conflict understand more clearly the sacrifice citizenship can entail. As veterans come home demanding their due, and as politicians proclaim the nation's gratitude to its fallen and to the survivors, such societies grow particularly conscious of the relationship between citizenship and service.[115] Finally, these three factors may not be entirely independent of one another. Polities that have recently survived the horrors of war may be more likely to employ republican rights talk. Republican societies may more often exhibit militaristic tendencies. However, even the few cases examined in this book suggest that if such relationships do exist, they are loose.

Although signals are ubiquitous in social life, not all will shape a minority's political behavior. The preceding section has laid out several hypotheses regarding the conditions under which the manpower-policy signal will prove strong (see table 1).

The Consequences of Signaling

When the military manpower-policy signal is strong, it exerts important effects on the objectives, the tactics, and the timing of minority political mobilization.[116] I hypothesize that inclusive manpower policies encourage minority elites to pursue "integrative voice," while exclusive policies foster "separationist quiescence."[117] The meaning of these terms and the causal logic of the hypotheses are elaborated in the passages that follow (and are represented in the top half of figure 1, p. 29).

When considering the problem of military service for minorities who pose a threat either to national security or to the prevailing social and political order, state elites have a wide range of options, with exclusionary and inclusionary ideal-types at either end of the continuum. For minorities weighing mobilization, however, the precise position of the manpower policy matters less than the trend. Imagine a group barred from service in the armed forces and confronting widespread discrimination in other social, political, and economic arenas. Should the state then decide to subject this minority to military service, even on discriminatory terms, the minority would, faced with the imposition of full duties, seek the other half of the citizenship bargain: equal rights, or complete integration. Imagine now a minority group already serving in the armed forces but in a discriminatory arrangement. Should the state liberalize its manpower policies—by sending minority units on combat missions they had previously been denied or by opening professional opportunities to minority specialists and officers—the minority would again pursue the objective of integration, believing that this goal was now achievable.

In principle, the minority fully excluded from military service would prefer to continue paying none of the costs of citizenship while receiving the full complement of rights. But in most cases this option is simply a nonstarter, and the minority consequently adjusts its ambitions to the next best option: separation. By developing autonomous institutions—such as, among others, labor unions, colleges and universities, political parties, and cultural and charitable organizations—the minority reduces its dependence on the state and mainstream society. Consider now the case of a minority group that once tasted something approaching equality in the armed forces but then observes retrogression in the military's manpower policy. For this group as well, separation may be attractive, for the military manpower policy suggests that any broader social and political change is far off. Separation does not, however, necessarily imply separatism—that is, an independent political unit. Separatism is not normally feasible unless the minority is geographically concentrated, but separation is more flexible, capable of accommodating a more widely dispersed social and economic network.

Strong manpower-policy signals shape not only the minority's objectives but also the timing of mobilization. When state leaders refashion policies in an inclusive direction, they signal that the balance of power has shifted in favor of those who welcome incorporating the minority into full citizenship. Aware of new political possibilities, minority elites update their estimate of the costs of agitation and mobilize their populations to achieve equality. When structural shifts render established orders vulnerable to challenge, and when groups awaken to these new realities, contentious collective action enters the realm of possibility. Manpower policy can help mediate between "objective" structural conditions, such as economic depression or demographic change, and groups' perceptions of the net costs of action.[118] An inclusive military participation policy thus encourages minorities to exercise "voice," and successful minority efforts to achieve effective citizenship recast the ties linking minorities to both state and nation. Such voice is integrative, for it seeks not to create deeper lines of division but to demand formal and informal equality, including the minority within the unifying bonds of citizenship.

Manpower policies that exclude minority groups, however, signal that the opportunity structure remains closed, that the dominant powers oppose efforts to widen the boundaries of citizenship. Confronted with state-led resistance to its claims-making, and fearing repression, the minority is likely to opt for quiescence, tolerating its subordinate status and rarely protesting its position. However, the excluded are silent, not mute. Their acquiescence is limited and calculated, for they will voice their discontent when their fears of a repressive response have been alleviated—either because the state no longer seems to possess the will to repress or because the minority is sufficiently powerful that challenging even a repressive state seems less costly. The excluded minority thus waits for other signs that the opportunity structure has cracked open, but when the excluded minority does mobilize, its objectives will differ greatly from those of the included minority. Convinced that integration is impossible, the minority creates exclusive ethnic spheres free of discrimination and develops separate institutions to represent its interests.

Even when the military's manpower policies are strong signals, they at most generate *incentives* for or against mobilization. Because minority groups draw on numerous sources to ascertain whether the political opportunity structure is open or closed, other factors may overwhelm the military manpower signal. Because minorities have different exogenous levels of motivation, included minorities may be reluctant to mobilize while excluded minorities may shrug off the signal and demand first-class citizenship regardless. Theoretical analysis alone cannot specify a priori either the relative importance of the manpower-policy signal or the strength of the minority's inclinations. It does, however, yield expectations of how an included or excluded minority would behave, all else being equal.

Finally, included and excluded minorities employ different political tactics. As befits a minority confident that its appeals will receive a fair hearing in the halls of power, the included group exerts pressure through that system's standard avenues—through "conventional" politics. Its mobilization is less likely to take the form of mass protest or violence; it does not seek to achieve its ends by threatening the state with disorder. Minorities with substantial standard political resources at their disposal utilize them, while weaker minorities invoke the sacrifice of their young men (and less commonly young women) in the hope of rhetorical coercion. In contrast, the excluded minority eventually mobilizes not because it believes that its appeals will be heartily welcomed, but because it perceives chinks in the discriminatory armor. With no faith in

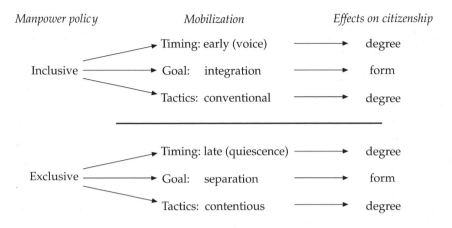

Figure 2. Manpower policy and mobilization

the state's openness to its demands—in fact, just the opposite—the minority adopts more radical modes of mobilization. Challenging the standard rules of the political game, it engages in "contentious" politics.[119] This is consistent with the suggestion that there is a curvilinear relationship between the incidence of protest and the structure of political opportunities: protest activity is minimal at the extremes of repression and responsiveness and is most common when structures are partially open.[120]

In short, when the manpower-policy signal is strong, one would expect to observe three differences between included and excluded minorities, with corresponding implications for the form and degree of effective citizenship they may achieve. First, the two groups should develop divergent objectives—integration and separation—which imply very different future relationships with the surrounding political community. Second, the included minority should mobilize relatively early in response to the signal, while the excluded minority opts for silence in the short to medium term. The earlier a minority mobilizes, the sooner it places pressure on the state to redress wrongs, and, ceteris paribus, the greater its progress toward effective citizenship. In the long run, however, these gaps in minorities' degrees of effective citizenship may shrink, in part because the late mobilizer will have learned from the early mobilizer's mistakes, allowing it to make up for lost time, and in part because the final barriers to effective citizenship are often both deeply entrenched and well concealed, rendering them particularly resistant to change. Third, the included minority should generally obey the accepted rules of the political game, while the excluded minority should embrace contentious politics. Different tactics may, in a more contingent fashion, prove more or less effective in winning concessions (see figure 2).

Assumptions of the Signaling Model

These hypotheses regarding the effects of manpower-policy signaling hinge on a number of assumptions. First, only those minorities whose behavior is contingent—neither unconditionally irreconcilable nor unconditionally pliant—will shift their objectives based on the signals. This scope condition does not, however, greatly limit the universe of germane cases. The ubiquity of communally heterogeneous political units combined with the relative rarity of large-scale communal violence suggests that few groups are truly unwilling to compromise. At the same time, the prevalence of intercommunal tensions indicates that groups are protective of their unique identities and will not readily concede.[121]

Second, this informal signaling model speaks to only an intermediate phase in the development of communal cleavages. On the one hand, it leaves aside cases in which minorities have yet to think of themselves as such or in which social stratification is nonexistent. Many residents of Brittany, for example, discovered only in the twentieth century that they were Bretons, and only then did regional ethnic organizations arise.[122] On the other hand, at times group conflict is so intense that only separation or partition is acceptable, and military inclusion could not possibly improve matters.[123] For instance, were Israel today to draft Christian and Muslim Arab citizens for the first time, it would accomplish nothing other than to infuriate these alienated groups and provoke widespread civil disobedience and even violence. In such situations of "lock-in," inclusion would lead not to conventional mobilization for integration but to contentious resistance in the service of a separationist agenda.

Third, the model holds only when populations perceive themselves as citizens, not as subjects.[124] Implying that ruling authorities and populaces have mutual obligations, citizenship enables claims-making. Relatedly, the state must be engaged in a national, not an imperial, project. The latter is typically a nonconsensual arrangement, and imperial subjects rarely presume that they can gain anything more than a subordinate position as long as they remain within the empire.[125]

The model rests on four additional analytical assumptions. First, the ethnic/racial/religious majority controls the institutions of the central state. While minority-dominated states are hardly rare (contemporary Syria, apartheid-era South Africa, Sunni-ruled Iraq) and are not necessarily short lived, they do represent the exception rather than the rule. Second, the minority is subject to social, political, and/or economic discrimination in society at large. Minorities that enjoy a substantial degree of effective citizenship either have lacked a reason to mobilize along communal lines or, alternatively, mobilized in an earlier period to achieve their gains.

Third, the state moves first, revising its manpower policy before the minority mobilizes. However, the symbolic import of the armed forces has historically rendered discrimination within them a target for minority activists. If the minority is already mobilized, measuring subsequent effects on the level and nature of its activity will be difficult. Moreover, if the new policy was largely the product of political pressure, this raises the question of endogeneity. In the United States, for example, because women and gays have been politically organized for well over a generation, any liberalization of military policies would presumably be more the result of these groups' efforts than the trigger for further activism. Such cases do not falsify the hypotheses, but they do prompt two methodological points. First, cases must be selected to avoid the taint of endogeneity, focusing preferably on situations in which the minority has not yet elected to mobilize. Second, tracing the sequence of events is unusually important.

Finally, inclusion of the minority in the military must pose a dilemma for the state. If arming this group does not somehow threaten the state or at least the social order, the signal will not be credible. Consequently this model cannot speak to cases in which such dilemmas have been absent but in which state decision makers have still worried about national cohesion. Thus, while the framework has relevance for Israel's relationship with its Arab minorities, it cannot yield insight into either the consequences of service for Jews of North African descent or the ramifications of widespread exemptions for the ultra-Orthodox.

Research Design and Case Selection

To assess the plausibility of these hypothesized dynamics, I examine the effects of military service on the citizenship struggles of minorities in two multiethnic democracies, Israel and the United States. Both countries have long been treated as "exceptional" by country and area experts, but each is also increasingly being brought into fruitful comparative dialogue. This work proceeds from the premise that there is a basis for productive comparison.[126] Both Israel and the United States are "settler" societies that have historically been defined around their central communal groups (Jews in Israel, whites in the United States) and in opposition to present Others (Arabs in Israel, African Americans and Native Americans in the United States). Both nations' rhetorical spaces have also contained diverse strains, ranging from the most civic to the most exclusive. Both have historically excluded certain communal groups from military service, and for both the eventual turn to a more inclusive policy was costly, though in different ways.

The claim is not that Israel and the United States constitute "most similar" cases, for they obviously do not: The United States is among the largest countries in the world, in terms of both population and landmass, while Israel is among the smallest. For much of its history, the U.S. homeland enjoyed relative freedom from insecurity, while Israel faced an existential threat at least through the 1970s and arguably beyond. Israel's political structure is uni-cameral and highly centralized, and a single political party dominated its po-litical system between 1948 and 1977; U.S. politics is marked by a separation of powers, a federal structure, and a high rate of party turnover. The Israel De-fense Forces occupy a central place in the country's symbolic fields, while through at least World War II the U.S. military resided in the hinterlands, physically and symbolically. The claim rather is that these two "macro" cases are similar enough to permit comparison but different enough and in the right way—as they are situated at opposing poles with regard to several critical in-tervening variables—so that one may explore and illustrate the full range of their framing and signaling dynamics.

These countries are also particularly useful as case studies because they supply revealing comparisons across time and across claimant groups. Stu-dents of collective action as well as area experts have emphasized how mod-ernization prompts political activity by creating capabilities and sociopolitical awareness; how larger, wealthier, better-educated, and better-organized groups have greater capacity and incentives to mobilize; and how the long-standing preferences of minority groups determine the objectives for which they strive. The "structured-focused" comparisons[127]—Druze versus other Arabs; African Americans during and after World War I, World War II, and the Ko-rean War; African Americans versus women (after World War I) and Japanese Americans (after World War II)—counter these alternative arguments re-garding the processes and outcomes of group political mobilization. These in-tracase comparisons also yield insight into the power and limits of rhetorical coercion, as these groups have framed their rights claims in different ways and advanced them in different discursive milieus.

Yet such comparisons are by themselves insufficient, for only by exploring the processes through which the causal mechanism *actually* operates can one make a more than circumstantial case. Charles Tilly has urged social scientists to move beyond conducting correlative tests and positing merely *plausible* mechanisms by "breaking down big events into causally connected sequences of events, and examining each link in the chain."[128] Tilly's advice is particu-larly relevant to this book, given the dual threats of endogeneity and epiphe-nomenality. On the one hand, a skeptic might argue that that which explains the origins of manpower policy might also account for its political conse-quences; for example, the state may demand military service only of minori-ties it perceives as loyal, and this assumption may further explain why the state is relatively responsive to certain claimants and unyielding to others. On the other hand, a skeptic might also argue that military participation policies are more the product than the cause of citizenship struggles. Given these con-cerns, the above hypotheses are particularly sensitive to sequence and con-text and demand the careful tracing of causal processes. A rigorous analysis requires rich historical research, and the case studies draw on primary sources ranging from published works to archival collections to oral histories and interviews.

An analysis structured around mechanisms has a further advantage.[129] While the earlier theoretical discussion treated the two mechanisms as if they were largely independent, it is obvious that they are in practice often related. But there is no consistent or systematic relationship. Some minorities, inspired by an inclusive military participation policy to mobilize intensely, may devote their energies to rhetorical contestation centered around the performance of the supreme civic duty: this was, and still remains, the Druze way in Israel. Other groups, despite massive mobilization, may shy away from emphasizing their battlefield experience: despite their service in the recent world war, African Americans in the late 1940s rarely invoked their collective sacrifice to prick white Americans' consciences. In contrast, in the wake of World War I, some African American leaders, notably those affiliated with the NAACP, sought to take advantage of blacks' service to press their case, even though they lacked mass support and failed to mobilize intensely. In short, while I treat the mechanisms themselves as generalizable, I expect that different cases will display different configurations of mechanisms. I favor an epistemology that aims not at the discovery of covering laws, but at "the identification of causal chains consisting of mechanisms that reappear in a wide variety of settings but in different sequences and combinations, hence with different collective outcomes."[130]

Theories require simplification, which the complexity of history naturally resists. Like all models imposing order on an untidy world, my own theoretical framework represents a stylized version of messier actual events. Real human beings often do think strategically, but they also react emotionally. Rarely presented with single moments of decision, they often improvise and innovate. Alfred North Whitehead once said, rightly, "There is only one difficulty with clear and distinct ideas. When we finally achieve them, we can be sure that something has been left out."[131] However, large questions of past and present are intractable without analytical categories and stylized narratives.

Case studies, however, are a different beast. They must not be so analytical that they simply retell the theory with proper names substituted for more abstract concepts,[132] and they must do justice to contingency while highlighting critical variables. Case studies should exceed theory's grasp and raise questions that theory did not anticipate. The chapters that follow demonstrate not only the value of the theoretical framework but also the deviations from its idealized, too neat presentation of the politics of citizenship and military service.

PART I

THE IDF AND THE MAKING OF ISRAEL

The Jewish State and Its Arab Minorities

Introduction

On May 14, 1948, David Ben-Gurion, the longtime head of the Jewish Agency, proclaimed the establishment of the State of Israel.[1] This was to be not just a political entity with a Jewish majority or a haven for oppressed Jews but, in the words of the new state's Declaration of Independence, a Jewish state. Its soul was forged in the pogroms of Eastern Europe and Russia and was further steeled by the Holocaust. It looked backward, rooting its central concerns in the tragedies of Jewish history and learning its lessons from the passivity of the traditional Jewish leadership. And it simultaneously looked forward, celebrating Jewish self-help and sporting an aggressive pride in military prowess and in "making the desert bloom." Palestine, and later Israel, became a magnet for Jewish refugees—Jews from Europe (Ashkenazim), whose eyes had seen what they would not speak, and Jews from North Africa and the Middle East (Mizraḥim), whose habits and ways the state's Ashkenazi leaders disparaged. At its birth, Israel pronounced itself a liberal democracy and promised equal rights for all the country's inhabitants, regardless of class, ethnicity, or religion. But its ethno-religious character overwhelmed its liberal assurances.[2]

Today numbering well over a million and amounting to nearly 20 percent of the country's population, Israel's Arab citizens[3] are divided by religion and tradition, with the Muslims, the Christians, and the Druze being the three largest groups.[4] A secretive religious community that began almost one thousand years ago as an offshoot of Islam and whose members are today dispersed across Syria, Lebanon, and Israel, the Druze account for under 10 percent of Israel's minority population and live primarily in mountainous redoubts in the country's north.[5] The entire Arab community has, since its incorporation into Israel, made great socioeconomic strides relative to Palestinians in the West Bank and the Gaza Strip and to Arabs throughout the

Middle East. Yet, despite possessing basic civil and political rights, they have suffered discrimination at the hands of the state and the majority Jewish population.[6] Israel is a *Jewish* state, and thus Jews, no matter what their country of origin, are favored in countless ways, while non-Jews are consigned to second-class citizenship. This tension is neatly encapsulated in the contrast between the country's modern-secular name—the State of Israel (*medinat yisrael*)—and its still widely used historical-religious title—the Land of Israel (*erets yisrael*).[7] While "democratic Israel" can effortlessly accommodate a substantial Arab minority, "the Jewish state," embodying the Zionist impulse for a purely Jewish homeland, casts *all* Arabs as a threat. In the struggle of Israel's Arab citizens for full citizenship, in their insistence that Israel abide by its liberal democratic commitments, lies the battle over the meaning of Israel and the nature of Israel's democracy.

Although Israel's ethno-religious ethos has unquestionably driven the country's policies and priorities, the experience of the country's Arab citizens has not been uniform. Exclusion is often a matter of degree, and the Druze notably have succeeded in winning an intermediate place in the polity—above other Arabs, well below Ashkenazim, a notch below Mizraḥim.[8] The fact that Jewishness and Zionist ideology have been embedded in state institutions cannot account for such variation.[9] How did this Arab minority group come to acquire a distinct status? The most persuasive existing argument suggests that Israel co-opted the Druze, offering them individual and communal benefits in exchange for their quiescence, in the hope of fragmenting the Arab community and limiting its political potential.[10] Although co-optation was certainly part of Israeli policy, it was limited to occasional symbolic gestures. In the state's early years, the Druze generally confronted levels and forms of discrimination that were equivalent, more or less, to those faced by other Arabs, and when the Druze demanded equal treatment, the state resisted substantial concessions. In short, Israel did not pursue a systematic strategy of co-optation, and the Druze by no means behaved like a model co-opted minority.[11]

States may attempt to dictate the nature of citizenship, to impose sociopolitical and socioeconomic arrangements, but populations often resist: citizenship emerges from continual negotiation between populations and authorities. Consequently, explaining citizenship regimes requires examining the political process in which the contending articulations (as well as the preferences and power) of states and populations are brought to bear. From this perspective, four puzzles come into view. Why did the Druze mobilize earlier than the larger, wealthier, and better-educated Christian and Muslim communities? Why, given their similar grievances, did the Druze not join forces with their fellow Arabs? Why did the Druze adopt a more moderate set of political tactics than their Christian and Muslim neighbors? Why were the authorities more receptive early on to Druze than to Christian and Muslim claims? At least part of the answer lies in the manpower policies of the IDF.

Israel's male Druze citizens have been subject to mandatory conscription since 1956, and over the succeeding decades barriers to equal service in the IDF have steadily crumbled. Christian and Muslim citizens have been exempt from the draft since it was first instituted in 1950.[12] Comparing the political pathways of Israel's Arab minorities, this case study illustrates the difference that military service can make.

If the design of the armed forces is to shape the politics of citizenship anywhere, it should be Israel. Despite a raging debate in the Israeli academy and even the public sphere over whether Israel can be classified as militaristic,[13] there is general agreement that who has and who has not served in the IDF has been and remains critical to setting the boundaries of effective citizenship and nationhood in Israel. "Participation in the national security effort," one scholar notes, "defines the extent to which an individual is 'in' the social-evaluative system of Israel—a system whose boundaries are not identical to those of the formal political system."[14] This perspective is shared by more critical observers who, even as they emphasize (and seek to promote) the voices of dissent undermining the dominant ideology, acknowledge that the IDF is "the central arena for the inculcation of citizenship and membership."[15] Even though—or perhaps because—this claim underpins much scholarship and public discourse in Israel, it is more often unreflectively invoked than argued.

The theoretical framework elaborated in the previous chapter can help shed light on the divergent patterns of Arab political activity and on the role of the IDF in bounding the Israeli political community. The decision to draft the Druze and then gradually to open increasing professional opportunities to Druze soldiers and officers was a strong signal—by virtue of its credibility, clarity, and cultural availability—of how the Israeli state would respond to Druze demands for equal rights. Although the Druze, like other Arabs, had suffered discriminatory treatment, only they had been welcomed into the central institution of Israeli society. They consequently no longer felt as constrained by their minority status, no longer as apprehensive that the Israeli security apparatus would respond with repression. Thanks in part to their inclusion in the IDF, the Druze grew increasingly politically active, but they sought integration into Israeli society and played by the accepted rules of the political game.

In contrast, the rest of the Arab population, with but minor exceptions, was exempt from mandatory service, and, on those occasions when some sought to volunteer, they were typically rebuffed. Israel's resistance to including Christian and Muslim Arabs within the bonds of military service, even when it had evidence that younger Arabs were eager to prove their loyalty to the new state, powerfully signaled that the political opportunity structure remained closed and that the state would not countenance Arab demands for full citizenship. Christian and Muslim Arabs thus hunkered down, refraining from overt challenge and waiting for a more opportune moment. Their eventual mobilization in the mid-1970s—after they were rejoined with their Palestinian brethren as a consequence of the 1967 war, after Israeli society had been rocked by social upheaval in the early 1970s, and after the debacle of the 1973 war—bore, in its objectives and tactics, the imprint of their exclusion from the IDF: Christian and Muslim Arabs favored autonomy, and they engaged in mass, at times violent, protest. In short, the included Druze mobilized earlier than other Arabs, pursued integration into Israeli society, and employed conventional political tactics, while their Christian and Muslim neighbors grew politically active later, espoused separationist aims, and embraced contentious politics.

Moreover, despite their lack of conventional political resources, the Druze have proved a potent force in Israeli politics. As Druze activists invoked their community's military sacrifice in framing their demands for rights, Jewish-Israeli leaders were bound by the terms of Israel's narrowly republican citizenship discourse and lacked the rhetorical materials with which to rebut the Druze's claims. Exempt from the draft, other Arabs couched their appeals in liberal terms. They thus left Jewish politicians with a republican escape hatch: Arabs deserve less because they have not been willing to endure the greatest of sacrifices for their fellow Israelis. Today the Druze dream of first-class citizenship still remains unfulfilled, for formal and informal discrimination against minorities is entrenched.[16] Nonetheless, the Druze's achievements, made possible by their service in the IDF and the power of republican forms of argument in Israel, have been remarkable. As Virginia Dominguez insightfully observes, it is not accidental that Israelis refer to the Druze population as an *edah*—a term meaning "community" that is typically reserved for Jewish groups. The Druze, she suggests, are an "internalized other," "on the margins of the Israeli Jewish collective self and with a special relationship to Jews and Judaism."[17]

For schematic representations of these claims, layering the details of these Israeli cases onto the basic theoretical framework, see figures 3 and 4. These figures should not be interpreted as implying that decisions regarding military service are entirely determinative of the fate of Israel and its various Arab minority groups. No single factor could bear such causal weight. State policies in other domains, processes of modernization, and cultural practices undoubtedly played a role, and they receive due consideration in the historical narrative. But the policies of the IDF rarely make such a list. Widely viewed as critical to welding together the Jewish community in Israel, the IDF's policies vis-à-vis the Arab minorities are generally portrayed as at most mirroring the state's exclusionary nature. The comparison between the Druze and other Arabs, however, suggests that the military institution may also shape—not just reflect—the politics of citizenship.

In many respects, this account is consistent with the literature published over the past two decades on Israel's relationship with its Arab minorities. Scholars, both Jewish and Arab, have uncovered much evidence of discrimination against Israel's Arab citizens, and they have laid at least part—and of-

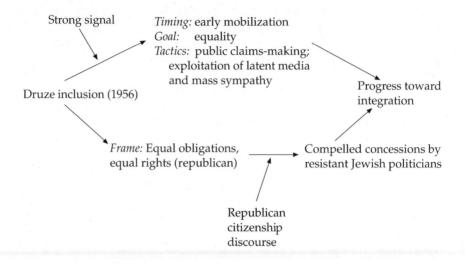

Figure 3. The consequences of drafting the Druze

ten the bulk—of the blame at the feet of the central state. However, whereas this conventional wisdom treats the Druze as culturally exceptional, manipulated, or even passive, I accord the Druze meaningful agency: they are neither cultural dopes nor the puppets of an omnipotent state. Whereas the conventional wisdom frames the subjection of the Druze to the draft as purely *reflective* of the state's will, in this book I treat that move as *productive* of Druze political behavior and identity. Whereas the conventional wisdom identifies Muslim and Christian exclusion from the IDF as just another instance of exclusion from the Israeli polity, I suggest that their exclusion was of far greater import.

In these chapters I argue that Israel missed an opportunity in the 1950s and 1960s to win over its Christian and Muslim citizens. Had Israel drafted Christian and Muslim Arab youth, inequities would undoubtedly have persisted, and resentment would still likely have bubbled over. But the counterfactual suggests at least the possibility that Israel could have forged a relationship with Christians and Muslims akin to that which it has developed with the Druze. Rare is the Druze politician today who expresses sympathy for those engaged in attacks on Israeli civilians; among other Arab politicians, in contrast, this is all too common. Counterfactuals of this nature are essentially contested, and, in the midst of the second intifada, this one is not likely to resonate with either Jewish or Arab citizens of Israel. Perhaps, however, in calmer moments, such a dose of historical perspective could help the parties achieve mutual understanding, prompt changes in state policy, and even heal some wounds.

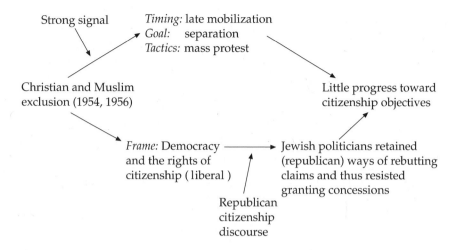

Figure 4. The consequences of excluding Christians and Muslims

The Israeli case presents scholars with intriguing puzzles, but conducting research in Israel on sensitive questions can be immensely frustrating. Occasionally, relevant data simply does not exist. For example, the Central Bureau of Statistics did not generally break down information on the Arab minorities by religious affiliation until the 1972 census. Whatever data does exist is often inaccessible. At the State Archive, files from the most relevant offices remain partly or entirely classified—notably the Office of the Adviser to the Prime Minister for Arab Affairs (fully classified) and the Department of Minorities in the Ministry of the Interior (classified after 1960). At the IDF Archive, documents from before 1956 have been systematically declassified, but only very partially: an archivist confided to me that only 1 percent of the documents associated with the military administration (*mimshal ha-zva'i*) that governed Israel's Arab citizens from 1948 through 1966 has been declassified. An equivalent to the U.S. Freedom of Information Act has had little impact because it includes a national security exemption, which the authorities have interpreted broadly.

As closed files are gradually declassified and exposed to public scrutiny over the coming decades, histories of Israel's relations with its Arab minorities will have to be rewritten. The claims advanced here are therefore necessarily somewhat tentative. However, revealing documents have slipped into the archives' open files, offering a glimpse into the richness of the full documentary record,[18] and key Jewish policy makers in the Arab sector have disclosed much information in interviews and public forums.[19] Thus the broad outlines of Israel's policies are known, providing a solid foundation for the arguments put forward in the chapters to come.

CHAPTER 3

Confronting a Land with People

It was hardly inevitable that the Druze would carve out a distinctive path toward citizenship, separate from their fellow Arabs, in the new state of Israel. The Druze had long exhibited particularistic tendencies, but there was no "natural" alliance between the Zionists and the Druze. It is true that the Druze did not, by and large, join in either the Arab Revolt of the late 1930s or the 1948 war, and some sought alliance with the Zionists as early as the 1930s. But Druze behavior did not, on the whole, differ markedly from that of many other rural Arabs to whom the language of nationalism was still alien as were its urban, educated adherents. Most rural Arabs were residents of Palestine but not Palestinians: unmoved by the nationalists' appeals, they were at most passive supporters of the cause who ultimately cared less about who ruled than about being able to plant their crops and tend their fields.

Despite earlier Zionist efforts to exploit communal cleavages among Arabs, the State of Israel did not, in its first decade, systematically draw distinctions between Druze and other Arabs when it came to substantive policy. As Arabs, all ran afoul of the Zionist vision, all fell victim to the young state's priorities and prejudices, and all remained suspect from a security perspective. They shared common grievances—the expropriation of land, subjection to military rule, rigidly enforced restrictions on travel, societal penetration by the General Security Services (GSS),[1] exclusion from the giant labor federation (the Histadrut), and unequal access to water resources. Some Druze villages, notably the two on Mount Carmel above Ḥaifa, were spared the worst of these oppressive measures. But, for the most part, Christians, Muslims, and Druze occupied the same (Arab) social space in the Jewish state, and all had much about which to be resentful during Israel's early years.

Jews and Arabs under the Mandate

The early Zionist settlers lived more or less—at times, much less—in peace with their Arab, largely Muslim, neighbors. They typically founded their settlements in uninhabited and swampy areas; they depended heavily on Arab labor; and their numbers remained small. But, with the second great wave of Jewish immigration shortly after the turn of the century, Zionist-Arab tension intensified. Mostly from Eastern Europe and Russia, the new arrivals came in larger numbers and with a more ambitious vision. Driven by nationalist ideals, they developed a flourishing agricultural economy and incipient industry while refusing to hire low-wage Arab workers.[2] In the late 1920s and 1930s, Jewish immigration skyrocketed, presenting the Arab inhabitants of Palestine with a multidimensional threat. The Zionist pioneers and European refugees were often skilled laborers and had access to foreign capital. They threatened the almost uniformly Arab character that Palestine had retained through the centuries. And, as Jewish individuals and agencies bought large swaths of Arab-owned land and evicted the current tenants, they embittered displaced Arabs and fed the emerging nationalist movement. Arabs sought to stanch the Jewish inflow, in part by periodically threatening the public order, but they were never successful for very long. British restrictions on Jewish immigration, imposed in response to the violence, were either evaded or eventually rescinded.

To Zionist leaders, the Arabs of Palestine were an obstacle, regardless of religion. Zionist propaganda regularly described their enterprise as settling a people without a land in a land without a people, and many Jewish immigrants were surprised to discover that Palestine was not nearly as empty as they had been led to believe.[3] But leading Zionist thinkers recognized early on that the most desirable areas of Palestine were teeming with human life, and they understood that territorial conflict was inevitable, that it would have a zero-sum character, and that a negotiated solution would be impossible. David Ben-Gurion warned the governing body of the prestate Jewish community (the *yishuv*) in 1919, "Everybody sees a difficulty in the question of relations between Arabs and Jews. But not everybody sees that there is no solution to this question. . . . We, as a nation, want this country to be *ours;* the Arabs, as a nation, want this country to be *theirs*." And the revisionist Ze'ev Jabotinsky similarly concluded that "the tragedy lies in the fact that there is a collision here between two truths. . . . The Arab is culturally backward, but his instinctive patriotism is just as pure and noble as our own; it cannot be bought, it can only be curbed by . . . *force majeure*."[4]

Publicly, however, most Zionist spokesmen argued that the Jewish immigrants posed no threat to the native population but would bring education, modern industry, and prosperity to all. Zionism would simultaneously make the Jews into a "normal" nation and civilize the Arabs. In recognition of their common class interests, Arab peasants might even join forces with Jewish la-

borers against the effendi (land-holding urban notables). Before various international bodies, Zionists affirmed that the Arab citizens of a future state of
Israel would enjoy the full range of civil, political, social, and economic rights.
When pressed on the tension between his nationalist and liberal commitments, Ben-Gurion offered only elusive platitudes: "I am unwilling to forego
even one percent of Zionism for 'peace'—yet I do not want Zionism to in-
fringe upon even one percent of legitimate Arab rights."[5] Aware that their
movement's fate hinged on international opinion, Ben-Gurion and his fellow
Zionists denied that there was any potential contradiction.

Privately, in contrast, Zionists recognized the intractability of the conflict
and even toyed with population transfer.[6] In general, most Zionist leaders dismissed critics who questioned them about the "Arab problem": as one put it
bluntly in 1925, "Listen, is it because you've already solved the Jewish problem that you pester me with the Arabs?"[7] While Pinḥas Lavon, a rare exception, envisioned Arabs working together with Jews even in the military, his
colleagues in the dominant political party, Mapai, rejected his proposals to
open the Histadrut to Arabs and to create a joint school system. In private settings, they candidly maintained that the future state would be premised on
preference for Jews, not equality; at the same time, they conveniently assumed away problems, asserting that few Arabs would ultimately choose to
remain in the new state or that whichever Arabs did stay would eschew integration.[8] Most refused to extend their gaze beyond the establishment of a majority Jewish state, and they devoted little concentrated thought to the sizable
Arab minority that would reside within that state's borders.[9]

Both Zionist and "revisionist" histories—in an unusual point of agreement—have portrayed the Arab population as unremittingly hostile to Jewish settlement, with the notable exception of the Druze. Their alliance with the
Zionists was predictable, for the two groups faced a common Muslim threat.
In this vein, one standard text asserts that the Druze, "traditionally the persecuted victims of Moslem Arabs, . . . accepted their new Israeli rulers with
gratitude and assurances of ironclad loyalty."[10] There is some evidence to
support this view. Some Druze, notably a handful of ḥamula (clan) leaders in
Ussafiya and Daliyat-al-Carmel near Ḥaifa, had enjoyed close relations with
Jews since the 1930s. When, during the Arab Revolt at the end of the decade,
insurgents murdered two Carmel ḥamula chiefs who refused to toe the nationalist line, more Druze joined the Zionist camp. Some ten years later, as the
British prepared to leave Palestine in the spring of 1948, several dozen Carmel
Druze joined the mainstream yishuv military force, the Haganah, and fought
alongside Syrian Druze who had defected to the Zionists after their unit in the
Arab Liberation Army (ALA) had been defeated. By June 1948 the IDF had
enough Druze soldiers to form two platoons, which participated in the liberation of the Galilee. The Druze cast the conflict in religious (Muslim-Jewish)
rather than nationalist (Arab-Jewish) terms: they consequently sympathized
with the Zionists, and few were attracted to the Arab nationalist movement.
Or so many historians would have one believe.[11]

But this conclusion extrapolates too readily from the Druze who lived near Ḥaifa to the larger Druze population, which lived in the central and upper Galilee and was very much a part of an almost exclusively Arab world.[12] Many Druze opposed closer links with the Zionists, and some took up arms alongside their fellow Arabs during the Arab Revolt and then again in 1948. Even during the revolt, the Druze atop the Carmel remained deeply split.[13] In 1936 Yosef Naḥmani of the Jewish National Fund (JNF) sought to persuade Druze *shaykhs* (religious and political leaders) to prevent further attacks, attesting to significant Druze participation in the Arab Revolt.[14] As the 1948 war approached, many Druze made common cause with the larger Arab population. In the winter of that year, the Haganah noted that indigenous Druze gangs had carried out raids on Jewish convoys, and a Druze wing sprang up under the auspices of the Arab National Committee. When the ALA's Syrian Druze battalion swept into Palestine that spring, it was welcomed even on the Carmel, and many local Druze flocked to it and were killed in battle with Zionist forces.[15] Some Druze brokered deals with the advancing Israeli forces, but no communitywide consensus emerged in the summer of 1948, leading to the failure of an IDF operation that had targeted the Galilee; and in August, two Druze villages permitted the ALA to position its soldiers there. Only in September and October 1948, as the Israelis' military superiority became apparent to all, did the Druze generally allow their bloodless conquest by the IDF.[16]

In the 1930s and 1940s, most Druze at least passively identified with their fellow Arabs and the nationalist cause. The Druze's neighbors were not co-religionists, but they shared a culture, historical experiences, and social ties.[17] Neither of the Carmel ḥamulas allied with the Zionists was a major force in Druze politics before 1948, and when, at the Zionists' request, the two clan leaders embarked on a tour of the Druze villages in 1946 with the aim of establishing a Jewish-Druze friendship association, they were not well received. Shaykh Amin Tarif was the recognized leader of the Druze community in Palestine: he maintained a position of strict neutrality and was, by some accounts, inclined to support his fellow Arabs in the battle against Zionism and its encroachment on Arab land.[18] As Ezra Danin, the Israeli Foreign Ministry's senior adviser on Arab affairs, observed in July 1948—in response to another official's complaint that, as the IDF's forces entered the Galilee, "Druzes and Christians are seen as 'kosher' and Muslims as 'non-kosher'"—"we have not ignored for a moment our previous experience and knowledge of the Druze and the Christians. They are not different from the Muslims and perhaps they are even worse."[19] Once Israel had clearly gained the upper hand, many Druze flocked to the Israeli side, but among such actors guided by realpolitik, no pact is a "steadfast alliance."[20]

Zionist (and later Israeli) leaders sought to fragment Arab unity by cultivating relationships with religious and ethnic minorities across the Muslim-Arab Middle East.[21] As part of this strategy, prominent Zionist figures advocated close relations with the Druze of Palestine, if only as a vehicle for approaching the larger Druze communities of Syria and Lebanon. Representatives from the Jewish Agency and the Haganah seized whatever opportunities arose to nurture trust, and the Zionists time and again showered the Druze with favors and even intervened with the British on the Druze's behalf. During the 1948 war, they continued to pursue this strategy, and Christians and Druze received better treatment at the hands of the IDF than did Muslims.[22] While the Druze appreciated Jewish assistance with the British authorities, there is little evidence that the strategy won their loyalty. As late as August 1948, although some Israeli observers claimed to be confident that the Druze's "friendship and alliance with us are sincere and stable," even they acknowledged that "outwardly [the Druze] appear neutral or even pro-Arab."[23]

Although the strategy called for the co-optation of Arab minorities, it was often superseded by the goal of clearing the land of Arabs—Druze as well as Christians and Muslims—so that future generations of Jews might comfortably settle. From a Zionist perspective, even the small Druze community was problematic. In the late 1930s, largely in response to the Peel Commission's proposals,[24] Abba Hushi (then secretary of the Workers' Council in Haifa and later the city's longtime mayor) sought to drum up support for transferring the Druze of Palestine to Syria. Chaim Weizmann, then president of the Zionist Organization and later the first president of Israel, endorsed the plan, encouraged Hushi to persist in his negotiations, and provided him with monies to tempt local Druze to sell their land and to promise to their Syrian hosts as settlement assistance. After several frustrating years, Hushi had still made little progress. Funds dried up with the outbreak of World War II, and the plot was dropped.[25]

A religious minority within the Arab majority, the Druze of Mandatory Palestine bore no great love for their Muslim neighbors, but neither were they the Jews' natural allies. The Druze were typical of Palestine's rural Arab population. While rural Arabs grew increasingly politically conscious during the 1930s and 1940s, their primary allegiance remained to the hamula. Largely isolated from national affairs, they recoiled from nationalism after the Arab Revolt, in part because of the Mandate's harsh suppressive tactics and in part because roving insurgents had imposed a brutal discipline on *all* villagers.[26] As one historian puts it, before 1948 "politics and the national struggle were remote, playthings of sophisticated city folk. . . . Much of the Arab population had only an indistinct, if any, idea of national purpose and statehood."[27] For the Druze, as for other rural Arabs, Zionism was a threat but usually an abstract one. Some Druze joined in combating Jewish encroachment; the majority remained neutral, although their sympathies likely lay with their fellow Arabs; and some wisely placed their bets on the Jewish horse. Zionist efforts to sway the Druze to their side were less than successful. One cannot read the later Druze relationship with the Israeli state back into the time of the Mandate.

In the winter and spring of 1948, after the United Nations General Assembly approved the partition of Palestine, the conflict escalated. Yet rural Arabs often displayed little interest in fighting the Zionists: some villages, whether dominated by Christians or Muslims or Druze, approached their Jewish neighbors to design strategies for peacekeeping, and many engaged in more passive forms of cooperation. Many of these feelers came to naught because of the Haganah's suspicion of all Arabs—a source of great frustration to the Arab Division of the Jewish Agency's Political Department, which asserted that there was a "possibility of distinguishing between good and bad Arabs."[28] As Israel extended its reach over the Galilee in the summer and fall of 1948, many Arabs, including Muslims, sued for peace and stayed on their land, particularly in the far north, which had been spared much of the war. Rural Arabs, regardless of their religious commitments, often had greater priorities than hewing to the nationalist agenda.[29]

While the Druze shared much with other rural Arabs, they were nevertheless unusual in discerning relatively early that the momentum had shifted to the IDF, that Israel would not be easily eliminated in a second round of fighting, and that holding on to their land required accommodation. They, therefore, tendered uncommon levels of cooperation with the advancing IDF, and, unlike the Muslims in particular, hardly any Druze fled in fear of retribution from the Israelis.[30] But the Druze leadership did not make a conscious strategic choice to ally with the Jews against the Muslim majority with which the Druze had long had tense relations. Rather, the Druze were simply more astute (or perhaps just more lucky) in their reading of the political tea leaves and were as a community more capable of coordinated action.

The big winners in the 1948 war were of course the Jews, and the biggest losers were the local Arabs. Eighty percent of the Arab population of Palestine had emigrated, fled, or been expelled, and the first to leave were the intellectual, political, and religious leaders, followed by the rest of the educated classes.[31] The vibrant Arab civil society—newspapers and magazines, political parties and federations, unions, clubs—collapsed. War was, as ever, disruptive to Druze life, but the Druze could have done much worse. Unlike many urban residents and Christians and especially Muslims, few Druze had abandoned their homes or land and thus they could not be assigned the legal (if bizarre) status of "present absentees"—a tactic that permitted Israeli authorities to confiscate much Arab-owned and Arab-occupied land. During the summer of 1948, Israeli officials usually allowed Druze farmers in areas under their control to harvest their crops, while Muslims were often prohibited from leaving their villages.[32] And, in a (short-lived) concession to Druze pride, the Druze were initially permitted to keep their weapons, as long as they registered them.[33] Nevertheless, the Druze too soon found themselves the victims of the discriminatory policies of the new Jewish state.

Democracy and Discrimination, 1948–1957

On May 14, 1948, David Ben-Gurion, surrounded by the leaders of the yishuv in the Tel Aviv Museum, announced the establishment of the State of Israel.

Although the declaration repeatedly proclaimed Israel "the Jewish state," it also promised that the new country would promote the welfare of all who lived within its boundaries:

> The State of Israel . . . will foster the development of the country for the benefit of all its inhabitants; it will be based on freedom, justice and peace as envisaged by the prophets of Israel; it will ensure complete equality of social and political rights to all its inhabitants irrespective of religion, race or sex; it will guarantee freedom of religion, conscience, language, education and culture; it will safeguard the Holy Places of all religions; and it will be faithful to the principles of the Charter of the United Nations.[34]

Although the document lacked legal standing, it did possess moral authority, as an expression of the bedrock principles on which the state had been founded. Israeli diplomats regularly invoked it in countering Arab states' accusations that the Arab citizens of Israel were the targets of persecution and discrimination.[35]

Although Israel's leading figures rarely wavered publicly from the liberal creed, in practice the new state waffled between treating the Arabs—Druze, Christians, and Muslims alike—as a "fifth column" and as a minority deserving full equality. Even apparently sincere advocates of the latter position occasionally mused about the dangers posed by the Arab citizens, and, in private, many expressed views and recommended policies that bore little resemblance to their public pronouncements.[36] Ben-Gurion, for example, who tirelessly defended Israel as a democratic state that safeguarded the rights of its minorities, opposed granting citizenship to the Arab residents of the so-called Little Triangle, an all-Arab region transferred to Israeli authority under the terms of the 1949 armistice agreement with Jordan: "These Arabs should not be living here. Anyone who thinks that the Arabs have the right to citizenship in the Jewish State is saying that we should pack our bags and leave."[37] Contradictory state policy was in part the consequence of bargaining among Jews, but it also resulted from a tension between the desire to integrate the country's Arab citizens and the pressing need to control them.[38]

The minority communities' standard of living improved dramatically under Israeli rule, an achievement that Israel's propaganda organs never tired of touting.[39] Health clinics were established throughout the Arab sector, producing an almost instantaneous decline in mortality. The educational system was revamped and vastly expanded.[40] Isolated villages became accessible by paved roads and were attached to the national electricity grid; water towers, wells, and other public works were built by the central government as well. Arab agricultural productivity increased thanks to the introduction of new seed strains, increased irrigation, and farm machinery—all facilitated by government loans and grants.[41] Although Arab laborers were not permitted to

join the Histadrut, which controlled access to jobs and provided a host of social and economic benefits, separate affiliated Arab trade unions were organized, and labor exchanges were established to distribute local jobs.[42]

In the political arena, Arabs enjoyed full suffrage, and often a greater proportion of Arab than Jewish citizens turned out to vote.[43] In January 1949
three Arab representatives entered the Knesset, elected either through Arab
lists affiliated with Mapai or through the Communist Party, Maki; when the
left-leaning Zionist party Mapam welcomed Arab citizens into its ranks in
1954, yet another avenue was opened.[44] Although it never achieved the status and ubiquity of Hebrew, Arabic was an official language for the purposes
of communication with government offices and in the courts. It was the language of instruction in the state-sponsored Arab school system, and official
publications appeared in both tongues.

But that is only half the story. Throughout the 1950s infiltration along Israel's borders was widespread, as refugees sought to return to homes now occupied either by other Arabs or more often by new Jewish immigrants, and
groups supported by the Arab states regularly wreaked havoc on the civilian
Jewish population. Israelis and Arabs alike anticipated a second war, and, in
this tense environment, Israeli leaders feared "their" Arabs would serve as an
intelligence network for Israel's Arab enemies, harbor terrorists and returning refugees, and conduct guerrilla activities.[45] Ben-Gurion, as usual, did not
mince words: "The IDF seeks to deter the external enemy, and the [military]
administration seeks to deter the internal enemy. Do you really believe the internal enemy does not exist? . . . I see three dangers to the Jewish people in its
land: the armies of Nasser, the refugees, and the Arabs in Israel."[46] A year
later, he told the Knesset that "at the moment, the internal danger is greater
and must take priority." The Arab citizens, he maintained, "should be judged
according to what they might do, and not according to what they have
done."[47] Guided by that standard, Israeli policy toward its Arab minority was
in equal parts repressive and well meaning. Uri Lubrani, the prime minister's
adviser on Arab affairs, indicated which of these values took precedence: "If
there were no Arab university students, it would have been better. If they had
remained woodcutters, maybe they would have been easier to control."[48]

Fear of Arab betrayal was no doubt real,[49] but the Israeli government also
put in place measures that were only tangentially linked to legitimate security concerns. The responsibilities of the military administration (MA), established over nearly all areas where Arabs lived, included not only keeping
"dangerous elements" under surveillance and foiling cross-border infiltration
but blocking Arabs' use of state lands and absentee properties designated for
Jewish settlement, preventing the reestablishment of abandoned Arab villages, thwarting Arab laborers from capturing labor markets intended for
new (Jewish) immigrants, preparing land for cultivation by Jewish farmers,
and encouraging the industrial development of the Galilee and the absorption of (Jewish) immigrants.[50] The military governors also worked closely

with the GSS to inhibit political activity among the country's Arab citizens, especially by hampering the Communist Party (Maki).[51] They sought to undermine all independent Arab organization, viewing it as an instrument of "nationalist agitation."[52]

These various missions could not be defended on narrow security grounds. In 1962 the head of the IDF General Staff's research department admitted as much: "From 1949 until today, there has been no evidence that the Arab states have prepared to exploit the Arab minority in Israel for the sake of military missions . . . during war or approaching the outbreak of war." Arabs were occasionally recruited for spying, but "information and espionage did not receive high priority in the Arab intelligence services with regard to the allocation of monetary resources, professionals, or technical equipment."[53] By the mid-1950s only a broad definition of security—so broad that it appeared coextensive with the interests of the regime and its Jewish constituents—could justify the administration.

Military governors exploited an extensive system of permits to ensure compliance. The most onerous were the limits on travel, ostensibly designed to identify and capture dangerous Arabs but also actually intended to protect immigrant Jewish labor from Arab competition. Initially, with the region divided into forty-five zones, most Arabs could hardly get beyond their own villages without permits, which the governor tightly controlled. Over the years, the number of zones was reduced, restrictions were eased, and permits were distributed more freely, so that by 1966, when the MA was finally dissolved, few Arabs were constrained.[54] For much of the 1950s, however, these regulations exerted a powerful effect. Moreover, all economic activity in the Arab sector required the permission of the governor, and the GSS burrowed into every nook and cranny of Arab life. Sometimes the governor distributed these permits himself, in consultation with the GSS, but often, particularly in later years, he delegated this task to the *mukhtar* (village chief). Thus was established a chain of debt and obligation running from the villagers to the mukhtar to the governor.[55]

The government's public defense of the MA against charges of discrimination was disingenuous.[56] It asserted that the administration was established in certain areas not because the residents were largely Arab but because this was where infiltration was most likely and where the security concern was greatest; when Jews came under its jurisdiction, the government claimed, the rules were applied equally strictly.[57] In practice, however, Jews did not have to wait in humiliating lines at the governor's office or approach the mukhtar for a permit. Jews did not worry that their requests to open shops or factories would be denied. Just the opposite: Jewish settlements within the MA were priorities for development, and special funds were allocated to rapidly industrialize and Judaize the Galilee.[58]

By the late 1950s, a political figure as prominent as former prime minister and Mapai leader Moshe Sharett could openly declare the MA "such a monster that it is worthwhile killing."[59] Yet it survived for another decade. This was partly because it was self-sustaining. "The need for the Military Administration," said one Knesset member, "springs largely from the Military Administration itself."[60] Periodically the prime minister would ask the IDF chief of staff whether the MA was still necessary, and he would in turn ask the military governors, who would naturally confirm that indeed it was.[61] Second, the MA served Mapai's partisan interests.[62] The administration's powerful levers were often applied to undermine the challengers to Mapai's left and to ensure high voter turnout for Mapai.[63] By the late 1950s parties across the spectrum recognized that the MA had given Mapai a huge advantage in tapping Arab electoral potential, and they banded together in opposition.[64]

The MA was, however, only the tip of the discriminatory iceberg. Using cleverly designed legal instruments, the young state seized the bulk of Arab-owned and Arab-controlled land and eventually turned much of it over to Jewish immigrants.[65] The amount of land thus expropriated cannot be precisely ascertained, but the total clearly climbed into the millions of *dunams* (1 dunam = approximately one-quarter of an acre).[66] Officials in the government and in quasi-public institutions like the Jewish National Fund cared little for fine distinctions among the Arab religious communities, as all fell victim to the state's ravenous hunger for land.[67] Some Druze villages lost as much as 60 percent of their holdings. Even in Daliyat-al-Carmel and Ussafiya, the laws were applied without mercy.[68] Jewish protectors of "loyal" communities could rarely save them from their legal, if unjust, fate.

These land seizures aimed at furthering *yehud ha-Galil*, the "Judaization of the Galilee," and they were underpinned by a mélange of considerations.[69] Security, narrowly construed, was one: in 1948 Jews owned little land in the central Galilee, and that region, one officer reported in the mid-1950s, "remains today the only area in the state in which there exists a continuous and dense concentration of the Arab population, almost all of whom are hostile to the State of Israel."[70] But planners were also jealous of the region's fertility and were eager to transform it into "the primary supplier of our fruit baskets."[71] Finally, they were also inspired by the Zionist vision of an Arab-free Israel, which Ben-Gurion stated succinctly in 1960:

> The trees whose fruit we eat, the roads on which we travel, the houses we live in, the factories where we work, the schools where are our children are educated, the army in which they are trained, the ships we sail in and the planes in which we fly, the language we speak and the air we breathe, the landscape we see and the vegetation that surrounds us—*all* of it is Jewish.[72]

The most straightforward way to advance this program was to establish new Jewish settlements along the northern border and at critical nodal points, but that required land. In addition to legal expropriation, the authorities prevented Arab cross-border and internal refugees from returning to their homes and expelled individuals as well as entire villages.[73] They even explored re-settling Israel's Arab citizens in Argentina.[74] IDF Chief of Staff Moshe Dayan defended his forces' aggressive action against infiltration on such grounds: "There will perhaps be another opportunity to transfer these Arabs from Eretz Israel in the near future, and as long as this possibility exists, we must do nothing to foreclose it."[75]

Many discriminatory measures, however, bore only the most indirect relationship to security concerns. Compared to their Jewish competitors, Arab farmers faced severe water and electricity quotas. They were excluded from powerful marketing, credit, and purchasing cooperatives, and they received poor loan terms. When the state did compensate them for the land it had seized for "public purposes," they received between one-fourth and one-fifth of what the state paid to Jewish owners.[76] Employment officers favored Jews and shunted educated Arabs into poor-paying low-skilled work. As Abba Ḥushi acknowledged in the early 1960s, "The claims regarding discrimination in work and business are largely justified. . . . There is no shortage of work among Arab workers, but there is discrimination regarding places of work, types of work, and profession."[77] Finally, public and private companies and institutions declared military service a criterion for jobs or benefits, thus excluding Arab citizens.[78] As early as 1953 some officials voiced their misgivings:

> We are not upholding the principles of democracy, the equality and patience of which we always speak, among our Arab residents. . . . I suspect that we have not done all we can in this area—and especially regarding those points that are more obvious, more emotional, more infuriating, *and sometimes they are particularly the issues that are not important from a security perspective.*[79]

Not only were Israel's policies toward its Arab minorities in the state's first decade deeply discriminatory in numerous areas, but they were, as a rule, applied without regard to religious affiliation. Although some officials, including Ben-Gurion and his advisers on Arab affairs, inclined toward the older Zionist practice of showing preference for the Druze and other minorities (thereby fragmenting the Arab population), this did not carry over much into practice. When Israeli decision makers spoke of Arabs, they usually meant the Druze as well; the Arab Departments of the ministries and the Histadrut, and the Office of the Adviser to the Prime Minister for Arab Affairs, were the addresses for *Druze* appeals. With the exception of the two villages on the Carmel, the Druze were subject to the same restrictions on movement as other Arabs until the late 1950s. Their land was expropriated with the same legal mechanisms and to the same extent, and, even through the 1970s, development plans failed to differentiate between the Druze and other Arabs. While the Ministry of the Interior and others supported the establishment of Druze local councils, those responsible for security—the MA and GSS—dominated decision making, and they opposed all independent political activity in Druze villages.[80] Israeli decision makers did draw distinctions between "positive" and "negative" *individual* Arabs, between those who had shown themselves worthy of trust and those who had sided with Arab nationalism. The former not surprisingly received preferential treatment, but whether an Arab was Druze or Muslim mattered less than his stance on Arab nationalism and Israeli rule.[81]

In short, the fundamental policy baseline for the Druze and other Arabs was, in practice, the same.[82] While Ben-Gurion repeatedly and seemingly sincerely said he wished to close the gap between Jews and Druze, his underlings consistently refused to implement his broad policy guidelines. As the historian Shimon Avivi summarizes Israeli policy toward the Druze from independence through the late 1960s, "Government officials failed, in many cases, to distinguish between Druze and Arab [sic]: they looked the same, spoke the same language, lived next to each other, and had the same names. These similarities made the Druze seem to them like an Arab, and so they treated him."[83]

The Arab population was, after 1948, in no position to protest its mistreatment. The war had deprived it of its religious and political leadership as well as of its intellectual and business elites—that is, of all those who might have mounted a challenge to Israeli rule. An urban population that would have totaled nearly three hundred thousand without the 1948 war amounted by 1951 to under just forty-five thousand. The remaining Arabs were, according to Ben-Gurion's adviser on Arab affairs, "like a headless body."[84] Only the hamula chiefs could take the reins, and these traditional local leaders were easily co-opted.[85] The Arab Knesset members (MKs) affiliated with Mapai were, through the 1970s, typically wealthy notables with a vested interest in the status quo. They mobilized electoral support for Mapai, voted with the party, and avoided all criticism of the government. Arab Mapam representatives were more independent, and those of Maki still more so, but they, like the parties to which they belonged, were marginal.[86] Muslim religious institutions had been decimated, and the new Muslim authorities were indebted to Israel for their positions. However, Archbishop George Hakim, the highest-ranking Greek Catholic (or Melkite) prelate in the country, was an articulate spokesman for his flock's plight and a thorn in Israel's side, although some thought him insufficiently assertive.

Without a national leadership, political activity among Israel's Arab citizens was in these early years occasional and brief. This was particularly true of the Druze, the most rural and least educated of the Arab groups. According to the 1961 census, the first that carefully examined the Arab population, 91 percent of Druze continued to live in rural areas, compared with 83 percent of Muslims and just 39 percent of Christians.[87] There are no statistics regarding literacy and education among the various Arab communities before 1961, but in 1957 Christians (around 20 percent of the Arab population) constituted 46 percent of all teachers in government-sponsored Arab schools, Muslims (70 percent) accounted for 40 percent of teachers, and the Druze (10 percent) contributed a mere 5 percent of educators. Of 214 Arabs in government service in June 1953, only 7 were Druze (3 percent), compared with 117 Christians (55 percent) and 88 Muslims (41 percent).[88] The lack of education left the community not only impoverished but also firmly in the grip of the traditional leadership, which was as pliant as (but not more so than) that of other rural Arab communities. Those few Druze who did come politically of age by the mid-1950s identified fully with the pan-Arabist discourse common among the Arab intellectual classes, and they faced the same Israeli-imposed barriers to political organization.[89]

This first decade was, for the Arab community, marked by the slow process of communal reconstruction and reorganization. Despite occasional outbursts, flashes of resentment, and insecurity, the Arab community was generally quiet and obedient. With a dependent and relatively uneducated leadership at the helm, and with Israeli state policies designed to reinforce the ḥamula and religious heads' dependency, quiescence reigned.

Military Service for Minorities?

In the fall of 1949, the Knesset took up the question of the draft, and in 1950 it approved an unusually universal conscription law. Technically neutral with respect to both gender and ethnicity, it called on men and women, Jews and Arabs, to defend their country. But the law also authorized the defense minister to grant exemptions, and, despite the insistence of the Communist Party's Knesset delegation that the law be fully applied, the entire Arab population was not—and, with the exception of the Druze, has never been—drafted.[90]

But the question of conscripting Arabs would not go away. The most serious effort came in 1954 when Defense Minister Pinḥas Lavon ordered the registration of minority youth. According to a ministry official, this was to be "part of the process of freeing the Arab population from the feeling of discrimination by extending rights and obligations to all the residents of Israel."[91] With Prime Minister Sharett's support, the Ministry of Defense announced in July that registration would commence imminently, and Lavon's experiment even received the public endorsement of Reuven Barakat, the head of the Histadrut's Arab Affairs Department. During November and December 1954, a lively debate erupted in the Hebrew-language press, but the process ground to a halt when Lavon was forced to resign in February 1955 for unrelated reasons. Sharett invited Ben-Gurion to return as defense minister, and Ben-Gurion's predictable opposition, joined with that of the IDF

General Staff and the ḥamula leaders, compelled the suspension of Arab registration. It was never again to receive anything more than passing consideration.[92]

Lavon's experiment did not last long, but it was, in a sense, a surprising success. Since January 1950, when Maki's Tewfik Toubi had on the floor of the Knesset demanded the inclusion of Arabs in mandatory military service, the party had not raised the issue in a public forum, sensing little popular enthusiasm. Yet, when summoned, young Arabs flocked to the registration stations—perhaps, Jewish observers thought, because they found the prospect of battle exciting, perhaps because they were attracted to military drill and discipline, perhaps because they saw military service as a way to escape stultifying village life, perhaps because they truly believed that equal obligations would bring equal rights.[93] Many expressed strong preferences regarding their unit of choice and asked how they could ensure entry into it. Many over the age of twenty, who had been exempted from registration, showed up anyway, hoping somehow to slip in, and others who were too young sought to register as well. Like draftees the world over, some resorted to absurd tricks to evade service, but the feedback from the Arab youth was overwhelmingly positive. Despite poor coordination between the IDF and the Ministry of the Interior, around 90 percent of the Arabs subject to the order had been registered within two months—a success by any standard.[94]

In contrast, older Arabs and clan leaders were from the first opposed to Lavon's program and sought to undermine it at every turn.[95] They raised economic, political, and social concerns. Conscription would interfere with their sons' ability to contribute to the family livelihood, and it would ruin the community's standing with fellow Arabs across the border. But, in seeking to persuade their sons, they primarily argued that military service would force young men to delay marriage. The unspoken, but palpable, fear among the older generation was that patriarchal Arab society would never survive conscription. After their exposure to secular, modern Israeli society, Arabs drafted to the IDF would return prepared to rebel against the existing power structure centered on the family patriarch and the ḥamula. The local leadership of Maki, despite the party's official support, sided with the forces of tradition, as did Archbishop Hakim. To Israeli promises, they replied, "Without rights, there is no draft."[96] But in Israel, dominated by a republican citizenship discourse, such a declaration seemed the opposite of civic virtue and was consequently fated to have little impact.

Among Lavon's opponents on this issue, as on many others, was the professional military. As late as the summer of 1954, the commander of the Minorities Unit refused to accept Muslims even as volunteers, and a 1955 rejection letter explained to a Muslim applicant that "until now the IDF has not mobilized Muslim youth."[97] In September 1954 Dayan expressed annoyance and dismay that the question of registering Arabs had been raised first not with the General Staff but with a civilian body, the Supreme Council for Arab

Affairs. Dayan further informed Lavon that "the general atmosphere in the [General] Staff (and this was also my first reaction) is against the establishment of Arab units in the IDF."[98] He argued that the Muslim minority was too great a security risk, but this position conveniently complemented the IDF's interest in maintaining its autonomy. Lavon was at loggerheads with the IDF throughout his tenure, as he sought to impose strict civilian control over a military to which Ben-Gurion had often given free rein; and in the wake of the botched sabotage operation by Israeli agents in Egypt that led to his resignation—the first stage of the so-called Lavon affair—the entire country became aware of the crisis in civil-military relations.[99]

The conventional wisdom is that the Druze uniformly welcomed military service while other Arabs uniformly opposed it, but the record does not support that conclusion. At the end of the 1948 war, most Druze serving with the Minorities Unit left the IDF. Those who remained were generally Syrian Druze who could not return home and had few other ways of earning a living. The Minorities Unit was woefully undermanned, and Druze volunteers rarely came forward to fill the ranks. Just twenty-five Druze from villages in Israel volunteered for service between January 1950 and June 1953.[100] Low pay and the unit's assignment in the country's south, far from the Druze's homes in the Galilee, made service unattractive, but many were also dissuaded by the opposition of religious and ḥamula leaders. These recruitment problems were not a passing phase: they persisted until conscription began among the Druze in May 1956. The unit's commanding officer even sought the help of the Galilee's military governor, requesting that he make life difficult for Druze who did not volunteer. Druze notables now and then interceded and raised limited numbers of troops, but they always exacted a price for their assistance.[101]

In 1953 the authorities announced the imposition of mandatory reserve duty, but the religious leadership, with the exception of MK Shaykh Salaḥ Khnayfes, resisted such recruitment. Shaykh Amin Tarif not only feared the younger generation's exposure to Israeli culture and suspected that the Druze would be exploited as cannon fodder but he was reluctant to burn the Druze community's bridges to its fellow Arabs in Israel and neighboring states. Tarif's vociferous opposition raised questions about his loyalty in the minds of Israeli officials, who were generally inclined to support him and other traditional leaders.[102] In short, the Druze were not as willing servants of the state as they have usually been portrayed.

Although Israeli officers and officials often asserted that the Druze, unlike other Arabs, were trustworthy, their treatment of the Minorities Unit belied that claim.[103] At first, in 1949, the Minorities Unit operated in the north countering infiltration, but it was soon transferred to the Negev to patrol the southern border.[104] The purpose was clear: to prevent the largely Druze Minorities Unit from confronting Syrian or Lebanese Druze in battle and to shield the Druze from the temptation to betray Israel. As Amnon Yanai, the commander of the Minorities Unit, observed in 1953, "Their permanent work in the Negev seems to them—and justly so—discriminatory compared to the Jewish soldiers that serve only for short periods in the Negev and on a rotation basis." Nor were Druze permitted to serve outside the Minorities Unit. This policy was the joint product of paternalism and continuing distrust: Yanai argued that the Druze soldier "suffers from feelings of inferiority and from suspicions that he would not be able to overcome were he to serve in a single unit with Jewish soldiers," and his blunt successor defended the segregated status quo, maintaining that "it is also desirable, for security reasons, that there should be separate units to improve supervision of them."[105] Discrimination against the Druze was rampant: numerous specialties remained closed to them, few became officers, and the Minorities Unit did not see combat again until 1967. In his diary, Ben-Gurion swore to solve this problem—"We must firmly uproot all discrimination. We must allow every Druze to progress like the Jew"—but it persisted nonetheless.[106] Until the mid-1970s the Druze served in a very different army than did their Jewish counterparts, but at least they served.

In May 1956 mandatory conscription of Druze youth commenced. The official version is that the Druze leaders requested that the military service law be applied to their community.[107] But enough documentation has surfaced to warrant the conclusion that the initiative lay with the Israeli government. Immediately after the 1953 reserve recruitment, the commanding officer of the Minorities Unit proposed obligatory conscription for Druze males. In late 1954, Druze MK Jabber Mu'addi met with Dayan and requested that the Druze be drafted. A year later, in November and December 1955, Druze leaders dispatched a wave of stilted formal requests for conscription to the Minorities Unit, the minister of defense, and the adviser to the prime minister for Arab affairs. Written in an identical tone and nearly identical language, nearly all invoked the equation of rights and obligations, and most indicated that the letters had been composed at Mu'addi's request—a sure sign that the state had solicited the letters to ensure a proper paper trail.[108] Army plans for drafting the Druze, however, appeared as early as February 1955 and were discussed in the IDF throughout that year, long before any Druze request (other than Mu'addi's) appears in the records. By late November 1955, as the first Druze requests flowed in, IDF officials had already decided how many Druze were to be drafted in each wave in the coming year.[109]

To the extent that the authorities' motives can be discerned, domestic and international political interests—not strategic or ethical concerns—appear to have been paramount.[110] Conscription of the Druze, they believed, would forestall nationalist mobilization among Israel's Arab citizens by fragmenting the Arab citizenry and would effectively counter foreign critics of Israel's minority policies.[111] Although the Druze were small in number, admitting them to the IDF would assuage Jewish Israelis' consciences and, even more important, neutralize those at home and abroad who claimed that the state persecuted Arabs without cause.[112] The Druze would serve as evidence of Jewish liberalism and of the perfidy of other Arabs whose irreconcilability had unfortunately deprived them of full citizenship. No one, however, ascribed much weight to the Druze's military contribution. Only political considerations during the state's first decade had saved the Minorities Unit from repeated efforts to disband it on grounds of inefficiency. Even in 1949, one official from the Ministry of Religion commented that, despite the publicity attached to the Druze unit, "as far as numbers and military importance are concerned, they do not amount to much."[113]

Concerns about the social and political consequences of military service sparked vigorous opposition to conscription among the Druze, and protests began before the first class had been drafted. There were even unconfirmed rumors that some religious leaders would not participate in the feast of the prophet Shu'ayb—a traditional Druze religious festival held at the supposed tomb of Moses' father-in-law, Jethro (in Arabic, Shu'ayb), which soon after 1948 had been infused with Israeli nationalist content and transformed into a militaristic quasi-official ceremony in which the Minorities Unit figured centrally—and were instead declaring it "a day of mourning, not a holiday, since the conscription law is unacceptable to the Druze religion." The Interior Ministry's regional representative reported that "a state of tension prevailed regarding the mandatory conscription."[114] Opposition intensified in late 1956 and early 1957, as the restive religious leadership organized demonstrations, appeals to the press, meetings with Knesset members, and the distribution of leaflets. Shaykh Farhud Qasim Farhud of Rama arranged a mass protest, and some three hundred shaykhs traveled to Jerusalem to protest the draft across from the Knesset. Petitioners from Abu Snan argued that the new policy "had been motivated by the political considerations of leaders who sought to be rewarded by the authorities." In February 1957 residents of Ussafiya—a town known for its strong relationship with the Israeli establishment—held protests against the draft in Haifa, across from the American Consulate, the British Consulate, and the Mobilization Office. With rare exceptions—for example, Druze from Shfar'am who argued that they were part of the Arab nation—Druze who opposed conscription appeared to be motivated by local economic, political, and social calculations, not deeply held nationalist commitments.[115]

The Israeli authorities leaned heavily on the traditional leadership and the resisters.[116] Although Israeli intelligence reported that the consensus in the Druze community was that Mu'addi's efforts had been for his own gain, relatively few shaykhs were willing to oppose the draft publicly, and Shaykh Amin Tarif in particular, who had led the opposition in 1953 to reserve recruitment, worked to undercut the vocal opponents of conscription. Noncompliance with draft orders was initially widespread, even in the Carmel villages, but levels soon improved.[117]

By mid-1957, only a whisper of protest could be heard, for the state had appeased religious authorities with two concessions. The first was a system of exemptions for Druze who had committed themselves to religious study, to joining the select group of *ukkal*. Shaykhs who had feared that mandatory service would dilute their authority and reduce the number of religious adherents were now reassured. Over time, this system has, with some shaykhs' approval, been exploited by Druze seeking to avoid military service for whatever reason. Second, the Druze had long sought recognition as a *millet*, an autonomous religious community. This standing, which carried with it the right to supervise communal religious endowments (*waqf*)—usually farmland whose revenues finance houses of worship and study and religious schools—and to maintain religious courts in matters of personal status, had been denied the Druze under the Ottomans and the British, and it does not seem accidental that they were granted their wish in 1957. Ben-Gurion had apparently considered Druze religious autonomy "a magnificent idea" as early as 1948, but nothing had come of it over the next decade. Over the course of several years, the Druze waqf was institutionalized, a personal status law was adopted by the Druze, and Druze religious courts were set up and judges appointed. The religious leadership now had behind it not just the force of tradition but the power of a legal institution.[118] Given the only partial declassification of documents, such horse-trading remains speculative, yet it is intuitively persuasive.

Both traditional and revisionist historians have maintained that the Druze were, from well before 1948 and certainly thereafter, more accommodating to the Zionists (and later to the Israelis) than were their Christian and Muslim neighbors and that they were compensated accordingly. Some explain the Druze anomaly as a product of the Druze's vulnerability as a small group desperate to survive and retain a shred of autonomy. Others suggest that the Druze identified with the locally dominant Jews as a fellow minority among the regionally dominant Muslims. Both reasons have been advanced to explain why the Druze were targeted for military service and why they came to occupy an intermediate position in the Israeli polity.

The conventional wisdom is based on a selective reading of the complicated and often contradictory historical evidence, however. Zionist leaders certainly did seek to fragment the local Arab population in Palestine, but they pursued this objective fitfully at best. After the establishment of the state, official policy was less than consistent, but it generally continued to emphasize the importance of distinguishing among the various Arab communities, and the Druze occasionally benefited from the authorities' petty favors. On the whole, however, the Druze suffered similar forms and levels of discrimination, manipulation, and oppression in the young ethnic democracy. While Ben-Gurion differentiated between Druze and other Arabs, many other officials did not set the Druze apart—either rhetorically or substantively: they cast all Arabs, including the Druze, as a security threat, and they designed uniform and universal policies based on that presumption. The record of Arab military service in the 1950s suggests that the most important cleavages were less communal and religious than generational. With the exception of a handful of committed nationalists, younger Arabs, regardless of religious affiliation, generally welcomed military service; the traditional leadership opposed military service because it threatened their status within the village's patriarchal political and social system. In the first decade after Israel's independence, the Druze were not the beneficiaries of unusual state largesse in the arenas that mattered most, they did not escape suspicion despite their service in the IDF, and they did not differ much from their rural Christian and Muslim counterparts in their attitudes toward the state.

The chapters that follow systematically trace differences that emerged by the mid-to-late 1960s, in the wake of the imposition of military service, between the Druze and other Arabs. By demonstrating that Israel's policies toward the Druze did not differ radically from its policies toward other Arabs and by showing that the Druze did not differ radically from other rural Arabs in their attitudes and stances toward the Zionists and later the new state, this chapter has laid the critical foundation for the ensuing analytical narrative. It has established an essential baseline from which to measure the difference that military service can make.

CHAPTER 4

Two Roads to Jerusalem

The newly formed State of Israel and its Arab citizens eyed each other warily after 1948. The young state was surrounded by adversaries, and it doubted the loyalty of nearly one-fifth of its population. During the war, the IDF had proven itself, but it remained undermanned, undertrained, and underequipped. Conscripting Arab youth would alleviate the manpower shortage, but it would also entail risk, providing a possibly irreconcilable minority with military training and arms. The Arab citizens, on the other hand, had to grapple with their own questions. Israeli officials spoke of equality, and the state funneled resources into the Arab sector. But such talk seemed Orwellian, as Arabs found themselves subject to military rule, restrictions on travel, land seizures, and exclusion from the major political parties. Every Arab leader, and even potential participant, must have estimated how the state would respond to political protest, to efforts to hold it to its promises of meaningful citizenship. Would it grudgingly concede, admitting the injustice of its policies? Would it deny Arab claims? Or would it use Arab demands as a pretext for broadening the expulsions and land expropriation, for rooting out agitators, even for ridding Israel of its Arab minority? Both sides wrestled with these complex calculations.

Military manpower policies can serve as strong signals of the state's intent, helping cautious minorities sort through contradictory data. In the early 1950s Israel considered drafting its Arab citizens, but a bungled covert operation and its political fallout stopped this plan in its tracks. In 1956, however, Druze males became subject to the draft, and in welcoming the Druze into the military, Prime Minister Ben-Gurion invoked the familiar equation of rights and duties. Should Israel's manpower choices have proven powerful signals capable of shaping the political behavior of Druze and other Arabs, or should they have seemed weak and been ignored? As we have seen, strong signals display some combination of credibility, clarity, and availability, and Israel's manpower choices exhibited all three. They therefore should have had a substantial impact on the timing, goals, and tactics of Arab citizens' political activity and ultimately on the degree and form of effective citizenship they achieved. And, in fact, they did. The strong Israeli manpower-policy signal helps explain why the (included) Druze mobilized earlier than did other (excluded) Arabs, why the Druze employed conventional political tactics while other Arabs embraced contentious (in addition to parliamentary) politics, and why the Druze consistently pursued integration while other Arabs were regularly attracted to separationist aims.

Signaling in Context

The manpower-policy signal was certainly *available* in Israel in the 1950s and beyond because Israeli society has been deeply militaristic. Such militarism has not manifested itself in the usual ways: through glorifying violence, romanticizing the military lifestyle, or emulating military customs.[1] But the IDF has inhabited a central site in the country's cultural complex, notwithstanding challenges to its sterling record after 1973.[2] Most Jewish Israelis have seen military service not only as an essential rite of passage but as the crucible of citizenship, as the primary institution through which individual and collective identities are formed.[3] The link between service and citizenship is so often articulated that it has become rhetorically ritualized. Claims to citizenship were, and still are, buttressed by military service—whether one served, in which unit, and how greatly one was decorated.[4]

Israel's political and social structures have imparted *clarity* to the manpower-policy signal. First, Israel's political system in this period spoke with one voice. The executive and legislative branches normally moved in lockstep, and local councils and municipalities possessed little coercive authority. Most important, Mapai dominated the political scene for nearly three decades, until it was finally displaced by the Likud in 1977. Its partisan concerns penetrated all levels of the bureaucracy, and its supporters and opponents alike viewed party, government, and state as nearly indistinguishable.[5] The centralization of the state structure, the stability of Mapai's rule, and the party's firm grasp on the bureaucracy bolstered not only the signal's clarity but its credibility, for there was little room for involuntary defection.

Second, like other militarist polities, Israel has historically lacked a bright line dividing the military and civilian spheres.[6] Revisions in the military's manpower policies have consequently suggested not the preferences of a narrow segment but a broad bulwark of political support. Before and especially after the 1973 war, Israel had a single integrated economic, political, and social network: senior officers were swiftly absorbed into civilian life, and military rank tended to translate into civilian status.[7] At the mass level, the reserve system, organized along the regimental model, served a similar function, for reservists often lived near one another and socialized outside of *miluim* (reserve duty). The result was that—as Yigael Yadin, the IDF chief of staff who designed the system, famously put it—the Israeli civilian was a soldier on eleven months' annual leave.[8]

Third, the nature of the Israeli recruitment system further boosted the signal's clarity. A rarity among contemporary states, Israel still conscripts the majority of its male citizens, and until relatively recently nearly all Jewish men in each cohort were called to active duty.[9] Although a small number of individuals were declared unfit, members of an ethnic or religious group could not be systematically excluded without the message coming across loud and clear.

Finally, the Israeli manpower-policy signal appeared *credible.* With the exception of the few Druze who condemned conscription because it separated the Druze from the broader Arab community, most appear to have taken Israeli officials at their word, believing that citizenship rights would follow the fulfillment of military obligations. Although in retrospect Israeli leaders appear to have had no intention of conceding much of consequence, the new manpower policy had qualities that suggested that Jewish politicians were sincere and that offered recourse to the Druze even if they were not. First, while the inclusion of the Druze does not appear to have met much resistance within the IDF and thus was not politically costly, it was costly in a more basic strategic sense. Like other Arabs, the Druze had reason to be dissatisfied with their lot under Israeli rule, and their feelings toward the new state were mixed at best. Moreover, their coreligionists were important actors across the border, and several even served in the Syrian high command. Given the Israeli fear of Arab betrayal, the expected costs of drafting the Druze were plain to see. As late as 1966 Amnon Lin warned that "all the training given to young Druze in the army, all the weaponry, all this is likely to prove dangerous to the state if the young Druze do not know why they must support the state."[10] Second, the public nature of the Israeli commitment created potential domestic and especially international costs to defection. Pinhas Lavon perceptively predicted in 1948 that "this state will in some ways be a glass house, and every time we yawn, and anything that we do, big or small, will be photographed by the entire world."[11] Nearly a decade later, the Foreign Ministry's Walter Eytan confirmed Lavon's insight and complained that the MA undermined Israel's international position: "If we are to wave the banner of democracy, they want us to be a true democracy. Any deviation from the principles of democracy makes a poor impression, especially because the world expects something different from us."[12] Israel's diplomats at the United Nations parried the fusillade of criticism by portraying the country's Arab citizens as a potential threat to the state and by demonstrating that these groups had, despite their antagonism, made great strides since 1948. But the former argument was, after 1956, not sustainable publicly with regard to the Druze.

For other Arabs, excluded from service in the IDF, questions as to the credibility of the signal were less salient, for there was no possible deceptive motive. The events of the mid-1950s—when Ben-Gurion's return to power had doomed Lavon's plan to extend conscription and when the Druze alone had been drafted—settled any niggling doubts about the Jewish core's deep distrust of the Arab minority. However, Christian and Muslim Arabs had been excluded from numerous Israeli institutions: Why ascribe much causal power to the IDF in particular? The critical role for the manpower-policy signal in shaping Christian and Muslim politics emerges out of the comparison with the Druze. The Druze shared a great deal with their fellow Arabs—from a common culture and socioeconomic structure to a shared experience of oppression at the hands of the Israeli authorities—but their political path had nevertheless diverged substantially from that of their neighbors by the mid-1960s. The Druze's inclusion in the IDF, and Christians and Muslims' exclusion from that central Israeli institution, proved to be the difference.

Slouching toward Integration: The Druze in the Jewish State, 1957–1995

Mobilization Delayed, 1957–1965

For several years, notwithstanding the inclusive signal, Druze politics underwent little change. With Jewish patrons supporting ḥamula leaders,[13] the extended kinship group remained the basic unit of political affiliation and mobilization.[14] The Druze MKs were ḥamula heads who had cultivated ties to the central government and upheld the status quo. And officers' billets were typically bestowed on Druze from prominent families, who had little incentive to challenge the traditional power structure.[15]

The first wave of conscription came and went in May 1956, but the state took no substantial steps toward granting the Druze first-class citizenship. Druze villages were still subject to the rule of the military governors and the oversight of the GSS, the local councils and schools suffered from inadequate and unequal funding, and most travel restrictions remained in place. Ex-soldiers also found themselves excluded from full membership in the Histadrut and Mapai and deprived of many benefits to which they were legally entitled. The Arab Departments of the ministries continued to be assigned the task of serving Druze communities.[16] What followed conscription was consequently inconsistent with systematic co-optation, which would have dictated an overhaul of the state's policies.

The Druze did win some limited gains in the first decade after the draft. The establishment of official Druze religious institutions solidified the power of the shaykhs, but it also satisfied the popular Druze desire to escape Muslim religious control.[17] In February 1957 most Druze were granted long-term travel passes, and Druze veterans could, by presenting evidence of reserve status, travel freely, alleviating the MA's greatest burden. That same year, they were admitted as full members into the Histadrut.[18] Finally, in 1962 all Druze—veteran and nonveteran alike—were exempted from the MA's travel regulations. The price: Druze had to abandon official identification with their fellow Arabs by replacing "Arab" as the "nationality" option on their identity cards with "Druze."[19] But the practical import of this new policy was limited. While strict enforcement of the MA's rules had prevented Arabs from integrating into the national economy for many years, the system had become more permissive by the early 1960s. The vast majority of Arab citizens could travel at will during the day to major urban centers, and long-term overnight permits were readily dispensed. In 1962, a classified government review observed that "if in the past travel permits were issued only after investigation, today they are given almost automatically to anyone who requests one—except elements known to be dangerous to national security."[20] Once again, the authorities had tossed the Druze but a crumb, seeking to satisfy them with petty gains while refraining from more substantive concessions. With regard to economic development, for example, the Druze continued to be lumped in with other Arabs in five-year plans approved in both 1962 and 1967.[21]

What little Druze political activity there was took two forms. First, university students and graduates protested, sometimes in league with other Arabs, against discriminatory state policies. Given the small number of educated Druze, their membership was necessarily diverse, and settling on a common agenda was a difficult, at times impossible, task. United in youthful rebellion, they were unable to agree on the basic elements of their vision—integration vs. separation, Druze particularism vs. Arab nationalism. In the late 1950s and early 1960s, however, the leading figures typically celebrated the Druze's Arab identity and struggled against particularist Druze tendencies and the Israeli policies that nurtured them, especially military service. As one Israeli official recalled, when Christian and Muslim students "engaged in nationalistic activities, it was difficult for the Druze to stand on the sidelines, because they did not want to appear to be traitors. . . . The Druze very quickly joined the choir of Arab nationalism."[22] Internal discord combined with the opposition of the established Druze leadership and of the authorities to undermine these organizations' political capacity. Second, Druze veterans formed local associations to lobby for the democracy and equal rights they had been promised.[23] Although they rarely addressed the deeper questions of identity that exercised and fractured their university-educated coreligionists, even their faint calls for reform posed a threat to the ḥamulas and the state, which sought to weaken their cohesion, appeal, and exposure. Generally relatively uneducated, the ex-soldiers were incapable of creating lasting institutions that would transcend the locale or the moment.[24] Both groups, however, remained politically marginal.

Despite the inclusive manpower-policy signal, the Druze did not immediately mobilize. The shaykhs were well acquainted with the politics of personal patronage that had served them and prior generations well under the Ottoman Empire and the British Mandate, but they were unfamiliar with pressure-group tactics and were therefore poorly equipped to navigate Israel's democracy. Moreover, they had little incentive to challenge the status quo.

By the middle of the 1960s, however, a new generation of leaders—better educated, better acquainted with the Israeli political scene, more knowledgeable about Israeli society, more aware of their political advantages, and better prepared to exploit an opening in the opportunity structure—was ready to demand the Druze community's rightful place in the polity. Emboldened by the manpower-policy signal, these Druze paved the way for their fellow Arabs. In the words of one well-known Druze, "When the Druze did something, the Arabs came after. We were like the laboratory for the others."[25] One military governor recalled, "The Druze started shouting first . . . and slowly the others joined up too."[26] Service in the IDF nurtured expectations of membership in the Israeli political community: the Druze had integration in their sights, while their fellow Arabs, hopelessly excluded, embraced separationist goals. The Druze, moreover, were more confident that their political protest would be efficacious and would not be met with repression. According to one Druze mayor, military service empowered the Druze: "The moment you have greater awareness of your needs and rights, you demand more. And Druze demand more than Arabs."[27] As a prominent Druze editor put it, "Service in the military gave us a feeling of power. Perhaps this was an illusion, I do not know. . . . We proceeded, perhaps under an illusion, that we would attain equality of rights."[28]

A New Generation Awakens, 1965–1975

In the latter half of the 1960s, inspired by Druze military service, a concerted effort to forge an active Druze political presence took off. During the 1965 Knesset elections, the dysfunctional alliance between Druze radicals and moderates (or, if one prefers, Arab nationalists and Druze integrationists) finally collapsed, and the two groups went their separate ways. While the former lobbied the Druze electorate on behalf of the new Arab-dominated Communist party, Rakaḥ, and embraced its nationalist agenda, the latter focused more narrowly on the status of the Druze community. Even in this early incarnation, they framed their demands in terms of their people's loyal service in the IDF and pressed for integration and equal rights—not for the entire Arab population, but just for the Druze. The following year, further land expropriations triggered a wave of protest that swept across the Druze villages of the northern Galilee. Perhaps its most important legacy was the new vehicle to which it gave rise: the Druze League.

Although the leadership of the newly formed organization consisted largely of educated Druze associated, professionally or otherwise, with the authorities, they were hardly the stooges of Israeli officials. Calling for real equality with Jewish citizens, the league's spokesmen most often articulated two concrete demands.[29] First, they called for the mainstreaming of the Druze within Israeli public institutions, for their removal from the custody of the Arab Departments of the ministries and of the Office of the Adviser to the Prime Minister for Arab Affairs. Partly a matter of principle, this insistence on full administrative integration had more instrumental roots as well: these departments' lower ranks were staffed largely by Christian and Muslim Arabs, who, the Druze believed, were less sympathetic than Jews to Druze pleas for special consideration on the basis of their collective military sacrifice.[30] Second, they sought to highlight the imbalance in central government investment in Jewish settlements and Druze villages. Even when both were located in rural regions, the former were far more likely to be connected to the national electricity grid and water system, to have a functioning sewage system, and to be awarded the status of a "development town," which made it more attractive to private industry. These forms of discrimination were subtle compared to the inequities in central government funding: Jewish settlements received more money per capita than did similarly situated Arab, including predominantly Druze, villages. The Druze League insisted that equal development resources be channeled into the "Druze sector." After Israel's stunning victory in 1967, in which Druze soldiers had played a major combat role for the first time since independence, the Druze League intensified its criticism of the state's policies—while fully playing within the rules of the Israeli political game and refraining from challenging the Jewish character of the state. Lacking conventional political resources, it crafted resonant public appeals, exploited the sympathy of the Jewish media and masses, and dared Jewish politicians to lay bare the ethno-national basis of their discriminatory policies.[31]

Israeli officials should have welcomed the rise of the Druze League, which even sought a new school curriculum stressing the historical ties between the Jewish people and the Druze and which at times adopted a radically particularistic stance denying the Druze's Arab identity. But the relevant officials were by and large ambivalent, when they were not simply opposed. The police and the prime minister's adviser on Arab affairs were eager to distance the Druze from Arab nationalism, as was the more powerful GSS, but the GSS opposed any but local Arab (including Druze) political organization, fearing that such institutions would ultimately be put to rebellious purposes.[32] Parochial bureaucratic interests no doubt played a role, but GSS officials also feared that concessions to the Druze would signal weakness to the far larger but still quiescent Christian and Muslim populations and prompt a more radical and organized minority politics than Israel had yet confronted. Finally, by empowering the individual and thereby weakening the ḥamula, integration threatened to undermine the reigning system of control.

In 1968, reflecting this view, Amnon Lin of the Labor Party recommended rejecting Druze demands to join the party. Acceding to the Druze would strike Christians and Muslims as an affront, Lin argued, and would undermine the party's standing among those populations. More important, Lin charged all politically active Druze reformers with "incitement." He labeled as "radicals" those who protested "(a) a separate Druze unit in the IDF; (b) discrimination in the educational field; (c) refusal to grant them equal membership in the Labor Party; (d) the lack of development in the villages." But the demands of such alleged radicals were in fact those of the relatively moderate Druze League.[33] Lin's report was unusually explicit, but its thinking was typical of the state's specialists on Arab affairs who viewed Druze moderates and radicals as equally dangerous.[34] These officials sought to harness the power of the hamulas against the young rebels, warning the clan heads that the league's success would come at their expense.[35] Amnon Lin apparently was persuasive, for the party decided to continue to restrict membership to Jews.

Despite the Druze League's largely elite membership and relatively small size, it succeeded in garnering attention from mainstream Hebrew-language media outlets. The activists skillfully hammered at the injustice of the Druze's predicament: performing the same duties as other citizens of the state of Israel, the Druze were manifestly not treated equally. A resistant government finally conceded not long after the conclusion of the June 1967 war.[36] In October, Prime Minister Levi Eshkol announced that, as a consequence of their brave service on the battlefield, the Druze would henceforth be fully integrated into Israel's public institutions and that they would, for better or worse, be treated just like Jewish citizens. Linking the fate of the two peoples, Eshkol declared "kamonu kamokhem"—as it is with us, it will be with you.[37] The Druze League praised this "positive historical step," but it noted that Eshkol had failed to make any commitments regarding the more important and costly measures on the league's agenda. It also observed that Eshkol had delivered these assurances not to representatives of the league but to those of the traditional religious and clan leadership, which had played no role in the campaign. Concerned that the government had little intention of following through on its pledges, the league set a one-year deadline for substantive progress.

Their skepticism proved warranted, as one year came and went with little forward movement. The Druze League was true to its word. It mobilized its youthful cohorts to campaign for immediate integration and sent out a flurry of letters and appeals to government ministries and the media. To its original program, it added an additional demand: the desegregation of the IDF—that is, allowing Druze to serve in the unit and service arm of their choice. As the campaign for integration intensified, coordination suffered; egos, historical rivalries, and intense personal animosities hampered the Druze's capacity to exert concentrated political pressure. But the disorganization served only to emphasize the larger lessons: the clans were no longer capable of containing discontent, the Druze demanding integration would not be placated with fine words, and this new generation promised to be politically formidable. These events constituted the first round in what became a cyclical pattern. The young Druze protested, Jewish politicians issued promises, bureaucrats dragged their feet, and the Druze grew ever more noisy.[38]

The 1969 Knesset elections shook Israeli officials out of their complacency. Although most Druze continued to vote for the mainstream Zionist parties and their affiliated lists, Rakaḥ made unprecedented inroads that year among the Druze and the Arab population as a whole. Blaming the state and its discriminatory policies for Rakaḥ's success, the Druze moderates came forward with renewed vigor, promoted their cause in the Hebrew and Arabic press, and raised awareness of their people's plight.[39] At first, the government sought to stem the tide by appointing Druze to prominent posts: Faris Falaḥ was named the first Druze judge in the secular legal system, and Kamal Mansour was dispatched by the Foreign Ministry to the United States on a lecture tour. But such gestures failed to satisfy the increasingly restive Druze. In May 1969 Amnon Lin reversed his position and publicly endorsed Druze membership in the Labor Party, arguing that political considerations should not override the imperatives of justice "when Druze are fighting shoulder to shoulder with Jews in defense of the homeland." One year later, while the War of Attrition degraded Israeli defenses across the Suez Canal and continued to eat away at the nation's morale, Lin's views had not changed: "Especially now we must emphasize to those who have tied their fate to us that they are our partners. Brothers are equal in everything."[40]

In 1970 Prime Minister Golda Meir felt compelled to reaffirm her predecessor's pledge, and she declared that the Druze would be "administratively . . . Israelis in every respect." Where Eshkol had publicly ignored the Druze League, Meir pointedly acknowledged that the locus of power among the Druze had shifted. But her announcement brought little change in policy. Druze demands mounted in the early 1970s, and as the trail of promises made and broken grew, it played into the Druze's capable hands. They continued to demand membership in the Labor Party, they publicized the fact that neighboring Jewish municipalities received much larger government grants than did their local councils, and they called for the inclusion of Druze villages in the "development zones" through which the state directed large transfers of public funds and substantial investments of private capital to underdeveloped areas. They insisted that their coreligionists in the Knesset work to resolve the question of land expropriations, remedy the inequity in grants and loans to local councils, and equalize agricultural prices for Jewish and Druze cooperatives.[41] At all times the Druze activists reminded their Jewish audiences that their people regularly made the supreme sacrifice for the political community.

Unyielding Druze pressure did lead to some preferential treatment in the early 1970s. Thanks to the "protracted struggle of the Druze youth," the Druze were *collectively* declared eligible for membership in the Labor Party, in contrast to Muslims and Christians, who were admitted only on an individual basis: because the military obligation was framed collectively, the corresponding civic right had to be extended to all.[42] Government and private investment in Druze villages increased, and a disproportionate number of the factories established in the Arab sector in those years were in predominantly Druze villages. A government committee discovered in 1973 that the Interior Ministry was giving twice as much, on a per capita basis, to the local councils of mainly Druze villages as to mainly Christian and Muslim villages, although that still amounted to between only one-sixth and one-half the funds granted per capita to Jewish villages and towns. Access roads were built, water pipes laid, health clinics launched, the electric grid extended, and new local authorities established.[43]

The 1973 Knesset elections confirmed that these halting steps had been insufficient. With the government continuing to stall, the radicals' appeal grew and the moderates' tone became more strident, particularly after April 1974. That month Palestinian guerrillas snuck into Israel and killed Jewish civilians in Kiryat Shemona, near the Lebanese border. Coming not long after the October 1973 war, the deadly attack signaled Israel's vulnerability and led to recriminations in the Knesset. But, from the perspective of the Druze, it was the events following the raid that were most troubling. On the assumption that local Arabs were sympathetic to and perhaps had even abetted the terrorists, the town's Jewish residents took out their frustration and anger on nearby Druze from the Golan as well as on Druze soldiers in uniform who happened to be present.

This incident threatened to drive discouraged moderates into the radical camp, and the authorities moved swiftly to prevent that outcome.[44] Later that year, two government-sponsored bodies were established to investigate the community's problems and grievances. One was a Knesset committee composed entirely of Jewish MKs and chaired by Avraham Schechterman. The other brought together a well-known Jewish expert on the Druze, Gabriel Ben-Dor of the University of Haifa, and two prominent Druze activists under the auspices of the Office of the Adviser to the Prime Minister for Arab Affairs. Both groups' recommendations largely paralleled the agenda that Druze moderates had articulated over the last decade. Both rejected demands to abolish mandatory conscription in the Druze community. Both recommended removing the Druze from the ministries' Arab Departments, fully integrating Druze soldiers and officers into mainline IDF units, providing equal benefits for Druze veterans, displaying flexibility and even sympathy for Druze in addressing land disputes and illegal construction in the overpopulated villages, sponsoring a new Druze settlement in the Galilee, and supplying increased development funds for the Druze villages. Significantly, both cast their proposals as the Druze's just recompense for their willing sacrifice— mirroring the Druze's claims-making frame, justifying preferential treatment relative to other Arabs, and reinscribing the dominant republican citizenship discourse.[45] The Druze integrationists were on the verge of seeing their dreams become concrete realities, but celebration was premature. The government's endorsement of these recommendations had a pro forma ring to it.[46] Much would depend on their implementation.

Moderate activists dominated the Druze political scene, mobilizing relatively effectively by the mid-1960s—that is, just a few years after mandatory conscription had commenced. After a somewhat greater lag, smaller groups at either extreme responded to the opening in the political opportunity structure. In 1973 Yusuf Nassr-al-Din founded the Druze-Zionist Circle, but over two decades it never attracted more than a handful of Druze adherents. For most Druze, loyalty to the State of Israel was one thing; Zionism, which seemed to imply that the Jewish people had a right to Druze land, was quite another.[47]

More popular and certainly more troubling to the government was the Druze Initiative Committee (DIC), founded in 1972. Backed by Rakaḥ, its leaders argued that the Druze were a religious, not a distinctive ethnic, community and thus were fully part of the Palestinian nation, along with Muslims and Christians. The DIC gave voice to the entire panoply of Druze complaints, but its distinctive centerpiece was its opposition to conscription, which it portrayed not as a blood covenant, but as a blood tax. It exploited a groundswell of resentment toward military service: young Druze increasingly saw the draft as hindering their social and economic prospects, particularly relative to Muslim and Christian young men who could complete an undergraduate degree or learn a craft while the Druze performed his military duties. As one discontented Druze told a journalist, "If I require assistance from a government agency, does my twelve years of service help me in any way? The answer is no. Can I get farming loans? No! Can I find useful work? No! Do I have any advantages over the same Arabs who are sworn to the destruction of Israel? No!"[48] In the attempt to avoid military service, some DIC members have even renounced their Druze affiliation and converted to Islam: by one estimate, they accounted for one-quarter of all Druze conversions to other religions between 1952 and 2002, and over three-quarters eventually requested that they be readmitted to the Druze community.[49]

In 1974 the DIC hijacked the festival at the tomb of Nabi Shu'ayb, which had for two decades served as an annual ritualized renewal of the Druze-Jewish covenant. The Minorities Unit was always a key element of the ceremony, and new recruits were initiated there. The young radicals insisted that their leader, Shaykh Farhud Qasim Farhud—who had opposed conscription twenty years before and who had founded the DIC when his son came of draft age—be permitted to address the audience, but Shaykh Amin Tarif refused. The DIC vanguard was, however, in no mood to take no for an answer and seized the stage from Prime Minister Yitzhak Rabin, placing Farhud at the podium in his stead.[50] The effectiveness of the DIC as a social movement climaxed that year, and afterwards it fell victim to typical movement growing pains, eventually merging with Rakaḥ.[51]

Although the organization succeeded in attracting the authorities' attention, the Druze public was not generally receptive to its message, and the integrationists have long appeared to have had their finger closer to the pulse of the Druze populace.[52] During Arab protests in 1961 against the MA, most Druze—though equally subject to its oppressive whims—refused to join, for nationalist demands had been grafted onto the quest for first-class citizenship. While Druze university students railed in the early 1960s against the state's efforts to fragment the Arab minority, local branches of their organization more closely identified with the struggle for equality. Druze voting patterns have tended to resemble those of Jews more than other Arabs, as far larger numbers of Druze shunned the Communist Party.[53] Finally, data on Druze opinion are consistent with the conclusion that the DIC spoke to a narrow subset of the Druze community. In the late 1970s, when Arab opinion in Israel began to be regularly surveyed, Druze fell closer to Jews on most questions—ranging from Israel's right to exist to the equation of Zionism with racism to support for independent Arab national political parties—than to other Arabs. In 1976, though 10 percent of the Arab population, the Druze accounted for over 20 percent of the "accomodationists" identified in one survey, and around 75 percent of Druze fell into categories associated with integrationist aims. Ten years later, nearly 80 percent of polled Druze continued to endorse integrationist aims and policies.[54]

Pressure from Within and Without, 1975–1995

To oversee the implementation of the Ben-Dor and Schechterman Committees' recommendations, a permanent committee composed of the directors-general (the highest-ranking unelected ministry officials) was formed in October 1975. Although incapable of direct action, this group (hereafter, CDG—the Committee of the Directors-General on Druze Affairs) required ministries to explain discrimination and inaction in a quasi-public forum, urged them to speed development efforts in the Druze villages, and ultimately compelled them to devote resources they might otherwise have withheld. At its meetings, the ministries typically fell over one another in their eagerness to take credit for the favors showered on the Druze and in their willingness to acknowledge and promise to rectify failings. Thanks to the CDG, the Druze came to occupy a middle position in this ethnic democracy, lagging behind their Jewish counterparts but clearly better off than their Christian and Muslim neighbors. This, however, had substantial costs: working within the state bureaucracy, the Druze retreated from the arena of public contestation and stopped employing the claims-making strategy that had served them so well.

Although bureaucratic resistance continued to undermine substantive reform, the CDG was a boon to the Druze in three ways.[55] First, it empowered the new generation of Druze leaders, replacing the politics of patronage with a more institutionalized form of political activity. By giving Druze civil society and the local councils an address of their own, separate of either the Arab Departments or the MKs, it conferred legitimacy, fostered independence from the traditional leadership, and pressured the hamula heads to adopt a more forceful style of claims-making.[56] Second, the committee served as a clearinghouse for the grievances of local Druze veterans' organizations, the increasingly assertive Druze local councils, and the rest of Druze civil society— with which it maintained a vigorous correspondence.[57] It forwarded these demands to the appropriate ministry with the imprimatur of the bureaucracy's highest-ranking officials and also often arranged meetings between local Druze political leaders and Jewish politicians and officials. Third, the CDG created pressure for change by drawing attention to the Druze's plight within an institutional framework that encouraged reform and provided oversight. Even after the Likud came to power in 1977, the CDG continued to serve as the linchpin of a system of accountability—by serving as a forum within which ministry representatives had to demonstrate progress toward their stated objectives or account (quasi-)publicly for the lack thereof.

The CDG's accomplishments were not insubstantial. Its efforts resulted in increased funds for Druze schools, the allotment of new land for Druze villages, a vast building initiative in the Druze sector, the resolution of Druze land claims, the full integration of Druze across the IDF, greater employment opportunities for Druze veterans, countless public welfare projects, and so on. But progress still came at a snail's pace. The ministries faced some real impediments, but—guided by inertia and ethno-national priorities—they also stalled. Faced with such opposition, the Druze community had little recourse. Their turn from public protest to internal lobbying had undercut their chief political asset: their ability to mobilize the sympathies of the Jewish masses and rhetorically put Jewish politicians in a difficult spot. A cynic might claim that this was precisely the purpose of the CDG, but there is no evidence of such conspiratorial intent. The Druze learned that sometimes one should beware what one wishes for.[58]

Although the Druze's position rose relative to that of other Arabs, they remained far behind their Jewish neighbors. In the villages of the upper Galilee, sewage and water systems remained inadequate through the early 1990s. Even though most Druze villages had completed development plans by the early 1980s, approval was slow in coming, and thus nearly all construction in the villages was deemed illegal. Despite the effort to build schools in the Druze sector, the budgets were never sufficient to meet the ministries' own goals. Retired army officers continued to have difficulty finding appropriate work, and the same was certainly true of other educated Druze. Few Druze occupied senior government positions. Finally, the Interior Ministry's grants to equivalent Druze and Jewish settlements were obviously not equal, and Druze villages could not access special development funds as well as those monies disbursed by quasi-public institutions such as the Jewish Agency.[59]

Despite the CDG's achievements, many Druze perceived a persistent, and even widening, gap between themselves and their Jewish fellow citizens. The government's internal documents frankly admitted that "the noticeable difference in the levels of development, on the one hand, and the system of benefits, on the other, creates a feeling of serious discrimination in the Druze and Circassian communities, whose sons serve in the military." Zeidan Atashe, a Druze first elected to the Knesset in 1977 as a member of Dash (the Democratic Movement for Change), was among those who gave voice to the frustration of the Druze leadership. In 1985 he wrote to Prime Minister Shimon Peres that "the covenant of blood and shared fate between the [Druze] community and the Jewish people . . . is in danger." After reviewing the Druze's complaints, Atashe warned, "If steps are not taken and solutions suggested, the community will see itself as free from any obligation that does not promise full rights and will leave to the free will of every Druze the question of whether he wishes to volunteer for the IDF."[60] The Druze community remained relatively quiet during the first intifada. But in the early 1990s, perhaps inspired by the Palestinian uprising and sensing an opportunity in the easing international situation, the Druze community abandoned the quiet hallways of government and returned to the public arena.

The local leadership initiated this new wave of public political activity in 1991 in the Galilee, and it culminated in a 1995 sit-in across from the prime minister's office. The mayors were eventually joined by the Druze MKs and by the religious leadership. On the one hand, their rhetoric bore the signs of the changing times: "The rift between our communities and the state is widening. Before us stands the danger of an intifada that nobody wants." But it also invoked the older motifs of military sacrifice and civic virtue, implicitly recognizing why the broader public continued to listen and why the authorities would ultimately concede. As MK Salaḥ Tarif put it in 1994, "The Druze have been fooled for too long. We cannot and will not put up with any more empty promises and hollow gestures in return for the blood of our sons."[61] After much political maneuvering, the government finally committed to providing five years of increased development funds and to equalizing grants to Druze and Jewish villages and towns.[62] These supplementary budgets are universally acknowledged to have tremendously reduced (though not eliminated) the gap between Israel's Jewish and Druze citizens.

Druze Mobilization and Manpower Signaling

Druze political behavior is puzzling, especially compared with that of the rest of Israel's Arab population. "So long as you are a tender young plant," one older Druze advised, "you must protect yourself against every gust of wind. But once you grow strong and strike roots in the soil, you need not fear even the gales of winter!"[63] Under 2 percent of Israel's total population, without access to conventional political resources, and the target of discriminatory policies, the Druze initially resembled that seedling, but by the late 1960s they

were acting more like a firmly planted cedar. With regard to the timing of political activity, the Druze began to mobilize in the mid-to-late 1960s, nearly a
decade before other Arabs. When politicians' pledges remained unimplemented, the Druze engaged in increasingly strident protest, confident that the
state could not and would not silence them. With regard to their objectives,
the Druze put integration at the top of their agenda. With regard to their tactics, the Druze played by the rules of the Israeli political game; they did not
threaten the state with disorder, but rather invoked their history of military
service. The Druze's tactics resembled those of Jewish immigrant interest
groups in Israel who similarly have sought formal contacts with government
officials, exploited personal relationships with decision makers, and brought
their grievances to the media.[64] Their political activity reflected the liberalization of the IDF's participation policies—beginning with the conscription
of the Druze in 1956 and culminating in their eventual integration into nearly
all units and service branches. Jewish politicians had their own motives, but,
for the Druze, the extension of the draft was a powerful signal as to how the
Israeli state and its Jewish majority would respond to demands for equal
rights.

Scholars often argue that the moderate objectives and tactics of mainstream
Druze political activity reflected that population's co-optation by the Israeli
regime. Relatively uneducated, poor, and politically weak, the Druze were
fertile soil for the authorities' gestures, and given its small size, the group
could be incorporated into the polity without fundamentally challenging its
character. Druze who identified with the Palestinian cause have leveled similar allegations, deriding the proponents of integration as "new props, look-
ing younger but carrying the same registered trade-mark" as the traditional
leadership, a group of "shaky wooden pillars . . . which have been infested by
woodworm and need to be replaced."[65]

But this charge and, even more important, this interpretation were off the
mark. Israeli officials wanted a subdued and subordinate population, but
these Druze refused to strike an obsequious tone. They drew attention to inequities and contradictions in Israel's ethnic democracy, and they continually
presented Jewish decision makers with uncomfortable dilemmas. Not only
had the experience of military service failed to ensure their quiescence, it had
in fact inspired them to press for true equality. Although the Druze politician
Kamal Mansour often kowtowed to the authorities, he fully grasped Druze
frustration and its source: "The Druze veteran does not compare his lot with
the neighboring Arab—that would be too simple. His framework for comparison is provided by the Jews with whom he served and fought. . . . How
can you be equal one day and less equal the next?"[66] Or as the Druze journalist Rafiq Ḥalabi put it, "The Druze may have earned the moral right to demand equality, but in actuality they found it hard to dispel their feeling that
they were 'Jews' when it came to obligations and 'Arabs' when it came to
rights."[67] One MK in the late 1970s warned his colleagues, "We may not mea-

sure the progress [in Druze villages] by comparing it to current levels in Arab countries. . . . The problems emerge from the comparison with the state's Jews."[68]

Unlike other Arabs, the Druze were confident that their political voice would not be silenced, that they could effectively protest their subordinate status—albeit within the standing rules of the Israeli political game. This was not the way a co-opted minority would speak, and it was hardly what the authorities envisioned when they compelled the Druze to serve. One influential decision maker recalled that the activities of these Druze were "not always comfortable for us. You know that when you occupy the seat of power, you want them to do exactly as you wish. Here the problem was that at times they did not do [what we wanted]."[69] Nor did the state systematically seek to co-opt the Druze. Symbolic gestures were common, but the truly substantive advances the Druze achieved were the product of their struggle, not Israeli largesse.

Radicalism Unbound: Christians, Muslims, and the State, 1957–1995

Foundations, 1957–1973

Although 1956 brought the draft to the Druze, for Christians and Muslims, life went on as before. The young state was democratic but hardly liberal, and most Arabs fell into line. Sustained efforts to challenge the state were few and far between, and those that did emerge were crushed. As Druze political activity was growing increasingly intense, one foreign journalist observed that the Arab citizens of Israel were "an inarticulate minority in an alien society. . . . There are no powerful champions of the Israeli Arabs, neither within their own ranks nor in foreign capitals, near or far. No one takes up their cause; they have produced no rebels."[70] Co-optation and repression no doubt contributed to Christian and Muslim quiescence, but both featured (though the latter to a lesser extent) in state policy vis-à-vis the Druze. The most obvious difference in these communities' experiences lay in the realm of military service. While it does not seem plausible to place the full weight of explanation on Christian and Muslim exclusion from the IDF, the military's policies promoted quiet within the Arab community even as they planted the seeds of the mobilization that would burst on the scene in the mid-1970s.[71]

Arab protests against the MA and other restrictions erupted only intermittently. In the 1950s and 1960s, Arabs accounted for just 4 percent of demonstrations in Israel, far below their proportion of the population.[72] Yet beneath the surface calm lay radicalism in gestation. On those occasions when Arabs did protest, they framed their demands not in the language of integration but in the nationalist pan-Arabism current outside Israel.[73] In 1961 five young Arab citizens were shot by an Israeli border patrol as they sought to cross illegally into the Egyptian-held Gaza Strip, triggering four days of mass demonstrations. In Nazareth, the largest exclusively Arab city in Israel, the crowds were kept manageable only by roadblocks. Several thousand school-boys crowded into Nazareth's central square, shouting slogans such as "Down with Ben-Gurion and his government of murderers!", "Long live Nasser!", and "May Israel be destroyed!" In Acre, Arabs marched toward the Jewish quarter chanting "Death to Ben-Gurion" and "Palestine is Arab."[74] As an Israeli diplomat ruefully observed, "It is clear that these Arabs wish to live physically in the state, but from a spiritual perspective, they live with 'the Arab side,' with the enemies of Israel."[75] It is hard to believe that, less than a decade before, the younger generation of Arabs had enthusiastically wel-comed the draft.

Whatever institutionalized politics existed in the Arab sector reflected such nationalist leanings. Well into the 1970s, nearly all organization of conse-quence among Israel's Arab citizens occurred under the aegis of the Com-munist Party. Maki's largely Jewish leadership, sensitive to the constraints of Israeli politics, opposed pan-Arabism and continued to embrace at least ele-ments of Marxist-Leninist internationalism.[76] But the same cannot be said of the Arabs who constituted the overwhelming majority of Maki's and later Rakah's supporters. As a GSS representative noted of Maki in 1962, "The fact is that its activities among the Arab population are not communist activities from a socialist perspective, but national-Arab activities, and often extremist. The emphasis is not on equal pay for the Arab worker or his acceptance into Histadrut; the struggle is national-Arab."[77] The Israeli establishment not sur-prisingly saw Maki and later Rakah as hostile not only to the state's Jewish character but to its very existence.[78] The Communist Party's status shielded it from overt repression, but Communist-backed organizations enjoyed less legal protection. Several efforts to establish an all-Arab political party, from the early 1950s through the mid-1960s, ended in failure, in large part because the authorities took steps, coercive and co-optive, to undermine them.[79]

The official line was that, if not for the conflict between Israel and the Arab states, all of Israel's citizens, regardless of ethnic or religious origin, could live in harmony.[80] Public opinion surveys suggested, however, that ethno-reli-gious antipathy was deeply rooted. In the wake of the Holocaust, most Jews had little sympathy for Arabs who denied the legitimacy of the Zionist cause and proclaimed the Israeli state grounded in injustice. In the late 1960s over three-quarters of Jewish Israelis, both Mizrahim (Jews of North African and Middle Eastern descent) and Ashkenazim (Jews of European descent), agreed that "every Arab hates Jews," and well over 90 percent thought "it would be better if there were fewer Arabs." Social prejudice was also intense, with clear majorities objecting to some extent to having an Arab as a neighbor, let alone as a son-in-law. Anti-Arab sentiment grew even more prevalent after the 1967 war.[81] Surveys of Israel's Arabs conducted just before the war revealed a gen-erational divide that boded ill for the future: Arabs who had been born or come of political age in Israel—and were therefore more likely to be sensitive to its exclusion of them—were far more likely than their parents to voice hostility toward the state.[82] Over half of younger Arabs reported feeling more "at home" in one of the Arab states, which few had visited, than in Israel, and close to three-quarters either denied or expressed reservations about Israel's right to exist. Some 81 percent of Arab high school students preferred to be "a separate but equal people" within Israel, and 13 percent favored a separate state entirely.[83] These were the seeds from which the later mobilization would grow.

Israel's conquest of the West Bank and Gaza Strip in 1967 rejoined its Arab minority with fellow nationals, among whom a Palestinian identity had taken hold and among whom political activism was rife. In 1970 even moderate Israeli Arab leaders felt compelled to at least pretend to grieve when Nasser died; thousands turned out in Israel's Arab villages, towns, and cities to mourn the leader of pan-Arabist nationalism. Meanwhile, increasing, though still very small, numbers of Israel's Arab citizens began to take part in terrorist activity.[84] This remained the largely uncoordinated behavior of motivated individuals, but it reflected the nationalistic tendencies Israel had nurtured among its Arab citizens.

Politicization, Palestinization, and Mobilization, 1973–1995

On Israel's northern border, two humble Christian Arab villages, Ikrit and Berem, had welcomed the invading Israeli forces in 1948, and their residents had willingly evacuated the area at the request of the IDF, which promised that they would be allowed to return once it had ceased military operations there. But the IDF reneged, even ignoring a Supreme Court of Israel ruling upholding the villagers' petition. Invoking emergency regulations, and this time supported by the court, the army continued to turn the former residents away. During the appeals process, it leveled the villages. When, twenty years later, Defense Minister Moshe Dayan suggested that the closed security zones along the borders might be opened, the villagers came forward and demanded the right to return to the rubble they still called home. For several months in 1972, they protested their ill-treatment while averring their loyalty to the state and playing on Israeli guilt. Jewish liberals flocked to their cause, and a sympathetic press aired their case. The government was divided, but Prime Minister Golda Meir, decrying the "erosion in Zionist faith," gathered enough support to reject the villagers' claims. They failed to achieve their immediate aims, but the villagers, with their powerful charges against the quality of Israeli justice, seized the political agenda and helped pave the way for further Arab mobilization.[85] The fractured Jewish Israeli response indicated to other Arabs that—as Meir rightly feared—the consensus was beginning to crack.

The pointed exclusion of Christian and Muslim Arabs from military service in the 1950s had signaled that the state would reject their demands for first-class citizenship, employing repression if necessary. Under such circumstances, vocal claims-making was out of the question. In the absence of strong reasons to revise their estimate of the costs of agitation, Israel's Arab citizens would likely have remained quiet. But three events combined in the early 1970s to signal that the opportunity structure was inching open. First, and perhaps most concrete, was the very public and tortured debate over the past and present of Ikrit and Berem. Second was the political awakening of the Mizrahim, who in the early 1970s gave voice to their own discrimination and cultural marginalization at the hands of the dominant Ashkenazi elites. By launching a vigorous challenge to Israel's prevailing social and political hierarchies, the self-labeled Black Panthers demonstrated that rebellion was possible and inspired the country's Arab citizens. Finally, and arguably most powerful of all, was the social upheaval and disillusion that followed the 1973 Yom Kippur War. Widely known in Israel as the *mehdal* (the blunder), the war marked the end of the country's innocence and shattered its unity. With these events as the backdrop, Israel's Christian and Muslim citizens raised their collective voice in the mid-1970s. They mobilized for separationist objectives and engaged in contentious politics—outcomes consistent with a powerful exclusionary military-manpower signal. This signal cannot account for the timing of Christian and Muslim protest, but it deeply influenced the character of Arab political activity—that is, the objectives they pursued and the tactics they employed.

Abandoning the politics of caution, Israel's Arab citizens became more assertive in the mid-1970s. Arabs had engaged in protest in fewer than two events a year before 1972, but between 1973 and 1979 that figure rose to an average of over nine events annually; there were seventeen Arab protests in Israel in 1979 alone. Between 1950 and 1975, Arabs accounted for just over 3 percent of all protests in Israel, but in the following decade they organized nearly 11 percent. These protests have more than twice as often entailed violence against property or persons than have demonstrations involving mainly Jewish citizens.[86] In opinion surveys, Arabs have, particularly in the 1980s, expressed both confidence in the efficacy of parliamentary politics and enthusiasm about extraparliamentary strategies, with large majorities endorsing without reservation licensed demonstrations and general strikes and with a somewhat slimmer majority supporting boycotts.[87] Arabs did not abandon "conventional" politics, but at the same time they increasingly ardently took up "contentious" politics in its various forms.[88]

The period from the mid-1970s into the 1980s also witnessed an institutional explosion among Israel's Arab citizens.[89] As early as 1970 the heads of Arab local councils in the Galilee had banded together, irregularly and informally, to lobby the government. In 1974 these local leaders formed a more lasting body, the National Committee of Heads of Arab Local Authorities. Initially nurtured by the government as a counterweight to Rakah, the committee early on revealed an independent streak. It began with exclusively local matters, but after 1976 it expanded its scope of concern and ratcheted up the level of activity. Through meetings with top-tier officials as well as mass action, its representatives demanded recognition of the Arab citizens as a *national* minority, strengthened ties with Palestinians in the Occupied Territories, expressed support for the Palestinian nationalist struggle, and protested land seizures as well as discrimination in government allocations and employment. To sustain the campaign, the committee created several substantive follow-up committees—in such areas as education, health care, social services, and agriculture—staffed with professionals as well as political figures. By the early 1980s it had seized the mantle of nationalist leadership from Rakaḥ and was widely viewed as the "parliament of Israel's Arabs."[90] The committee was typically responsible for organizing the largest demonstrations and general strikes among the Arab population, with a particular focus on citizenship and national questions.[91]

Beyond the committee, Arab civil society was reborn in the mid-1970s. Arab student associations sprang up at all the universities, and a national student union took shape as well. After 1980 Arabs increasingly founded nongovernmental organizations, with the pace picking up particularly in the 1990s.[92] New political parties, notably the Progressive List for Peace, came into being a few years later and cut substantially into the Communists' electoral base. The PLP's 1984 platform called for national and civil equality for Arab citizens, the separation of church and state, and a written constitution; affirmed Palestinian refugees' right to return; and demanded negotiations with the Palestine Liberation Organization. Far more radical groups came out of the woodwork as well. The Sons of the Village emerged at the local level, and a few years later the National Progressive Movement, which eventually folded into the PLP, came on the scene. Both identified fully with the Palestinian national movement, rejected the legitimacy of Israel as a Jewish state, and called for a binational secular state occupying the entire territory of Mandatory Palestine. Denying the relevance of the Green Line—the boundary designated in the armistice ending the 1948 war—to national identity, these organizations all but declared themselves wings of the PLO—then viewed by most Israelis as a terrorist entity unsuitable as a negotiating partner.[93]

Finally, capitalizing on popular frustration with Arabs' stagnating material standard of living, the Islamist movement surged after the 1979 revolution in Iran. At first it took the form of a paramilitary unit waging a jihad against both the Jewish state and secularism among Israeli Muslims. Penetrated by the GSS in 1981, its leaders were sentenced to long prison terms, but, just a few years later, Islamism resurfaced. The new Islamic associations preached nonviolence and strict religious observance, combined with a message of self-help: promoting local action for social and economic development, their motto was, "If the state is not ready to help us, we shall help ourselves." By the late 1980s the Islamist movement had grown into a major force in local politics, winning over 30 percent of the seats in local elections in the Little Triangle.[94]

The critical turning point in Arab political practice came after the Israeli government announced a series of land expropriations in February 1976. Most of the land seized this time was slated to come from Jewish owners, but the move nevertheless triggered an explosion of long-repressed resentment over the state's land policies. Rakaḥ took the lead in forming the National Committee for the Defense of Arab Lands, which designated March 30 "Land Day" and called for a general strike. In the chaos of the day, Israeli security forces killed six Arab citizens. The six became martyrs, and their deaths became a focal point for the Arab community: nearly every March 30 since then has been commemorated on both sides of the Green Line, but especially the Israeli side, as Land Day—often with a general strike and mass demonstrations, expressions of Palestinian nationalism, and the occasional burning of the Israeli flag. As the 1980s wore on, and especially during the first intifada, Israel's Arab citizens regularly engaged in strikes and large-scale protests with the aim of addressing both their own grievances as well as those of the Palestinian nation as a whole.[95] Sensing the shifting political winds, even Arab politicians affiliated with Zionist parties began to adopt more independent stances, especially on questions related to Palestinian national aspirations. The Labor MK 'Abd al-Wahhab Darawsha was typical in describing himself as "Palestinian by nationality and Israeli by citizenship."[96]

Evidence of *separationist* objectives among Israel's Christian and Muslim Arab citizens has been available in abundance and takes three forms.[97] First, the agendas of the most popular political parties and figures have been explicitly or implicitly separationist. In the mid-1970s Rakaḥ and its non-Communist nationalist competitors moved from the margins to the center of Arab politics. In 1975 a Communist-led list won the municipal elections in Nazareth for the first time. This startling local development heralded national trends. For much of the 1960s, the Communist Party had received between 20 and 25 percent of the Arab vote in national elections, but it jumped to 37 percent in 1973 and to 50 percent in 1977. After the 1979 Camp David accords, which temporarily tripled Arab support for the Labor Party, the two Arab-dominated parties, the DFPE (the Democratic Front for Peace and Equality, which succeeded Rakaḥ) and the PLP, recovered in 1984 to win half the Arab vote. At the same time, the Arab lists affiliated with Labor went into terminal decline.[98]

A separationist political program has, in one form or another, been central to the Arab nationalist agenda from the state's earliest days. Not long after 1948, Maki abandoned its call for an independent Arab state and instead advocated the Arab citizens' "autonomous management of their national, political, and economic affairs."[99] After Rakaḥ's formation in 1965, it adopted a new objective: ridding Israel of its Jewish character and transforming the

country into a secular binational "state of all its citizens."[100] Many Jewish Israelis have feared that this civic rhetoric is but a trimming hiding fundamentally national branches, and their concern may be well founded. When Azmi
Bishara, a leading proponent of this vision, complains that "here in Israel you
can have individual rights, but not collective rights," he invokes a language
of collectivities that is very much in tension with the liberal ideals of a secular binational state.[101] He has called for the recognition of Israel's Arab citizens as a national minority—including an elected council that would run the
Arab population's educational system, oversee its media, and supervise its
economic development. In the absence of a binational solution to the larger
Israeli-Palestinian conflict, Bishara insists that "Israeli Arabs will have to run
their affairs by themselves."[102]

Other Arab leaders have espoused separation equally openly. As early as
1984 the PLP endorsed a wide range of separate institutions, and its 1990 program was still more explicit:

> Our Arab masses demand . . . their rights as a national minority, which
> is distinct nationally, culturally, and in way of life. . . . We have to con-
> duct our special life by forming cultural, social, and political institu-
> tions, to administer our own educational and cultural affairs, to launch
> an Arab university for strengthening our national Arab-Palestinian
> identity.

The leading PLP MK argued that "we must give up the demand for unat-
tained equality and call instead for self-rule."[103] The electoral performance of
the PLP and similar parties suggested the popularity of the separationist vision. Today, Bishara's party, Balad (the National Democratic Assembly), demands the Arab minority's "self-rule in matters that distinguish it from the
national majority," especially education and the media.[104]

Those who advocate separation, in principle and in practice, typically also
press for civic equality, but the latter is at best a secondary theme. As the
scholar As'ad Ghanem, hardly hostile to the Palestinian cause, points out,
whatever emphasis there has been on equality has been "tactical": "The struggle for equality was only an avenue for helping the Arabs in general, and the
nationalists in particular, reach the ultimate strategic solution to the Palestinian problem." The competition for local support has, however, over time
compelled even the nationalists to devote more attention to improving the circumstances of life on the ground for the Palestinian citizens of Israel—and
therefore to achieving civic equality.[105]

Second, separation has lain not just in the realm of aspiration, as part of an
abstract political program, but from the 1970s rapidly acquired the status of a
fact on the ground. Even liberal Hebrew media have portrayed the National
Committee of Heads of Arab Local Authorities as the foundation for Arab institutional autonomy, and they noted that its substantive follow-up commit-

tees bore a marked resemblance to the yishuv and its "state in the making."[106] The Zionist movement in Mandatory Palestine had, in response to a variety of constraints, sought "to insulate Jews from Arabs and create islands of political and infrastructural autonomy."[107] Similarly, seeking to carve out spaces free of Jewish discrimination and mirroring the ethnoreligious shape of the surrounding public sphere, Arabs have since the mid-1970s been building autonomous institutions in the social, economic, and political arenas. The Islamist emphasis on Arab self-help has reinforced that trend since the 1980s, even if Islamist leaders studiously avoided endorsing separationist ideas.[108] Collective rights emerged as a central element in the Arab citizens' political consensus, and autonomous institutions have been both the manifestation of that desire and the means to that end.[109] Whether Israelis—Arabs or Jews—admit it openly or not, the Arab mobilization beginning in the 1970s, embodying a "strategy of segregation," laid the institutional groundwork for autonomy.[110]

Third, polls of Arab public opinion have captured both increasing Arab alienation from Israeli society and the increasing desire for autonomy. Since 1967 Israel's Arab citizens have steadily downgraded the Israeli component of their national identities and highlighted the Arab and Palestinian element.[111] Moreover, "whereas the terms 'Palestinian' and 'Arab' denote sentimental or affectively loaded identities, . . . 'Israeli' denotes for Israeli Arabs an identity limited to instrumental concerns such as equal rights and material improvements."[112] In the words of one Palestinian citizen, "I belong to the State of Israel only in the geographical sense. . . . But in the spirit, in soul, I belong to the Palestinian people."[113]

Surveys have also found direct evidence of the popularity of a separationist agenda among Israel's Arab citizens. Large majorities of Arabs—typically in the vicinity of 70 percent, and reaching as high as 90 percent—have consistently expressed skepticism that Arabs can ever achieve equality in Israel as long as it remains a "Jewish state." They have supported Arab control over their educational system and over the Arab Departments in the ministries as well as the formation of an independent Arab trade union, press, university, and political party. When asked in 1985, 65 percent agreed that Arabs should organize independently, like ultra-Orthodox Jews, to advance their interests. These numbers would be significantly higher if one excluded Druze and Bedouin from the sample.[114] Israel's Arab citizens have wanted to be central players in the nation's politics, and they have grown increasingly powerful. But their political program has very little in common with the integration that the Druze have sought.

Explaining Arab Political Activity

A largely quiescent minority during the country's first quarter-century, Israel's Arab citizens suddenly impressed themselves upon the nation's political consciousness in the latter half of the 1970s. That first Land Day in 1976 was just the opening bell in a period of intense Arab political mobilization that regularly took the form of general strikes, noisy and sometimes violent demonstrations, and even rioting.[115] Although the stated goal was equality, Arab leaders and demonstrators did not envision integration on Israel's terms but rather sought to design the state anew—as a secular de-Judaized entity. Uninterested in linking their fortunes to a future Palestinian state in the West Bank and Gaza Strip, they also did not wish to link their fortunes to the Israeli polity any more than necessary: over the course of the 1970s and 1980s, they developed a wide range of autonomous social, economic, and political institutions to satisfy their needs without reliance on the state. Their aims were not usually secessionist, but they were nonetheless separationist; they did not turn to terrorism to further their political ends, but they did adopt a strategy of mass protest that stretched the rules of the game. What explains the political objectives, timing, and tactics of Israel's Arab citizens?

The comparison with the Druze reveals the importance of military participation policy in shaping Christian and Muslim political activity. From 1956 on, the Druze were subject to mandatory military conscription, while their fellow Arabs were rarely accepted into the IDF even as volunteers. The Druze mobilized relatively early, struggled within the rules of Israeli politics, and remained committed to integration. In contrast, Christians and Muslims, pointedly excluded from this central Israeli institution, mobilized about a decade later, embraced a more radical political agenda, and engaged in mass, at times violent, protest. Exclusion from the IDF signaled to Christian and Muslim Arabs that they were outsiders in the Israeli polity, compelled their silence until later events suggested that mobilization would be safe and possibly beneficial, and drove them toward autonomy and contentious politics.

Israel's Arab citizens, however, rarely drew particular attention to military exclusion. When they protested their treatment at the hands of the state during its first two decades, they normally pointed to the military administration, land expropriations, unequal allotments of government assistance, or continuing inequities in the labor exchanges.[116] Yet these same issues would have appeared on any Druze's list. Only very occasionally did Arabs identify their exclusion from obligatory military service as something that rankled, and the authorities, perhaps self-servingly, typically viewed such complaints merely as attempts to score propaganda points.[117]

There are several reasons that military exclusion would rarely make an Arab's top-ten list of oppressive state policies, even if it critically shaped his or her political perspective. First, the most commonly named Israeli misdeeds were the stuff of everyday life, policies that confronted Arabs as they plowed their fields and gathered their crops, as they traveled to their workplaces far from home, as they visited Jewish towns and cities and compared the infrastructure and services to their own villages. Second, Arabs were understandably more likely to list things the Israelis did to them (they seize our land, they give us the jobs they do not want, they assign us to positions inappropriate for our skills, they compel us to wait in humiliating lines) than things they did not do (they did not draft us to defend the state). Third, the sources typically consulted to compile such lists, informants and newspapers, were the least likely to mention exclusion from military service. The co-opted traditional leadership, which often served as a valuable source of information, feared that conscription would undermine its capacity to exercise influence and that support for military service would render it vulnerable to charges of betrayal. At the opposite end of the spectrum, the nationalists, who published the most widely read independent newspapers, ideologically opposed service in the IDF. In short, neither of these groups was a likely candidate for mentioning mass disappointment at exclusion from conscription.

While inclusion led the Druze to believe that the state would not refuse their demands and thus prompted early mobilization, exclusion stifled Christian and Muslim political activity. Whereas the Druze thought that they could count on the Jewish public for support, their fellow Arabs had to wait for other signs that the political opportunity structure had opened. Only after the political awakening of the Mizrahim, the public outcry over the plight of Ikrit and Berem, and the "defeat" in the 1973 war would Israel's Arab population mobilize politically. Patterns of military inclusion and exclusion cannot explain why Israel's Arab citizens finally summoned the courage to organize in the 1970s, but they can help us understand why they did not in the mid-1960s—when the military administration was on its last legs, when the educational system was producing large numbers of educated and frustrated young people, and when the Druze began to bombard the Israeli media and political establishment with their demands. Patterns of military inclusion and exclusion cannot, therefore, account fully for the timing of Christian and Muslim mobilization, but they can help explain the goals for which these Arabs strived and the tactics which they embraced.

CHAPTER 5

Military Rites, Citizenship Rights, and Republican Rhetoric

Long neglected and often manipulated, Christian and Muslim citizens made some headway in the 1980s because they controlled a critical asset: votes. After the Likud unseated Labor in 1977, the Jewish Israeli electorate was severely divided. By the early 1980s, the mainstream Zionist parties were for the first time competing intensely over this last remaining bloc of uncommitted voters. This explanation of how Israel's Arab citizens acquired influence is consistent with a well-established understanding of political power in democratic regimes.

The success of the Druze in securing attention, promises, and ultimately policy change from central decision makers is, in contrast, curious. The usual calculus of political resources is of little help in accounting for this outcome. The Druze's potential voter base has been tiny; their per capita income has remained relatively low; they have historically eschewed violent confrontation with the authorities; and they have often had difficulty creating and sustaining effective organizations. Yet the Druze have proven surprisingly effective, in large measure because they have plied their rhetorical trade in a welcoming milieu. Relying on the power of ethical argument and Western citizenship norms, they have framed their demands for equality around their history of military service. Faced with such claims, Jewish politicians could not follow their ethno-national inclinations without contradicting the civic republican conception of citizenship that they themselves had endorsed and without consequently running afoul of key domestic and international audiences.[1] Whether their desire to integrate the Druze was sincere or not, Jewish politicians lacked sustainable ways of rebutting Druze demands for first-class citizenship. In short, the Druze found success by engaging in rhetorical coercion.

Despite their superior numbers, their higher levels of education, income, and wealth, and their greater organization, Christians and Muslims confronted an imposing rhetorical barrier. Excluded from mandatory conscription and the concomitant claim to military and civic virtue, they could not credibly invoke republican rhetoric to bolster their claims-making. Rather, in challenging the state's policies, they insisted that Israel abide by its commitment to liberal democracy. While this liberal citizenship frame also drew on Israeli commonplaces, it left Jewish politicians with room for rhetorical maneuver. They justified discrimination against Christians and Muslims by invoking the inverse of the Druze claim: those who do not perform civic duties cannot lay claim to equivalent public rights and benefits. In short, the history of Arab claims-making in Israel nicely illustrates the power and limits of rhetorical coercion.

"Shaveh Ḥovot, Shaveh Zekhuyot"

Since 1956 the Druze, both traditional leaders and their challengers, have consistently framed their demands around their people's military service.[2] The Druze League naturally gravitated to this rhetorical mode, complaining that "we still do not enjoy full equality with our fellow citizens who fulfill the same obligations, and we perceive this as injurious to our rights."[3] As one member recalled, "We give without receiving; equality of obligations deserves equality of rights. This was our motto."[4] In 1967 the League circulated widely a similarly framed appeal: "Since we have done our duties [i.e., military service] . . . and see in the lack of equality . . . an infringement and denial of our rights, we urgently demand correction of this wrong." Three years later, it proclaimed that among the state's foundational principles was that "equality of obligations obligates equality of rights."[5] In the same vein, Kamal Mansour called for a Druze deputy minister in 1971: "When one speaks of residents who serve in all the security services, who sacrifice their blood and strength for the security of the State of Israel—are they not worthy of a position of leadership?"[6] The secretary of the Bet Jan local council similarly complained, "We fulfill all the state's obligations—and willingly. But when it comes to our rights, we are not the top priority. In all matters related to budgets and grants, we have serious problems."[7] Surveying Druze claims-making, one scholar noted that "injustices to individual Druzes are usually attacked as ingratitude toward a man who was willing to shed his blood for his country, but now his country turns against him."[8]

When the Druze turned once again to public claims-making in the 1990s, their preferred frame remained the same. According to two observers, they "usually denounce[ed] the Israeli government for its broken promises, and stress[ed] the price paid by the community in the form of hundreds of Druze soldiers killed during their service in the Israeli army."[9] The Druze mayors that initiated these protests were less likely than their predecessors to continually affirm their loyalty to the State of Israel, but they still resisted an alliance with their fellow Arabs, and they continued to invoke their military service to explain why they deserved preferential treatment.[10] Even the minority that has objected to mandatory conscription has accepted these basic terms. As Mohammed Naffa, a Communist Druze MK, has argued, "If this is a blood covenant, then give us the feeling that we are living in our state, in our homeland, with full rights like all citizens. . . . And if there is to be no equality of rights, then do not demand equality of obligations, and allow Druze to choose—to serve or not to serve in the IDF."[11] Among Druze, the Hebrew slogan *shaveh hovot, shaveh zekhuyot*—the performance of equal obligations deserves the bestowal of equal rights—is axiomatic. It often seems that no Druze can even casually discuss his citizenship status without uttering this phrase.

The Druze, however, did not invent this equation of obligations and rights. Not only did it reflect a norm of citizenship deeply rooted in Western culture but it has been regularly reinforced over the decades by Jewish politicians. Explaining the Histadrut's decision to admit only Arab (typically Druze) veterans as full members, one policymaker argued, "Those who elected to identify themselves with the state by serving in the armed forces deserve the rights of full citizenship, and that includes the right of membership in the Histadrut."[12] In December 1963, at the swearing-in ceremony of the Druze court of first instance, President Zalman Shazar similarly greeted the three newly appointed judges:

> The State and its institutions have the sacred duty to pay special attention to your community . . . since the members of the Druze community have willingly undertaken all civic obligations, including service in the Israel Defense Forces, and are thereby making a considerable contribution to the security of the state. This is the supreme sign of civic loyalty.[13]

Four years later, Prime Minister Levi Eshkol announced the administrative integration of the Druze, pointedly praising the Druze contribution in the 1967 war.[14] As a senior IDF officer put it at a public ceremony honoring the Minorities Unit, "The covenant between the Druze and the Jewish nations is not written only on a piece of paper. It has been sanctified in the blood of Druze fighters."[15] Similar claims might be heard every Memorial Day at the Druze military cemetery in Ussafiya and, through the 1970s, at the annual festival of the prophet Shu'ayb.

Rights, Obligations, and Israeli Political Culture

The discourse of citizenship in Israel contains multiple strands, ranging from an exclusive ethno-national strain to a maximally inclusive liberal one.[16] For much of the country's history, first-class citizenship in Israel has, however, been rooted less in the liberal notion of citizenship as a bundle of rights than in the republican conception of citizenship, with its greater emphasis on public obligation and civic virtue.[17] Thus Christian and Muslim Arabs enjoy basic civil and political rights, but, denied the opportunity to perform their civic duty, they remain otherwise consigned to second-class status. They are within the state but outside the political community.[18]

The prevailing republican citizenship discourse has roots stretching back at least to the prestate Jewish community, the yishuv.[19] Although participation in the yishuv was necessarily voluntary, the essence of *halutsiyut* (literally pioneerism) was individual and group commitment to the public good, defined as the historical mission of the Jewish people to rebuild the Land of Israel and epitomized by the kibbutz movement.[20] The new state preserved this emphasis on civic commitment as the basis for membership, grafting a statist ideology (*mamlakhtiyut*) onto the earlier discourse. The sacrifice of individual wants to communal needs continued to be prized, but now it was the state that constituted the relevant community.[21] In an early Knesset debate over the place of women in the IDF, Ben-Gurion gave voice to the essence of the Israeli republican tradition: "There are no rights without obligations. And above all is the obligation of security, the obligation of defending our existence, our freedom, our independence, and our growth."[22] Later that year, in a Knesset debate over a written constitution, Ben-Gurion expressed himself in characteristically blunt terms: "In a free state like the state of Israel there is no need for a bill of rights. . . . We need a bill of duties . . . duties to the homeland, to the people, to aliyah [the Hebrew term for the immigration of Jews to Israel, literally 'ascent'], to building the land, to the security of others, of the weak."[23]

This republican discourse on citizenship established itself as hegemonic.[24] In the late 1980s, a survey of Israeli interest groups found that their leaders generally believed that material resources were far less determinative of success in Israel's political system than was "a group's social contribution." The reason, it was suggested, was that "devotion to the collective is highly legitimized" in Israel.[25] Even dissidents have protested *within* the terms of this discourse: one conscientious objector from the 1982 Lebanon War defined citizenship as "military service, paying taxes, and obeying the law. . . . That is what makes you a citizen and makes you eligible to enjoy the defense and the fruits that [the state] equally distributes."[26]

This civic republican tradition has long sat uncomfortably alongside a substantial ascriptive component in the definition of the Israeli political community. Laws (e.g., the Law of Return), policies (e.g., the close relationships between the state apparatus and quasi-public institutions like the Jewish Agency and the Jewish National Fund), and official discourse (e.g., the Declaration of Independence's repeated references to "the Jewish State") have clearly indicated to Israel's Arab minorities their liminal place. At one level, "Jewish ethnicity is a necessary condition for membership in the political community, while the contribution to the process of Jewish national redemp-

tion is a measure of one's civic virtue."[27] Yet this formulation ignores the potential contradictions between these discourses. Such tensions are muted
when only Jewish citizens are drafted; then Israeli leaders can publicly embrace civic republicanism while preserving ethno-religious priorities. But the
inclusion of the Druze and their claims-making framed around their collective military sacrifice challenged the peculiar Israeli amalgam that Yoav Peled
calls "ethno-republican" citizenship. The Druze confronted Jewish Israelis
with an uncomfortable choice: the latter either had to acknowledge their exclusive definition of the political community or had to open (grudgingly) the
community's doors. Returning repeatedly to the equation of obligations and
rights, the Druze have plumbed the republican depths of Israel's soul.

Israeli political culture has been not merely republican but militarist, so
that "civic virtue has been constructed in terms of and identified with military virtue."[28] Initially the province of elite groups in the yishuv, militarism
spread among the masses as an integral component of mamlakhtiyut. Ben-
Gurion turned especially to the IDF, among state institutions, to overcome the
ethnic and class divisions among Israel's immigrants and build the new Israeli nation. Certainly the instrument of national defense, the IDF was also the
first option of choice for numerous "nonmilitary" tasks, from road building
to remedial education.[29] In the early 1950s, one minister of education told a
conference of teachers that the new Israelis must be "a nation of soldiers," an
image far removed from the biblical vision of "a nation of priests."[30] Over
time, military service became "the single most important test . . . for individual and group acceptance in[to] the mainstream of Israeli society governed by
[the] Zionist civil religion."[31] Even after the army's prestige had declined in
the wake of the Yom Kippur War and, especially, the invasion of Lebanon,
even after Lebanon and the first intifada had made conscientious objection a
recognizable element of the Israeli political scene, the IDF lost little of its
politico-cultural centrality.[32] Only in very recent years has the IDF's social significance begun to wane.[33]

Militarism has so deeply pervaded Israeli society that the armed forces' influence can be spotted in nearly all spheres—politics, the economy, even the
arts.[34] Debates over group exemptions from service still exercise the Israeli
public, and the refusal of the *haredim* (the so-called ultra-Orthodox) to serve
was central to Ehud Barak's successful campaign for the premiership in 1999.
Moreover, as in other militaristic environments, the boundary between the
military and the civilian spheres has been highly permeable.[35] From the very
beginning senior officers have moved smoothly into key political posts, many
negotiating with political parties while still in uniform. These trends intensified in the 1960s and 1970s, and there was little public outcry: in fact, just the
opposite, as some criticized parties that hindered officers' efforts to penetrate
the political system.[36] Finally, one critic noted in the 1950s that "one has only
to mention the word 'security' for all protests to be silenced. 'Security' is the
Holy of Holies, and nothing connected with it can be criticized."[37] Exploiting

Israel's siege mentality, the country's leaders have deployed the rhetoric of security to justify substantial deviations from the rule of law. Only in recent years has the public begun to question such an expansive definition of security.[38]

The armed forces have also been the focus of many of Israel's public rituals. Well into the 1970s, the highlight of the annual Independence Day celebration was a parade that displayed Israel's military might and technological sophistication. Popular expressions and banners cast the IDF in the role of God: "The guardian of Israel neither sleeps nor slumbers"; "Israel trust the IDF, it is your help and defender"; "In the beginning the IDF created the soldier, and the IDF created the nation."[39] The metaphor not only suggested the infallibility of the army but implied that it was more responsible than any other institution for the nation's fate. Nearly every Israeli town has a monument to its war dead, and the annual memorial day is commemorated according to a set of relatively fixed rites. Nor is it coincidental that Israel's memorial day immediately precedes Independence Day and that the official ceremony opening the latter is at the same time the closing ceremony of the former.[40]

Naturally, Israel's militarized republican citizenship discourse was not the only terrain on which claims-making might be conducted, nor did it go unchallenged. Dissenters abounded—from Christian and Muslim Arabs and leftist Jews inspired by liberal visions of citizenship to Jews on the right who eschewed ethnically neutral terms—for republicanism always competed with other citizenship discourses. But this was a lopsided competition, for the alternatives had less traction.

"Our Ears Were Open"

With few conventional political resources at their disposal, the Druze citizens of Israel had little choice but to place their bets on the power of the military sacrifice frame. Ideally, Jewish politicians would be persuaded by their ethical argument, but the Druze understood that this was unlikely in Israel's ethnic democracy. They recognized that few Jewish decision makers would, if left to their own devices, pay much attention to the Druze's condition.[41] In fact, while the Druze squeezed concessions out of Israeli officials beginning in the late 1960s, there is no evidence that their appeals were persuasive: the limited and incremental nature of Israeli concessions, as well as the grudging manner in which they were offered, is not consistent with a narrative centered around persuasion. Rather, the Druze hoped to twist Jewish politicians' arms by forcing their tongues, to fashion a frame that had coercive potential in addition to persuasive possibilities. Such a frame might force Jewish politicians to endorse the Druze program against their will and their better ethnic judgment.

Faced with Druze claims, Jewish leaders could have (a) admitted openly the discriminatory nature of "the Jewish state," (b) claimed that the Druze were not relatively disadvantaged, or (c) argued that the Druze community's problems were of their own making. The first alternative was unappealing: aside from the likely international repercussions, it would have contradicted both Israel's self-proclaimed status as the sole democracy in the Middle East and its dominant way of speaking about citizenship.[42] The second put forward a claim widely known to be false. The third possible response, while perhaps plausible with regard to general questions of economic development, could not justify administrative segregation. This was, whether cleverly or serendipitously, among Druze activists' first targets,[43] and it was, by some accounts, that which most rankled the Druze in the late 1960s and early 1970s.[44]

There was, however, a fourth option: Jewish politicians could simply have refused to reply. If relevant audiences were unaware of the Druze's plight, the Druze could not credibly threaten to bring those audiences into the struggle on their side, and Jewish politicians would consequently have felt no pressure to accede to Druze demands. The Druze's capacity to engage in rhetorical coercion was consequently dependent on garnering attention from the Hebrew-language media. As a general rule, the Hebrew press only rarely covered the Arab population, for its readers and writers were almost entirely Jewish.[45] But unlike the politicians, the Jewish public and, more important, the media were basically sympathetic to the Druze's principled arguments, which were couched in terms consonant with the dominant republican rhetorical practice. As one Druze editor observed:

> No one gets anything in Israel without pressure: not the Sephardim [a broad category encompassing Jews of Southern European, North African, and Middle Eastern descent], not the ultra-Orthodox, not the immigrants. If you just sit on your chair, you will get nothing. But, in truth, there are those, particularly in the broad public, who believe that the Druze deserve without pressure . . . ; there are those who believe that they have obligations to the Druze and search for ways to give.[46]

When the Druze made noise, the press amplified it, helping the Druze compensate for their lack of political clout and ensuring a hearing in the halls of power.[47] In news stories, reporters would often implicitly endorse the Druze's complaints and demands and sometimes even give voice to them in the first person.[48] As the Druze began to mobilize in the mid-1960s and broadcast their appeals to a wider audience, this marginal minority succeeded in commanding a place on the government's agenda.

In short, the Druze trapped Jewish leaders in a rhetorical cul-de-sac: there was no sustainable response at their disposal. The Druze unquestionably fulfilled the same obligations as other citizens, and thus it was not clear how their claims could be denied. Wary of calling forth punishment either from sympathetic Jewish domestic audiences or from international audiences eager to find fault, Jewish leaders believed they had little choice but to concede, at least publicly. The Druze thus found that concessions from the Israeli leadership came relatively easily. When Druze complaints garnered media coverage, Jewish politicians readily adopted the frame the Druze had deployed and acknowledged the justice of Druze claims, appearing to grant them because they seemed "objectively justified."[49] According to a long-serving adviser to the prime minister, "When the Druze demanded something, the ears were much more open."[50] The Druze themselves recognized this to be the case: "It is impossible to argue: you are right that you give like any Jew, so why do you get less? So, they cannot tell you [the Druze] that you are not right. There is no reason, and therefore, in general, they give support."[51]

Despite the Druze community's electoral insignificance, cases of alleged discrimination against individual Druze received attention even at the level of the Knesset.[52] The Druze demand in the late 1960s for full membership in the Labor Party was ultimately irrefutable: as a prominent Labor Party functionary wrote in a major newspaper, "How can we explain to that Druze, Circassian, or Arab that he is good enough to endanger his life for the state but that he is not good enough to be a member of the Labor Party?"[53] Confident of the frame's efficacy, the Druze have invoked it year after year. In the words of one local elected Druze official, "The Druze will not be able to determine whether [Ehud] Barak becomes prime minister, but they can say we serve, we are brothers, we ate out of the same ration plates."[54]

For all their skill at extracting promises from Jewish politicians, the Druze have found realizing them a greater challenge. Their influence has been greatest when they have waged their struggles publicly, but implementation comes about through mastery of bureaucracy's byways. Years have sometimes passed before these pledges acquired substance. Prime Minister Eshkol, for example, affirmed his commitment to the Druze's administrative integration in 1967, but there was little real progress until the mid-1970s. As late as 1974, one journalist observed that the only change had been the addition of the word "Druze" to the title of the prime minister's adviser on Arab affairs.[55] A 1987 government decision to equalize the grants to Jewish and Druze villages and towns had limited practical import until further Druze pressure several years later. As Shmuel Toledano recalled, "To say that if the ears were open, things were done—there is a difference." Or as Salman Falaḥ put it, "My impression . . . is that everything that was accepted by Jewish public opinion and by the government authorities, everything related to the Druze, was accepted willingly. . . . But between such acceptance and operational policy lies a great gap."[56] Noting the persistent chasm between promises and action, many Druze believed that Jewish Israeli leaders had paid only lip service to their concerns.[57] But even a sincere politician might not be able or willing to expend the political capital necessary to ensure implementation in the face of bureaucratic resistance and in the absence of substantial outside pressure.[58]

The problem the Druze faced was that as the reform process moved into the bureaucracy, journalists typically lost interest. Once the government had to all appearances put into motion an apparently just process, there seemed to be little to report. Moreover, the prosperous economy and continuing government initiatives rectified many infrastructural weaknesses, thereby appearing to gainsay charges of discrimination. To make headway, the Druze needed to return to the public arena, where they enjoyed a comparative advantage and where they could put Jewish leaders on the rhetorical defensive.

On balance, were the Druze's efforts at rhetorical coercion all for naught? The Druze have certainly not thought so. Certain that their rhetorical resources have bequeathed disproportionate influence, they have been reluctant to join forces with Christians and Muslims: an alliance with other Arabs would bring the strength of numbers, but the Druze would also no longer be able to deploy the military sacrifice frame. As Kamal Mansour has noted, "There is one overriding difference that no one can overlook—we have totally empathized with the State of Israel and we've proven our loyalty on the battlefield."[59] Former MK Zeidan Atashe, who early on publicly embraced his Arab ethnicity, related a typical dialogue with his fellow Arabs: "The Arabs were criticizing me, 'Why do you speak about the Druze, [and not] the Arabs? We are proud that you are representing our case in the Knesset, but why do you specify the Druze?' . . . I replied, 'I am an Arab. I spoke for you always. But I have some distinctions. My people serve in the army.'"[60] Even those Druze otherwise critical of Israel's policies have normally supported continued conscription so that this frame would remain available.[61] They would point to even the partial implementation of these commitments as proof of their strategy's success. But they would also argue that these rhetorical successes are themselves of immense value, for they create a solid foundation for further claims-making.

Falling on Deaf Ears

Exempt from the draft and as a general rule excluded from the IDF, Christians and Muslims could not provide compelling evidence of civic virtue and thus could not frame their claims in the republican terms that the Druze had found so effective. Political contestation, however, is impossible in the absence of framing, and they consequently turned, for the purposes of political struggle, to the language of liberal democracy.[62] Christians and Muslims challenged Israeli officials to live up to their own commitments, dating back to the very beginning of the Zionist enterprise. Ben-Gurion and his colleagues often promised that citizenship, not ethnic or religious identity, would be the chief determinant of rights, and that Arabs could expect a fair shake in the Jewish state. After the establishment of the state, Israeli diplomats upheld this claim against persistent Arab allegations to the contrary. While this frame was hardly alien to Israelis, Arab efforts to engage in rhetorical coercion were bound to fail because Jewish politicians had rhetorical options.

First, Israeli leaders often argued, especially in international forums, that conditions in the Arab sector had developed rapidly under Israeli sponsorship, and they invited comparisons to either the Arab world or Mandatory Palestine. Abba Ḥushi of Mapai responded in this vein to the Arab activist Elias Koussa:

> You complain about the lack of legal equality, of rights and obligations? I do not want to say that our government is all perfect and never makes a mistake and has never done any evil, but try to compare the condition of the masses in Egypt, Syria, Iraq, and Jordan to that of most Arabs in Israel. . . . The Arab citizens of Israel are in the Garden of Eden compared to the condition of Arabs in lands under the rule of Nassers.[63]

Given the backward state of the Arab population, they maintained, patience was required, for an advanced society and economy could not emerge overnight or even over a couple of decades.

Second, particularly for Israeli domestic consumption and occasionally for outsiders, they retreated into a republican defense: Arab rights were not sacrosanct, for those who did not fulfill their civic obligations deserved less than those who had made the supreme sacrifice. In seeking to convince a wavering Knesset member to support the military administration, Ben-Gurion invoked the usual formula: "I have recognized all these years that rights are dependent on obligations, except for children and the aged who have only rights and no duties. . . . I do not understand why I may limit the freedom and steal the time of young Jewish men and women when they are in the army, but why it is forbidden to limit much less the freedom of those who do not serve in the army."[64] A decade later, writing in a popular newspaper, Amnon Lin justified the exclusion of Arabs from the Labor Party on similar grounds:

> I asked them [close Arab friends] how they could sit in the party central committee . . . next to a bereaved father or mother, next to a party member who had just returned from the front, next to a member who stands ready to leave the next day for reserve service, while they still do not fulfill this obligation. I asked them, 'What would you say to a bereaved mother, a member of your party's central committee, and how would you console her while you do not participate in this war?', and they lowered their eyes.[65]

Decades later, this rhetorical move continued to frustrate Arab efforts to attain first-class citizenship. In the late 1980s, a proposal to subject Arab citizens to military and/or national service sparked a vigorous debate. A former adviser to the prime minister for Arab affairs, Ra'anan Cohen, claimed that he and his colleagues had "regularly recommended that Arab Israelis be put to the test. If they are interested in equality of rights, they must fulfill all the obligations, like other Israeli citizens." He predicted that they would refuse to serve and thus would "establish that they are not ready to fulfill all their obligations to the state."[66] More recently, one Arab activist complained, "They are trying to link our rights as citizens to performing military service. That's not how a real democracy works."[67] Never mind that Jewish Israelis have never been supportive of extending the draft to the Arab population. The bluff has been a safe one: Arab citizens have, at least since the 1970s, vociferously opposed conscription, and nearly half have objected even to mandatory non-military national service.[68] Nevertheless, to parry Jewish politicians' rhetorical moves, Arab leaders have continually considered encouraging masses of Arabs to volunteer their services and skills to the army.[69]

With this standard republican response so readily available, Christians and Muslims, unlike the Druze, could not control the terms of debate, and their demands consequently met with greater resistance. As one observer has noted, explaining the Arabs' lack of effective citizenship, "Equal to the Jews in political rights and before the law, the Arab communities are unequal both in obligations . . . and in effective claims on public resources."[70] A second reason, however, lay in the difficulty Israel's Arab/Palestinian citizens had squeezing their calls for collective rights into the individualistic language of liberalism. Although liberal principles required redress of individual Palestinian citizens' grievances, liberalism provided little succor to Palestinian citizens' demand that they be recognized and dealt with as a *national* minority. Drawing on older Zionist themes,[71] "Palestinian *individuals* are often treated leniently, in accord with the ethos of personal equality and meritocracy; when it comes to *The Palestinians* as a collective, the application of these values is arrested."[72] Since the 1970s, Arab citizens' demand that they be accorded equal treatment has increasingly gone hand in hand with the assertion of their Palestinian identity, the struggle for an independent Palestinian state, and the recognition of their collective rights. Yet whereas the former can be framed comfortably within the terms of liberalism, the latter cannot. Israeli officials have thus been free to paint the entire canvas of Palestinian citizens' demands with a broad brush. The protests and strikes organized by the National Committee of Heads of Arab Local Authorities, even those focused on local matters, have generally been cast by the government as "unjustified, needless, and politically motivated."[73]

Although Christians and Muslims could not control the rhetorical playing field, they did make significant gains in the mid-1980s thanks to their raw political power. As Arab citizens increasingly identified with the Palestinian national cause after 1967, Jewish Israelis grew nervous about their loyalty. Uncomfortable or not, however, Israeli politicians, on the left and the right alike, began to cozy up to the Arab population. After the breakdown of Labor Zionism's stranglehold on the political system, the Jewish electorate was fractured, and national unity governments became the norm. As the electoral competition tightened, all sides scrambled for whatever advantage they could muster, and the Arab population was actively wooed.[74] The Labor Party disbanded its affiliated Arab lists after the 1981 elections, and by the mid-1980s its Arab candidates were no longer selected by its "experts" but by the Arab delegates to the party's central committee. In recognition of Arabs' growing political strength, in 1982 the Likud established an Arab Department for the first time. Candidates from across the political spectrum stumped in Arab villages, each seeking to outdo the other in demonstrating his or her commitment to improving the Arabs' lot.

Demographic and economic trends also contributed to Zionist parties' courting the Arab vote. Over three-quarters of the Arab population was Muslim at that time, and their fertility rate exceeded that of all other social groups except ḥaredim and the Druze. Arabs constituted no greater a portion of the population than they had immediately after the 1948 war, but, despite the waves of Jewish immigration since, they were no smaller either. And projections suggested that, the annexation of the West Bank and Gaza Strip aside, the future of Israel as a Jewish state was, at least demographically speaking, bleak. In addition, Arabs within the Green Line had climbed up a notch on Israel's socioeconomic ladder, increasingly working in skilled and professional jobs. Unskilled workers, as the Palestinians from the Occupied Territories discovered during the first intifada, could easily be replaced with foreign labor, but Israeli industry was ever more dependent on its Arab citizens.

Both short-term and long-term political and economic interests thus dictated greater receptivity to Arab demands. Arab MKs forged an alliance with the Labor opposition in the early 1980s to reverse discriminatory university fees and to defeat a bill linking suffrage to military service. Land seized in the past from Arabs for Army training grounds was returned; orders to demolish illegal buildings in Arab towns and villages were frozen. The National Committee of Heads of Arab Local Authorities was accepted informally as the population's representative, and its leadership met regularly with top government figures. By the early 1990s Arab parties had wrung further commitments from fragile governments—including promises to grant Muslims autonomy in the management of the religious endowment, to accord municipal status to unrecognized Arab settlements, and to close the gap in expenditures for social services—and there was a relatively high level of implementation. The ethno-religious rules of the Israeli political game have prevented the formal inclusion of Arab parties in the governing coalition, but they have not prevented narrow Labor governments under Shimon Peres and Ehud Barak from depending heavily on Arab parliamentary support. And the realities of Israeli politics have compelled Jewish politicians from Labor and the Likud alike to pay increasing attention to Arab demands.[75] Resonant rhetoric—the Druze way—is naturally not the sole means of placing one's concerns on the agenda: occupying a critical site in the Israeli political system after 1977, Arabs have acted at times as spoilers and as kingmakers.

Back to the Future?

Over the past twenty-five years, Israeli culture has undergone a sea change. The republican ideal of nondomination has gradually given way to the liberal vision of non-interference; the emphasis on collective sacrifice and the common good has been replaced by the primacy of the individual. The economy has been liberalized, the once all-powerful Histadrut has been transformed into a far weaker trade union, universal social services have been challenged by proposals for means-testing, and the sale of public land to private owners has found its way onto the agenda. That distinctive Israeli collective, the kibbutz, has entered a state of seemingly terminal decline, and those kibbutzim that remain viable have survived by abandoning collective living and socialist values—in short, by deviating, often quite far, from the kibbutz ideal.[76] A new generation of academics and intellectuals has challenged the Zionist narratives of their intellectual mentors, and their "revisionist" or "post-Zionist" versions of Israeli history were the basis for a highly controversial television series marking (but not entirely celebrating) the fiftieth anniversary of Israel's establishment; post-Zionism also found its way into the latest editions of the state-run educational system's textbooks.[77] And, in the surest sign of a potential changing of the country's ideological guard, these struggles within the academy have burst into far more public forums, both in Israel and abroad.[78]

Reflecting this cultural shift, there have been major attitudinal changes with regard to military service. Through the 1980s over 90 percent of male Jewish Israeli high school students routinely reported that they looked forward to enlistment and would serve even if there were no draft. After years of anecdotal evidence suggesting cracks in the consensus, by the mid-1990s public opinion surveys revealed that only three-quarters of Jewish males now embraced military service, and even the normally tight-lipped IDF admitted that motivation to serve had declined 2 percent per year since 1992. As IDF Chief of Staff Amnon Lipkin-Shahak worried, "We are witnessing a preference for the individual over the collective in the age of liberalism."[79] The increasing cultural influence of liberalism has also been reflected in Israel's popular music. Whereas Israel's Top 40 had once reinforced the Zionist consensus, it now came to be dominated by songs calling for draft evasion or yearning for freedom from responsibility.[80]

As these two traditions squared off in Israel's culture wars, the standard republican reply to Arab claims became increasingly untenable. Ever larger numbers of male Jewish Israelis were either opting out of military service or finding that the IDF did not want them.[81] At the same time, the growing political power of the ḥaredim resulted in a redistribution of resources toward a population that not only refused to defend the state but typically ostracized those of its number who did. With fewer Israelis donning a uniform than ever before, invoking the equation of rights and obligations strained the bounds of credibility, and Arab demands for equal treatment could no longer be dismissed out of hand on republican grounds. At the same time, the Druze found that their rhetorical tactics were no longer as effective. Druze local and national leaders complained that the left-wing Meretz Party—a crucial member of Ehud Barak's governing coalition—denied that they deserved special consideration on the basis of military service. As a result, the Druze asserted, they failed at the end of the 1990s to win renewal of the five-year disbursement of additional development funds that had begun in 1995.[82]

The second intifada, which began in the fall of 2000, at least partly reversed some of these trends. Support for negotiations with Yasir Arafat or any other likely Palestinian leader plummeted. Jewish Israelis remained desperate for peace but increasingly despaired of achieving it. Israel's Left was eviscerated, and unilateral withdrawal and defensive measures drew broad and deep support.[83] Perhaps most important, Jewish Israelis again openly spoke of the country's Arab citizens as a fifth column—IDF Chief of Staff Moshe Ya'alon called them a "cancerous threat"—and at least one government minister proposed stripping Arab suspects of their citizenship and demolishing their houses, as Israel routinely did in the West Bank and the Gaza Strip.[84] Sympathetic (and at times violent) demonstrations by Israel's Arab citizens, evidence that Arab citizens had occasionally abetted terrorists, and Arab politicians' public stances that seemed to encourage violence against Jewish civilians even within the Green Line all contributed to a collapse of Jewish understanding for the plight of Israel's Arabs. In 2002, a startling 31 percent of Israelis (up from 24 percent in 1991) favored "transferring" the country's Arab citizens, and three-quarters or more of those surveyed questioned Arab citizens' loyalty, opposed including Arab parties in a coalition government, and thought that Arabs had no place participating in crucial national decisions (such as those regarding the country's future borders)—substantial increases over 2000 and incremental increases over 2001. Revealingly, in 2002 only 10 percent believed that Israel was solely or mostly accountable for the Arab citizens' situation, while 43 percent thought that the Arabs themselves were solely or mostly responsible.[85]

Less clear are the cultural consequences of this political backlash and how long it will last. The second intifada has not rekindled in Israelis an old-time Zionist fervor, and Israeli youth do not seem suddenly enthusiastic about serving in the IDF. Perhaps just the opposite, as conscientious objection has been on the rise. The upheaval has damaged Israel's formerly thriving high-tech sector, but it has hardly dampened the zeal for capitalism and privatization. The continual terrorist attacks have not led to massive emigration, and they do not appear to have prompted enduring cultural shifts. Although there is some evidence that Israeli opinion on security has begun to pull away from the extremes of 2002, it is overall quite mixed. On the one hand, there was substantially more support for abandoning all but the largest settlement blocs in the West Bank and even Arab neighborhoods of Jerusalem in the framework of a peace agreement in 2003 and 2004. On the other hand, Israelis were in 2004 equally pessimistic that a peace treaty was truly workable, and slightly lower numbers thought that a Palestinian state should be, or was likely to be, established.

Yet there is also evidence that relations between Israel's Arab and Jewish citizens were more than superficially harmed and may even have been poisoned. Despite the population's more optimistic and conciliatory mood in 2003, greater or at least equal numbers thought the government should "encourage the emigration of the Arabs from Israel," supported the transfer of the country's Arab citizens, and opposed Arab participation in crucial national decisions. By 2004, more Israelis objected to the inclusion of Arab parties in a governing coalition and believed Arab citizens to be disloyal. Perhaps most important, nearly half of all Israelis in 2003 thought that the Arabs were solely or mostly responsible for their troubles, with only 11 percent ascribing to Israel sole or predominant blame; by 2004, the latter number had fallen to just 7 percent.[86]

No one can prophesy with confidence when Israel and the Palestinians will negotiate a permanent arrangement, but the current instability is unsustainable in the long run. As in the past, such instability will eventually be followed by periods of relative peace. When that happens, Israelis will have to come to terms with unresolved questions about their country's identity as a democracy and as a Jewish state. And it seems likely that such debates will transpire on a terrain that is increasingly dominated by a liberal discourse of citizenship. Even if the effects of the second intifada prove lasting, even if relations between Israel's Arabs and Jews never fully recover, continued discrimination against the country's Arab citizens would likely be difficult in such a context.

However, this is only one arrow in the Arabs' well-stocked political quiver. Although the recent Russian and Ethiopian immigrations have slowed the "Arabization" of Israel, they have not rendered it a mirage. The underlying demographic trends are the same, particularly because the Russians, like other Jews of European descent, reproduce at levels below the replacement rate. Given the growing strength of Arabs' conventional political resources, isolating the effects of their frame is impossible: they enjoy a happy confluence of favorable demographic, organizational, and cultural developments. Arabs may not ultimately prove successful in making Israel into a "state of all its citizens." But, regardless, Arab claims-making will likely increasingly powerfully shape the Israeli political agenda.

Conclusion

Israel undoubtedly remains a Jewish state in the deepest sense of the word.[1] Its central symbols—from the menorah that is the state's official emblem to the Star (or Shield) of David that is pictured on the national flag to "Ha-Tikvah" (The Hope) that serves as the national anthem—are drawn from and speak to the heritage of the Jewish people. To be an Arab in Israel is necessarily not to feel entirely at home. Arab citizens playing for Israel's national team kept the country's World Cup hopes alive in March 2005 by scoring late goals and temporarily became heroes to Israel's soccer-crazy public. Just weeks before, however, cries from the stands of "no Arabs, no terrorism" greeted one of these new heroes every time he touched the ball, and the following week, in league play, Jewish fans hailed him with a large sign proclaiming, "Abbas Suan—you do not represent us."[2] Even in the mid-1990s, when many were still hopeful that the Oslo process would bear fruit, Israel's Jewish citizens showed little inclination to include the Arab minority symbolically, socially, institutionally, or even economically and politically. A large majority believed that the state should show preference for Jewish over Arab citizens, opposed any modification in the major national symbols, and was unwilling to live in a religiously mixed neighborhood. Half treated "Israeli" as synonymous with "Jewish." Substantial minorities thought that only Jews should hold civil service jobs and favored the expropriation of Arab land to further Jewish development.[3] Such views have only hardened and grown more extreme since the outbreak of the second intifada.[4] Yet, despite the prejudice woven into Israel's very fabric, the experience of the country's Arab minorities has varied dramatically.

In Israel's complicated relationship with its various Arab minorities lies a controlled comparison demonstrating the difference military service may make. The subjection of the Druze to military conscription in 1956, and the gradual subsequent liberalization of the IDF's participation policies, sparked early Druze mobilization, encouraged the Druze to pursue integration, and led the Druze to play within the rules of the Israeli political game. In contrast, Christians and Muslims were exempt from the draft. Permitted to volunteer but rarely accepted, they remained politically quiescent well into the 1970s: the IDF's policies had signaled that repression, or at the very least the cold shoulder, would greet Arab political agitation. When Israel's Christian and Muslim citizens did finally come forward to demand their due, they pursued separationist goals and employed more aggressive tactics. If the Druze battle cry was "Integration Now," other Arabs opted for "Separate but Equal." Furthermore, despite the Druze's dearth of conventional political resources, they proved surprisingly effective actors on the Israeli political stage. Operating within discursive fields dominated by republican conceptions of citizenship, the Druze put their sacrifice in uniform to their political gain and compelled reluctant Jewish politicians to concede Druze claims. Christians and Muslims, however, could employ only a liberal rights frame, and Israel's politicians denied their demands by retreating into republican rhetorical forms. Christians and Muslims did eventually make headway, but only when they came to occupy a critical electoral position.

My emphasis on signaling and framing challenges conventional explanations of Israel's relations with its minorities. Both alternative accounts of the *timing* of Arab political activity fail the comparative test. First, some point to processes of modernization that created a minority capable of challenging the state.[5] However, the Druze—the most rural, least educated, and least wealthy Arab subgroup—enjoyed the fruits of development no more, and possibly even less, than did other Arabs, yet they mobilized earlier. A second popular explanation argues that the Arab minority remained politically quiescent for nearly thirty years because of Israeli policies that prevented united Arab political action, generated dependence on the Jewish economy, and co-opted groups and individuals.[6] However, according to this argument, the Druze were the most prominent co-opted Arab subgroup, and one would therefore have expected the Druze to be the last to challenge the discriminatory system, not the first.[7]

The scholarly literature suggests four explanations for the Druze's more moderate *goals* and *tactics,* though again all are lacking in one way or another. First, many have argued that Arabs' political attitudes were forged by state predation, exploitation, and suppression.[8] Although this is doubtless true, it cannot be the whole story, for the Druze also suffered from oppressive policies, precisely in that early period that many have considered a critical juncture. Second, and closely related, others have argued that the Druze pursued a different path because, unlike other Arabs, they had been co-opted. But the Druze faced nearly equivalent discrimination, and, except for token gestures, the state resisted granting them the first-class citizenship they craved. Whether because state policy was bedeviled by incoherence or because officials believed the Druze could be kept quiet with less, Israel failed to pursue a systematic strategy of co-optation. While a co-opted minority would have been content with the favors the state bestowed, the Druze became dissatisfied with their status and continually presented Jewish politicians and officials with uncomfortable choices. The Druze may not have been as aggressive as their fellow Arabs would have liked, but their behavior was not consistent with that of a co-opted minority.

Third, others have attributed the Druze anomaly to their predilection for *taqiyya,* or the art of concealment. Long viewed as heretics by their Muslim neighbors, the Druze had shielded themselves from persecution by hiding their religious observances. Inclined to adapt to powerful majorities, the Druze adopted an ultrapragmatic political doctrine that prescribed neutrality when possible and bandwagoning—allying with the expected victor—when necessary.[9]

This argument has some merit, but it is ultimately not satisfying. One would thus have expected the Druze generally to have avoided challenging stronger parties, but in fact the Druze displayed a rebellious streak during Ottoman and European colonial domination of the region. Despite a long history of tension with both Christians and Muslims in Lebanon, the Druze made common cause with their fellow Arabs in the struggle for Lebanese autonomy early in the twentieth century. During a 1908 confrontation between Lebanese notables and the Ottoman governor-general, the latter refused even to meet with the delegation until local Druze issued a not-so-subtle threat by surrounding his palace. Those Arabs plotting rebellion usually assumed that they could count on the support of the Lebanese and Syrian Druze communities. In 1915 Sultan al-Atrash—one of the leaders of the Jabal al-Duruz, the "Druze mountain," in Syria—promised Druze assistance in an Arab revolt against the Ottomans, and he renewed that pledge the following year despite a less favorable distribution of power. During World War I, when the long-planned revolt finally began, the Druze played a key role in the final assault on Damascus.[10] In the mid-1920s, frustrated that one foreign ruler had simply replaced another, al-Atrash initiated a nationalist revolt against the French—with disastrous consequences.[11] The Druze were not protonationalists, but they were at times willing to set aside intra-Arab differences and rebel against stronger parties, compelling one to ask why they did not cast their lot with other Arabs in Israel in the decades after 1948. Taqiyya is obviously of little help in answering this question, for it lacks analytical bite. The doctrine is so flexible that it is less an explanation for Druze behavior than a tidy description of it.[12]

A different version of the cultural argument, which Druze and Jews alike have relished, argues that the two peoples are natural allies as fellow non-Muslim minorities. Shaykh Jabber Mu'addi, the longtime Druze MK, expressed this view: "From the beginning we felt a rapport with the Jews. They were a small, persecuted people, and so were we. They were vulnerable to the

Moslem majority, as were the Druze. They gave the world the Ten Commandments, and we cherished these laws. The Jews created no problems for the Druze, and we wished to live in peace with them."[13] Yet while the Druze have long been a community apart in a Middle East dominated by Muslims, the assertion of a natural Jewish-Druze affinity is propagandistic rhetoric that has, since the founding of Israel, served the interests of both Israeli officials and Druze leaders.[14] Druze religious texts are typically dismissive of other religions, and while particularly disparaging of Islam, they are hardly admiring of Judaism. Consider that, in the allocation of curses, Shiites are to receive fifty, Sunnis forty, and Christians thirty, but the Jews still are to receive twenty. These texts may display less venom toward the powerless Jews, but there is little indication of any particular affection or respect.[15] Nor was a Jewish-Druze alliance in any way foreordained. Many Druze, including from the villages atop Mount Carmel, joined the Arab nationalist forces in 1948, and the Druze in the central and upper Galilee were at best neutral and probably sympathetic to the nationalist cause. Jewish decision makers continued to view the Druze as a security threat well into the 1960s, even after conscription to the IDF had commenced.

Finally, a "realist" might argue that process variables, like signaling and framing, were less important than structural factors. Precisely because the Druze were so small, so weak, and so moderate, Israel could countenance their inclusion in the IDF and grant them a modicum of effective citizenship without threatening these institutions' or the state's Jewish character. Because the Druze were a minority within a minority, nationalism was beyond their reach; Christians and Muslims could dream nationalist dreams—and did. Had the Druze's population been as large as Israel's Christian or Muslim communities, concessions would have been unthinkable. Relatedly, others might argue that the Druze occupied a different social space in the new Israeli polity: regardless of whether the Druze were truly of a different nature than the country's other Arabs, Israel's Arabists had long emphasized the political as well as the religious distinctiveness of the Druze community.[16]

The Druze's small size presumably did make them an attractive target for co-optation. But if this argument were correct, the state should have flung its doors wide open, for the costs would have been negligible and the propaganda advantages substantial. Yet the Druze had to fight for every small step of progress they achieved: Israeli decision makers resisted acting on their rhetorical concessions and grudgingly offered only small increments of meaningful citizenship. Moreover, such an account would not have expected Christian and Muslim youth to register enthusiastically for the draft in 1954, and it would not have anticipated the opposition among Druze religious and ḥamula leaders to the extension of reserve duty in 1953 or to the draft in 1956–1957. This evidence suggests that, at least early on, religious divides in the Arab community were perhaps less politically salient than other cleavages, notably generational divides. Size figures in the story, but it is not determinative.

Moreover, there are good reasons to doubt how unique was the place the Druze occupied in the Israeli sociopolitical system during the periods explored here. Like other Arabs, the Druze threatened the Zionist project, which had nearly from its inception been centrally concerned with Jewish ownership of territory.[17] The dominant security authorities—the military administration and the GSS—were ever reluctant to grant the Druze special dispensation and often crafted policies implying that the Druze posed as great a security threat as did other Arabs. Even in matters of development, at least for the state's first quarter century, policy was designed for Druze and other Arabs alike. The Druze have, over the decades, carved out an unusual space in the Israeli social imaginary, but this has been the *product* of their framing work, enabled by their service in the IDF.

The policies of the IDF were then not only reflective of Israel's citizenship regime but productive of it as well—for Arabs as well as Jews. Although the army's minority policies did not emerge from a vacuum, they nevertheless had an independent causal effect, as the comparison between the Druze and other Arabs has suggested. Israel may then have missed a golden opportunity in the 1950s and 1960s to forge a very different relationship with its Arab citizens. As the longtime Communist MK Tewfik Toubi once told Ben-Gurion, had Arabs been granted first-class citizenship and even been drafted to the IDF, "the Arabs in this country would have felt themselves partners with equal rights in the creation of state institutions [and] the life of the state."[18] Today, as Arab MKs regularly approach and increasingly cross the line of acceptable dissent, Israel finds itself coping with a problem of its own making.

Suddenly reversing course and demanding that Arab citizens serve in the armed forces is not the solution, however. Some conservatives suggest doing precisely that, though one suspects that they are interested less in promoting a just society and a more inclusive Israeli identity than in scoring political points and demonstrating Arabs' ostensible disloyalty.[19] After enduring a half century of discrimination, however, Arabs would not flock to the armed forces to display their allegiance but would protest vigorously, and even violently, against a new effort to exploit them without giving them the equal rights of citizenship. Although the Druze have made headway in Israeli society, even they have grown so frustrated with the pace of change that the first Druze cabinet member, appointed to his post in 2001, urged fellow Druze not to serve in the IDF until the state followed through on its promises.[20] While the elimination of all vestiges of discrimination in public policy and the rigorous enforcement of laws prohibiting discrimination in the private sector must be a top priority, that alone will not achieve the desired effect.[21] The problem of Israel's Arab citizens is today deeply intertwined with the broader Israeli-Arab and Israeli-Palestinian conflicts. In the 1950s Israel could have won over its Arab citizens even in the absence of those conflicts' resolution. Today that is not possible.

PART II

THE PERPETUAL DILEMMA

Race and the U.S. Armed Forces

Introduction

As the U.S. Civil War came to a close, black and white Americans alike recognized that their relations had been radically reshaped by the war and, more specifically, by blacks' service in the Union army. In 1864 one U.S. senator observed that the "logical result" of blacks' military role was that "the black man is henceforth to assume a new *status* among us." A black delegate to the 1868 Arkansas Constitutional Convention defended his people's right to the vote by invoking their spilled blood: "Has not the man who conquers upon the field of battle, gained any rights? Have we gained none by the sacrifice of our brethren?"[1] Nearly eighty years later, Walter White, the longtime executive secretary of the National Association for the Advancement of Colored People (NAACP), was among those leading the charge for racial equality in the armed forces during World War II. After investigating the conditions of African American service, White noted, "At times it is evident that some Americans have a mortal fear lest, given an opportunity to prove his mettle as a soldier, the Negro do so."[2] He did not need to explain to his audience why racist Americans would not want to see blacks succeed on the battlefield.

Throughout U.S. history, black leaders have perceived a tight bond between military service and civil rights. They have usually urged their fellow blacks to volunteer and to obey the call to the colors—even though the United States, both North and South, has violated the most basic terms of the social contract. Whenever war beckoned, African Americans flocked to the armed forces, despite segregation and limited opportunities for promotion. During the conflict and afterward, they contended that their collective sacrifice must be repaid, that the country was obligated to grant them first-class citizenship. Informed by the theoretical framework, in Part 2 I pose two central questions. First, how did blacks frame their citizenship demands during and after the twentieth century's two great wars, and what role, if any, did those frames

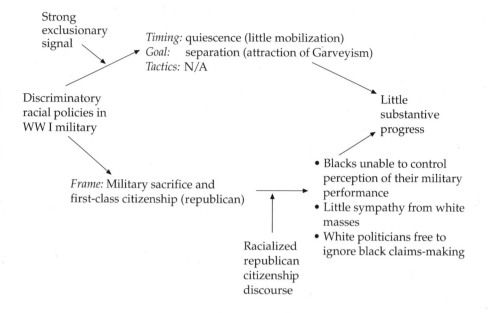

Strong exclusionary signal

Timing: quiescence (little mobilization)
Goal: separation (attraction of Garveyism)
Tactics: N/A

Discriminatory racial policies in WW I military

Little substantive progress

Frame: Military sacrifice and first-class citizenship (republican)

Racialized republican citizenship discourse

- Blacks unable to control perception of their military performance
- Little sympathy from white masses
- White politicians free to ignore black claims-making

Figure 5. African Americans and World War I

play in the success or failure of their claims-making? Second, did the U.S. military's racial policies shape African Americans' quest for civil and political rights in the twentieth century?

To explain why blacks proved more influential after the Second World War than after the First, most accounts stress their greater electoral strength due to interwar and wartime migration. However, the interaction between the frame of black claims and the U.S. discourse on citizenship deserves a place in the narrative (see figure 5). After World War I and well into the 1920s, blacks sought to turn the fact of military service to their political advantage by implicitly or explicitly invoking the classic equation of obligations and rights. But they made little headway. Black leaders astutely identified the centrality of republican strains in U.S. citizenship discourse, but they failed to grasp that this was a racialized republicanism that left them outside the republic of virtuous citizens. Black claims-making thus failed to find a sympathetic ear among the majority white populace, and white politicians could safely ignore black demands. African Americans confronted imposing barriers to first-class citizenship in the first decades of the twentieth century, so imposing that their failure might seem overdetermined. But their political strategy might have been more effective in a different environment. To build plausibility for this counterfactual, in chapter 6 I compare African Americans and women.

Women did not generally serve in the military, but their participation in the war effort—on the factory floor, in nurses' uniforms, and in other ways—undermined the common republican rebuttal to the suffragists' demands and helped pave the way for passage of the Nineteenth Amendment to the U.S Constitution.

Although African American political leaders and newspaper editors again employed the military sacrifice frame during World War II to mobilize their followers and readers, they abandoned it in favor of a liberal rights frame in the war's aftermath. Black activists rarely invoked their people's history of service on the nation's behalf but appealed instead to America's liberal heritage, the principles of freedom and equality of opportunity for which the country had fought in the recent war, and the emerging global competition with the Soviet Union. Their efforts bore some, not entirely satisfying, fruit: although Southern senators blocked far-reaching legislative proposals, civil rights became a central accomplishment of the Truman administration. The Great Depression, the war against Nazi Germany and imperial Japan, and the anticommunist crusade effected a deep and lasting change in U.S. political culture, laying the foundation for the dominance of a liberal citizenship discourse and for an expanded conception of the federal role. At the same time, however, the rhetoric of the cold war compelled black leaders to emphasize their anticommunist credentials and to avoid pressing for the socioeconomic changes many believed were necessary to address the race problem (summarized in figure 6). Chapter 7 further suggests counterfactually that had African Americans employed a republican rights frame after the war, they might have felt less pressure to narrow the scope of their claims.

The second angle of inquiry focuses less on the efficacy of blacks' claims-making than on its pattern. Did exclusion from the armed forces lead African Americans to refrain from loudly demanding their rights and to embrace a separationist program after the First World War, as one might expect? I answer yes, but with qualifications. The encounter with a deeply discriminatory armed forces during and after World War I powerfully reminded blacks in the service and on the home front that they remained less than fully American and signaled that the state would not respond favorably to black demands for full citizenship. With the exception of some highly educated and highly motivated African Americans, most blacks opted for a quiescent political posture—even in this age of the "New Negro." At the same time, the military's policies drove many into the arms of Marcus Garvey and far from the fledgling NAACP (see figure 5). The racist policies of the armed forces cannot claim exclusive credit for these outcomes, however, for equally important were the postwar white-initiated racial violence and the authorities' passivity in the face of such violations of the rule of law.

The second case jumps forward to the early cold war. Did Truman's support for the desegregation of the armed forces spark the vast civil rights mobilization that erupted within a decade? Here, contrary to the conventional

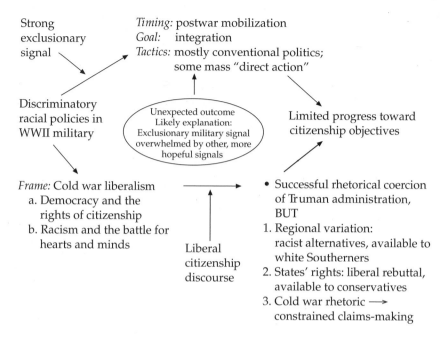

Figure 6. African Americans after World War II

wisdom, I answer no. While the civil rights movement came on the heels of military desegregation, it was plotted not from above, by those who might have been sensitive to signals embedded in national policies, but from below, by Southern blacks attentive primarily to local conditions. The theoretical framework helps us understand why this purported link lacks explanatory power. Although Truman's stance was politically costly, the decentralized structure of the U.S. political system curbed the signal's strength. With the legitimate means of violence shared by federal and state governments, and with the former divided into three independent branches, African Americans were well aware that, no matter how costly this inclusive signal, it revealed at most how the federal executive might respond to their demands. The opposition of the Congress and the Southern state governments was only too clear. The causal relationship between military desegregation and the civil rights movement is spurious (see figure 7).

In their sweeping analysis of African Americans' quest for civil rights, Philip Klinkner and Rogers Smith suggest a "theory" of the ebbs and flows of race reform that differs in important respects from the perspective presented here. They point to three factors as historically important for racial progress: a large-scale war that created white dependence on black manpower, a

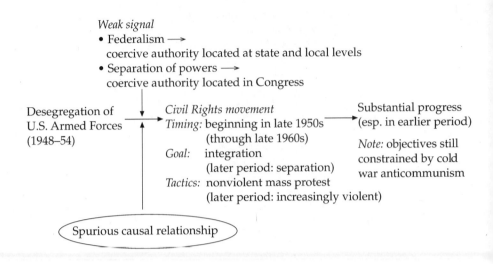

Figure 7. Military desegregation and the civil rights movement

wartime mobilization rhetoric that was inclusive and egalitarian, and the existence of well-developed black protest movements. Thus they argue that blacks' appeals fell on deaf ears during and after World War I because it was not a large-scale war requiring substantial mobilization of the black population, its rhetoric was more often racist than inclusive, and the black protest vehicles of the time were elitist. In contrast, they would paint World War II as the best-case scenario for race reform: a total war marked by inclusive rhetoric and during which organizations such as the NAACP, the Urban League, and the March on Washington Movement developed mass memberships.[3]

Though persuasive, this account leaves a number of questions unanswered. First, some important moments of civil rights progress, such as during the Truman administration, did not come during total war. Second, in such cases, wartime rhetoric per se mattered less than the postwar rhetorical context. Furthermore, while Klinkner and Smith divide the universe of citizenship discourse into inclusive (liberal) and exclusive (racist), the fate of African American claims-making can be understood only if one is sensitive to the differences *within* the inclusive category—that is, between liberalism and republicanism. Third, their account lacks a systematic explanation for the pattern of black protest, leaving open the possibility that whatever explains the emergence of well-developed protest vehicles also accounts for blacks' political influence.

In the following chapters, I do not seek to replace one grand narrative of the African American struggle for civil rights with another. Rather, drawing on the theoretical framework developed in chapter 2, I focus more narrowly on the role that military service has played in African Americans' quest for first-class citizenship during and after the twentieth century's two world wars. Whereas the Druze case highlights the possibilities created (and, to a lesser extent, the limits imposed) by that Arab minority's service in the Israeli armed forces, black Americans' experience with military service is, for the most part, a more sobering one. African Americans' sacrifices on the battlefield did not yield the civil rights they sought, but those failures are themselves instructive.

CHAPTER 6

Great War, Great Hopes, and the Perils of Closing Ranks

Woodrow Wilson's election in 1912 marked the return of the South to the center stage of American politics. Born in Virginia and raised in Georgia, Wilson had been president of Princeton University, a bastion of the Southern elites, and he counted four Southerners among his closest advisers. Although Wilson had early on identified more closely with the Union than with his native region, he had embraced the South as his political prospects grew bright.[1] Nevertheless, Wilson had garnered substantial support from black leaders during the election, largely on the strength of a handful of discreet statements promising a fair deal for African Americans and of growing black frustration with Republican hypocrisy.[2]

But black Americans were soon disappointed. Like other post–Civil War presidents, Wilson suffered from a case of the "slows" when it came to America's race problems.[3] Not only did he fail to use the powers of his office to ensure that blacks received the fair treatment he had promised but he presided over the expansion of segregation in the federal government.[4] During his administration, new policies—from the denial of traditional patronage posts to the introduction of applicant photographs—further limited blacks' employment opportunities in federal agencies.[5] In a 1913 meeting with Monroe Trotter, the fiery black editor of the Boston *Guardian*, Wilson pleaded for patience: "Things do not happen rapidly in the world, and prejudices are slow to be uprooted. We have to accept them as facts, no matter how much we may deplore them in their moral and social consequences."[6]

Americans entered World War I acutely conscious of the challenges of nation building. The country's leading intellectuals had for years vigorously debated how the immigrant hordes could be purged of alien values and transformed into true Americans, and the impending conflict only intensified those concerns.[7] Yet, for all the Progressive hand-wringing over immigrant assimilation, they paid little attention to the problem of race, and Wilson refrained from publicly addressing the issue throughout his presidency. As the war approached, even Booker T. Washington observed, "I have never seen the colored people so discouraged and bitter as they are at the present time."[8]

In 1912 W. E. B. DuBois was ambivalent about Wilson, but he ultimately concluded that the Democratic nominee held out the best hope because he was a "cultivated scholar" from whom blacks might expect "farsighted fairness."[9] Woodrow Wilson may have been erudite, but African Americans should not have expected much while he sat in the Oval Office. Neither Wilson's personal inclinations nor, more important, the political environment boded well for racial reform. The new Southern presence in the nation's capital reflected the reintegration of the South into the political system as part of a grand sectional bargain.[10] Even if Wilson had been a sincere advocate of racial justice—which he was not—he would have had to adjust to a political milieu deeply inhospitable to reform.

Gambling with Loyalty

For activists on behalf of African Americans' rights, the central problem was how to move from the country's blind spot into its field of vision, and with the decision to enter the war, they thought they had found the way. Most well-known African Americans urged their fellow blacks to join the war effort without reserve, so that they might prove their worthiness for full citizenship. Black newspapers reported on Liberty Loan drives, loyalty day parades, Red Cross work, and food conservation, and gave abundant space to inspiring stories of patriotism. When the board of directors of the recently founded NAACP—at the time considered radical agitators—discovered that the military had no intention of drafting blacks, it urged young men to enlist voluntarily. Those stalwart integrationists even endorsed a *segregated* officers' training camp. Although DuBois bemoaned the "perpetual dilemma," in the end he reasoned that the benefits of black representation in the officer corps warranted the sacrifice of principle.[11]

Underpinning black elites' support for the war effort was their belief that their loyalty would be amply repaid at the war's conclusion.[12] Blacks, wrote the NAACP's James Weldon Johnson, really had little choice: "To perform the duties and not demand the rights would be pusillanimous; and to demand the rights and not perform the duties would be futile." In 1918, before a Carnegie Hall audience, he roared, "The record of black men on the fields of France gives us the greater right to point to that flag and say to the nation: Those stains are still upon it; they dim its stars and soil its stripes; wash them out! wash them out!"[13] The link between citizenship and military service was seen as incontrovertible: "Wearing the uniform of a Federal soldier," declared NAACP cofounder Mary White Ovington, "is prima facie evidence of citizenship."[14] Those who served in the armed forces, whether they volunteered or were drafted, saw themselves as the vanguard of the fight against discrimination at home. The NAACP's William Pickens imagined that "when a black American shot a German in France he hoped he saw a lyncher die a spiritual death in the United States."[15] "Our second emancipation," the Texas grand master of the Negro Masons foresaw, "will be the outcome of this war."[16] Black college students and graduates flocked to the controversial officers' training camp, and by the end of the war even the camp's critics were proudly touting the accomplishments of black officers and soldiers.

Endorsing Wilson's declaration of war, DuBois characterized the Allies as the more benign imperialists—that is, the lesser of two evils. Like many, he saw the war as an opportunity to reshape the American (and the international) political, social, and racial order.[17] DuBois was hardly alone, especially after the United States officially joined the battle. The Baltimore *Afro-American*, which just four months earlier had excused blacks' reluctance to volunteer and had predicted that the war would set back the cause of racial equality, urged its readers to contribute any way they could: "Help—or by not helping handicap your boy at the front." The Chicago *Defender*, the most widely circulated black weekly, similarly affirmed, "It matters not what reasons we may harbor for withholding our support, they pale into insignificance when compared with the reasons why we should go into this struggle . . . with our whole heart and soul."[18]

But this was where the consensus ended. Many wanted to combine participation with pressure; they hoped to exploit the state's reliance on black manpower and achieve gains during the war, before their collective sacrifice had become a distant memory. DuBois continued to attack racial discrimination, violence, and inequity in his usual manner. Meeting with Secretary of War Newton Baker in 1917, he implied that blacks' loyalty was contingent:

> It must be remembered that Negroes are human beings, that they have deep seated and long continued grievances against this country; that while the great mass of them are loyal and willing to fight for their country despite this, it certainly will not increase their loyalty or the spirit in which they enter this war if they continue to meet discrimination which borders upon insult and wrong.[19]

Byron Gunner, the president of Trotter's National Equal Rights League, wrote to DuBois that "now, 'while the war lasts,' is the most opportune time for us to push and keep our 'special grievances' to the fore."[20]

Others maintained that the cause would be best served by a posture of greater accommodation. The editor of the Chicago *Defender* put it well in May 1918:

> In common with white American citizens let us put our shoulders to the wheel and push with might and main to bring this war to a successful conclusion. If we have any grievance at home—and we have many of them—we will set about the task of solving these after the greater task

of winning this war is over. . . . The colored soldier who fights side by side with the white American in the titanic struggle now raging across the sea will hardly be begrudged a fair chance when the victorious armies return.

Most surprisingly, DuBois, who had been so critical of Booker T. Washington's willingness to accept halfway measures, notoriously advised blacks in the summer of 1918 to "forget our special grievances and close our ranks shoulder to shoulder with our white fellow citizens and the allied nations that are fighting for democracy. . . . We make no ordinary sacrifice, but we make it gladly and willingly with our eyes lifted to the hills."[21] This editorial touched off a bitter controversy, in which DuBois was accused of having abandoned his own principles to obtain a military commission. In Trotter's estimation, DuBois was "a rank quitter in the fight for equal rights" who had "weakened, compromised, deserted the fight, betrayed the cause of his race."[22]

These disputes should not, however, obscure the more fundamental point of agreement: black elites were united in the strategy of earning rights after the war by earning America's gratitude during the war. The black masses, though, were another matter, for many deemed this a "white man's war." More interested in winning democracy at home than in securing it abroad, many blacks would have agreed that "since [whites] weren't willing to accept us as civilians, then let them fight it. It was something that didn't concern Negroes."[23] Apathy prevailed, creating a ripe audience for those who counseled blacks to evade service. That the black draft delinquency rate was two-and-a-half times that of whites may have indicated greater ignorance, illiteracy, and migration—as government officials claimed—but it may also have reflected the true sentiments of black citizens.[24]

As mainstream black leaders traded military service for citizenship, dissenters accused them of "criminal incompetence and cringing compromise" and derided them as "mental manikins and intellectual lilliputians." A. Philip Randolph, then on the radical fringe, branded DuBois a "hand-picked, me-too-boss, hat-in-hand, sycophant, lick spittling" Negro. Chandler Owen, Randolph's colleague at the socialist magazine the *Messenger*, ridiculed the notion that participation might lead to full citizenship: "Did not the Negro fight in the Revolutionary War with Crispus Attucks dying first . . . , and come out to be a miserable chattel slave in this country for nearly one hundred years after?"[25] From the moment Congress declared war, however, these voices, asserting the bankruptcy of the dominant strategy, were solitary ones. That truth would ultimately be on their side was little consolation.

Fighting to Fight

African American leaders expected that the postwar battle for civil rights would be fierce, but they did not anticipate the hurdles that would be placed before their very entry into the army. "It is beginning to look," one commented, "as if the Negro will, as a burglar, have to break into this War."[26] Southern congressmen, fearing the implications for their region's social, political, and economic order, sought to exclude blacks from Selective Service.[27] Secretary of War Baker, relatively liberal by the standards of the day, squashed these efforts, but his priority was getting the best army to France, not meeting the demands of racial justice. While the military on occasion accommodated the NAACP, it generally indulged white racial prejudice so as to avoid undermining the war effort. When not in dialogue with race activists, however, Baker often whistled a different tune. In 1917 he wrote to the House Judiciary Committee chairman, who was a Southerner, that the riots in Houston by black servicemen had revealed that "these elements of our population did not have the necessary capacity for the high service of military duty, the respect for constituted authority, and the due appreciation of the obligations of a soldier."[28]

Some 380,000 African Americans ultimately entered the U.S. armed forces in World War I, but they hardly enjoyed anything approximating equality. Draft cards instructed registrants to indicate their "African descent" by tearing off one corner. Various branches—notably the artillery, the aviation corps, and the U.S. Navy—remained almost entirely off-limits to blacks. Few made it into combat; most were relegated to engineer, quartermaster, or pioneer (construction) battalions. Just forty-two thousand were assigned to combat units, and half of these saw action only as part of the French Army. Though 9 percent of the U.S. Army and 8.15 percent of the American Expeditionary Force (AEF), blacks were only 2.87 percent of the army's combat strength. In the navy, blacks accounted for just 1 percent of all sailors.[29] Most black volunteers and draftees remained stateside, however. Under the "Work or Fight" laws enacted across much of the South beginning in 1918, many were put to work as manual laborers on large plantations to alleviate labor shortages.

After the Armistice, the racism that was part of the normal order in the U.S. military returned with a vengeance. While the black troops of the Ninety-second and Ninety-third Infantry Divisions awaited their return home, Jim Crow was imposed at the request of the U.S. Army all over France. Black soldiers were prevented from socializing with the local population, especially the women, and they were almost sequestered in their camps. DuBois, on a postwar investigative mission, discovered a galling French memorandum, issued with U.S. approval, that instructed French forces to "prevent the rise of any pronounced degree of intimacy between French officers and black officers. . . . We must not eat with them, must not shake hands or seek to talk or meet with them outside of the requirements of military service." They were warned not to praise black troops and were ordered to keep the local population from "spoiling" the black American forces.[30] Matters became still worse as the military downsized. Although a survey of the Army War College's students and staff found them relatively open to assigning blacks to combat branches and technical arms, the army pursued every available means to limit the enlistment of blacks, shrink the size of the legally mandated black regiments, and consign those forces to demeaning duties.[31]

During the postwar debates over universal military training, some members of Congress, particularly from the South, opposed the plan, less because they feared the spread of societal militarism or an unbearable fiscal burden, than because the large-scale conscription of blacks threatened to undermine their familiar world and their interests.[32] NAACP chairman Oswald Garrison Villard gave credence to such fears:

> I hear it said that there is no longer time for patience and humility; that where the Ku Klux walks, there blood shall flow; that where the colored soldier has learned how to fight, he shall fight against his compatriots who do him wrong; that he has come back from the shores of France in a fighting mood, that like a lion's cub, having tasted blood once, he will taste it again.

Even racial moderates like Joel Spingarn, who had championed the segregated officers' training camp and worked hard from within the military to ensure a modicum of racial fairness, confessed that when he read of the wave of postwar lynchings, he said to himself, in the heat of the moment, "By God, there is only one way to deal with these people: the only thing to tell the black to do is to arm and defend himself." Spingarn's wife calmed him down, but he was nonetheless "very glad that two or three hundred thousand black men have had the soldier's discipline and learned to use weapons."[33]

Sacrifice, Race, and Resonance

Germany accepted the Allies' terms on November 11, 1918. Race activists in the United States wasted no time seeking to reap the political advantages of their sacrifice. Within a year, at least three books appeared extolling African Americans' contributions to the national cause, and DuBois too had begun a multivolume history of the black soldier in the Great War. "Negro leaders in all parts of the country recognized at once," wrote Emmett Scott, who had served during the war as a special assistant on racial matters in the War Department, "that the national crisis demanded . . . that, without bargaining, there must be a pledge on the part of the Negro of his undiluted and unfaltering loyalty." He continued:

> Negro editors, with but few exceptions, rallied to the Nation's call and wrote in a martial spirit; the Negro clergy put on the whole armor of patriotism and awakened the Negro laity to a sense of its duty, opportunity, and responsibility; Negro educators in all sections taught loyalty as

a cardinal virtue and representative Negro public speakers sought dili-
gently to maintain a healthy morale among the rank and file of colored
Americans.

Their reasoning was clear: "The moment the American Negro failed to perform all the duties of citizenship, he immediately abdicated the right of claim-
ing the full privileges of citizenship."[34] These early postwar writings exuded
optimism. Inspired by Wilson's rhetoric, Kelly Miller hailed "the new democratic spirit" that was taking hold and asserted that the "gallant part" played
by black Americans would help "liberalize [white] feeling and sentiment."[35]
Through these works and countless articles and speeches, black elites hoped
to shape collective memory, to mold how the public perceived and remembered African Americans' part in the Allied victory. They shared an unshakeable belief that the fate of their struggle hinged on the success of these efforts.
As DuBois wrote to the NAACP board during his fact-finding trip to France,
"The greatest and most pressing and most important work for the N.A.A.C.P.
is the collection, writing, and publication of the history of the Negro troops in
France."[36]

Debates over African Americans' record in uniform raged into the mid-
1920s.[37] Senior military personnel charged their black soldiers, and especially
officers, with cowardice and ineptitude, implying that they had thereby
proven themselves unworthy of citizenship.[38] One white officer reportedly
confessed that "there was a concerted action on the part of the white officers
throughout France to discredit the work of the colored troops in France,
and . . . everything was being done to advertise those things that would reflect discredit upon the men and officers, and to withhold anything that
would bring to them praise or commendation."[39] The NAACP and its allies
mounted a vigorous defense, alleging that "the colored soldier's own white
countrymen not only stole all possible opportunity for distinction from him,
but actively sought to poison European and American public opinion against
their brothers in black."[40]

Over the next decade, race activists tried to bolster their claims-making by
alluding to blacks' military sacrifice and consciously invoking the classic republican frame. Countless addresses at NAACP annual conferences from
1917 on framed blacks' demands in terms of their contributions to the common good, particularly in World War I and earlier conflicts. With the war over,
Emmett Scott declared, "those who have fought and sacrificed in the Common Cause" had a rightful place in America: "We have met the high expectations of American citizenship. Our men have fought, bled, and died for the
Stars and Stripes on foreign battlefields 'to make the world safe for democracy'. . . . I think we have the right to demand that democracy shall also be
made safe for the world." Moorfield Storey, the NAACP's white president,
proclaimed that "nothing more imperatively requires attention in this country than the demand of twelve million American citizens, who are taxed as

citizens, called to arms as citizens and made to perform all the duties of citizens[,] for the rights of citizens." The educator Mordecai Wyatt Johnson sounded this same note:

> The Negro people of America . . . have cut our forests, tilled our fields, built our railroads, fought our battles, and in all their trials until now they have manifested a simple faith, a grateful heart, a cheerful spirit and an undivided loyalty to our nation that has been a thing of beauty to behold. . . . They ask for the bread of liberty, of public equality, and public responsibility. It must not be denied them.

Most clearly and simply, the NAACP declared in 1919, "The country has recently called on us to perform unusual duties; we demand that we have the usual rights of American citizens."[41]

This republican rights frame found its way into more popular forums as well during and after the war. One uneducated soldier complained to the NAACP, "We are out here for the same purpose [white soldiers] are out here for, so why is it that we cannot be treated like men." A black lieutenant explained to a journalist:

> If we can't fight and die in this war just as bravely as white men then we don't deserve equality with white men, and after the war we had better go back home and forget about it all. But if we can do things on the front; if we can make ourselves felt; . . . then I am sure it will be the biggest possible step toward our equalization as citizens.

At the war's close, newspapers sympathetic to black claims also adopted this frame. The Chicago Post editorialized, "It will be a great pity if our black Americans do not receive their full share. They have earned it by their conduct as soldiers. . . . When [the Negro soldier] comes home it is to be hoped that his valor will be remembered to his credit and that some of the rough places along his path will be accordingly smoothed."[42]

Blacks across the political spectrum justified their rights claims in this fashion. Robert R. Moton, who had succeeded Booker T. Washington as principal of the Tuskegee Institute, sought to inspire an audience of white servicemen to embrace race reform:

> These black soldiers, officers and men, have with you willingly and gladly placed their lives at the disposal of their country. . . . What a wonderful opportunity you have therefore, and what a great responsibility[,] for you to go back to America resolved that as far as it in your power lies, you are going to see that these black men and the twelve millions of people whom they represent in our great country, who have stood so loyally by you and America in peace and in war, shall have a

fair and absolutely equal chance with every other American citizen, along every line—this is your duty and sacred obligation.

Even Monroe Trotter, who had opposed black participation in the war, employed such arguments. In a September 1919 telegram to Wilson, Trotter argued that the country's black soldiers would have "died in vain" unless Wilson would "grant to their kin and race at home protection of right and life" and urge Congress to make lynching a federal crime.[43]

Invoking the equation of obligations and rights, race activists hoped to leave their opponents without a sustainable way of refusing blacks' citizenship claims. At the same time, however, they threatened that blacks would no longer feel the weight of these obligations if the country failed to hold up its end of the bargain. After cataloging the disparity between blacks' recent sacrifices and "poor schools, Jim Crow methods of travel, little or no justice in courts or in things economic," the NAACP warned that disappointment would invite blacks "to grasp the hands which the Bolsheviks, the I.W.W., and other kindred organizations hold out to him." A favorite expression of Moorfield Storey was that the country was "sowing dragon's teeth." He elaborated: "Can we afford to cultivate just discontent in our midst? These twelve million men must seek friends elsewhere if the governments under which they live and the men among whom they dwell deny them justice and safety."[44]

Though no frame was deployed as frequently as the republican one, black claims-making wove together other threads from the country's discursive quilt.[45] Drawing on America's liberal tradition, blacks routinely invoked the language of natural rights and the equality of man. Race reformers also seized on the very ideals with which Wilson had mobilized the nation for war. Assailing the United States for its hypocrisy, James Weldon Johnson had little patience for "holding up our hands at German 'atrocities' . . . while the wholesale murder of American citizens on American soil by bloodthirsty American mobs hardly brings forth a word of comment."[46] But the hypocrisy frame could not long outlast the war, and liberal arguments were bound to fall flat in a country that had, in its wartime treatment of German-Americans, proved willing to abrogate the rights of those it deemed potentially disloyal.[47]

Black leaders were astute observers of the country's cultural and political scene, and their choice of a republican rights frame was wise. The first decades of the twentieth century witnessed a vibrant public debate over the meaning of citizenship, with some four hundred articles on the subject published in leading magazines between 1900 and 1918. "This public discourse about citizenship," historian Kimberly Jensen notes, "focused, above all, on participatory citizenship by emphasizing the duty and the privilege of citizens to act in support of the nation."[48] The Great War reinforced these trends. Americans were urged to tighten their belts for the good of their boys fighting overseas, the country, and even Western civilization, and those who did so freely were touted as heroes. Grounded in the vast U.S. network of voluntary organizations, a coercive program took shape to compel reluctant citizens to do their part on the home front, creating a paradoxical milieu in which people were obliged to volunteer.[49] President Wilson sought to reconcile these themes by suggesting that, if the United States was to win the war, "it needs each man, not in the field that will most pleasure him, but in the endeavor that will best serve the common good." The draft, he continued, was "in no sense a conscription of the unwilling; it is, rather, a selection from a nation which has volunteered in mass."[50] Many Americans tried to evade their wartime commitments, but this in no way undermined the power of the republican citizenship ideal. It is not accidental that opponents of anti-immigration legislation regularly made mention in the mid-1920s of the wartime contributions of newcomers from Southern and Eastern Europe.[51]

Blacks advanced appeals framed in republican terms on what should—at first glance—have been a favorable discursive terrain, but they were rebuffed. In the summer of 1919, as white veterans returned home and competed for work with blacks who had migrated to the North, riots broke out nationwide in more than twenty-six cities, and more than one hundred blacks were killed. But the federal government was silent. Presented with a petition protesting attacks in the District of Columbia, Wilson dismissively replied that the murderous mobs were a lesser priority than the League of Nations. As Storey ruefully observed, rampant lynching and mob violence were tolerated: "Silence, indifference, acquiescence prevail. No one approves the barbarism and injustice . . . but few indeed are the men who condemn it." But that same summer also gave blacks reason for optimism, for presidential aspirant Warren Harding, greeting the NAACP's annual conference, hoped that "the splendid part played by the colored citizenship of America, in the winning of the great world war, will bring to full appreciation, in all sections of our common country, their capacity for citizenship and their indisputable rights to all the privileges which American citizenship conveys to any of our people."[52]

In the years that followed, black Americans were as politically impotent as ever, notwithstanding their wartime sacrifice: the military service gamble had failed.[53] In February 1920 the NAACP circulated a survey among seventeen prospective presidential candidates, requesting their views on questions of concern to blacks. Only three, Harding among them, replied at all, but none offered a substantive answer.[54] When the NAACP's James Weldon Johnson met with Harding during the 1920 campaign, he found the nominee pleasant, even cordial, but without a strong commitment to racial justice. Harding agreed "as a matter of principle" with nearly all the NAACP's demands but retreated behind a pragmatic logic in refusing "to make campaign issues of any of them," with the exception of Haiti. When Johnson tried to play political hardball, asserting that blacks held the decisive vote in several Northern states, Harding bluntly replied that "the injection of the details of the Negro question into the campaign would lose the Republican Party more votes than it would gain." The most Johnson could report was that the visit "was not an entirely lost effort."[55] While Johnson did succeed in securing an appointment with the president in April 1921, this meeting was perfunctory.

President Harding's public pronouncements initially gave heart to politically aware blacks—Johnson commended them as "the most practical, the most concrete and at the same time the strongest ever made"—and, in his first State of the Union address, he called on Congress "to wipe the stain of barbaric lynching from the banners of a free and orderly, representative democracy."[56] But Harding took no action on a promised interracial commission, refused to put the weight of his office behind antilynching legislation, appointed few blacks to public office, and countenanced the extension of racial segregation in the federal government. By 1922 Johnson, who had spent many an hour roaming the halls of Congress lobbying for the Dyer antilynching bill, was frustrated: "Each time I get up to talk on the subject of lynching . . . it becomes more and more difficult. . . . I find that my vocabulary has about run out. I have damned and double damned lynchers until there are no more words with which to do it." "Sometimes," he later recalled, "my heart was as sore and weary as my feet."[57]

Harding's premature death brought Calvin Coolidge to office, but Coolidge was even less willing than his predecessor to speak publicly on racial matters. Outside of brief condemnations of lynching in his State of the Union messages, Coolidge suggested that the federal government's role was necessarily limited: "These difficulties," he told the nation, "are to a large extent local problems which must be worked out by the mutual forbearance and human kindness of each community. Such a method gives much more promise of a real remedy than outside interference." And, as presidents would for many decades, he blamed the lack of progress on Senate Democrats.[58] When it came to African Americans, Silent Cal lived up to his nickname.[59]

Black activists learned that they would never make progress by placing their faith in ethical argument alone. Just after the war, they adhered to the following dictum: "Base your appeal to those in authority on grounds that will arouse their indignation, as it has yours, and you'll get a response." Now, however, Johnson asserted that "no change has ever come about except through a force of some kind. . . . A cause may be just and a cause may be right, but it does not win merely of its justness and righteousness. . . . A right is not a thing issued out on a silver tray and that you can put in your pocket like you can a gold piece." As the editor of the New York Call put it, "There is only one virtue in any race that is worthy of respect and that is power, power, power, and the only power that is worth anything is organized power; and when you stop asking, when you stop protesting, when you organize for political power, your problems will be solved."[60]

But why had the claims advanced by African American activists failed to move white politicians? Their arguments were unassailable on republican grounds, and they tapped into the dominant language of citizenship. What had gone wrong? Unlike Jewish politicians in Israel who deflected Christian and Muslim complaints by denying or even justifying discrimination, white politicians in the United States only occasionally resorted to such moves. African Americans' problem in the 1920s was more basic and more severe, as leading politicians rarely felt compelled to publicly address their concerns at all. Although blacks' sacrifices in uniform had bequeathed them a rhetorical advantage, they could not surmount the initial hurdle. Jewish politicians in Israel did not have the option of ignoring the Druze, who enjoyed the sympathy of the Hebrew-language media, but American white politicians in the 1920s for the most part could and did ignore African Americans. Whereas the Druze effectively plumbed the contradiction between Israel's civic republicanism and exclusionary ethno-nationalism, African Americans worked within the terms of a racialized, noncivic republicanism. Unlike the Druze, African Americans could not credibly threaten to bring critical audiences into the struggle on their side, and white politicians were free to pay their protests little heed. The result was that African American grievances were simply rarely on the agenda. Had African Americans held the electoral balance, been represented by an organization with mass backing, or enjoyed greater wealth, they might have warranted a hearing. But such conventional political resources were equally beyond their grasp.

Racial categories grew increasingly prominent in American academic and popular discourse in the latter half of the nineteenth century. By the 1890s the nation's egalitarian ideals had come to seem increasingly antiquated, and many were attracted to social Darwinism, which articulated a clear racial hierarchy and associated the "darker races" with savagery.[61] In the wake of the 1898 Spanish-American War, the United States acquired an overseas empire populated by such "darker races." U.S. imperialism was interpreted and justified not in terms of national power but as the responsibility of a superior Anglo-Saxon nation shouldering the white man's burden.[62] By the turn of the century, even the "party of Lincoln" had grown comfortable with the language of white supremacy.[63] As John Higham puts it, American politics after 1890 became obsessed with "fears of impurity, pollution, corruption, and depravity."[64]

In the years before the First World War, labor unions embraced republicanism, but they often excluded African Americans, contending that blacks had failed to give "evidence of a possession of those peculiarities of temperament such as patriotism, sympathy, sacrifice etc. which are peculiar to most of the Caucasian race, and which alone make an organization of the character and complicity of the modern trade union possible."[65] At the same time, national reconciliation, which had begun to take shape in the 1890s, reached its full maturity, as all sections shared in a racist and nationalist popular culture.[66] Despite universalistic elements in Wilson's rhetoric, World War I was fought largely as an Anglo-Saxon campaign against the vicious Huns, further reinforcing the culture of race. And, in the war's aftermath, the boundaries of the nation were hardened. Court rulings in the early 1920s declared Japanese immigrants ineligible for citizenship and upheld state laws forbidding Japanese resident aliens from owning property. Congress, committed to keeping the country racially "superior," and fearful of admitting anarchists and Communists, passed a series of laws restricting immigration from Southern and Eastern Europe and from Asia.

This melding of republicanism with race prevented African Americans from making gains toward first-class citizenship equivalent to those achieved by the Druze in Israel. Druze claims, framed in terms of military sacrifice, resonated with the Jewish majority. Once the media amplified Druze demands and compelled policymakers to respond, the Druze's claims could not be gainsaid. In contrast, African Americans lost the battle over how their wartime service would be remembered. Racialized republicanism created rhetorical possibilities for white politicians, furnishing them with a sustainable counternarrative with which to parry African Americans' appeals. Embedded in a racist popular culture, whites were predisposed to believe the worst about blacks' capabilities, courage, and record, and thus the efforts of white military commanders to portray blacks as shirkers, cowards, and/or incompetents found a receptive audience.[67] If necessary, white politicians likely could have with impunity deployed explicitly racist rationales for exclusion, but they rarely had to play the race card. Rather, because white Americans did not give blacks the same boost that Israel's Jewish majority gave the Druze, U.S. politicians could continue ignoring their black citizens' plight.

A skeptic would contend that African American weakness after World War I, not America's racist culture, was the most powerful factor hindering blacks' political prospects. There is some truth to this, and had African Americans possessed conventional political strength, they would in fact likely have earned a place on the national agenda. But this would have been neither necessary nor sufficient for meaningful progress toward first-class citizenship. Even if African Americans had succeeded in securing more attention from white politicians, the latter had rhetorical resources at their disposal with which to turn black demands aside. And, as the example of the Druze suggests, minority groups can compensate for a dearth of standard influence assets when the rhetorical stars properly align. This also proved to be the case for another U.S. group of this era outside the national core of white males: during and after the First World War, American women also sought to exploit the rhetoric of sacrifice to bolster their citizenship claims.

World War I, Civic Virtue, and the Nineteenth Amendment

Suffragists saw in the Great War an opportunity to change minds—that is, men's minds—about the capacities of women to exercise citizenship. At the very least, they hoped through their work for the war effort to counter an argument long invoked by their opponents.[68] Historically, the association between military service and citizenship had prevented women from enjoying full membership in the civic life of the nation. Speaking of the early American republic, Linda Kerber has observed that "the connection between the republic and male patriots—who could enlist—was immediate. The connection between the republic and women—however patriotic they might feel themselves to be—was remote."[69] In the nineteenth century, suffragists typically framed their claims around the liberal tradition of individual rights, but their adversaries had little difficulty rebuffing these arguments by drawing on republican rhetorical forms. As a delegate to the 1879 California constitutional convention clearly stated, "What is political sovereignty? It is the fruits of the sword," and women, he noted, had not taken up weapons in the nation's defense.[70]

Before the turn of the twentieth century, many activists shifted gears, cleverly invoking essentialist arguments and stressing the unique sensibility women would bring to the public sphere.[71] The vision of a "maternalist commonwealth" promised to rid politics of corruption and bring renewed attention to social welfare, education, and public health. This politics as "extended housekeeping" accepted that women had distinct social roles and broke with the protofeminist spirit of Seneca Falls. Despite this conservative turn, the suffrage movement remained stymied, unable to counter effectively the republican arguments that opponents advanced.[72]

World War I, however, created an unprecedented opportunity for women to contribute to the common good, rendering implausible republican rebuttals—and women seized it.[73] Rather than transform the paradigm of citizenship, most women associated with the largest and best organized group, the National American Woman Suffrage Association (NAWSA), worked within that republican framework. They created home defense organizations, learned to fire rifles, sold bonds and thrift stamps, knitted clothes, and distributed food; others joined the AEF, typically as telephone operators and nurses. Some one million women worked in the war industries and claimed equal participation in the war effort. President Wilson himself had buttressed suffragists' claims, even as his gendered language excluded them from the militarized nation: "In the sense in which we have been wont to think of armies, there are no armies in this struggle, there are entire nations armed. Thus, the men who remain to till the soil and man the factories are no less a part of the army that is in France than the men beneath the battle flags."[74]

Although the postwar reality fell far short of feminists' aspirations regarding women's place in the public sphere and the industrial economy, the suffragists did finally succeed in securing the vote with congressional passage of the Nineteenth Amendment in 1919 and its ratification the following year. Their turn to a republican frame played no small role in helping to bring about that favorable outcome. During and after the war, suffragists regularly stressed their wartime record, and Wilson became a convert to the cause, personally intervening when the proposed amendment came before the Senate and again during the ratification process.[75] Wilson portrayed the extension of the vote to women as part and parcel of the war:

> We have made partners of the women in this war; shall we admit them only to a partnership of suffering and sacrifice and not to a partnership of privilege and right? This war could not have been fought, either by the other nations engaged or by America, if it had not been for the services of the women—services rendered in every sphere—not merely in the fields of effort in which we have been accustomed to see them work, but wherever men have worked, and upon the very skirts and edges of the battle itself.[76]

The suffragists' republican rhetoric did not sweep away all opposition, and the battles in the Senate and for ratification were long and hard fought. But, if not for the war and the republican rhetoric it made available, it might have been many more years before they enjoyed this triumph. Women's war work precipitated a major shift in public opinion on the suffrage question in the United States and in Britain.[77] As the historian David Kennedy concludes, the Great War was for American suffragists "the final push over the top."[78]

This brief account in no way seeks to diminish the essential role of NAWSA and other suffragists in winning passage of the Nineteenth Amendment. Under the leadership of Carrie Chapman Catt, NAWSA was increasingly well organized, well funded, and politically sophisticated. Suffrage was—thanks to the adoption of moderate tactics, the sanitization of the movement's past, and a narrowing of NAWSA's agenda—no longer associated with a radical feminism that sought to reshape the entire gendered division of labor. At the same time, NAWSA cultivated an impressive network of state organizations that coordinated their activities with national headquarters, and it brokered an alliance with the Progressive movement, apparently profiting from public support for that broader agenda.[79] But until the United States entered the war, the association had enjoyed few successes in passing state legislation giving women the vote, in generating pressure on antisuffrage federal representatives and senators, and in getting a federal constitutional amendment out of committee. The war had given suffragists a powerful citizenship claim, and they had exploited it, proving more effective than their material power base alone would indicate.[80]

NAWSA differed in fundamental ways from the NAACP. The latter was a much younger association with a smaller and less geographically diffuse constituency, a less focused agenda, less secure funding, less coordination with local branches, and less experience with pressure politics. These differences in the organizations' circumstances help explain why suffrage was on the political agenda even before the United States entered the war, whereas African American concerns received little play. But there were important similarities as well. Both, before the war, saw little prospect of imminent success. Both threw themselves into the war effort. Activists in both were divided over whether to continue to agitate for their respective causes as long as the war raged. And both sought to engage in rhetorical coercion. But the outcomes differed dramatically. Despite blacks' service in the armed forces, most white Americans held them to be unworthy of full citizenship, and their claims were consequently turned aside. Suffragists' war work was rewarded with a surge in public support and a growing sense that victory was inevitable.[81]

Military Discrimination and the Lure of Garvey

The policies of the U.S. armed forces during and after World War I combined with postwar racial violence to puncture the optimism with which African Americans had joined the war effort and to nurture the economic, social, and political environment in which the black leader Marcus Garvey would achieve great popularity. The treatment of black soldiers and veterans signaled that the U.S. political community was still defined in racial terms. As one observer noted two decades later, "The Negroes' hope in a better future as a consequence of an allied victory dissipated soon after the war and gave way to latent cynicism and overt despair."[82] Garvey was a skilled showman, but he would never have acquired a mass following without the deep postwar disillusionment. As the theoretical framework would anticipate, a strong exclusive manpower-policy signal led many African Americans to embrace a leader who espoused separationist goals.

During and immediately after World War I, African Americans looked to the military's treatment of black soldiers as an indication of how the country would respond to their citizenship demands. "Did the Negro Soldier Get a Square Deal?" asked Emmett Scott. "That is the thing, I think, that is in the minds and . . . the hearts of the colored people throughout this whole country."[83] If the military's policies were diagnostic of the health of the nation's liberal ideals, however, the prognosis was not good. Blacks had reluctantly reconciled themselves to segregation in the armed forces, but they had not foreseen that black soldiers would be virtually excluded from combat, that the few black combat units would be used like cannon fodder, that Jim Crow would be reborn in Europe, that the postwar military would recommit itself to the prewar racial norm, or that the black troops' record would be viciously attacked. At the NAACP's 1919 annual conference, protests against discrimination in the military, especially "the campaign of lies" smearing black officers and enlisted men, surfaced repeatedly. To many, these events revealed the stark truth about their country for the first time. With the end of the war, wrote Mordecai Wyatt Johnson, "the Negro's faith in the righteous purpose of the Federal Government has sagged."[84] Some, such as Rayford Logan, who would later become a distinguished historian, were so disturbed that they became at least temporary expatriates.[85]

What made this signal so powerful? First, the *credibility* of such exclusionary military participation signals is rarely in question: it is hard to imagine what state interest such a deception might further. Second, the signal was also relatively *clear.* The U.S. armed forces were generally open about the racial basis of their policies regarding the recruitment and deployment of African American troops. This was reinforced by DuBois's postwar investigations and by testimony from returning soldiers about those racist practices the army had sought to conceal. That these policies were approved by civilian, and not just uniformed, decision makers was hardly in doubt. The efforts of Southern congressmen to prevent blacks from enlisting in the first place had been only too public, as had been their concerns about the ramifications of black military training for the South's postwar social, economic, and political fabric. Finally, U.S. military participation policy was *available* as a signaling device. The United States was not a deeply militaristic polity like Israel, but, as we have already seen, republicanism was the dominant mode of citizenship talk in this era. Moreover, the war had been the country's most intensive military engagement in half a century.

After the collapse of Reconstruction, blacks had confronted a wide range of discriminatory institutions and practices, and black nationalists, most notably Bishop Henry Turner, again won some backing. But no black nationalist before the twentieth century—including David Walker, the Reverend Henry Highland Garnet, and Martin Delany—had acquired a truly mass following.[86] Before Marcus Garvey burst onto the scene, such figures had attracted "little more than tepid support."[87] A charismatic figure, with a flair for ritual and pomp, Garvey succeeded in creating a movement with mass appeal less because of blacks' accumulated resentment or his own prodigious talents than because of blacks' recent experiences, particularly in the armed forces. Critics charged that his United Negro Improvement Association (UNIA) was a predominantly West Indian phenomenon,[88] but this allegation was probably off base. Although the organization's leadership was disproportionately Caribbean in origin, the rank-and-file members were typically native born from the middle and working classes. At the height of its popularity, the association spanned the nation with seven hundred branches, 60 percent of them in the South, which had little Caribbean presence. The circle of sympathetic admirers was no doubt larger. When Garvey visited Los Angeles in 1922, nearly half of southern California's black population turned out to see him—ten times the membership of the local UNIA branch. His newspaper, the *Negro World,* had a circulation that, at its zenith, was exceeded among black publications only by the Chicago *Defender.*[89] Garvey's drawing power lay not only in his personal magnetism but in an environment that had been primed for his message. As Winston James concludes, the betrayal by the United States of the military service–citizenship bargain is the key to understanding the Garvey movement: "The time was ripe for Garveyism; Garveyism was ripe for the times."[90]

Perhaps the clearest sign of Garvey's popularity lay in the vitriolic attacks other black leaders launched against him. They found Garvey's methods distasteful, his ideology unappealing, and his praise of the Ku Klux Klan repugnant. But they would not have let fly such ad hominem broadsides if they had believed Garvey marginal. DuBois, for example, ridiculed Garvey's appearance ("a little, fat black man, ugly, but with intelligent eyes and a big head"), assailed his integrity ("a demagogue, a blatant boaster who with monkeyshines was deluding the people") and his qualifications ("Garvey had no thorough education and a very hazy idea of the technic of civilization"), and disparaged his character ("he was inordinately vain and egotistic, jealous of his power, impatient of details, a poor judge of human nature"). If Garvey's base had been small, DuBois would not have expressed so much concern about the havoc "the Demagog" would wreak: "He will gather large followings and then burst and disappear. Loss and despair will follow his fall until new false prophets arise."[91] Surely individuals with little else in common, from avowed socialists at the *Messenger* to bourgeois officials at the NAACP, would not otherwise have joined forces and urged the U.S. attorney general to deport Garvey and to "disband and extirpate" his "vicious movement."[92]

Disabused of their dreams of a new postwar racial order, again aware that white America would never welcome them as full citizens, many African Americans found Garvey's vision appealing.[93] Drawing on Booker T. Washington, Garvey emphasized self-help, but, more so than Washington, Garvey was an economic nationalist. He spurned white investment, and he founded the UNIA as the jewel in the crown of an all-black economic empire that would end black dependence. Garvey warned that "the Negro is living on borrowed goods." He envisaged "a self-contained world of Negro producers, distributors, and consumers who would deal with or be independent of the rest of the world as necessity and circumstances dictated."[94] His emphasis on autonomous black institutions was not itself distinctive, for historically blacks had of necessity developed an elaborate "counterpublic sphere" in response to racial segregation.[95] But Garvey was unusual in making this necessity of black life into a virtue and in hardly concerning himself with African Americans' citizenship status.

Garvey's separationist ideology, rooted in a deep pessimism about the possibility of racial harmony, extended beyond the economy to the entire realm of social relations. In 1921 Garvey congratulated Warren Harding not for his defense in the South of blacks' political and civic equality but for his stand "against every suggestion of social equality." Obsessed with racial purity, Garvey even praised and made common cause with the Ku Klux Klan. Despite withering criticism from within the black community—A. Philip Randolph bestowed on him the moniker the Honorable Black Kluxer—Garvey refused to apologize for meeting with the Klan and instead hailed it for its honesty: "I was speaking to a man who was brutally a white man, and I was speaking to him as a man who was brutally a Negro."[96]

Garvey's association with the Klan put him beyond the pale, his populism had always rubbed black elites the wrong way, and questions dogged his business practices. But his ideas were, in and of themselves, not offensive. Even leading figures in the NAACP found Garvey's aims more attractive than they usually cared to admit. DuBois's confrontation with the military's racism so profoundly disappointed him that he was initially complimentary of Garvey. The Jamaican leader, he wrote, was "a sincere, hard-working idealist" who propounded "worthy industrial and commercial schemes." DuBois criticized Garvey's penchant for "bombast," but commended the substance of his plans:

> What he is trying to say and do is this: American Negroes can, by accumulating and ministering their own capital, organize industry, join the black centers of the south Atlantic by commercial enterprise and in this ultimately redeem Africa as a fit and free home for black men. This is true. It is feasible. It is, in a sense, practical.

Two years later, in the middle of an anti-Garvey screed, DuBois still described the program as "in many respects original and alluring."[97] And once Garvey had disappeared from the scene, DuBois would confess that they had had much in common. The latter's authoritative biographer has concluded that the dispute had less to do with contending ideas than with the struggle for leadership. In the end, writes David Levering Lewis, "it came down to the threat posed by the messenger, rather than to the crux of the message."[98]

What made Garvey's program "practical" in the eyes of DuBois was the truth, revealed by the war and its aftermath, that racial integration was but a pipe dream. Four decades later, DuBois's writing still throbbed with fury:

> With the Armistice came disillusion. I saw the mud and dirt of the trenches; I heard from the mouths of soldiers the kind of treatment that black men got in the American army; I was convinced and said that American white officers fought more valiantly against Negroes within our ranks than they did against the Germans.

DuBois's postwar pessimism was increasingly at odds with the integrationist ideal he had long cherished. The program of attaining first-class citizenship, he concluded in 1933, "has failed—flatly and decisively failed."[99] By the early 1930s DuBois proposed that blacks engage in "voluntary segregation" and form a cooperative economy in response to the Depression—though he waffled on whether this was tactical or principled, whether the ultimate goal was integration or autonomy. He now believed that the "thinking colored people of the United States must stop being stampeded by the word segregation." Rather than "beat futile wings in an impotent frenzy" protesting their exclusion from American society, African Americans had to focus on building their "nation within the nation."[100] As Mark Tushnet has concluded, DuBois now "defined equality primarily as black autonomy."[101]

Out of step with the NAACP leadership, DuBois was forced to resign as editor of the *Crisis* in 1934, but his personal ideological journey was hardly atypical in the decade after the First World War. As Joel Spingarn wrote to NAACP Secretary Walter White, "Self-imposed 'segregation'" was "a strong contemporary trend" among "most of the Negro intelligentsia."[102] This was apparent at the 1933 Amenia Conference, which brought together the brightest stars among the younger generation of African Americans. The final report and recommendations reflected the conferees' Marxist leanings but ultimately converged on a program for black economic independence that would supplement, if not supplant, the traditional NAACP agenda.[103]

Spingarn, DuBois's close friend and NAACP colleague, underwent a similar, if less complete, transformation. He too had been disillusioned by his experiences in France. There he had confronted for the first time the callousness of wealthy Southern white officers and the resentment of poor Southern white enlisted men. But what made the deepest impression on him was the lack of training and equipment given to the black Ninety-second Infantry Division, which he interpreted as a deliberate effort to undermine its performance: "Who were the traitors that betrayed their country, who would rather see it lose in battle than have any social change at home? . . . Everywhere white officers seemed to care more about social changes at home than efficiency in the field, when black men were concerned." So ingrained was the racism and so deep seated was the belief that black achievements on the battlefield would translate into equality at home that, in Spingarn's view, there had emerged a "conspiracy among all the men of the American Expeditionary Force to blacken the record of the colored soldier." Spingarn's sense of injustice was compounded on his return home, where gruesome tales of lynching awaited him. "Never was any deed done by our foes in Europe and Asia," he railed, "more cruel or treacherous than is being done to-day to black men in our own South."[104] In 1934, when the controversy erupted over DuBois, Spingarn defended the editor, writing to White that segregation "has become a sort of shibboleth." Once the board had endorsed White's rigid stance, Spingarn registered his opposition, sarcastically arguing that the organization must henceforth oppose all black institutions in the South, deny them funding, and even break off relations.[105]

Even William Pickens, the association's field secretary in the early 1920s, was generous in his assessment of Garvey. He admired Garvey's efforts to galvanize the masses, and Garvey's assault on integration struck a chord. "Is not that like the Ku Klux Klan?" Pickens asked rhetorically. But it was not, for "the only thing wrong about the Klan is its lawlessness, its secret judgments and executions, its assumption of the functions of the state, and the exercise of authority over the conduct of people who are not members." The racial divide was here to stay, and blacks must make the best of it. Within six months, however, Pickens broke with Garvey over the latter's association with the Klan.[106] Prominent figures, black and white, did not object to Garvey's separationist vision per se, but rather to the irresponsible management of his enterprises, the threat this posed to black investors, and—the final straw—his praise of the Klan. Most of all, though, they objected to his audacious bid for power in the black community.

Although the military's exclusionary policies pushed African Americans toward separation, blacks, at least at first glance, did not adopt a quiescent posture, as the theoretical framework would lead one to expect. DuBois, for one, returned from France more militant than ever. He rallied his readers to the cause:

> By the God of Heaven, we are cowards and jackasses if now that the war is over, we do not marshal every ounce of our brain and brawn to fight a sterner, longer, more unbending battle against the forces of hell in our own land. We return. *We return from fighting. We return fighting.* Make way for Democracy! We saved it in France, and by the Great Jehovah, we will save it in the United States of America, or know the reason why.[107]

More generally, the end of the war ushered in the era of the "New Negro"— determined to resist oppression "with stiffened back bone, dauntless manhood, defiant eye, steady hand and a will of iron." The war, it was thought, had inspired young blacks to return "erect and straight like free men. They had a new light in their eyes, a new vision in their souls and instead of the tradition[al] fear, they had courage in their hearts. They had taken their own measure and realized that they were men."[108]

But the New Negro, for all his public acclaim, represented just the thinnest slice of black society, just a portion of even the "talented tenth" that DuBois had identified as the future leadership of the African American community. Intellectuals and artists who participated in the Harlem Renaissance and published in the *Messenger* might welcome the New Negro with open arms, but the perspective of the Old Negro still dominated the black masses and the NAACP's officials, who remained highly sensitive to the costs of protest. Acutely aware of the state of tension in the South, Moorfield Storey recommended that executive secretary John Shillady not pursue a particular case legally because "our attempt to employ counsel might result in the death of our client and the death of his counsel, and simply add to the horrors of the situation."[109] With normalcy returning and disillusion spreading, most blacks once again lost interest in the larger world and even the cause of civil rights.[110] The *Crisis,* whose circulation had skyrocketed in the months after the United States entered the war, saw a fall nearly as dramatic after the war's end.[111] The same period had witnessed an explosive rise in the NAACP's membership, followed by a rapid decline after the Armistice.[112] Prewar African American political action had been strikingly elite centered, and postwar black politics was nearly equally so. The NAACP had made little effort even during the war to organize the black masses, and although Garvey's UNIA made substantial strides in that direction, one should not exaggerate the depth and breadth of its mass support.[113] Among African Americans in the 1920s, quiescence remained the norm. Political action was too narrowly based to warrant counting it as "mobilization"—particularly in comparison to the far deeper and broader mass involvement that was to come during and immediately after World War II and then again during the civil rights movement. In short, the pattern of African American mobilization after World War I was generally consistent with a strong exclusionary military manpower-policy signal.

As the United States readied itself to join the Great War, most African American leaders thought they had come upon a unique opportunity: if blacks proved their worth on the battlefield, the white majority would be hard-pressed to deny their citizenship claims. After the Armistice and well into the 1920s, blacks framed their appeals in classic republican terms, stressing their historical contribution to building the United States, their young men's recent sacrifices in uniform, and the entire community's part in the war effort.

Given the dominance of a republican citizenship discourse, one might have expected (based on the theoretical framework presented in chapter 2) that such claims would be well received, but they fell flat. Unlike the appeals of female suffragists in the United States or the Druze in Israel, those of African Americans were usually ignored. Blacks were typically unable to secure a place on the agenda—not only because of their political weakness, measured by conventional metrics, but also because of the intertwining of republicanism with race in early twentieth-century America. The Druze exploited Israeli leaders' commitment to civic republicanism to make gains despite ethno-religious preference. But that option was foreclosed to African Americans, who struggled within an environment that was marked by republican commonplaces but was hardly civic. These racist strands in American citizenship discourse were rarely treated by white politicians as an escape hatch, much as Israeli politicians eager to deny Christian and Muslim Arab citizenship claims had turned to republican commonplaces. Rather, although racist discourse might have facilitated such rhetorical possibilities, it also meant that white politicians were free, more often than not, to disregard black pleas for justice and first-class citizenship. Recall that efforts at rhetorical coercion can succeed only when the claimant can credibly threaten to bring some public into the argument on its side. For African Americans after World War I, that was simply not an option. White politicians did not have to proffer explicitly racist arguments to defend the citizenship status quo because they felt little pressure to respond in the first place.

Blacks were to be disappointed during the war, as discrimination pervaded the military charged with making the world safe for democracy, and afterward as well, as the armed forces reverted to the prewar racial norm. Such exclusion was a powerful signal that the postwar United States would not tolerate black mobilization, and it should, in line with theoretical expectations, have resulted in "separationist quiescence." And that is what one observes. Many blacks found Marcus Garvey's separationist agenda attractive, and the vast majority, rather than being energized by the war, returned to their quiescent ways.

For two reasons, however, one cannot attribute the timing and goals of African American political activity in the 1920s to the manpower-policy signal alone. First, prior to World War I, blacks overwhelmingly lived in the rural South and backed Booker T. Washington's accommodationist approach. Unlike Northern black elites, they knew firsthand the dangers of protest, and they grasped that "the desire to protest had to be tempered by a disciplined caution."[114] Quiescence was prevalent before, during, and after the war. Second, even as details drifted back home in the summer of 1919 regarding the treatment of blacks in the armed services, whites across the country went on a rampage. Racial violence engulfed nearly every city that had seen sizable African American inflows during the war. Such physical coercion may have dwarfed the implications of the army's racial policies, though the violence was even more galling to blacks because newly returned veterans were often its consciously chosen targets.[115] Postwar violence followed too closely on the heels of military discrimination for either observers at the time or historians after the fact to clearly distinguish their impact. At the very least, however, the military's participation policies were an important factor that led African Americans to return to their quiescent ways and that rendered Garvey's vision appealing.

The armed forces' discriminatory policies engendered great bitterness among African Americans, and it lingered. Fifteen years later, Emmett Scott, "as one who recalls the assurances of 1917 and 1918," admitted to "a deep sense of disappointment, of poignant pain that a great country in time of need should promise so much and afterward perform so little." He was representative. "Besides angering DuBois," Bernard Nalty has written, "the treatment of black soldiers angered the 'talented tenth' for whom he served as spokesman," and their disenchantment reshaped their political identities and behavior.[116]

As another European war loomed in the late 1930s, blacks recalled the previous conflict as a cautionary tale. On behalf of the NAACP, attorney Charles Houston, whose brush with the military during World War I had deeply soured him, wrote to President Franklin D. Roosevelt that the Negro population would "not again silently endure the insults and discrimination imposed on its soldiers in the course of the last war."[117] African American leaders swore that they would not call on the black masses to "close ranks," as DuBois had in 1918. Yet they continued to believe that they could not expect to receive the fruits of first-class citizenship unless they were willing to bear its burdens, and they continued to embrace a faith in the power of military service. African Americans' behavior during World War II was surprisingly similar to their behavior during World War I, despite the palpable anger and frustration that had been the latter's legacy. But their postwar political activity departed dramatically from the earlier pattern: their claims-making was more vibrant, more committed to integration, and more engaged with the grass roots, and it usually adopted a liberal, rather than a republican, rights frame.

CHAPTER 7

Good War, Cold War, and the Limits of Liberalism

What E. H. Carr famously called the "twenty years' crisis" ended in September 1939.[1] Europe was again at war, and it would not be long before the United States intervened in that conflict and before the building tensions with Japan came to a head. World War II was a defining experience for Americans. With its truly global stage, greater military commitment, deeper state penetration of society, more intense mobilization of national resources, longer involvement, and ultimately more prominent location in the nation's collective memory, the Second World War outstripped the First in its impact on the American home front. For African Americans, however, the legacy of the "good war" was more mixed.

First, while African Americans encountered discrimination within the armed forces and on their return home during and after both world wars, they embraced an assertive politics aiming at integration after World War II (an outcome that runs counter to theoretical expectations). Second, African American claims-making met with greater success after World War II. The advances of the late 1940s have often been attributed to shifting demographics, increased black electoral strength, and the cold war. Although such factors were important, rhetorical coercion was also at work in compelling the Truman administration to embrace civil rights. Third, many have credited the desegregation of the military with contributing to, if not sparking, the civil rights movement of the late 1950s and 1960s, yet I maintain that military desegregation's long-term impact has been inflated.

The Puzzle of Postwar Mobilization

As the United States geared up for war, it became clear to blacks that their role in the war machine would be as limited as it had been two decades before.

Since Versailles, the black presence in the regular army and navy had been steadily reduced. As late as 1940, when blacks constituted nearly 10 percent of the population, they accounted for less than 2 percent of the ranks and a tiny proportion of the office corps.[2] The Selective Service Act of 1940 assured blacks a place in the expanding military, but it neither guaranteed a combat role nor challenged segregation. During a 1940 meeting with African American leaders, President Roosevelt had expressed enthusiasm for military integration. But less than two weeks later, the War Department declared, with the president's explicit approval, that segregation had proven "satisfactory" in the past and that any change would be "destructive to morale and detrimental to the preparations for national defense."[3] This belief would underpin the military's racial policies for the duration of the war.

The military defended segregation much as it had during World War I. Army Chief of Staff George Marshall characterized desegregation as an "experiment . . . in the solution of social problems" that was necessarily "fraught with danger to efficiency, discipline, and morale." Rectifying inequities within the armed forces took a backseat to winning the war, and thus the military had to abide by the terms of "the social relationship between Negroes and whites which has been established by the American people through custom and habit."[4] Military officials simply could not fathom blacks' obsession with this matter. "I do not think that the basic issues of the war are involved in the question of whether colored troops serve in segregated units or in mixed units," wrote Assistant Secretary of War John McCloy to William Hastie. More important, cautioned McCloy, "if the United States does not win this war, the lot of the Negro is going to be far worse than it is today."[5]

To placate restive African Americans, Hastie, a black attorney and later federal judge, had been appointed civilian aide to the secretary of war, but he was hardly the restrained voice the War Department had desired. His 1941 assessment of the military's racial policies repudiated the military's logic, concluding that the armed forces' acceptance of "the traditional mores of the South" had undermined the mobilization effort. He warned that black soldiers were increasingly of the opinion "that since they have been called to fight they might just as well do their fighting here and now."[6] Frustrated by stonewalling, Hastie resigned in January 1943, half a year before racial violence erupted—between black and white soldiers, between black soldiers and white military police, and between black soldiers in Southern training camps and local townspeople—and compelled the military to address discrimination in the ranks.[7]

Despite the efforts of Hastie, other black appointees to federal posts who advised the administration on racial matters (the so-called Black Cabinet), and activists outside government, most blacks found little of redeeming value in their military experience. Dispatched to the South for basic training, Northern blacks confronted rigid formal segregation for the first time. They were subject to the worst of Southern racism when they went off base, and their uniforms offered scant protection against slights, slurs, and bodily assault.

Sent overseas, they typically labored in service units under white officers. In 1945 African Americans made up 20 percent of the engineering corps, 33 percent of the transportation corps, and 44 percent of the quartermaster corps. The war years did bring some progress for African American soldiers, but every two steps forward in principle were usually negated by nearly two steps back in practice. Advances were generally only symbolic, and none came close to challenging the overarching system.[8]

At war's end, as after World War I, the U.S. military preserved the segregated status quo and even took steps back toward the prewar norm.[9] Three studies, conducted independently by the army's major components, unreservedly endorsed segregation. The Army Ground Forces even questioned the very utility of black soldiers: "The history of the Negro soldier, both in peace and wartime, indicates that his greatest concern is that of race. In many instances, they have put advantage to race before service to their country." That same year, at the order of Secretary of War Robert Patterson, the army appointed a committee, headed by Lt. Gen. Alvan Gillem Jr., to review and revise its racial policies. In line with the earlier reviews, the Gillem Board envisioned a segregated force down to the mess hall and barracks. Perhaps to protect blacks, the board also instituted a quota so that the postwar army's racial ratios would mirror those of society. While the Gillem Board never questioned segregation, it did recommend increased black representation in the officer corps and combat units and close working relationships between segregated units.[10]

But a more traditional mind-set swiftly took hold. Fearing a flood of African American soldiers, the army banned almost all black enlistments and imposed a ceiling on black participation, effectively requiring black applicants to score thirty points higher than others on the admittance test. By the middle of 1947, the black share of the army's enlisted force had declined below the required ratio. In general, the Gillem Board's effort to create career opportunities for blacks remained unimplemented—partly because no special staff were appointed to facilitate it, partly because few officers were aware of it even months after its promulgation, but most important because segregation closed many options.[11] Originally warmly received by the black press, the Gillem Board report came to be seen as emblematic of postwar army racism. As the *Amsterdam News* (New York) noted, "All [the board] did was to slice jim crow a little thinner and spread it around more so it wouldn't make such a stinkin' heap in the middle of the national floor."[12]

Black soldiers abroad and blacks at home were acutely conscious of discrimination in the armed forces during and after World War II. Although blacks had acquired much political and economic clout since World War I, they again served disproportionately in the support arms, racial segregation continued to be the norm, and postwar army policies had once more regressed toward the prewar status quo. Yet this time African Americans would not be quiescent, waiting for a Garvey to lead them to the promised land. Despite mistreatment at the military's hands and despite the failure to compel major wartime reform in society at large, they remained optimistic. After World War II, African Americans mobilized in pursuit of integration.

In the postwar years, civil rights activism intensified. At the center of the postwar surge was the NAACP, which had over the course of the war solidified its position as the leading black organization but which had remained as committed as ever to integration. During the war, its membership had grown ninefold to nearly half a million, and the readership of the *Crisis* had multiplied fivefold—and would remain at those levels into 1949.[13] Emboldened by its newly acquired power, but also afraid of losing its wartime base, the normally staid association embraced more assertive tactics.[14] Alongside this vibrant national politics, local civil rights organizations with ideologically diverse roots sprang up across the nation and mustered their members for goals ranging from voter registration to social welfare services.[15] Blacks were, according to Representative Adam Clayton Powell Jr., "ready to throw [themselves] into the struggle to make the dream of America become flesh and blood."[16] The postwar period witnessed the emergence of an insistent rights consciousness that replaced gradualism "with a new immediacy and sweeping vision."[17] Why did broadly similar military policies during and after the two wars not have the same effects?

A Weaker Signal?

One possible explanation is that the armed forces' exclusionary policies during and after World War II were a weaker signal. But the signal was, if anything, stronger. Although exclusionary military participation signals are by nature *credible*, this one should have been even more so. The strategic costs of racial discrimination in the armed forces were higher: World War II had demanded the full mobilization of America's resources, while, at least for the United States, World War I had not been a total war. Such policies were more politically costly as well, for wartime rhetoric stressed America's tradition of tolerance in contrast to Nazi Germany's racist weltanschauung. Second, there is no reason to think the signal was any less (or more) *clear* than during World War I, for the armed forces' racial policies continued in general to be a matter of public record. It is revealing that Hollywood's wartime movies mythologized the ethnic (European) diversity of American forces but rarely portrayed them as racially diverse. Finally, the signal was even more *available*. War mobilization completely penetrated the U.S. economy, and the draft touched civilian society as never before. The United States had not engaged in total war since the Civil War—and never a war as total as this.

Not surprisingly, African Americans' experiences during World War II in fact engendered a keen disappointment. The military's refusal to make full use of its black soldiers had proclaimed, "with a baldness and a bluntness that matched any anti-Semitic decree of Nazi Germany," the exclusion of black citizens from the polity. After the 1943 Harlem riots, Robert Weaver, a member of the Black Cabinet, identified military discrimination as "the primary, fundamental cause"; the NAACP ascribed the riots to "the fury born of unchecked, unpunished, and often unrebuked shooting, maiming, and insulting of Negro troops." Reflecting on blacks' postwar prospects, one observer was not hopeful, in part because "the unwillingness of white Americans even to permit Negro Americans to participate fully in the war itself on an equal basis" indicated that there had been no change of heart.[18]

After the war, Truman's Committee on Civil Rights observed that discrimination within the armed forces was "a peculiarly humiliating badge of inferiority." Its report echoed the testimony of the prominent black attorney and former head of the NAACP legal department Charles Houston, who had warned that "many of the returning service men felt they were not coming home but . . . going to a foreign land." The poet Langston Hughes linked the military's policies with the future of black citizenship: "Jim Crow Army and Navy, Too / Is Jim Crow freedom the *best* I can expect from you?"[19] In the judgment of the historian John Morton Blum, the many forms of civilian discrimination "created less bitterness than did the unchanging policies of the armed services."[20]

Nor did African Americans quickly forget what they had endured. A. Philip Randolph accurately gauged black sentiment when he warned in 1948 that blacks were of the "mind and temper of not wanting to shoulder a gun to fight for the protection of democracy abroad until they have democracy at home." Walter White of the NAACP, who criticized Randolph for advising black men to dodge the draft as long as segregation persisted, nevertheless confirmed that blacks could not be "enthusiastic fighters" because "their memories of mistreatment in the last war are bitter green."[21] In short, the military's participation policies did not pass unnoticed: they shaped African Americans' views of military service and the body politic, and military racism was as bitterly resented as it had been over twenty years earlier.

Extension of Wartime Mobilization?

Another possible explanation is that the postwar mobilization derived from wartime patterns. According to the conventional wisdom, African Americans were more contentious during World War II, in part because "closing ranks" had gotten them nowhere during World War I. However, in both world wars activists followed a strikingly similar path: before U.S. entry into the ongoing conflict, they vigorously protested discrimination in the public and private sectors while affirming their loyalty, but, after the United States became a combatant, pressure abated. By the end of 1942, even the Pittsburgh *Courier*'s famed "Double V" campaign—urging African Americans to fight with equal vigor against racism at home and abroad—had been succeeded by less ambiguous declarations of patriotism.[22]

From 1940 through 1942—while the country's industrial war machine revved up but before large numbers of Americans had died overseas—criticism of the Roosevelt administration and of discrimination in the armed forces and the defense industries was intense. Recalling bitterly the broken promises of World War I, many blacks resolved to exploit the dependence on black manpower. As one Harlem leader wrote in early 1943, "If we don't fight for our rights during this war, while the government needs us, it will be too late after the war."[23] This militancy did not escape the notice of official Washington. Assistant Secretary of War McCloy early on observed that "an alarmingly large percentage of Negroes in and out of the army . . . do not seem to be vitally concerned about winning the war."[24] The Office of War Information, charged with bolstering the nation's morale, was keenly aware of pervasive apathy in the black community, and it concluded that "racial grievances have kept Negroes from an all-out participation in the war effort." Blacks were reportedly even sympathetic to Japan, hoping that they might receive better treatment at the hands of their fellow people of color.[25]

The first years of the war witnessed a surge in political activism among African Americans—a "boom period," as the NAACP put it.[26] Randolph threatened a massive march on Washington in 1941 and, backed by organizations that had previously shunned mass action, wrung from FDR the Fair Employment Practices Committee (FEPC).[27] The NAACP greeted the bombing of Pearl Harbor with "unqualified support" for the nation's defense but swore that it would not "abate one iota our struggle for full citizenship rights." Similarly, a black activist from California declared to his colleagues, "As long as I have two arms, I will use one to fight for my country and the other to fight for my race."[28] Inspired by Roosevelt's rhetoric against "Hitlerism," blacks invoked parallels between Nazis abroad and racists at home.

But such radicalism was both skin deep and short lived. During World War II, black elites saw it as their responsibility to raise the masses' morale, mobilize them for the war effort, and prevent a paroxysm of violence. The Double V campaign, often portrayed as indicative of blacks' conditional loyalty, channeled mass anger in safe directions.[29] After 1941, the dominant theme among black leaders and in the black press—as during World War I—was that only an unquestionable commitment to the war effort would garner them the full citizenship they desired. Despite his earlier brush with army racism, Rayford Logan headed the Committee for the Participation of Negroes in the National Defense Program because African Americans "could demand nothing if there was even an aroma of their evading their military obligations in a time of war."[30] George Schuyler of the Pittsburgh *Courier* revealingly lamented:

Supposedly intelligent Negroes are swallowing hook, line and sinker the same bush-wah at which their fathers snapped during World War No. I, to wit that once victory is achieved, the colored brethren as a reward for their patriotic efforts and sacrifices will be promptly invested with all the rights and privileges of citizenship now denied them.[31]

The fight for the right to fight may not have seemed critical to blacks' daily lives, but it was, as the *Crisis* explained in 1940, of great symbolic import: "a struggle to take democracy off of parchment and give it life."[32]

Furthermore, support for mass action declined in step with deepening U.S. involvement, for reason dictated that aggressive protest would be self-defeating. Once the United States declared war, the black press's enthusiasm for the March on Washington Movement dissipated; in early 1943 most failed to endorse a new civil disobedience campaign. Black leaders abandoned mass action in favor of more "acceptable" tactics in league with white liberals. As Randolph's hopes for all-black direct action faded, even he turned to mobilizing the black vote and campaigning for a permanent FEPC. Harvard Sitkoff nicely summarizes these developments: "Gradual reform, through legislation and court decisions, became the order of the day; capitalizing on the conscience of white America, the major tactic; and integration, the most sought objective."[33] Despite black leaders' promise to fight unceasingly for equality, it became a lesser priority as the war wore on. The flame of protest was gradually extinguished, replaced by patriotic ardor. Postwar protest cannot, therefore, be explained as an extension of wartime mobilization.

The Postwar Political Opportunity Structure

That African Americans mobilized after World War II for racial integration runs counter to theoretical expectations. Neither the strength of the manpower-policy signal nor wartime patterns can account for it. It is worth remembering that the military's participation policies are just one indicator of the shape of the political opportunity structure. Although African Americans were deeply disappointed by the armed forces' stubborn adherence to racial discrimination, they nonetheless had faith that the political system as a whole was more pliable. In this case, it appears that the implications of the military's policies were overwhelmed by the cumulative effect of other strong signals.

Since the late 1930s, blacks had made steady, if slow, gains, and this trend—despite its frustrating pace and despite the Roosevelt administration's preference for symbolic, rather than substantive, concessions—gave blacks hope for the future, encouraged the postwar mobilization, and built support for integration. Roosevelt had reversed the long-standing tradition of segregation in federal agencies. Just prior to the start of World War II, the Justice Department had established a civil rights section charged with enforcing existing civil rights legislation. And during the war, the administration had proven even more responsive. Black appointments to high-profile government positions, the creation of the FEPC, the further liberalization of the military's racial policies: these had been the product of Roosevelt's efforts to reconcile his electoral imperatives with the priority of national security. As partial measures, all had fallen far short of blacks' demands and of the promises implicit in wartime rhetoric attacking racism. But half steps, black leaders believed, were better than nothing.[34] Moreover, the Supreme Court had taken a major step toward protecting black voting rights; in *Smith v. Allwright* (1944), the Court had ruled that in Southern states in which the Democratic primary was effectively the election, the party was not a private association and thus could not disqualify voters on account of race.[35] With the death of FDR, few knew exactly what to expect of Harry Truman, but the new president soon gave Southerners much reason to worry and blacks enough reason to be sanguine.

Perceptive African American leaders were aware that Roosevelt and Truman were not fearless moral lions eager to do battle against racism at home. They would have agreed with one historian's assessment that Roosevelt's "political instincts told him to ignore racial dilemmas whenever possible, to split the difference between [prominent black leaders] Walter White and Phil Randolph and [notable Southern politicians] Tom Connally and Jimmy Byrnes, to delegate authority to his experts."[36] They recognized that FDR hardly deserved the accolades and even adoration blacks sometimes reserved for him. But black leaders across the spectrum nonetheless believed at the close of World War II that, regardless of Roosevelt and Truman's inclinations, further erosion of the racist bulwarks was inevitable.

With so much progress made (though with so far still to go), it was inconceivable that such trends would be reversed. This was partly because of African Americans' increased political strength thanks to demographic changes.[37] Blacks had also gained valuable political experience during the 1930s and 1940s, honing their skills at organizing and politicking through Roosevelt's New Deal programs and the labor movement.[38] Finally, as Gunnar Myrdal noted, blacks had recently played an important role in a total war in which antiracist rhetoric had, at least in the European theater, been a dominant theme.[39] Black leaders believed that decision makers could not go back to the prewar world even if they wished to do so. Such confidence underlay the postwar mobilization.

Framing Civil Rights: Cold War Liberalism

Scholars seeking to explain African Americans' relative success in the postwar years, have justifiably focused on electoral and cold war politics. Truman, it is often argued, was a shrewd politician who understood that he could not win reelection without black votes in key industrial states.[40] Moreover, he and Secretary of State Dean Acheson were, as the bipolar contours of the postwar world took shape, sensitive to how foreign audiences perceived America's commitment to (its own) democracy.[41] These are essential components of the story, but rhetorical coercion also played a role: African Americans enjoyed greater influence in part because the way they framed their claims was compelling in the postwar milieu. Soon after the war, African Americans drew on a rejuvenated liberal tradition, hammering on the contradiction between racism and human rights. As relations with the Soviet Union grew increasingly acrimonious, they further argued that racism at home furnished Soviet propagandists with a potent weapon. Activists' embrace of cold war liberalism furthered the struggle against discrimination, but it also limited the depth and breadth of reform: wary of being painted as Communists, they concentrated their energies on formal civil and political rights, setting aside the deep political economy of race. The United States is still coping with the implications of that choice. African Americans did not deploy the military sacrifice frame after World War II—perhaps to the detriment of their cause, as a brief counterfactual analysis and a short study of Japanese Americans suggest—but the mechanism of rhetorical coercion nevertheless yields insight into the sources of their postwar success.

Race Reform under Truman

Although FDR had offered African Americans neither substantial concessions nor soaring rhetoric, his occasional gestures and the obvious sincerity of his wife Eleanor had made him much beloved among blacks. Many had their doubts about the vice president who stepped into Roosevelt's large shoes in 1945—and with good reason. He was the native son of a state in which segregation was the norm. He had been known to litter his speech with racial slurs. Rumors surfaced that he had once been a member of the Ku Klux Klan, and even when courting blacks, as during his 1940 senatorial campaign, he reminded them not to aspire to "social equality." Yet, as a senator and as an operative in the Pendergast machine in Kansas City, Truman had been solicitous of black interests and had stood against lynching and the poll tax and in favor of the FEPC. Despite persistent private ambivalence, he had been increasingly willing to associate publicly with civil rights.[42] Neither side knew what to expect from the newly installed president. Senator Burnet Maybank of South Carolina confided to a friend, "Everything's going to be all right—the new President knows how to handle the niggers." The *Crisis* meanwhile praised Truman's record and averred that he was "entitled to a chance to add to that record as president."[43]

Whether Truman was truly committed to civil rights or just to his political fortunes will never be resolved, but his administration was more responsive to African Americans than its predecessors and many of its successors. While racial issues were generally a lower priority than other elements of his program,[44] his advisers have uniformly listed civil rights as among the administration's greatest accomplishments, along with the rebuilding of Europe.[45] Unlike FDR, who had refused to take a public stand in favor of reform, Truman identified openly with the cause, focusing the public's attention on the gap between America's ideals and its practices. His rhetoric on race was not matched by achievements, but this was true of his Fair Deal as a whole.

The country would not have to wait long for President Truman to address civil rights. Asked in April 1945 whether he would pursue racial policies akin to FDR, Truman proudly replied, "I will give you some advice. All you need to do is to read the Senate record of one Harry S. Truman."[46] When the FEPC's funding prospects waned later that year, Truman publicly protested the committee's abolishment without so much as a vote. Surprised, a delegation of Southern congressmen requested a meeting, but Truman declined, noting to his personal secretary, "The answer is not enough time to get 'em in." A permanent FEPC was central to his plans for "reconversion" of the economy, from a focus on the production of war materiel to a civilian orientation more appropriate for peacetime, but, when it fell prey to a Senate filibuster, the president refused to intervene, believing it would be futile.[47] "The program," he lamented, "has been almost ruined by one filibuster and I think that is enough for a season."[48] Contemporary civil rights advocates and later historians accused him of hypocrisy, but in a Congress dominated by Southerners, FEPC had little chance, no matter what Truman did.[49]

The summer of 1946 brought both a wave of racial violence against African Americans and an unusual level of black political mobilization. Initially Truman and Attorney General Tom Clark did little more than express horror, order investigations, and promise legislative action. But civil rights activists kept up the pressure. In September a delegation met with Truman, described the grisly events, and implored the president to take action. In Walter White's recollection, a "visibly moved" Truman exclaimed, "My God! I had no idea it was as terrible as that! We've got to do something!"[50] Though Truman and his aides had earlier discussed forming a presidential committee on civil rights, the meeting convinced Truman that race reform must be a priority and that such a committee—with prominent members, public hearings, and a widely circulated report—would be an essential first step.[51] Soon thereafter, Truman asked Clark to appoint the committee, and he appended a more personal note: "I am very much in earnest on this thing and I'd like very much to have you push it with everything you have."[52]

Some have speculated that the President's Committee on Civil Rights (PCCR) was designed primarily to soothe black activists and white liberals while avoiding offense to the South.[53] However, on several occasions, Truman expressed enthusiasm for the project, and he charged the committee with making the Bill of Rights live "in fact as well as on paper": "We have been trying to do this for 150 years. We are making progress, but we are not making progress fast enough. . . . It's a big job. Go to it!"[54] Its remarkable 1947 report would serve as a blueprint for civil rights activity for the next two decades. At Truman's urging, the committee examined civil rights in the broadest terms. It established beyond question that blacks were second-class citizens, and it came down firmly against segregation. Given the reluctance of state and local authorities to protect these citizens, the PCCR called for federal intervention to eliminate such stains on American democracy.[55]

The other notable event of 1947 was Truman's address to the NAACP. With the Lincoln Memorial in the background, he delivered a stirring speech, promising to make the federal government "a friendly, vigilant defender of the rights and equalities of all Americans." As he returned to his seat, Truman told Walter White, "I said what I did because I meant every word of it—and I am going to prove that I do mean it."[56] The speech freed Truman from Roosevelt's long shadow. The Pittsburgh *Courier* observed that "we cannot recall when the gentleman who now sleeps at Hyde Park made such a forthright statement against racial discrimination. . . . Mr. Truman deserves high praise for his sincerity and forthrightness after a long era of double talk and political expediency."[57]

The PCCR report compelled Truman to make a strong public statement on civil rights. As Robert Carr, the committee's executive secretary, summarized the president's dilemma, "It would be utterly unrealistic of him to recommend everything that is contained in the Report of the Civil Rights Committee; on the other hand, he must not disappoint those people who have had their hopes aroused by the Report." One aide argued that the report was "so dramatically forthright that anything but the strongest Message will seem like a retreat."[58] The eventual address to Congress proposed a federal law against lynching, effective protection of voting rights, a permanent FEPC, and an end to discrimination in interstate travel and in the armed forces. Truman did not have high hopes for its reception, but he was also not prepared for the political fallout: the legislative proposals alienated the South while the rest of the country barely took notice.[59] When Truman, at the behest of his advisers, delayed introducing an omnibus civil rights bill or issuing the promised executive orders, he earned the distrust of white liberals and black leaders, while Southerners still feared for their way of life. With less than a year to go before the election, the incumbent faced an uphill battle.[60]

African Americans welcomed Truman's gestures, but they did not refrain from public protest. As universal military training came on the national agenda in 1948, race activists concentrated their fire on segregation in the armed forces—on which the president could act without congressional approval. A. Philip Randolph led the charge, threatening widespread civil disobedience unless segregation was abandoned. Mainstream black leaders and editors refused to endorse such tactics, but they confirmed that "there is sympathy in many hearts for the Randolph point of view." Randolph and his supporters, meanwhile, continued to picket the White House, drawing media attention, compelling the administration to respond, and reminding the president that blacks might abandon his camp in the coming election.[61] As the campaign wore on and the Dixiecrats rebelled, Randolph again threatened draft evasion if military Jim Crow were not eliminated, and he set a deadline of mid-August, coinciding with the first draft wave. Although the episode "bore the earmarks of [a] bluff," Truman issued his long-awaited executive order in late July.[62]

Swiftly submitting civil rights legislation to Congress after his surprising electoral victory that fall, Truman did not let African Americans down. Its passage, however, hinged on revision of the rules on cloture, for otherwise conservative senators—Southern Democrats and Northern Republicans—could filibuster to death any proposed legislation. The administration's failure on this procedural question ensured that its domestic legislative program had no chance, and civil rights bills rarely came to a vote. Many, noting Truman's legislative failures, have concluded that he was not serious about civil rights.[63] But this charge is off the mark. The administration did lack an effective congressional liaison, but Truman and his aides spent much time lobbying members of Congress in person and on the telephone.[64] Stephen Spingarn, whose familial connections to the NAACP ran deep, was brought on board to supervise the drafting of and fight for the civil rights bill.[65] Strong-arm tactics, however, were anathema to Truman who had resented White House interference when he was a senator.[66] His reluctance to play hardball reflected his personal experiences, not a shallow commitment to civil rights.

Whatever his inclinations, Truman did not have the votes. Even if he had led a moral crusade, it is not clear the outcome would have been much different.[67] As Senator Wayne Morse complained:

> I recognize how easy it is for people who do not sit in the seat of a Senator to jump to the conclusion that because civil rights legislation hasn't been passed it follows that a Senator who is for civil rights has not been doing all he can to get it passed. If some of these critics had to deal with the realities of the legislative process, they would recognize that it isn't a push-button affair.

Truman similarly objected to a black delegation: "You don't need to make that speech to me, it needs to be made to Senators and Congressmen. Every effort is being made by the executive branch of the Government to get action on these measures."[68]

Reflecting on Truman's civil rights legacy, historians have tended to take him and his administration to task for what they did *not* achieve. Some have even blamed him for the radical black nationalism of the late 1960s.[69] But lost in this presentist criticism is a sense of how much more responsive Truman had been than previous presidents. He undoubtedly left many areas untouched that he had the power to redress. But, as Donald McCoy and Richard Ruetten conclude in their balanced assessment,

> although Harry Truman often moved by fits and starts and left something to be desired, he was the first president to have a civil-rights program, the first to try to come to grips with the basic problems of mi-

norities, and the first to condemn, vigorously and consistently, the presence of discrimination and inequality in America. His endeavors, courage, and accomplishments far surpassed those of his predecessors.[70]

While the advances of the 1960s would dwarf those of the 1940s, African Americans enjoyed greater political success in the postwar years than they had before or during the war.

Rhetorical Coercion in Postwar America

During the war, black leaders had drawn on hoary republican commonplaces to mobilize blacks for the war effort, and Walter White for one believed that how blacks' military record would be written mattered to the civil rights present. Toward the end of the war, he, like W. E. B. DuBois before him, requested monies for a history of the black soldier in World War II: efforts to "smear even the limited amount of combat achievement by Negro units" would provide "the basis for slurs against the fighting ability and contribution of Negroes when the war is over." But the NAACP board refused to fund the proposal.[71] The association certainly did not ignore attacks on black soldiers' records, but rebutting them would no longer be among its most urgent activities.

After World War I, civil rights activists had—in the end, to little effect—regularly invoked African Americans' sacrifices on the field of battle, but after World War II they rarely drew on blacks' military service to bolster their rights claims.[72] This was not because they had lost faith in rhetorical coercion, or because they doubted the potential of resonant rhetoric to force those who were otherwise reluctant to endorse reform. Though they were well aware that blacks occupied a pivotal political position in the urban North, they did not think success would hinge on this alone. Activists continued to believe that the power of ethical argument would be critical, and they consequently took the framing of their case very seriously. As White urged, "We must pound and pound and pound the conscience of America."[73] But, in the quest for rhetorical coercion, they turned instead to two other rights frames—partly because their efforts after World War I had failed so miserably and partly because they saw other approaches as superior in the current rhetorical environment.[74]

First, activists framed their claims in the language of individual rights, drawing on the country's rich liberal tradition. In 1947 the chairman of the NAACP board, in a representative address, called on white Americans to endorse racial reform "for the sake of the Constitution and the Bill of Rights that we Americans profess to live by, and for the sake of common ordinary justice that is supposed to exist in civilized countries." Whereas republican frames had prevailed at NAACP conferences during the war, the 1946 convention saw a mix of republican and liberal arguments, and the following year liberal frames dominated. Resolutions adopted in 1948 argued that the struggle for civil rights was "in accord with the best traditions of American democracy, the Constitution, and the Bill of Rights" and demanded that Americans make these assurances more than "pious platitudes."[75] The report of Truman's Committee on Civil Rights was consciously framed in the liberal terms of the "American Creed" because, as a background memorandum reasoned, "the Committee's recommendations will carry more weight in the public mind if they are related to the average man's concept of the American way of life."[76] During World War I, that way of life was self-evidently Anglo-Saxon, but the rhetoric of World War II and the emerging cold war had replaced racialized republicanism with a race-free liberalism.

Second, civil rights activists regularly noted that racial discrimination hampered U.S. foreign policy by impeding U.S. efforts to win the hearts and minds of "colored peoples" the world over. Blacks turned to this foreign affairs frame more frequently after 1947 as the superpowers competed for international opinion. Testifying before the Senate Armed Services Committee in 1948, Grant Reynolds charged that military segregation was not "beneficial to anyone except the propagandists in the Kremlin." Shortly after the outbreak of the Korean War, the NAACP, while supportive of a military response, warned that only proof that "democracy is a living reality" would "win the support of non-Communist Asia and Africa."[77] Translating the costs of racism into a militarized calculus, White argued in 1952 that every racially motivated attack was "worth ten divisions of troops . . . to Soviet Russia." Published posthumously, his final book took this as its central motif.[78]

The shift from republican to liberal frames in African American claims-making reflected a profound change in U.S. political discourse that had occurred between 1930 and 1945 in response to two crises.[79] The Great Depression and the Second World War had combined to legitimize an expanded federal role. Presidents Harding and Coolidge had cowered behind the rhetoric of states' rights, and the dominant legal and political questions of the interwar period had centered on the proper extent of federal authority. But Presidents Roosevelt and Truman had overseen the greatest extension to date of federal power, and, by the time the war ended, there were few arenas which the federal government had not penetrated. Truman could hardly credibly claim to be particularly concerned about violating state prerogatives. The 1930s and 1940s saw the creation of an American order in which politics became "increasingly state-centered, executive-centered, and president-centered."[80]

The Second World War was also critical to a related move from obligations to rights, from republicanism to liberalism. World War II gave rise to a rhetoric that hailed America's defense of individual rights regardless of ascriptive characteristics.[81] Faced with the difficulty of publicly justifying political obligation, the country's leaders mobilized the nation through appeals to universal values, such as the "Four Freedoms," as well as to private duties, notably defense of the family and home.[82] If the United States held dear the rights of the individual, the same could not be said of its enemies: the Japanese, wrote the editors of *Fortune*, "have little opportunity for self-expression, simply because they do not exist as individuals at all."[83] The cold war solidified liberalism's place over its competitors: the Soviet Union was portrayed as Nazi Germany's twin, another totalitarian state that trampled on the individual.[84] The confrontation with Nazism and Soviet Communism underpinned a key shift in U.S. rights talk, as lawyers, politicians, and civil rights advocates now embraced foundational rights, prior to and irrespective of positive law, that attached to all human beings.[85]

The postwar consensus on "human rights" reflected liberalism's triumph. "The idea of human rights," according to legal scholar Louis Henkin, "is that the individual counts—independent of and in addition to his or her part in the common good[,] . . . as a matter of entitlement, not of grace or discretion."[86] Truman's rhetoric reinforced and reflected the links between human rights, liberalism, and democracy. In his 1948 State of the Union address, he declaimed, "Any denial of human rights is a denial of the basic beliefs of democracy and of our regard for the worth of the individual. . . . Whether discrimination is based on race, or creed, or color, or land of origin, it is utterly contrary to American ideals of democracy." Two years later, Truman approvingly claimed that "today men feel more deeply than ever that all human beings have rights, and that it is the duty of the government to protect them."[87] By 1950 Walter White had concluded that racism was on the run. Overt racist rhetoric was no longer tolerated, and the equivalents of racist governors Ben Tillman of South Carolina and James K. Vardaman of Mississippi were "either loathed or laughed at." Even if most Americans paid their foundational principles only lip service, the gap between rhetoric and performance was not sustainable. "The walls of segregation," White declared, "cannot be shored up much longer."[88]

Sensitive to shifts in the rhetorical toolbox, civil rights activists turned in the postwar years to new liberal drivers that they believed (or at least hoped) would be more effective than their now-worn republican ones in putting the screws to decision makers. And the move seems to have paid off. Though civil rights advocates were disappointed by paltry legislative accomplishments in 1950, they were buoyed by the fact that "public officials still felt the need to give at least lip service to equality."[89] Nearly all politicians—regardless of their personal feelings—felt compelled to condemn racial discrimination and to acknowledge, at least in broad terms, the justice of African Americans' demands. The liberal frame pervaded testimony before the PCCR, and its report embodied a clear statement of these principles. "The central theme in our American heritage," its opening paragraphs declared, "is the [belief] . . . that every human being has an essential dignity and integrity which must be respected and safeguarded. Moreover, we believe that the welfare of the individual is the final goal of group life." Its implicit historical narrative emphasized what Louis Hartz would call the "liberal tradition in America" and ignored illiberal streams. "We can," the PCCR affirmed, "tolerate no restrictions upon the individual which depend upon irrelevant factors such as his race, his color, his religion or the social position to which he is born."[90] So powerful was the liberal rhetorical imperative that when the NAACP in late 1947 contacted prominent figures from across the political spectrum—from heroes of the Right like General Douglas MacArthur and Senator Robert Taft to moderate Republicans like Governor Thomas Dewey to liberal stalwarts like Senator Wayne Morse—for comment on the report, the vast majority endorsed it without reservation.[91] Even conservative politicians, whose guiding philosophy was at odds with the report's conception of federal power, apparently felt that they had to give their imprimatur to this liberal document. The liberal turn generally threatened to impose heavy costs on those who would retreat into openly racist rhetoric.

Liberal frames did, however, have their limits as coercive tools. First, Southern politicians could comfortably advance arguments that deviated from the liberal ideal.[92] One Southern senator asserted to a national radio audience that "the Negro himself cannot make progress unless he has white leadership. If you call that 'supremacy,' why suit yourself. But I say that the Negro race as a whole, if permitted to go to itself, will invariably go back to barbaric lunacy." Others shared their fears that the end of segregation would mean the "creation of a mongrel race of people, instead of the pure Anglo Saxon race of which we are now so justly proud."[93] As a result, Truman's civil rights program made little headway in a legislature that awarded the South disproportionate power. "The record," civil rights groups lamented, "is entirely one of defeats. . . . The civil rights issue was no more than a political football."[94]

Second, liberalism is a capacious discourse that makes available an elastic compendium of rights. It provided opponents of equality for African Americans with rhetorical options with which they could justify inaction, declare entire arenas off-limits to government intervention, and frustrate meaningful reform. Thus Southern politicians argued, fully within the terms of liberalism, that Truman's program implied an illegitimate expansion of the federal government's reach. "The so-called civil rights program," one intoned, "provides the spade and the shovel with which to bury virtually every remaining right of the States of this Union and all the individual rights of the citizens."[95] The breadth of liberalism also gave conservatives, committed to a limited federal government, the capacity to reject ambitious claims. President Dwight Eisenhower promised to end discrimination wherever the authority of the federal government reached, and he in fact extended the Truman administration's steps toward desegregation of the armed forces and military installations, desegregation of the District of Columbia, and the elimination of discrimination in the civil service and in government contracts.[96] No less a figure than Representative Adam Clayton Powell Jr. hailed the administration for having "started a revolution which means an era of greater promise for Negro citizens."[97] But Eisenhower also protested that federal action, even for a just cause, could prove counterproductive. Well before the historic 1954 *Brown v. Board of Education* decision, he recorded in his diary that "federal law imposed upon our states in such a way as to bring about a conflict of the police powers of the states and of the nation, would set back the cause of progress in race relations for a long, long time." Or, as he eloquently stated in his first State of the Union address, racial inequality would erode through "the power of fact, fully publicized, of persuasion, honestly pressed, and of conscience, justly aroused."[98]

The president, Russell Riley, has argued, is typically "a protector of the inherited political and social order and a preserver of domestic tranquility."[99] Assume for the moment that Truman was no exception: Why could he not simply have endorsed African Americans' quest for justice, expressed sympathy for their plight, but then invoked states' rights? Because Truman had, along with FDR, overseen the greatest expansion of federal power in the country's history and had shown little concern for states' rights in the past. A short-lived controversy illustrates this point. In April 1946 Truman told reporters that he did not "see any immediate solution to the poll tax," that the states would have to "work [the matter] out for themselves," and that education would be the key to overturning it in the long run. Soon thereafter, his aide David Niles warned that the public response had been strongly negative. "There is," cautioned Niles, "a fear that you have abandoned your support of Federal action in favor of State action. The question of Federal vs. State action is in some ways even hotter than the question of the poll tax itself and I feel your position should be clarified for the record before too much use is made of it."[100] Fearing punishment, Truman quickly reaffirmed his support for federal initiatives. Historians have long debated whether Truman was a sincere proponent of first-class citizenship for African Americans. But the controversy is both unanswerable and largely irrelevant. Truman lacked the rhetorical materials with which to construct a sustainable argument to turn black demands aside. Even if he had wished to rebuff black claims, he would have fallen victim to rhetorical coercion.

The claim that racial discrimination impeded U.S. foreign policy also resonated with the administration. In 1946 Secretary of State Acheson had pleaded with Congress to give a sorely needed boost to U.S. foreign policy by creating a permanent FEPC. The PCCR report echoed Acheson in arguing that "an American diplomat cannot forcefully argue for free elections in foreign lands without meeting the challenge that in many sections of America qualified voters do not have free access to the polls." Truman relied in equal measure on both halves of cold war liberalism. In his 1947 NAACP address, he declared, "The support of desperate populations of battle-ravaged countries must be won for the free way of life. . . . Our case for democracy should be as strong as we can make it." Concluding his civil rights message, Truman implored Congress, "If we wish to inspire the peoples of the world whose freedom is in jeopardy, if we wish to restore hope to those who have already lost their civil liberties, if we wish to fulfill the promise that is ours, we must correct the remaining imperfections in our practice of democracy." More colorfully, Truman reportedly said, "The top dog in a world which is over half colored ought to clean his own house."[101]

Yet cold war liberalism was sufficiently flexible to undermine race reform as well. The country's obsession with Communist infiltration and national unity rendered those challenging the status quo vulnerable to red-baiting.[102] By the late 1940s, the NAACP found itself on the defensive. In the midst of an aggressive 1950 lobbying campaign, Roy Wilkins, the NAACP official leading the effort, felt compelled to assure presidential aide Clark Clifford that those affiliated with the National Emergency Civil Rights Mobilization were "not of the extreme left wing" and that Communists were trying (but failing) to "horn in on the proceedings."[103] Years later Wilkins would remark, "God knows it was hard enough being black, we certainly didn't need to be red, too."[104] The Congress of Racial Equality (CORE), already suspect because of its pacifist leanings, also fretted over its members' political affiliations and formulated instructions on how to exclude Communists.[105] The damage to the cause was immense. Leftists, who had brought great energy and commitment to the civil rights struggle, were no longer welcome. And the economics of race in the United States, to which they had not surprisingly devoted so much attention, was a casualty as well.

How African Americans framed their claims, I have argued, should figure centrally in the narrative of postwar contention over civil rights. Yet scholars have generally tended to focus on electoral and cold war politics. These more conventional explanations are important pieces of the story, but substantial room remains for an account that focuses the analysis on how claimants articulate their demands.

The Great Migration and Black Political Power?

It is often argued that demographic changes had rendered African Americans a crucial voting bloc in the urban North and that their postwar gains were the result of Truman's efforts to capture their vote. As his civil rights message was being drafted, an adviser argued that "everything [is] to be gained and nothing tangible to be lost by making the most forthright and dramatic statement on [civil rights] and by backing it up with equally dramatic and forthright action."[106] Clark Clifford maintained that no policy, "no matter how 'liberal,'" could drive the South away. The winning coalition would comprise minorities and labor, and he all but endorsed the view that blacks held the balance of power in the North. No longer easily satisfied, the black voter had become "a cynical, hardboiled trader," and Clifford took seriously black threats to swing back into the Republican column. Catering to black demands might estrange Southern Democrats, but that was "the lesser of two evils."[107] African

Americans naturally encouraged such thinking.[108] According to this view, Truman's willingness to indulge the black voter and ignore the South—epitomized by his February 1948 civil rights address and especially his July executive order desegregating the armed services—paid rich dividends. He received over two-thirds of the African American vote, more than FDR had ever won. J. Howard McGrath, the Democrats' national chairman, exulted afterward that the focus on black concerns "lost us three Southern states, but it won us Ohio, Illinois, would have carried New York for us if it had not been for Henry Wallace, and it was a great factor in carrying California."[109]

The problem is that this argument exaggerates African Americans' political strength and confuses Clifford's advice with how Truman ran his campaign. At the end of the day, Truman was not prepared to abandon the South, and he worked hard to avoid a break. After Southern Democrats reacted stridently to his civil rights address, he sought to avoid antagonizing them: much to blacks' dismay, he did not introduce an omnibus civil rights bill, nor did he issue the promised executive orders that winter or spring.[110] During his famed Whistle-Stop Tour, Truman never touched on civil rights, and at the Democratic National Convention, he and his aides preferred a weak civil rights plank, much like that which the party had approved in 1944. When Hubert Humphrey insisted on a plank embodying Truman's legislative program, Truman privately labeled Humphrey and the Americans for Democratic Action "crackpots" who had needlessly alienated the South. The president eventually embraced his own record, but only with great reluctance.[111] Truman, historian Zachary Karabell writes, "wanted to keep the party together, not split it apart, and if modest civil rights language would keep the South inside the party, that was a price Truman was willing to pay."[112]

Throughout the campaign, Truman marginalized civil rights, suggesting that he believed blacks were firmly in the Democratic camp. Outside of a handful of symbolic gestures, he broached civil rights only once, during a stop in Harlem, and he did not actively campaign among African Americans. Truman seems to have thought that his record in prior years "add[ed] up to a solid back-log of strength."[113] Moreover, both third party challenges worked to Truman's advantage: the Dixiecrats made Truman seem more progressive, and Henry Wallace, running to Truman's left, protected him from red-baiting.[114] Meanwhile, notwithstanding his popularity among the black elites, the Republican candidate, Thomas Dewey, failed to capture the hearts of the black masses, and most grasped that a vote for Wallace was in effect a vote for Dewey.[115] Truman's gamble was on the money: seeing little option, African Americans voted overwhelmingly for him. Truman could consequently "have treated the civil-rights problem with soft soap alone."[116]

The Great Migration nevertheless had two important implications. First, it spurred an unusually assertive postwar black politics. African American leaders were, rightly or wrongly, confident that politicians who hoped to capture the North would have to heed their concerns. Second, it assured blacks a place on the national political agenda. After World War I, without access to either a resonant rights frame or conventional political resources, African Americans had difficulty securing a response from white politicians. After the Great Migration, blacks may not have held the "balance of power," but they could not be ignored. A place on the agenda did not guarantee substantial reform, but it was a necessary first step toward that goal.

Cold War Civil Rights?

Others have identified the need to bolster America's lagging image abroad as the key factor motivating U.S. statesmen to push, if only halfheartedly, for racial reform. Yet even in the most extensively researched account, there is little direct evidence that the principal actors in the Truman administration—as opposed to ambassadors and State Department desk officers, who clearly cared a great deal—were *sincerely* concerned about how America's failings on race affected the country's foreign policy.[117] That narrative is consistent with an explanation in which, whatever the motives, the cold war *frame* was critical.

In fact, the battle for hearts and minds in the third world, which would be central to American strategy later in the cold war, was at best a muted theme in the Truman years. In the late 1940s the administration's leading thinkers on foreign affairs, notably George Kennan, identified critical nodes of power worthy of U.S. attention and investment, but thought it pointless to expend resources challenging the Soviets the world over. It was this premise that underlay Acheson's fateful omission of South Korea from the U.S. "defensive perimeter" in 1950. Proponents of the domino theory, which would underpin U.S. interventions in later years, rarely had a prominent voice. Although the Truman administration saw its vital interests as engaged in areas far removed from the homeland, it gave only slight economic and technological assistance to developing countries.[118] U.S. foreign policy in the Truman years was more the product of improvisation and intuition than deductive strategy, but it is hard to imagine the administration running the risk of having its foreign policy priorities fall victim to Southern vengeance in Congress—just for the sake of America's image in countries of little strategic import.

The cold war must nevertheless feature in the story of blacks' postwar gains, for the intensification of bipolar competition closed off possible avenues of rebuttal to African American claims-making. Denying that America's reputation was under siege was not an option, given the wealth of evidence activists had collected. Downplaying the intensity of the Soviet threat was possible but unattractive. This would have undermined the administration's efforts to mobilize national resources, impairing the ability of the United States to compete with the Soviet Union in areas that it believed *did* matter. Finally, U.S. leaders could have openly admitted that they cared not at all what the world's "colored peoples" thought. But the priorities so strongly and clearly voiced in confidential settings could not be articulated in more public arenas, as such an admission would have undercut morale in the United States and Western Europe. The cold war rendered African American claims-making powerful in the Truman years because it prevented administration officials from rhetorically squaring the circle. They could either mobilize their population or tolerate racial oppression, but they could not do both.

Military Virtue after World War II

In the cold war milieu, all who challenged the status quo were vulnerable to charges that they were Communists or at least fellow travelers. Civil rights advocates, who had earlier allied with a wide array of left-wing causes, recognized that the slightest leftist tinge would color their entire enterprise. As they transformed themselves into zealous liberal anti-Communists, they ceased agitating against colonialism, refrained from criticizing U.S. foreign policy, purged their organizations of suspected Communist Party members, and shunned alliances with the Left. Many had long argued that any real solution required probing the relationship between formal legal discrimination and socioeconomic class, between race and capitalism. But in the repressive cold war environment, they hesitated to broach such questions, focusing instead on the less ambitious and more "acceptable" goal of formal civic equality.[119] This narrowing of the civil rights agenda had unforeseen and ultimately disastrous consequences. The failure to address the deeper sources of inequity nurtured mass black alienation and the black nationalism of the late 1960s and early 1970s. A less constrained movement might have been more successful in confronting racial discrimination in all its dimensions.

African Americans' battlefield sacrifices in the recent struggle against fascism and the current struggle against communism were prima facie evidence of their loyalty. Had civil rights advocates more regularly invoked these experiences, had they invoked the classic military sacrifice frame as they had after World War I, they might have warded off charges of subversion and been free to work for deeper change in the U.S. political economy. In the United States, liberalism and republicanism have always been intertwined,[120] and the liberal turn of the 1930s and 1940s did not undercut the tradition of the citizen-soldier that lay at the heart of American republicanism.[121] Americans continued to pay homage to their veterans and regularly spoke of the gratitude the country owed them. The GI Bill emerged out of a popular sense of appreciation and obligation: "Everyone favored veterans' legislation; along with mothers, apple pie, and Old Glory, aid for veterans was accepted without dissent."[122]

Although much wartime rhetoric stressed liberal themes, republican strands still poked through. In American propaganda, the U.S. celebration of the individual was contrasted to Germany and Japan's stifling emphasis on the group, but the Office of War Information at the same time suggested that all citizens were members of "Uncle Sam's family," and familial solidarity pervaded corporate advertisements. Americans were called upon to fight to protect not just their children and homes but their way of life and the country's democratic institutions. Norman Rockwell's representation of "Freedom of Speech"—the painter's favorite of his Four Freedoms series—suggested that Americans were waging war to defend a participatory citizenship.[123] No matter how much Americans' behavior deviated from the ideal, the rhetoric of sacrifice and civic responsibility dominated the home front.[124] Finally, in 1942 Congress voted to provide absentee ballots to soldiers regardless of race and to waive poll taxes for those on active duty. One reason that Southern Democrats did not filibuster the bill was that "they found it difficult to justify the deprivation of the right to vote to men fighting for their country."[125]

After the war implicit republican frames may have done much of the work for civil rights advocates. If Truman was "converted" to a pro–civil rights stance in September 1946, after a summer of brutal racial violence, it was not a coincidence that it came after he was informed of attacks on black veterans. Walter White recalled that the blinding of Sgt. Isaac Woodard at the hands of a local sheriff and the murder of two couples in Georgia, one of the men a newly returned veteran, had especially outraged Truman, and these episodes had in fact made a lasting impression. When asked by Southern Democrats to "soften" his position on race, Truman replied that, although he was from a state where Jim Crow still prevailed, "my very stomach turned over when I learned that Negro soldiers, just back from overseas, were being dumped out of army trucks in Mississippi and beaten. Whatever my inclinations as a native of Missouri might have been, as President I know this is bad. I shall fight to end evils like this."[126] Indignation at the mistreatment of veterans was hardly confined to the president. The PCCR report was an extraordinary statement of liberalism, but this document and its mandate also drew attention to the fact that many victims of the breakdown of local law and order were ex-servicemen.[127]

Perhaps, though, this is overly optimistic. First, veteran status did not fully shield leftists from harassment. The rise of a progressive veterans group to challenge the more conservative American Legion and Veterans of Foreign Wars was undone in part by the cold war.[128] Second, even if a republican rights frame would have proven successful in the rarefied air of national politics, it might have made little difference to blacks on the ground. Whites generally opposed residential integration whether prospective black neighbors were veterans or not.[129]

Japanese Americans and the Politics of Sacrifice

The experience of Japanese Americans after World War II may lend further plausibility to this counterfactual. Like African Americans, they experienced substantial discrimination before, during, and in the immediate aftermath of the war. Like African Americans, they served in segregated units and were given only limited opportunities to prove their loyalty. After the war, they operated in the same postwar environment, but they lacked the conventional political resources that African Americans possessed in relative abundance. Yet when Japanese Americans challenged the prevailing order in the late 1940s and early 1950s, allegations of Communist sympathies did not surface to silence them. One reason was that, unlike African Americans, Japanese Americans regularly highlighted the valor they had displayed during the war. Opponents of equal rights for African Americans thus had rhetorical options that the opponents of Japanese Americans did not.

From the moment of their arrival in the United States, Japanese immigrants (Issei) had endured substantial discrimination. Although aliens were commonly made citizens as a quid pro quo for military service in World War I, the Issei were excluded as "aliens ineligible for citizenship." The 1924 Immigration Act forbade further immigration from Japan, and in California and elsewhere Issei were prohibited from owning land. Excluded from many unions and forced into the ethnic economy, their Japanese American children (Nisei) experienced significant occupational and residential discrimination. As late as 1950, there were over five hundred federal, state, and local laws and ordinances directed against resident Japanese—even though the Issei and Nisei combined amounted to less than 2 percent of the population of the Western states.[130]

After Pearl Harbor, both Issei and Nisei fell under suspicion, and there was broad support for anti-Japanese measures. The draft was immediately suspended among the Nisei, and those already serving were dispatched unarmed to the country's heartland. Nearly the entire population of Japanese origin and descent in the continental United States was evacuated to internment camps. Anti-Japanese opinion was so strong that in 1943 over 60 percent of Los Angeles residents favored a postwar constitutional amendment deporting all Japanese, regardless of citizenship. Ringing dissents aside, the U.S. Supreme Court affirmed the constitutionality of the internment policy. Not until January 1945 was the West Coast reopened to both Issei and Nisei, and the camps were finally closed in March 1946.[131]

But after the war Japanese Americans made moderate, yet important, progress in combating discrimination. Californians rejected a 1948 ballot proposition to make the alien land laws even harsher. That same year, the U.S. Congress passed the Japanese American Evacuation Claims Act, compensating mainland Issei and Nisei whose property had been damaged or lost as a consequence of the wartime internment. Seniority rights were restored to Japanese Americans who had lost their jobs in the federal civil service during the war. In 1952 the McCarran-Walter Immigration and Naturalization Act finally passed both chambers, eliminating race as a barrier to naturalization and immigration (while nevertheless preserving immigration's overarching framework of discrimination). The following year, Californians overturned the alien land laws by a more than 2–1 ratio.

The standard sources of political influence cannot explain these achievements. The Issei had generally been farmers and storekeepers, hard working but not wealthy. The Nisei were unusually well educated, but in the postwar period most were young and still faced lingering occupational discrimination. While Japanese Americans were a political force in Hawaii, the Nisei population in the continental United States, concentrated in the Western coastal states, was small. Finally, for much of their history, Japanese Americans have been politically quiescent. The Issei response to discrimination was typically "shikataganai": "it cannot be helped." The Nisei, desperate to prove they belonged, turned to self-help rather than activism. During and after World War II, the only Nisei political organization, the Japanese American Citizens League (JACL), adopted a nonconfrontational political posture, and it was poorly funded.

Japanese Americans overcame these obstacles by cultivating a reputation for unusual civic virtue. The shock of Pearl Harbor, followed by the equally shocking evacuation orders, shook Japanese Americans out of their political apathy, and membership in the JACL jumped. Recognizing that Americans would not be sympathetic to the grievances of those associated with the enemy, the JACL cooperated—and arguably was *overly* pliant—in the hope of proving its people's loyalty, thereby creating the basis for postwar claims-making. In a statement reminiscent of W. E. B. DuBois' infamous call during World War I for African Americans to "close ranks," the organization's national secretary, Mike Masaoka, recommended that the Nisei "temporarily suspend" their rights "in the greater aim of protecting them for all time to come."[132] The JACL encouraged Japanese Americans to hold loyalty rallies, purchase war bonds, and try to volunteer for military service. Rather than challenge the evacuation, the organization accepted it as long as the government deemed it essential for national security. Even more troubling, JACL leaders went so far as to spy on potential subversives and to use their institutional position to stifle dissent.

The centerpiece of this strategy was military service as proof of loyalty. In November 1942, not long after the last of the evacuees had been transferred to the permanent camps, Masaoka persuaded other JACL leaders that "the most effective weapon against this kind of persecution is a record of having fought valiantly for our country side by side with Americans of other racial extraction." "When the war is won, and we attempt to find our way back into normal society," he argued, "one question which we cannot avoid will be, 'Say, Buddy, what did you do in the war?'"[133] The JACL demanded that Japanese Americans be permitted to volunteer and that the draft be resumed. In early 1943 the War Department partially complied, announcing the formation of a volunteer all-Nisei combat unit. Few Japanese Americans volunteered from the camps, but in Hawaii they came forward in droves. A year later, the draft was reinstated, and, despite some resistance, the orders were generally obeyed.[134] Some were assigned to military intelligence in the Pacific theater, but their performance in Europe was widely acclaimed and proved more important to their postwar claims-making. The 442nd Regimental Combat Team—whose motto was "Going for Broke"—was the most highly decorated unit in the entire U.S. Army.[135]

After the war, the JACL lacked a mass following, and years passed before it achieved financial stability, yet, according to its chronicler, this was its "golden era." Its postwar agenda included naturalization without regard to ethnicity or race, reparations for discriminatory wartime treatment and the establishment of a claims commission, successful legal challenge of the alien land laws and of the escheat of Japanese American land, reexamination of the constitutionality of the evacuation, and readjustment benefits for Nisei veterans. Over the course of the next decade, nearly all these objectives were met. The emerging cold war probably played some role in the JACL's success, but it cannot explain the overwhelming support for Japanese American claims (the Evacuation Claims Act passed the Senate unanimously) or the breadth of the JACL's success (among local officials as well as among national officials sensitive to strategic imperatives). Its successes might also be attributed to the influence that a small, well-organized group can have on the legislative process, especially in the absence of a well-defined opposition. But this would have difficulty explaining either the favorable outcomes in popular referenda or the lopsided congressional backing for the Evacuation Claims Act.

An equally important, if not greater, cause of Japanese American political influence lay in the republican frame of their claims-making. The JACL had urged the Nisei to embrace military service because of its postwar uses, and they "seized every opportunity to tell the story of the loyalty of Japanese Americans, dramatically demonstrated by their record on both the military and home fronts."[136] "Despite the barbed wire and the armed sentries," declared one publication intended for a broad readership, "they could and would prove their loyalty to the country in which they were born."[137] Officials regularly alluded to the Nisei's war record in meeting their demands. When Truman addressed the 442nd Regimental Combat Team on its return home, he explicitly linked this fight on two fronts: "You fought not only the enemy, but you fought prejudice—and you won. Keep up that fight, and we will continue to win—to make this great republic stand for what the Constitution says it stands for: 'The welfare of all the people all the time.'"[138] The 1947 House Judiciary Committee report recommending passage of the Evacuation Claims Act stressed that Japanese Americans had demonstrated their loyalty despite severe hardships: not only were there no reported acts of sabotage or espionage by Japanese Americans but they had enlisted in numbers exceeding the national rate.[139] Almost every witness who appeared before the Senate Judiciary Committee adhered to this theme. John McCloy, who had as assistant secretary of war overseen the evacuation, testified that the 442nd's brilliant combat record was "eloquent of the loyalty of this portion of our population." It proved the *entire* population deserving of compensation: "Although this bill goes far beyond providing for recovery of loss of property of the citizens who were in those units, those citizens were part and core of the entire population which was moved, and I think that their loyalty is indicated as a group."[140]

Historians of Japanese American politics often assert that the Nisei's wartime record was critical in changing both popular and elite views and in making possible legislative successes. But, lacking a historical or comparative lens, they cannot explain why such claims framed around military sacrifice aided Japanese Americans after World War II but did little for African Americans a quarter century before. The liberal turn was critical in depriving Japanese Americans' opponents—both at the federal and state level—of the option of indulging in the racist rhetoric they had employed in the past. As the cold war intensified, the reliance on a republican frame was particularly fortuitous, for it shielded the Nisei from allegations of Communist subversion. Forty years later, this frame remained potent, figuring prominently in the debate over redress for all evacuees, independent of documentable damage or loss of property.[141]

Japanese Americans' victories cannot prove that African Americans would have enjoyed similar success if they too had framed their appeals in republican terms. There were sufficient differences between the two groups in size, potential political and economic power, and degree of political organization that such conclusions are necessarily tentative. Yet the Japanese American experience is suggestive. After World War II, African Americans shied away from republican claims-making, apparently because this tactic had utterly failed after the First World War. But the Japanese American case may indicate that civil rights activists had learned the wrong lessons. A frame's efficacy depends on the environment in which it is advanced. Since the 1920s, U.S. political discourse had undergone a radical transformation, and African Americans did not take full advantage of it.

Desegregation and the Limits of Signaling

In the years after World War II, civil rights advocates invested substantial resources in desegregating the armed forces because they believed that racial reform in the military would spread throughout society. William Hastie later complained, "Of all the sophistries about human relations I have ever heard, none is more false than that overworked pronouncement, 'The armed services are not a sociological laboratory.' The armed services . . . are tremendous sociological forces. It doesn't matter whether we wish it so or not." E. W. Kenworthy, the executive secretary of Truman's Committee on Equality of

Treatment and Opportunity in the Armed Services (better known as the Fahy Committee), similarly wrote in 1950 that the committee's work was critical: "What is going on is a kind of quiet social revolution about which the country knows nothing. We feel that over a period of time this opportunity for whites and Negroes to live and work together is going to have an incalculable effect upon the civil population." Civil rights activists, writes the historian Adam Fairclough, thought that "ending racial discrimination in the armed forces would have a powerful effect on civil society."[142]

Historians as well have often concluded that the desegregation of the military transcended that institution. The 1948 executive order establishing the Fahy Committee was "significant, not only for its political import at the moment but also in terms of its long-run impact." Richard Dalfiume's oft-cited book on the subject concludes by framing the broad significance: "By structuring a situation whereby the Negro finds his best chance for equal opportunity in the military services, white America has produced a powerful force that is working to destroy the racial barriers it is so reluctant to pull down on its own volition." Or as Philip Klinkner and Rogers Smith put it more recently, "Military integration undoubtedly percolated back home. During the Cold War, millions of Americans served in the military, and it was here that many whites had their first experience of living, working, and often fighting and dying on an equal footing with blacks."[143] What we today call the civil rights movement was undoubtedly the key to black progress, but neither its origins nor its timing can be attributed to the desegregation of the armed forces. While the latter had the potential to touch off that vast mobilization, the political structure of the United States undercut the signal's credibility and clarity, notwithstanding its cost.

Assessing the Signal: The Costs of Desegregation

Desegregating the U.S. armed forces was relatively cheap in strategic terms. The likelihood of African Americans sharing critical information with the enemies of the United States was low.[144] But desegregation was *politically* costly. As an overture to a constituency that seemed unlikely to bolt from the Democratic Party, it did not have a huge upside. Meanwhile, the professional officer corps saw the implementation of Truman's order as deeply threatening to the armed forces' traditions and to white troops' morale, and the order antagonized the military's civilian defenders, many of whom hailed from the South. When Truman persisted despite the political costs of opposing the uniformed military, many blacks inferred that he was sincere in his espousal of civil rights.

After Truman assumed office, African Americans carefully studied his administration's policies for evidence as to the depth of the Missourian's commitment. They greeted the appointment of the PCCR with a collective ho-hum, for the committee would have no powers of implementation; they feared that its report was nothing more than "a 'flash' to corral Negro votes." While the black newspapers universally lauded Truman's speech to the NAACP, they cautioned their readers not to embrace the president until he followed through.[145] As Truman's staffers crafted his civil rights message, they understood the scrutiny to which it would be subjected. "If no other action is contemplated than 'investigation' or 'eliminating segregation as rapidly as practicable,' no mention should be made of any action," warned one aide. "Such feeble stuff weakens the whole position and blurs the picture." The "real pay-off," he presciently suggested, would come with executive orders to eliminate discrimination in the federal government and the armed forces.[146]

By the end of his second term, however, Truman seemed to have passed the test. Although many of his former supporters had abandoned him, blacks were resolute. Though he criticized the president for at times seeming to "soft-pedal" civil rights, Walter White regretted Truman's decision not to run for reelection in 1952: "No occupant of the White House since the nation was born has taken so frontal or consistent a stand against racial and religious discrimination as has Mr. Truman." As Truman departed the White House, Roy Wilkins praised him for showing "sheer personal courage" on questions of race "when political expediency dictated a compromise course." Although he doubted that anything would come of Truman's legislative program, Wilkins wrote privately that "Mr. Truman personally is sincere, as Roosevelt never was sincere. I believe he believes that what he has advocated should come to pass."[147]

Yet such faith in Truman is puzzling. His concrete achievements in civil rights were few. His legislative package had run into impenetrable congressional opposition, and many questioned his commitment to it. One congressional civil rights advocate complained that "it is obvious to everyone that everybody wants civil rights as a campaign issue but not as a law and that goes for Harry Truman, the Democratic party, and the Republican party."[148] The most prominent—if not the only substantial—exception to this disappointing record was Truman's steadfast support for desegregation of the military.[149]

Truman's willingness in 1948 to champion civil rights pleased blacks, but they remained unconvinced in the absence of tangible progress. His February message to Congress was hailed for its "Lincolnesque" language, and the following month one columnist observed that "the present abuse of Mr. Truman by certain southern gentlemen is lifting the president to a new level in the estimation of Negroes and other liberals." When, several months later, Southern delegates walked out of the 1948 Democratic National Convention, his standing rose even higher.[150] But for most blacks, the political costs Truman had endured were not yet proof of his resolve. The NAACP praised Truman because he "did not flinch and duck and dodge" when presented with the PCCR report, but only once the president had acted on areas within his authority would he have displayed "a courage . . . complete and enduring." Defending Truman against the charge of political opportunism, Walter White argued that the president was the target of "the most determined lynching bee in American history." But, at the same time, White acknowledged that the most convincing evidence was still to come—in the form of the promised executive orders.[151]

Truman's July 1948 executive order was by itself a suspect signal. Released in the middle of the campaign and following A. Philip Randolph's threats of civil disobedience, it seemed a gambit to shore up the black vote. Moreover, an executive order was easily issued, but it was often implemented only with great difficulty. Although the order did pacify Randolph, silence the black press, and perhaps assure Truman of the black vote, the circumstances undermined its potency.[152]

Over the next several years, however, Truman and, later, Eisenhower pushed desegregation forward.[153] The navy and air force swiftly proposed policies that satisfied the Fahy Committee, but wrangling with the army dragged on for nearly two years. Secretary of the Army Kenneth Royall ardently defended segregation and threatened that he would resign before dismantling the existing system. Regarding the army, Kenworthy vividly recalled, "They were impossible! You had to cram it down their throat."[154] Faced with substantial resistance, Truman could have acceded to the army by leaving implementation to its judgment. But, to his credit, he did not.[155]

Truman's staff kept him apprised of the army's recalcitrance,[156] and, at critical junctures and always in support of racial equality, he and his aides intervened in the Fahy Committee's often-deadlocked negotiations. Truman had privately promised the committee's chairman, Judge Charles Fahy, any and all assistance, and, according to one Defense Department official, Truman had "made it very clear to [Secretary of Defense James] Forrestal that he wasn't kidding around and we were trying to implement this."[157] During the protracted negotiations, the White House's backing never wavered. Royall, who refused all compromise, was eventually forced to resign. At key moments, the White House made it clear that it would not accept any proposal to which the Fahy Committee had not agreed. Especially during the fall of 1949, when only the most difficult gaps remained, this bolstered the committee's resolve.[158] In January 1950, with only the racial quota unresolved, Secretary of Defense Louis Johnson recommended that the committee be dismissed, but Truman refused to dissolve the committee until the army had conceded on the quota two months later. As one historian has concluded, "The President's backing for all of the Fahy group's recommendations to the Army enabled the committee to overcome the almost total opposition to integration in this service."[159] Segregation would persist until the exigencies of the Korean War, combined with the racial quota's elimination at the committee's insistence, impelled commanders to experiment with integrated platoons. While generals ultimately did the heavy lifting in integrating the Korean theater and the entire army, creating an atmosphere in which opposition to integration was unsustainable, this consensus would never have taken shape without civilian pressure by way of the Fahy Committee. African Americans rightly gave Truman the credit he so richly deserved.

In African Americans' eyes, Truman's commitment to racial integration in the military confirmed his sincerity. William Hastie later recalled that military segregation was "of particular concern to the Negro, and a great irritant," and it meant much that Truman, in this matter, "moved very positively and effectively." When Roy Wilkins, as Truman was departing office, listed the president's achievements in the field of civil rights, he put at the top that blacks were finally "serving their country's armed forces in pride and honor, instead of humiliation and despair." During the campaign of 1952, Walter White, writing to a liberal Eisenhower supporter, focused on these gains in the armed forces and credited Truman directly. One year into Eisenhower's term, White reviewed the achievements of 1953 and enumerated four advances, of which two related to the continuation and extension of military desegregation. He was optimistic about what the future would bring: "NAACP is confident that we are now in a climate of opinion which makes America ready for calm acceptance of integration."[160] White could not have been more wrong, as "massive resistance" lay just around the corner. But his mood reflected the strength of the signal that Truman and later Eisenhower had sent.

Not only was this signal costly but it ranked high along a number of other dimensions. First, desegregation was not likely to be reversed. The top brass was now committed to an integrated armed forces. Moreover, returning to segregation would, while bringing few benefits, prove a public relations disaster. In short, the United States' hands were tied. Second, the signal was relatively clear. Although desegregation began in wartime, it extended beyond the end of the war and into theaters that had not been touched by hostilities. Moreover, although implementation depended on the cooperation of the officer corps, the policy was of civilian provenance. Third, the military was, in the wake of World War II and the Korean War, an available cultural symbol.

Assessing the Signal: Desegregation and Political Structure

The racial integration of the armed forces spoke to the commitment of Truman—and perhaps of the executive branch—to full citizenship for African Americans. But the U.S. political system, with its checks and balances and its federal structure, militates against strong manpower-policy signaling. Blacks could not be sure that the president spoke for the other actors who possessed substantial control over the legitimate means of violence. At the federal level, the large Southern delegation was rendered disproportionately powerful in the anti-majoritarian Senate, and it could (and would) effectively exploit committee chairmanships and rules of procedure to prevent significant civil rights legislation. Even more important, the reach of the federal government was limited, and local officials operated with a great deal of autonomy. The desegregation of the military, even if it revealed how the federal executive would respond to black demands, disclosed nothing about the likely response of state and local authorities.

Activists on behalf of blacks' rights had long grasped that "all politics is local." In 1927 James Weldon Johnson told an NAACP audience:

> It is worth a great deal more for a Negro in Mississippi to help elect the sheriff, the prosecuting attorney, the police judge, the board of education and the various other local officers than it is to help elect the President of the United States. Why? If you are a Negro in Mississippi[,] the President of the United States cannot help you one bit.[161]

That Johnson came to this realization was ironic, for the NAACP, under Walter White's leadership, would focus less on developing vibrant local branches than on lobbying the federal government and on pursuing legal challenges to segregation and discrimination.[162]

Civil rights activists and federal representatives had long observed that local officials were key protagonists in the theater of lynching.[163] The 1921 Anti-Lynching Conference, organized by the NAACP, found that "local and state authorities too often offer only the feeblest objection to the actions of the mob which is permitted to do its will unchecked."[164] FBI Director J. Edgar Hoover placed the blame squarely at the feet of local authorities for impeding federal investigations. State police would make only perfunctory inquiries, grand juries would not return indictments, those convicted of lynching would receive inadequate sentences, and local communities would refuse to divulge any information. Truman's Committee on Civil Rights went further, charging that state and local officials were often at least complicit and were sometimes active participants. Its call for federal intervention was premised on these officials' unwillingness or inability to right wrongs against black citizens.[165]

Civil rights activists and organizations needed to be sensitive to local conditions. Even a group as devoted to direct action and as generally optimistic about its possibilities as CORE believed in the mid-1950s that field work in the South was inadvisable without "cautious prior planning" and without local contacts. Roy Wilkins summarized well the South's race rules: "It cannot be repeated too many times that Negroes do not tell southern white people what they think about segregation and civil rights. . . . Negroes tell whites only what is necessary to keep the peace and get along in the little worlds we both inhabit."[166] Openness to black demands in the federal government by no means implied that forces at lower levels would be equally open, and their continued opposition weakened the military manpower-policy signal.

Consequently, the civil rights movement did not originate with the traditional bastions of organized black politics, with groups like the NAACP and the Urban League that were most likely to be sensitive to such signals. It came from below, from the religious institutions that were the backbone of Southern black society, from the individuals whose accumulated resentment and personal bravery (combined with a crucial dose of foolhardiness) led them to challenge the Southern racial order. There is no evidence that the 1956 Montgomery Bus Boycott, which garnered worldwide attention and was the movement's opening salvo, was even indirectly linked to the desegregation of the armed forces. The key organization initially was not the local NAACP, but the Women's Political Council, whose president seems, for personal reasons, to have been particularly resentful of bus segregation. More important than national trends was the 1953 election of a racial moderate to the Montgomery City Commission. One can only conclude, as has legal scholar Gerald Rosenberg, that "a host of local factors provided the inspiration for the boycott."[167] The same is true regarding the sit-in movement. The first sit-in, by four black students at a Greensboro, North Carolina, Woolworth's lunch counter, sprang from countless bull sessions, personal humiliations, and even the intervention of an eccentric local businessman—that is, factors other than national planning by national organizations. Stirred by the Montgomery boycott and by their fellow students' bravery, young blacks embraced the sit-in as a means of drawing attention to larger inequities in the South and across the country.[168]

Military desegregation excited the national NAACP and prominent activists such as A. Philip Randolph, but they were secondary players in the emerging civil rights movement. While Randolph at least was enthusiastic about mass action and had been a pioneer in exploiting its potential, the NAACP generally opposed civil disobedience and preferred lobbying and litigation.[169] It saw new actors, such as the Southern Christian Leadership Conference and later the Student Non-Violent Coordinating Committee, as challengers for the mantle of leadership, and it openly clashed with and even sought to undermine them. When blacks' quest for civil rights greatly intensified in the early 1960s, African Americans' status in the U.S. armed forces was barely on the radar screen, and the starchy organizations that had earlier taken the lead in combating military segregation were at best reluctantly pulled along by the wave of mass protest.[170]

Desegregation of the armed forces was of symbolic importance, and one should not underestimate the significance of reducing racial discrimination in the nation's single-largest employer. But it did not have the reverberations that some foresaw and desired. It was, as the theoretical framework would have expected, a relatively weak signal, and it did not spark the civil rights movement. The consequences of desegregation illustrate nicely the limits of the military's manpower policy as a signal.

Conclusion

With the intense passions of the Civil War swiftly receding, and with numerous voices calling for sectional reconciliation and for equal honor to be bestowed on both sides' soldiers, Frederick Douglass was livid. Just six years after the war's conclusion, in front of the Tomb of the Unknown Soldier, he protested that he was "no minister of malice," but he nonetheless swore "may my tongue cleave to the roof of my mouth if I forget the difference between the parties to that . . . bloody conflict," between "those who struck at the nation's life, and those who struck to save it—those who fought for slavery and those who fought for liberty and justice." But Douglass, engaged in a battle over the meaning of the Civil War, was fighting for a truly lost cause. Many years later, he bemoaned his fellow citizens' short memories: "We see colored citizens shot down and driven from the ballot box, and forget the services rendered by the colored troops in the late war for the Union."[1]

Douglass's feelings of abandonment after the Civil War, of sacrifice freely made and inadequately rewarded, were familiar to African American leaders before and after him. Whenever the United States has been threatened, blacks have come forward to bear arms on the nation's behalf, often in the belief that, in the war's wake, their claims for full and equal rights could not be denied. But, more often than not, they have come away disappointed. Were they foolish to think that any sense of obligation could override Americans' deep-seated racism and fear of black economic competition? Although black leaders might have been overoptimistic and certainly made their share of errors, they were neither stupid nor naive. In the past, minority groups have often framed their rights claims as the just deserts for their collective sacrifice, and they have at times thereby compelled state leaders to acknowledge the justice of their demands. The preceding two chapters have shown, in accord with the theoretical framework, how and when the armed forces' racial policies did (and did not) shape the pattern of black mobilization in the twentieth century and why black efforts to exchange military service for first-class citizenship have been frustrated.

The deeply exclusionary policies of the U.S. armed forces during World War I and the interwar period were disillusioning to a generation of African Americans that had placed nearly all their eggs in the basket of military service. When the extent of discrimination within the wartime armed forces became clear, when the military returned to its prewar ways after the Armistice, and when black veterans found their postwar world unchanged if not more vicious, blacks became the model of "separationist quiescence." With the exception of that relatively rare breed, the New Negro, most retreated to their own world and failed to press their case. Their distress at the same time underpinned the popularity of Marcus Garvey. During World War II and after, the situation of African Americans in the armed forces improved, but they were again discouraged by the confrontation with discrimination in uniform, their overrepresentation in support units, and the postwar turn toward the prewar norm. Nevertheless, in the immediate postwar years, blacks mobilized for integration—a surprising outcome from the perspective of the analytical framework; in this case, a host of other factors overwhelmed the exclusionary manpower-policy signal. Finally, the desegregation of the armed forces, ordered in 1948 and implemented several years later, had little impact on black politics for reasons highlighted by the theoretical apparatus. Desegregation was politically costly for Truman, but the country's political structure undercut the clarity and credibility of the signal. When the civil rights movement burst on the scene in the late 1950s, military desegregation had little to do with it.

What about African American efforts to deploy the rhetoric of military sacrifice and just rewards to their political advantage? While the Druze benefited from Israel's relatively narrow republican citizenship discourse, African Americans were not so lucky. After World War I, race was as central to U.S. citizenship discourse as was republicanism, bequeathing rhetorical possibilities to white politicians and allowing them to ignore black claims-making. After World War II, sensing the ascendancy of liberalism and learning from their earlier failures, blacks rarely played on their willingness to brave the bullets and instead became cold war liberals. While this move wrung some concessions from decision makers, the flexibility of liberalism presented their opponents with rhetorical options, and the cold war worked to limit the scope of black claims-making. In the postwar period, blacks might have been better off invoking their sacrifices for the nation, as this rights frame might have afforded them some protection from charges of Communist subversion.

For both fringe claimants and core elites, framing is central to politics. For weak actors, words are often nearly all they have. But, as I argue in the final chapter, the African American experience suggests the high barriers to rhetorical coercion. In the end, for African Americans, the appeal to accepted ideals and past rhetorical commitments proved most useful in combating formal discrimination and segregation in public institutions. It was far less efficacious with regard to discrimination in other arenas: the private sector, the distribution of public resources, employment and housing conditions, and so on. The turn to collective protest and especially violence in the 1960s produced immediate change even in the Deep South, but it was no panacea. Such costly and unconventional tactics were ultimately often self-defeating, as they alienated whites and sparked a political backlash.[2]

CHAPTER 8

Unusual Duties, Usual Rights: Soldiering and Citizenship

Since Bill Clinton's first days in the Oval Office, the question of whether gays should be permitted to serve openly in the U.S. armed forces has periodically roiled the American political scene. On the surface, the debate has pivoted on claims about the effects of sexual orientation on unit cohesion and of cohesion on combat effectiveness.[1] That much was relatively predictable. More puzzling was the passion on both sides.[2] The Clinton administration's acquiescence in "don't ask, don't tell" was understandably disappointing to gays, but what the former believed to be a reasonable compromise, the latter generally disparaged as an unforgivable sellout. Gay leaders' most vicious rhetoric was reserved not for the conservative Republicans and the top military brass who had submarined reform efforts but for the Clinton White House that had squandered its political capital on their cause. The reaction seemed out of proportion to the crime.[3] It is equally difficult to comprehend the depth of the opposition. There could hardly have been a better time than in the 1990s to experiment with a more liberal military policy on sexual orientation. The cold war was over, great power war no longer loomed, and while the United States regularly exercised its military muscle, it did so in a limited fashion—in situations in which, even if the purported harm to efficiency were realized, the costs would have been manageable. Cold arguments about efficiency can hardly explain the intensity of the conservatives' resistance.

Early on, however, both sides revealed that their stances were shaped by a deeper premise—that the inclusion of gays in the armed forces would have profound consequences for society at large.[4] For social conservatives and liberals alike, the struggle between the Clinton White House and the Pentagon was a bellwether battle in the culture wars. The nation's leading conservative magazine, the *National Review*, saw "don't ask, don't tell" as "a key victory. . . .

Had Mr. Clinton delivered on his pledge to the gay lobby, he would have opened the way to the next controversy: redefining the family to mean just about anything." For the columnist William Raspberry, the "basic, overriding anxiety" was that "gays in the military is the first wedge in what will become a series of demands for gay marriages, full civil rights as a protected category under the law, gay curricula . . . , and all that."[5]

On the other side of the political spectrum, the *Nation* argued that the campaign was "ultimately the only way to advance society in the direction of sexual tolerance and, more than that, liberation." Another observer, noting that "the ability to serve in the armed forces has been a defining characteristic of full citizenship," believed that Clinton's failure had demonstrated the hollowness of his broader campaign promise to gays. At the time, the journalist Andrew Sullivan placed the military's prohibition of gays at the top of the gay political agenda. "Its real political power—and the real source of resistance to it—comes from its symbolism," he wrote. "The acceptance of gay people at the heart of the state, at the core of the notion of patriotism, is anathema to those who wish to consign homosexuals to the margins of society."[6] Nearly a decade later, Sullivan's views had not greatly changed. After the terrorist attacks of September 11, he, along with much of the media, believed (incorrectly) that the military had stopped discharging gays, and he put great stock in it.[7] "This is the first major war in which the open visible presence of gay and lesbian Americans cannot be denied," he noted, and the war's gay heroes—from soldiers in the armed forces to the openly gay Catholic priest who died while ministering to firefighters at the World Trade Center—would point the way toward "a brighter, integrated day."[8] Given the imagined stakes, it is not without reason that the U.S. military's policies toward gays have become the battleground for a fierce struggle over social values.

The notion that militaries are more than instruments for the application of force, that they are fundamentally social institutions that both reflect and mold the character of their surrounding political communities, has a distinguished lineage. It prompted the German historian Otto Hintze, for one, to declare that "all state organization was originally military organization, organization for war."[9] It inspired Machiavelli as well as lesser luminaries across the ages to tout obligatory military service as a way to cultivate civic virtue and counter rampant individualism. And it has historically intensified debates over manpower policy. The call to the colors gives rise to the question of not only who will live and who will die but who will be denied full citizenship and who will enjoy its benefits. For gays seeking a place in the American mainstream, the military's discriminatory policies have loomed large, for they have believed—rightly or wrongly—that true acceptance would not come as long as they were denied an open place in the armed forces. Convinced that a more liberal military stance on sexual orientation would culminate in widespread libertinism, the contamination of American culture, and ultimately moral relativism, conservatives have rallied to the status quo's defense.

The experience of American gays, while in some ways unique, is nonetheless familiar. Conscious of their fringe status and influenced by the republican tradition, groups at the margins have often sought to move toward the center by embracing the preeminent obligation of citizenship. During the Boer War, for example, Gandhi organized Indians in South Africa, prohibited from fighting for Britain, into a frontline ambulance corps, so that they would seem more desirable citizens and so as to bolster their postwar claims-making.[10] Like those unambiguously within the nation, marginal groups have at times sought to avoid military service, but they have perhaps more often volunteered, insisted that they too be subjected to conscription, and demanded that they have the same opportunity to serve and, if need be, die for their country. They have recognized that whether and how they serve in the armed forces can have implications for the quality of their citizenship. Populations across the globe—from Dalits (formerly "untouchables") in India after independence to Indians in South Africa in the 1970s to Native Americans in the United States, especially in the twentieth century—have pursued this route in the quest for broader societal inclusion.[11] Patterns of military service may merely reflect current citizenship arrangements, but they may also provide otherwise weak minorities with a potentially powerful resource with which to achieve (or at least move toward) full citizenship.

Citizenship is characterized by the mutual claims individuals and authorities can legitimately make on their respective resources, by the balance political communities forge between the rights populations can assert and the public obligations they must fulfill. Understanding and explaining patterns of formal and effective citizenship is intrinsically important, but citizenship in the era of the nation-state has also defined—and will for the foreseeable future continue to define—membership in the political community. It is not accidental that nationalism emerged in the wake of the revolutions of the late eighteenth century, which reshaped the bonds between persons and powers and thereby replaced the subject with the citizen. As many students of citizenship and nationhood have suggested, to study citizenship in the modern era is to study an institutional practice with substantial implications for national identity.

What We Have Learned

For centuries, political philosophers, social theorists, military planners, and civilian leaders have held as an article of faith that the armed forces' participation policies are of great import for the politics of citizenship and nationhood. Contemporary historians and social scientists have often endorsed this proposition, but they have rarely subjected it to systematic analysis.[12] Unsubstantiated assertions consequently abound in the relevant literatures. In this book I have sought to place these claims on a more solid theoretical and empirical footing. I have not challenged the notion that the military's manpower policies may in fact shape citizenship and national identity, but I have raised questions about the *processes* through which and the *conditions* under which the military's policies exert such effects.

There are at least two mechanisms through which patterns of military service might shape the struggles of marginal groups for citizenship rights. First, groups excluded from full membership in the political community have sought, by fashioning a compelling rhetoric of military sacrifice, to verbally bludgeon the state into granting them first-class citizenship. They have believed—or at least hoped—that their battlefield contributions would highlight the inequity of their situation. They have sought to force the state's tongue and eventually its hand, to engage in rhetorical coercion. To make this frame available, African American leaders encouraged young black men to volunteer and to comply with the draft during the two world wars. Especially from Hawaii, but even from the internment camps on the mainland, Japanese Americans sought military glory during World War II so they might overcome expected postwar discrimination. Although they were denied service overseas—except as nurses, telephone operators, and the like—white American women contributed in countless ways to the war effort during World War I, in part so they might demonstrate that they were worthy of the vote. The Druze Arabs of Israel have consistently framed their claims in terms of military sacrifice, and they remain convinced that this has been the key to their relative success.

Persuasive rhetorical action seeks to convince targets of a claim's rectitude, but true persuasion is rare in the political arena, and it is not necessary to effect lasting change. Rhetoric may also be coercive. Although free in principle to say anything they would like, targets of such rhetorical efforts may in practice feel compelled to adhere to particular formulations regardless of whether they actually believe the words they are uttering. They may find themselves without access to the cultural materials necessary for a sustainable rebuttal. Israeli leaders regularly spoke of Israel as "the Jewish state" and generally worked to further Jewish (as opposed to common Israeli) interests, but domestic and international audiences prevented them from openly espousing preference for their coreligionists; the disjuncture between Israel's civic citizenship discourse and the reality of its ethno-national policies created a space for Arab, especially Druze, claims-making. Similarly, not long after World War II, African American civil rights activists deemed racism to be no longer acceptable. While racial prejudice remained prevalent, the war's rhetoric had transformed U.S. political discourse, so that overtly racist talk was politically costly, except perhaps in the South.

Claims-making employing the military sacrifice frame may be rhetorically coercive under three conditions. First, some public must be a party to the episode: a necessary condition for rhetorical coercion is that the claimant must be able to threaten credibly to bring that public into the conversation on its side. If this audience is not engaged or does not exist, targets often need not respond at all and certainly need not be consistent. Second, the universe of rhetorical commonplaces must be at least somewhat constrained. If actors are free in both theory and practice to say anything they wish, rhetorical coercion is impossible. Third, the prevailing citizenship discourse must be republican. When it is exclusive, there is no gap between reality and normative commitments that minorities might exploit. When it is liberal, minorities may make headway—but not because of their sacrifices for the common good.

The cases illustrate both the possibilities and the limits of rhetorical coercion based on military sacrifice. The Druze succeeded in wringing concessions from Jewish politicians because Israel's narrowly republican citizenship discourse left the country's leaders without a legitimate basis for relegating the Druze to second-class citizenship. Openly acknowledging the state's ethno-national bias was not seen as sustainable, domestically or internationally. Excluded from the IDF, Christian and Muslim Arabs could not credibly deploy a republican frame. Their appeals, couched in liberal terms, were easily swept aside, as Jewish politicians retreated into republican justifications for discrimination against Arabs who failed to perform the same duties as other citizens.[13] After World War I, blacks' efforts to invoke their loyal sacrifice came to naught, despite the prevalence of republican citizenship talk. Popular racism predisposed whites to belittle blacks' battlefield achievements and to credit allegations of black incompetence and cowardice. African Americans were thus unable to credibly threaten to appeal to a sympathetic audience. White American women, however, met with greater success in this racist republican milieu, as they too drew on their wartime (though rarely armed) sacrifices.

The path to rhetorical coercion is strewn with barriers. First, even the most incontrovertible argument will have little impact when authorities need not respond. African Americans overcame this problem after World War II because their conventional political resources were sufficient to warrant a hearing. The Druze surmounted this hurdle when the sympathetic Hebrew-language press lent itself to their cause and amplified their demands. In the wake of World War I, however, African Americans could not compel white politicians to address their grievances, no matter that they were framed in republican terms. Second, rhetorical universes are typically less constrained than claimants would like: they often provide authorities with options with which to rebuff the minority's claims. Jewish politicians could employ the republican logic of citizenship to deny Christian and Muslim demands. After World War II, Southern politicians justified discrimination against African Americans by resorting to language that was overtly racist or by alleging that civil rights organizations were Communist fronts. While political conservatives outside the South acknowledged the injustices perpetrated against African Americans, they argued at the same time, fully within the terms of liberalism, that little could be done without violating the equally sacred rights of states and local communities.

Third, rhetorical coercion, like other attempts to influence politics, is harder in decentralized political systems. The centralized structure of the Israeli state allowed the Druze to focus their energies and make the greatest use of the limited resources at their disposal. Operating within a federal system, African Americans, in contrast, had to direct their appeals at multiple power holders. They discovered that their reliance on the rhetoric of cold war liberalism, so effective with the Truman administration, carried less sway with local authorities. Finally, the immediate consequence of even successful rhetorical coercion is a favorable public statement by the relevant political leader(s), but this does not translate smoothly into implementation, which takes place behind closed doors. Both African Americans and Druze learned that getting policymakers to agree in principle was not the same as moving a bureaucracy to act.

Given these difficulties, why would marginal groups turn to this political strategy and have any hope in its efficacy? Partly because they lack other means of influencing politics. Partly because the strategy seems relatively low in cost, since the worst that can happen is that the powers that be will ignore or reject the appeal.[14] Partly, and most important, because they have an abiding faith that rhetorical commitments ultimately matter, that authorities cannot forever maintain the gap between rhetoric and reality, and that by engaging in rhetorical coercion they are creating the foundation for progress in the long run. The racial desegregation of the armed forces did not lead *directly* to the flowering of the civil rights movement, but Truman's rhetorical embrace of the civil rights agenda and his (and Eisenhower's) limited implementation of it helped reinforce a normative milieu in which racism was no longer tolerated. The young civil rights activists who came of age in the late 1950s and early 1960s confronted a very different United States than had the veterans of World War I and even World War II—one for which Truman was at least partly responsible.[15] There is a reason, in short, that Truman's advisers universally have, despite his meager tangible accomplishments, counted civil rights as among the most prominent elements of his legacy.

The second mechanism further fleshes out how the military's manpower policies relate to the minority's future status. Citizenship, claimants understand, is rarely granted without a fight, but such struggle is problematic. Because the state is normally relatively strong, the minority relatively weak, and political activity potentially costly, minorities will not mobilize without calculating, at least loosely, whether the state will respond with equanimity or repression to their demand for citizenship rights. Thanks to the traditional link between service and citizenship, minorities may treat the armed forces' participation policies as indicative of how the state will react to an increase in minority political activity. The strength of the signal is a function of its credibility, clarity, and availability.

The inclusion of the Druze in the IDF was a powerful signal. Israel's militarist culture and threatening international environment rendered the signal available. The dominance of Mapai made the signal clear and reduced concerns about involuntary defection. Finally, drafting the Druze was strategically costly, boosting the signal's credibility. In contrast, the desegregation of the U.S. armed forces, while politically costly for Truman, was a far weaker signal because of the federal and decentralized political structure of the United States. No matter how sincere African Americans believed Truman to be, they had to pay attention to local authorities in the South, whose feelings regarding civil rights were only too clear.

When the signal is strong, shifts in the military's manpower policy shape the objectives, tactics, and timing of the minority's challenge and in turn the form and degree of effective citizenship that the minority may attain. First, included minorities pursue integration, while excluded minorities pursue separation. These two objectives imply different relationships with the surrounding political community and thus different forms of citizenship. Second, included minorities, believing state repression unlikely, mobilize relatively early, while excluded minorities opt for silence in the short to medium term. The earlier a group mobilizes, the sooner it pressures the state to redress wrongs, and, all else being equal, the greater its progress. Third, included minorities generally employ conventional political tactics, while excluded minorities embrace contentious politics.

The Druze in Israel mobilized by the mid- to late-1960s for integrative aims and played by the rules of the Israeli political game: they appealed to the compassion of the Hebrew media and the Jewish public, crafted resonant public claims, and dared Jewish politicians to lay bare the ethno-national basis of discrimination. In contrast, their Christian and Muslim neighbors, despite their superiority in conventional political resources, remained quiescent until the mid-1970s. At that time, they began to build independent social, economic, and political institutions and to vote for Arab-dominated parties that identified with the Palestinian cause and that envisioned autonomy for Israel's Palestinian citizens. Although they participated vigorously in parliamentary politics, they also engaged in mass, and sometimes violent, protest. Similarly, even as most African Americans, deeply disillusioned by the mistreatment of blacks in the U.S. Army during the First World War and by the violence directed against black veterans in the war's wake, returned to their quiescent prewar ways, their disappointment fostered a milieu ripe for the separationist agenda of Marcus Garvey.

The empirical scope of this work has been limited to cases within two democratic regimes, the United States and Israel, but the theoretical dynamics are in principle generalizable. Statistical tests can establish a proposition's cross-national validity, but the proposed mechanisms—with their focus on the sequence and process of political contestation, on rhetorical interplay, and on cultural context—require careful process tracing. I cannot here make a strong case for the theoretical framework's portability, but I hope others will investigate the many other cases to which it may be applicable. Did Sikhs' overrepresentation in the Indian Army bolster their claims on state resources? Did blacks and mulattos in nineteenth-century Brazil undermine slavery by deploying the rhetoric of military sacrifice? Did the Batswa (formerly Pygmies) in Zaire in the 1970s successfully exploit military service to overcome their marginality, and did exposure to military service spark political activity among them? Have shifting military-participation policies transformed broader patterns of politics in postapartheid South Africa? The range of cases in which these dynamics might be explored is extraordinarily large.

Implications for Contemporary Affairs

We often tend to assume that debates over military service are a thing of the past. But, in fact, these continue to run hot in both the developing and the developed world. After World War II, Europe's major powers—notably France and Germany—instituted military recruitment systems based on mass conscription, less because of functional military needs than because of military training's assumed contribution to societal integration and civic socialization. In the late 1990s, despite the absence of a looming threat to European security and despite stagnant economies and persistent budget crunches, decisions to limit the size of entering cohorts or to abandon the mass-army model were extremely controversial. In Israel, military exemptions for ultra-Orthodox Jewish seminarians have aroused the ire of the country's secular majority as well as religious Zionists, and the issue has regularly emerged as an electoral football. The refusal of Israel's Arab citizens to volunteer for or be drafted to the IDF or even to perform nonmilitary national service figures prominently in national debates over their citizenship status. Beyond the world of industrialized democracies, the question of who serves is of even greater import, for who serves is often who rules. Nonrepresentative armed forces sustain nonrepresentative governing authorities, and the dominance of particular communal and kinship groups in the officer corps has paved the way for unusual degrees of political influence.

Even in the United States, the paradigmatic liberal state, such matters have continually risen to the top of the public agenda. Particularly since the inception of the all-volunteer force in 1973, the racial and ethnic composition of the armed forces has received much scrutiny, as African Americans and Latinos have become overrepresented. Although the military is often acknowledged to be the most racially integrated institution in the contemporary United States, allegations of racial and ethnic discrimination persist, for African Americans and Latinos lack a corresponding presence in the upper reaches of the officer corps. Some feminists have drawn attention to discrimination against women in the armed forces, particularly their exclusion from combat units. In recent years, gays have repeatedly taken aim at the military's policies on sexual orientation. Finally, for the first time in over thirty years, the nature of the U.S. military's recruitment system has again become a hot topic. The Bush administration's "war on terror" has stretched the army, in particular, very thin, and the National Guard and Reserves have been so exploited as to raise questions about the reserve system's long-term viability. Few are yet willing to contemplate seriously the imposition of a new draft, but the whispers are growing ever louder—at least in part because of alleged class and race bias in the composition of the U.S. armed forces.

Such debates are difficult to comprehend if one adopts the conventional realist view that military participation policies are devised primarily to meet foreign threats. In this book I have proceeded from the premise that the military is also a social institution, shaped by but also shaping social structures and values. This is the *only* plausible way to make sense of why the military's internal composition historically has been and today continues to be the subject of such intense debate.

The core arguments also have implications for understanding the role the military may play in democratic transition and consolidation. The classic question of civil-military relations has been how to guard the guardians: how to build a military strong enough that it can defend the nation but not so strong that it will encroach on the tasks properly assigned to civilian authorities. Such encroachment is tempting, and students of democratization have generally viewed the armed forces as a potential threat to fragile democratic institutions. Although this has much merit, it overlooks the positive contribution the military may make to the emergence of democracy. In a rarely noted passage, Dankwart Rustow argued over thirty years ago that democracy is impossible unless "the vast majority of citizens in a democracy-to-be . . . have no doubt or mental reservations as to which political community they belong to."[16] For many former Communist countries and developing nations, hovering somewhere between authoritarianism and democracy, these problems of "stateness" pose profound threats to their incipient democratic institutions.[17] If a more prominent military institution is better situated to foster more inclusive citizenship, it may help construct the sort of cohesive political community that democratic institutions require. This work, therefore, serves as a corrective to the common view that powerful militaries are entirely inimical to democracy.

Third, this study speaks directly to contemporary debates over the nature of citizenship. Communitarians have, particularly in the United States, launched a vigorous broadside against the postwar culture of rights. An emerging consensus is that Western democracies demand too little of their citizens: the well-intentioned effort to safeguard individual liberties has harmed the quality of democracy by nurturing a citizenry focused on pursuing private goods rather than on serving the public good.[18] In the absence of a more deeply participatory citizenship, populaces become disengaged from politics, and the result is the erosion of political community.[19] Communitarianism and republicanism are not identical,[20] but their adherents share a distaste for the atomistic world of liberalism and share an aspiration for a true community, marked by solidarity and belonging. And I am sympathetic to their argument that a renewed emphasis on civic duty and public service might reinvigorate American democracy.[21]

This book, however, raises questions about the communitarian and even the civic republican project. Contemporary republicans acknowledge that historically republicanism has imagined a citizenry composed of men, of men of substance, and of men in the mainstream, but they persuasively argue that republicanism, properly understood, can accommodate and contribute to feminist, socialist, and multiculturalist agendas.[22] But they have failed to confront adequately the tension between theory and practice and to come to grips with republicanism's unsavory history. In both Israel and the United States, republican citizenship discourse created opportunities for some groups at the margins but also silenced others. It frustrated white American women's efforts to gain the vote throughout the second half of the nineteenth century and into the twentieth, and it continues to stymie Arab attempts to garner first-class citizenship in Israel.[23] As the highest form of civic virtue, military service has often been treated as a prerequisite for full membership in the political community. When republicanism predominates, those who fail to risk their lives on the battlefield cannot persuasively lay claim to the full range of rights. Although there are alternative ways of demonstrating virtue, military service has often trumped such signs of commitment. The possibilities and limits of republicanism thus rest crucially on contingent intersubjective understandings of both who is a citizen and what is virtue. Given republicanism's dark side, one might reasonably conclude that it may be more productive to rectify the defects of liberalism than to call for the renewal of republicanism. The question is whether liberalism can be made compatible with obligation, and the sclerotic state of contemporary liberal democracy is reason enough for skepticism. What remains unclear is whether we face a true dilemma—forced to choose between the impoverished politics of liberalism and the potential exclusiveness of republicanism—or whether critical philosophical and political work can forge political cultures protective of liberty, dedicated to civic duty, supportive of solidarity, and committed to a broad citizenry.

This suggests two related questions. Are there other state institutions, such as the civil service, that might serve the same function in shaping minority political activity? Are there other ways through which citizens might demonstrate civic virtue and lay the foundation for potent citizenship claims? A civil service signal might be credible: civil service reform has in the past been costly, prompting protests from opponents within and outside the bureaucracy, and one would expect inclusive changes in appointment and promotion policies to spark resistance. More problematic though would be the signal's availability. The republican tradition links citizenship with the performance of public obligation. When government is resented, functionaries are usually viewed as bureaucrats: obstructionist cogs in a convoluted machinery. When government is hailed, they are often seen as technocrats: efficient and capable, but hardly civil servants working tirelessly for the public good. The availability of a signal depends on its cultural meaning, and a civil service signal would probably fall flat.

There are, however, more promising substitutes for military service. In particular contexts, paramilitaries and constabularies have been regarded as functionally and culturally equivalent to formal armed forces. In other circumstances—such as when only small numbers serve or when the military is not seen as performing a critical and salient function—military service may not confer any unusual status, and rights claims framed around military sacrifice may not carry any special weight. Other forms of national service may then be treated as comparable, perhaps even superior, to military service.[24] Civic virtue is a cultural construction: a shared understanding that, at least in republican polities, is often the subject of intense contestation. What precisely serves as evidence of civic virtue must be negotiated, and it is therefore historically contingent. This book has not problematized this socially significant category, but a fuller understanding of the politics of sacrifice requires grasping the shifting meaning of civic virtue and the place of military service in that complex.[25]

The Armed Forces in a Globalized World

At least two lines of argument—one stemming from the purported implications of globalization for citizenship and the other from the decline of mass military service—suggest that, regardless of this book's insight into past dynamics, its applicability to the present and especially the future is limited. However, these objections are, on the whole, not persuasive.

Globalization and the Alleged Irrelevance of National Citizenship

As early as the 1960s, theorists of globalization proclaimed the demise of the nation-state. More often joyously than mournfully, they have vigorously argued that global flows of information, money, and people have eroded the powers and even boundaries of the state. It is but a short step to the conclusion that national citizenship itself is outmoded. Insofar as globalization has promoted governance structures below and above the nation-state, it has also fostered a surge, or more aptly a resurgence, of transnational, supranational, and subnational identities.[26] Not only do communities of experience and meaning no longer reside exclusively at the level of the state but the implicit social contract binding states and citizens is under attack. Individuals submit to state authority and promise their allegiance in exchange for protection, but states are increasingly unable to hold up their end of the bargain. National citizenship is increasingly an anachronistic relic, and citizenship itself must be reconstituted on a regional or global basis.[27] Such arguments, once bandied about on the fringe, today increasingly represent the mainstream view.

Many years ago, Stanley Hoffmann famously noted that students of regional integration were getting far ahead of reality in heralding the end of the nation-state in Europe: in his oft-quoted formulation, the state is obstinate, not obsolete.[28] Forty years later, one might turn aside the more extravagant claims of globalization theorists with the same neat phrase. Certainly, over the intervening decades, the world has changed dramatically. Systems of transportation and communications have penetrated formerly isolated places, levels of foreign direct investment have reached remarkable heights, and multinational corporations have proliferated. After September 11, 2001, one hardly need argue that the world is replete with transnational threats requiring collaborative solutions. Renewed attention to transnational actors and networks is not a fad but a response to apparently enduring trends.

Yet no matter how avidly the nation-state's detractors might wish it to relinquish its authority to some global or regional body, no matter how fervently they might hope for some form of cosmopolitan citizenship, the nation-state remains the fundamental unit of the international system. Powerful regional organizations have not arisen of their own or of popular accord: they have been created through negotiations among nation-states seeking to advance their own interests, and they have been sustained by those states. At the same time, progressive transnational activists could not exert influence were there not liberal states in which to operate. States are ultimately responsible for much of the global governance that does exist, and the support of nation-states enables this world in which people, technology, information, ideas, products, and wealth flow relatively rapidly and freely across borders.[29] Across much of the globe, the state provides whatever domestic order and security exist and sets the rules of the political game. And it remains among the basic units of allegiance. Forecasts of the nation-state's death underestimate "both the staying power and the flexibility of the national form as a mode of organizing affiliation, political agency, and the global movement of people, money, and ideas."[30]

Nationhood and citizenship have proven durable not as stable entities but as fluid organizing discourses, as flexible categories through which people make sense of their worlds. Exclusion is implicit in the process of identity formation: to know who I am, I must be able to identify those whom I am like and those whom I am not like.[31] Cosmopolitanism, though seemingly appealing in the abstract, fails to grasp the fundamental human need to belong and thus to exclude. Civic forms of nationalism are particularly attractive because they are simultaneously inclusive and exclusive—open yet not infinitely expansive. As the legal institution embodying that ideal, national citizenship has proven resilient because it holds out the possibility of emancipation while demarcating the boundaries of membership.[32] The nation-state and its corollary national citizenship are thriving and will continue to thrive, even in an age of globalization.

In their more honest moments, writers on globalization have distinguished description from desire. Even so committed a global cosmopolitan as Richard

Falk has admitted that the "deterritorializing of citizenship seems presently, and for the foreseeable future, to reflect exceedingly 'thin' sentiments (either superficial and utopian or real . . . but engaging only a tiny fragment of society) as compared to the still 'thick' affinities that bind the overwhelming majority of generally patriotic citizens to their state and its flag." Global citizenship is the project of "a visionary, activist minority that organizes itself locally and transnationally . . . to construct a global civil society premised on an ethos of cosmopolitan democracy."[33] Imaginative, arguably admirable, perhaps prophetic, but nonetheless a tiny minority, probably no larger today than it was twenty-five years ago—and likely not to be much larger twenty-five years from now.

Liberalism and the Alleged Irrelevance of Military Service

Only when the military is a culturally available resource can shifts in its manpower policies serve as a signal of how the state would respond to demands for citizenship rights. Only when republicanism is central to the discourse of citizenship can military sacrifice serve as a basis for rhetorical coercion. A critic might argue that neither of these conditions holds in the present or will likely hold in the future.[34] On the whole, however, this critique reflects a teleological and ultimately ahistorical view, and it conflates recent developments in the industrialized world with broader global trends.

First, some might point to the contemporary culture of rights as evidence that military service would fail to resonate. Since the end of World War II, the links between citizenship and public duty have grown thin, and Western political culture is neither accustomed to nor appreciative of sacrifice. After the attacks of September 11, President George W. Bush urged Americans to express their patriotism not by laying their lives on the line but by laying their wallets on the store counter. Asked whether Americans would need to make sacrifices in the "war on terror," Bush declared, "I think the American people are sacrificing now." How? "I think they're waiting in airport lines longer than they've ever had [to] before."[35] This response, laughable on its face, was even more so in light of the repeated comparisons between the war on terrorism and World War II—between the continual small sacrifice of time and convenience and the continuous great sacrifice of blood and treasure.

Second, the military's cultural centrality has been receding for reasons only indirectly related to the triumph of liberalism. During the age of nationalism, wars were waged by immense, lightly trained, conscript armies. By the end of the twentieth century, however, militaries were smaller, increasingly professional, and better educated and trained. The battlefield had become heavily digitized and computerized, and warriors were replaced by managers and programmers. War was becoming "post-heroic," and conscription was seen as nearly unimaginable, with the result that the military operated ever more on society's margins. The mass army was dead, long live the "postmodern military."[36] The military's prominence as a societal institution may also be suffering because war, its central purpose, is arguably obsolete. The costs of conventional warfare, the impossibility of nuclear war, the economic benefits of peace, and the spread of liberal democracy: these are the pillars of the once and future security community.[37] If war is becoming a thing of the past, the military may become further marginalized and its capacity to reshape society may be correspondingly attenuated.

These arguments are attractive, but that is in no small measure because they flatter and reassure us. They suggest that the Euro-American path out of international anarchy is stable and portable—that it will survive unchanging far into the future and that this zone of peace will inexorably expand geographically. But this implicit view of history is teleological and thus flawed, for history has a way of surprising us. Perhaps September 11 was a last desperate gasp from history's losers, but it seems more likely that the end of history is not upon us, that Francis Fukuyama's optimism and triumphalism were misguided.[38]

It may be difficult to imagine war in the transatlantic space in the near future, but that hardly means that military force has lost its utility or that military institutions have been consigned to social marginality. First, even if one accepts Fukuyama's contentions, the inevitable victory of liberal democracy does not imply that there will not be resistance, often violent. As history's losers lash out, history's winners must defend themselves and their values. So one might interpret the turn to military force after the cold war by the West, especially the United States, from the Persian Gulf to the Balkans to Haiti to Afghanistan and back to the Gulf. Historical forces may need more than a little help from human agents ready to employ military power—particularly because globalization has arguably empowered the weak by spurring the proliferation of sophisticated weaponry and military know-how.[39]

Second, pace Fukuyama, one should not presuppose the identity of history's winners and losers. The history of ideological competition should give us pause before we proclaim one model of domestic order the eternal victor. At times such as these, it is natural for the winners to congratulate themselves for their possession of timeless verities. But often what is supposedly timeless has proven time bound, and what is supposedly universal has proven more limited in scope. Fukuyama's reading of human history implies an impoverished view of human ingenuity, but it would seem a poor idea to bet against our collective capacity for intellectual creativity. And while ideological rivalry need not be accompanied by military rivalry, it has often seemed that the war over ideas can be resolved only on a less elevated field of battle.

Third, one should be wary of extrapolating from the present transatlantic peace to the future and to the world as a whole. At least in the long run, it is likely that new powers will emerge to challenge the dominance of the United States and the rules of the game it has tailored to its advantage. Perhaps the contending powers will discover the long-sought secret to a peaceful realignment of the international pecking order, but the onus lies on those who would dismiss E. H. Carr's warning that in international politics "the use or threatened use of force is . . . a normal and recognized method of bringing about important political change."[40] Moreover, one can certainly imagine scenarios, such as severe economic recession, under which those stable pillars of the security community might collapse.

The above discussion also suggests avenues of reply to the dual challenge posed by the "postmodern military" and the triumph of liberalism. Small, technologically sophisticated armed forces are the norm today in the industrialized West, but poorer states, lacking satellite telemetry, modern information and telecommunications systems, and long-distance weaponry, will continue to rely on the "modern" military model and perhaps even on mass conscription. In such states, the military will likely remain an essential social institution.[41] Moreover, history is not linear. In the early modern era, military forces were small, well-trained, and relatively isolated from society at large. The mass army emerged first in the late eighteenth and, with greater staying power, in the mid-nineteenth century in response to changes in technology, doctrine, and social structure. After a long stretch of obsolescence, mercenaries—or, as they are now called, private military forces—are today on the rebound. Who can say that future developments will not prompt a return to large, lightly trained armed forces drawn from the nation at large?

Perhaps, however, the postwar supremacy of liberal citizenship discourse suggests that military service is and will be of little relevance to struggles for rights. But liberalism's victory is not universal and may not be lasting. The claim that the rights of the individual are paramount and that collectives lack status as rights-bearing actors is not universally accepted. The assertion of a distinct "Asian way" may be politically motivated, but it nonetheless reflects the existence of rhetorical alternatives to liberalism, which have been revived in recent decades, even in the United States. Rumors of liberalism's irreversible triumph are thus greatly exaggerated. Moreover, while the citizen-soldier is dead, at least in the West, his myth lives on. Even as the armed forces grow more professional, they remain symbolically potent.[42]

Implications for the Study of Politics

Students of civil-military relations have generally explored how to limit the threat that the military poses to civilian control. Concerned chiefly with the armed forces' overt influence over political decision making, they have devoted little systematic attention to the less visible means through which the military shapes social relations and produces politics.[43] In other words, the field of civil-military relations traditionally has examined the political influence of the military as an actor but not as an institution. I hope this work will help remedy that oversight.

More broadly, this book calls on political scientists and other scholars to take rhetoric itself more seriously and to think about rhetoric differently. Both materialist and ideational approaches have difficulty comprehending the energy with which political actors, both weak and strong, engage in public argument. Constructivists have usefully drawn renewed attention to public deliberation and the dynamics of persuasion, but, as I argued at length in chapter 2, they have not done sufficient justice to the realities of power and they have actually understated the importance of rhetoric and framing in political contestation. Drawing from, building on, and in ways taking issue with the recent rhetorical turn, the mechanism of rhetorical coercion explores how rhetorical choices can have causal effects even in more pedestrian moments. Thinking about rhetoric in such terms avoids the pitfalls of vulgar materialism, reductionist idealism, and deliberative constructivism.

Most broadly, cultural analysis has enjoyed a renaissance in recent years, and its return to the center of political science has provoked a vigorous debate. While the cultural turn has sparked useful discussion, it has also predictably led to exercises employing false dichotomies. Can material or ideational factors better explain the end of the cold war? Can cultural norms or rational calculation better account for why states have since World War I generally abstained from using chemical weapons against opposed combatants?[44] Such rigid either-or formulations have usefully compelled scholars to clarify the expectations derived from their favored causal factors and mechanisms, but they have also discouraged them from exploring how such factors might be productively conjoined without giving analytical priority to either.

One of this book's central claims is that cultural and rational modes of analysis are not merely compatible or complementary but mutually necessary. While the two mechanisms highlighted here appear at first glance to be in orientation predominantly cultural (framing) or rationalist (signaling), they are on closer inspection more difficult to classify, for the operation of each depends crucially on both cultural and rational presuppositions. Consider the politics of framing. This perspective suggests that political actors are not only deeply cultural creatures who are driven by the human imperative for narrative and conceptual order but also rational beings who normally select from among available frames that which seems most likely to achieve their ends. A similar mix of the cultural and the rational pervades the politics of signaling. The minority's leaders are rational actors, reasonably confident of their objectives, responsive to shifts in the incentive structure, and calculating to the best of their limited abilities the costs and benefits of mobilizing for first-class citizenship. But the interpretation of signals—and even what counts as a signal in the first place—is hemmed in by culture. Although the means through which the manpower-policy signal acquires credibility and clarity are consistent with rationalist reasoning, its very availability as a signal depends on the cultural context.

The story of the link between military service and the politics of citizenship could not be told without relying on both culture and rationality. Interwoven, they compose the basic structure of politics. And without equal attention to both, the study of politics is much the poorer.

Notes

Chapter 1. A School for the Nation?

1. David M. Kennedy, *Over Here: The First World War and American Society* (Oxford: Oxford University Press, 1980), 30–44.
2. By the "friendship of the peoples," Soviet ideologues meant the process by which nationalities' "common features grow and particularistic features gradually disappear." Brezhnev quoted in Teresa Rakowska-Harmstone, "'Brotherhood in Arms': The Ethnic Factor in the Soviet Armed Forces," in *Ethnic Armies: Polyethnic Armed Forces from the Time of the Habsburgs to the Age of the Superpowers*, ed. N. F. Dreisziger (Waterloo, Ontario: Wilfred Laurier University Press, 1990), 146; on "friendship," see Rakowska-Harmstone, "The Soviet Army as the Instrument of National Integration," in *Soviet Military Power and Performance*, ed. John Erickson and E. J. Feuchtwanger (Hamden, Conn.: Archon Books, 1979), 139. See also Ellen Jones, *Red Army and Society: A Sociology of the Soviet Military* (Boston: Allen and Unwin, 1985), 148–79.
3. See Maury Feld, *The Structure of Violence: Armed Forces as Social Systems* (Beverly Hills, Calif.: Sage, 1977), and Barton C. Hacker, "Military Institutions and Social Order: Transformations of Western Thought since the Enlightenment," *War & Society* 11, no. 2 (October 1993): 1–23.
4. See J. G. A. Pocock, *The Machiavellian Moment: Florentine Political Thought and the Atlantic Republican Tradition* (Princeton: Princeton University Press, 1975), 194–218, and Adrian Oldfield, *Citizenship and Community: Civic Republicanism and the Modern World* (London: Routledge, 1990), 31–49.
5. Weber, "The Meaning of Discipline," in *From Max Weber: Essays in Sociology*, ed. H. H. Gerth and C. Wright Mills (New York: Oxford University Press, 1946), 253–61.
6. On Russia, see Robert Baumann, "Universal Service Reform and Russia's Imperial Dilemma," *War & Society* 4, no. 2 (1986): 31–49, and Joshua A. Sanborn, *Drafting the Russian Nation: Military Conscription, Total War, and Mass Politics, 1905–1925* (DeKalb: Northern Illinois University Press, 2002). On Meiji Japan, see Marius B. Jansen, *The Making of Modern Japan* (Cambridge: Harvard University Press, 2000), 397–98. On Brazil, see Frank D. McCann, *Soldiers of the Pátria: A History of the Brazilian Army, 1889–1937* (Stanford: Stanford University Press, 2004), 158–66, and Peter M. Beattie, *The Tribute of Blood: Army, Honor, Race, and Nation in Brazil, 1864–1945* (Durham: Duke University Press, 2001).

7. Joseph A. Massad, *Colonial Effects: The Making of National Identity in Jordan* (New York: Columbia University Press, 2001), 180.

8. Peter Waldman, "In Its Basic Training, the Lebanese Army Reinvents a Nation," *Wall Street Journal*, 5 April 1994.

9. See William L. Ransom, ed., "Military Training: Compulsory or Volunteer," *Proceedings of the Academy of Political Science in the City of New York* 6, no. 4 (July 1916), and Paul Russell Anderson, ed., "Universal Military Training and National Security," *Annals of the American Academy of Political and Social Science* 24, no. 1 (September 1945).

10. See Andrew Bacevich, "Who Will Serve?" *Wilson Quarterly* 22, no. 3 (Summer 1998): 80–91, and James Burk, "The Military Obligation of Citizens since Vietnam," *Parameters* 31, no. 2 (Summer 2001): 48–60. Eliot Cohen argues that the link between citizenship and military service is all but obsolete today in developed countries. See Cohen, "Twilight of the Citizen-Soldier," *Parameters* 31, no. 2 (Summer 2001): 23–28.

11. See Gary Hart, *The Minuteman: Restoring an Army of the People* (New York: Free Press, 1998); Mickey Kaus, *The End of Equality* (New York: HarperCollins, 1992), 79–85; Charles Moskos, *A Call to Civil Service: National Service for Country and Community* (New York: Macmillan, 1988); and Thomas Ricks, *Making the Corps: Sixty-One Men Came to Parris Island to Become Marines, Not All of Them Made It* (New York: Scribner, 1997). See also Moskos and Paul Glastris, "This Time, A Draft for the Home Front, Too," *Washington Post*, 4 November 2001; Charles B. Rangel, "Bring Back the Draft," *New York Times*, 31 December 2002; Barry Strauss, "Reflections on the Citizen-Soldier," *Parameters* 33, no. 2 (Summer 2003): 66–77; William Broyles Jr., "A War for Us, Fought by Them," *New York Times*, 4 May 2004; James Dao, "The Option Nobody's Pushing. Yet." *New York Times*, 3 October 2004; Josiah Bunting III, "Class Warfare," *American Scholar* 74, no. 1 (Winter 2005): 12–18; and David M. Kennedy, "The Best Army We Can Buy," *New York Times*, 25 July 2005.

12. In this book I focus on the consequences—not the origins—of military participation policy. The latter has been the subject of much scholarship, but it figures here only insofar as the sources of manpower policy may also account for the purported consequences. Here it is therefore more productive to treat the origins of manpower policy as an empirical matter and then configure the cases so as to avoid problems of endogeneity and epiphenomenality. On origins, see Samuel P. Huntington, *The Soldier and the State: The Theory and Politics of Civil-Military Relations* (Cambridge: Harvard University Press, 1957); Alon Peled, *A Question of Loyalty: Military Manpower Policy in Multiethnic States* (Ithaca: Cornell University Press, 1998); and Stephen Peter Rosen, *Societies and Military Power: India and Its Armies* (Ithaca: Cornell University Press, 1996). For a critical view, see Ronald R. Krebs, "One Nation under Arms? Military Participation Policy and the Politics of Identity," *Security Studies* 14, no. 3 (Spring 2005): 529–64.

13. Cynthia H. Enloe, *Ethnic Soldiers: State Security in Divided Societies* (Athens: University of Georgia Press, 1980).

14. Morris Janowitz, "Military Institutions and Citizenship in Western Societies," *Armed Forces and Society* 2, no. 2 (February 1976): 185–204.

15. Geyer, "War and the Context of General History in an Age of Total War," *Journal of Military History* 57, no. 5 (October 1993): 152–53.

16. For representative works, see Davis B. Bobrow, "Soldiers and the Nation State," in *New Nations: The Problem of Political Development*, special issue, ed. Karl von Vorys, *Annals of the American Academy of Political and Social Science* 358 (March 1965): 65–76; John J. Johnson, ed., *The Role of the Military in Underdeveloped Countries* (Princeton: Princeton University Press, 1962); Ernest Lefever, *Spear and Sceptre: Army, Police, and Politics in Tropical Africa* (Washington, D.C.: Brookings Institution, 1970); and Daniel Lerner and Richard D. Robinson, "Swords and Ploughshares: The Turkish Army as a Modernizing Force," *World Politics* 13, no. 1 (October 1960): 19–44. Some were also sensitive to the military's conservatism. See Lucian W. Pye, "Armies in the Process of Political Modernization," in *Role of the Military*, ed. Johnson, 75–76, and Morris Janowitz, *The Mili-*

tary in the Political Development of New Nations (Chicago: University of Chicago Press, 1964), 26, 43–44.

17. For the former view, see Pye, "Armies," 81; Bobrow, "Soldiers," 75; and Edward Shils, "The Military in the Political Development of the New States," in *Role of the Military,* ed. Johnson, 32–33. For the latter view, see Janowitz, *Military in the Political Development,* 81, and Rupert Emerson, "Nation-Building in Africa," in *Nation-Building,* ed. Karl W. Deutsch and William J. Foltz (New York: Atherton, 1963), 115.

18. See Samuel P. Huntington, *Political Order in Changing Societies* (New Haven: Yale University Press, 1968), and Ali A. Mazrui, "Soldiers as Traditionalizers: Military Rule and the Re-Africanization of Africa," *World Politics* 28, no. 2 (January 1976): 246–72. See also Henry Bienen, "The Background to Contemporary Study of Militaries and Modernization," in *The Military and Modernization,* ed. Bienen (Chicago: Aldine, Atherton, 1971), 1–33.

19. Enloe, *Ethnic Soldiers.*

20. See Rosen, *Societies and Military Power;* Henry Dietz et al., "The Military as a Vehicle for Social Integration," in *Ethnicity, Integration, and the Military,* ed. Dietz et al. (Boulder, Colo.: Westview, 1991), 15–16; and Gwyn Harries-Jenkins and Charles Moskos, "Armed Forces and Society," *Current Sociology* 29, no. 3 (Winter 1981): 70.

21. Michael Howard, "Total War in the Twentieth Century: Participation and Consensus in the Second World War," *War and Society: A Yearbook of Military History* 1 (1975): 216–26. See also Theodore Zeldin, *France, 1848–1945* (Oxford: Oxford University Press, 1977), 2:905, and István Deák, *Beyond Nationalism: A Social and Political History of the Habsburg Officer Corps, 1848–1918* (Oxford: Oxford University Press, 1990), 4.

22. Charles C. Moskos and John Sibley Butler, *All That We Can Be: Black Leadership and Racial Integration the Army Way* (New York: Basic Books, 1996), 2.

23. For examples, see Everett Carl Dolman, *The Warrior State: How Military Organization Structures Politics* (New York: Palgrave Macmillan, 2004); David B. Ralston, *Importing the European Army* (Chicago: University of Chicago Press, 1990); Barry R. Posen, "Nationalism, the Mass Army, and Military Power," *International Security* 18, no. 2 (Fall 1993): 80–124; and Eugen Weber, *Peasants into Frenchmen: The Modernization of Rural France, 1870–1914* (Stanford: Stanford University Press, 1976).

24. Quoted in Richard Severo and Lewis Milford, *The Wages of War: When America's Soldiers Came Home—from Valley Forge to Vietnam* (New York: Simon and Schuster, 1989), 133.

25. Robert Weldon Whalen, *Bitter Wounds: German Victims of the Great War, 1914–1939* (Ithaca: Cornell University Press, 1984), 181–82; Eric J. Leed, *No Man's Land: Combat and Identity in World War I* (Cambridge: Cambridge University Press, 1979), 1.

26. For a comprehensive discussion and complete citation, see Ronald R. Krebs, "A School for the Nation? How Military Service Does Not Build Nations, and How It Might," *International Security* 29, no. 4 (Spring 2004): 85–124.

27. See John P. Lovell and Judith Hicks Stiehm, "Military Service and Political Socialization," in *Political Learning in Adulthood,* ed. Roberta S. Sigel (Chicago: University of Chicago Press, 1989), 176–78. On "total institutions," see Erving Goffman, "On the Characteristics of Total Institutions," in his *Asylums: Essays on the Social Situation of Mental Patients and Other Inmates* (Garden City, N.Y.: Anchor, 1961). On techniques of socialization, see P. E. Freedman and Anne Freedman, "Political Learning," in *The Handbook of Political Behavior,* vol. 1, ed. Samuel L. Long (New York: Plenum Press, 1981), 255–303.

28. Quoted in Beattie, *Tribute of Blood,* 230–31.

29. Gerhard Ritter, *The Sword and the Scepter: The Problem of Militarism in Germany,* vol. 1: *The Prussian Tradition, 1740–1890* (Coral Gables, Fla.: University of Miami Press, 1969), 118. See also Martin Kitchen, *The German Officer Corps, 1890–1914* (Oxford: Oxford University Press, 1968).

30. The last case is less well known. See Stephen D. Wesbrook, *Political Training in the*

United States Army: A Reconsideration (Columbus: Ohio State University, Mershon Center, March 1979).

31. Natan Eitan, "The *Hasbarah* Branch of the IDF Educational Corps," in *The Military in the Service of Society and Democracy*, ed. Daniella Ashkenazy (Westport, Conn.: Greenwood, 1994), 69–70.

32. For the seminal work on the contact hypothesis, see Gordon W. Allport, *The Nature of Prejudice* (Reading, Mass.: Addison-Wesley, 1954). For recent reviews, see Marilynn B. Brewer and Rupert J. Brown, "Intergroup Relations," in *The Handbook of Social Psychology*, 4th ed., ed. Daniel T. Gilbert et al. (Boston: McGraw-Hill, 1998), 2:576–83, and Thomas F. Pettigrew, "Intergroup Contact Theory," *Annual Review of Psychology* 49 (1998): 65–85.

33. See John Sibley Butler and Kenneth L. Wilson, "*The American Soldier* Revisited: Race Relations and the Military," *Social Science Quarterly* 59, no. 3 (December 1978): 451–67, and Charles Moskos, "From Citizens' Army to Social Laboratory," *Washington Quarterly* 17, no. 1 (Winter 1993): 83–94.

34. Breckinridge, "Universal Service as the Basis of National Unity and National Defense," in "Military Training," ed. William L. Ransom, 16.

35. Gary Gerstle, *American Crucible: Race and Nation in the Twentieth Century* (Princeton: Princeton University Press, 2001), 220–37.

36. John Gooch, *Army, State and Society in Italy, 1870–1915* (London: Macmillan, 1989), 1–35; Beattie, *Tribute of Blood*, 228–37, 270–71; and John Keegan, *The Face of Battle: A Study of Agincourt, Waterloo and the Somme* (London: Penguin, 1976), 221.

37. On France, see Forrest McDonald, "The Relation of the French Peasant Veterans of the American Revolution to the Fall of Feudalism in France, 1789–1792," in *The Military-State-Society Symbiosis*, ed. Peter Karsten (New York: Garland, 1998), 337–47. Ghana is the strongest case in Africa, but the counterarguments have been persuasive. See David Killingray, "Soldiers, Ex-Servicemen, and Politics in the Gold Coast, 1939–50," *Journal of Modern African Studies* 21, no. 3 (September 1983): 523–34, and Adrienne M. Israel, "Ex-Servicemen at the Crossroads: Protest and Politics in Post-War Ghana," *Journal of Modern African Studies* 30, no. 2 (June 1992): 359–68.

38. Enloe, *Ethnic Soldiers*, 199–209; David Carey Jr., "Who's Using Whom? A Comparison of Military Conscription in Guatemala and Senegal in the First Half of the Twentieth Century," *Comparative Social Research* 20 (2002): 171–99.

39. Philip A. Klinkner with Rogers M. Smith, *The Unsteady March: The Rise and Decline of Racial Equality in America* (Chicago: University of Chicago Press, 1999), 201–3, 205, 233–34. More broadly, see Christopher G. Ellison, "Military Background, Racial Orientations, and Political Participation among Black Adult Males," *Social Science Quarterly* 73, no. 2 (June 1992): 360–78, and Christopher S. Parker, *Fighting for Democracy: Race, Service to the State, and Insurgency during Jim Crow*, unpublished ms., Department of Political Science, University of California—Santa Barbara, 2005.

40. See Theda Skocpol et al., "A Nation of Organizers: The Institutional Origins of Civic Voluntarism in the United States," *American Political Science Review* 94, no. 3 (September 2000): 534, 538. See also the enormous literature on veterans' associations.

41. Veterans, once overrepresented in Congress, are today underrepresented, but military service continues to feature in U.S. political campaigns. The Democratic field in the 2004 presidential campaign had two candidates with distinguished service records, Senator John Kerry and retired general Wesley Clark, and both, while on the campaign trail, regularly drew attention to their service in Vietnam and elsewhere. See, for example, Robin Toner, "Still the Question: What Did You Do in the War?" *New York Times*, 15 February 2004.

42. See Richard E. Nisbett and Timothy D. Wilson, "Telling More Than We Can Know: Verbal Reports on Mental Processes," *Psychological Review* 84, no. 3 (May 1977): 231–59. A substantial literature has challenged aspects of this claim, but the larger point has withstood attack.

43. See James Scott, *Weapons of the Weak: Everyday Forms of Peasant Resistance* (New Haven: Yale University Press, 1985).

44. On the weaknesses of such models of socialization, see Timothy E. Cook, "The Bear Market in Political Socialization and the Costs of Misunderstood Psychological Theories," *American Political Science Review* 79, no. 4 (December 1985): 1079–93, and Stanley A. Renshon, "Assumptive Frameworks in Political Socialization Theory," in *Handbook of Political Socialization: Theory and Research,* ed. Renshon (New York: Free Press, 1977), 3–44.

45. Peter Karsten, *Soldiers and Society: The Effects of Military Service and War on American Life* (Westport, Conn.: Greenwood, 1978), 21.

46. If military educational programs have little impact on soldiers' views on matters so central to the war effort, a fortiori they cannot exert much influence on soldiers' attitudes on seemingly more peripheral matters, such as the definition of the nation. See Samuel A. Stouffer et al., *The American Soldier,* vol. 1, *Adjustment during Army Life* (Princeton: Princeton University Press, 1949), 458–85.

47. For salient examples, see Leo Bogart, ed., *Project Clear: Social Research and the Desegregation of the U.S. Army* (New Brunswick, N.J.: Transaction, 1992 [1969]), 125, and Robert B. Edgerton, *Hidden Heroism: Black Soldiers in America's Wars* (Boulder, Colo.: Westview, 2001), 182.

48. Moskos and Butler, *All That We Can Be,* 2.

49. This finding dates to the U.S. Army's earliest experiments with racial integration and has been a constant theme ever since. See Stouffer et al., *American Soldier,* 1:586–95, and Charles C. Moskos, "Racial Integration in the Armed Forces," *American Journal of Sociology* 72, no. 2 (September 1966): 142–43.

50. A subset of attitudes, notably partisanship, is increasingly stable at least through middle age, but it is unclear whether one can extrapolate to the beliefs of concern here. Few studies have been conducted on the question of socialization and national identity. See Virginia Sapiro, "Not Your Parents' Political Socialization: Introduction for a New Generation," *Annual Review of Political Science* 7 (2004): 1–23.

51. See Theodore M. Newcomb et al., *Persistence and Change: Bennington College and Its Students after Twenty-Five Years* (New York: Wiley, 1967), and Duane F. Alwin et al., *Political Attitudes over the Life Span: The Bennington Women after Fifty Years* (Madison: University of Wisconsin Press, 1991).

52. The impact of socialization may also be limited because genetics may have a sizable impact on political attitudes. See John R. Alford et al., "Are Political Orientations Genetically Transmitted?" *American Political Science Review* 99, no. 2 (May 2005): 153–67.

53. See Samuel A. Stouffer et al., *The American Soldier,* vol. 2, *Combat and Its Aftermath* (Princeton: Princeton University Press, 1949), 637–38, and George H. Lawrence and Thomas D. Kane, "Military Service and Racial Attitudes of White Veterans," *Armed Forces and Society* 22, no. 2 (Winter 1995–96): 235–55. For suggestive findings to the contrary, see Peter D. Feaver and Christopher Gelpi, *Choosing Your Battles: American Civil-Military Relations and the Use of Force* (Princeton: Princeton University Press, 2004).

54. See Lewis J. Greenstein, "The Impact of Military Service in World War I on Africans: The Nandi of Kenya," *Journal of Modern African Studies* 16, no. 3 (September 1978): 495–507, and Anne Summers and R. W. Johnson, "World War I Conscription and Social Change in Guinea," *Journal of African History* 19, no. 1 (1978): 33.

55. Stouffer et al., *American Soldier,* 1:449. See also M. Kent Jennings and Gregory B. Markus, "The Effects of Military Service on Political Attitudes," *American Political Science Review* 71, no. 1 (March 1977): 131–47.

56. Suzanne Mettler, *Soldiers to Citizens: The GI Bill and the Making of the Greatest Generation* (Oxford: Oxford University Press, 2005).

57. See Hugh D. Forbes, *Ethnic Conflict: Commerce, Culture, and the Contact Hypothesis* (New Haven: Yale University Press, 1997), and Walter G. Stephan, "Intergroup Relations," in *Handbook of Social Psychology,* 3rd ed., ed. Gardner Lindzey and Elliot Aronson (New York: Random House, 1985), 2:599–658.

58. Walter G. Stephan and Cookie W. Stephan, "Intergroup Anxiety," *Journal of Social Issues* 41, no. 3 (Fall 1985): 157–75.

59. Miles Hewstone and Rupert Brown, "Contact Is Not Enough: An Intergroup Perspective on the 'Contact Hypothesis,'" in *Contact and Conflict in Intergroup Encounters,* ed. Hewstone and Brown (Oxford: Blackwell, 1986), 10–12.

60. In their widely cited article published nearly fifty years after Allport's seminal work, Lee Sigelman and Susan Welch acknowledge this weakness; see their "The Contact Hypothesis Revisited: Black-White Interaction and Positive Racial Attitudes," *Social Forces* 71, no. 3 (March 1993): 781–95. Two studies employing sophisticated statistical techniques have claimed to have established that contact has a significant effect, but both take cross-group friendship as the *independent* variable. As this level of acquaintance greatly exceeds even Allport's standards, these studies cannot be taken as evidence of the hypothesis's validity. See Thomas F. Pettigrew, "Generalized Intergroup Contact Effects on Prejudice," *Personality and Social Psychology Bulletin* 23, no. 2 (February 1997): 173–85, and Daniel A. Powers and Christopher G. Ellison, "Interracial Contact and Black Racial Attitudes: The Contact Hypothesis and Selectivity Bias," *Social Forces* 74, no. 1 (September 1995): 205–26.

61. See Marc Howard Ross, "Culture and Identity in Comparative Political Analysis," in *Comparative Politics: Rationality, Culture, and Structure,* ed. Mark Lichbach and Alan Zuckerman (Cambridge: Cambridge University Press, 1997), and Ronald Jepperson et al., "Norms, Identity, and Culture in National Security," in *The Culture of National Security,* ed. Peter Katzenstein (New York: Columbia University Press, 1996).

62. On phenomenological individualism, see Charles Tilly, "Lullaby, Chorale, or Hurdy-Gurdy Tune?" in *The Rational-Choice Controversy in Historical Sociology,* ed. Roger V. Gould (Chicago: University of Chicago Press, 2001).

63. Benedict Anderson, *Imagined Communities: Reflections on the Origin and Spread of Nationalism* (New York: Verso, 1983).

64. See, among others, Rogers Brubaker, *Citizenship and Nationhood in France and Germany* (Cambridge: Harvard University Press, 1992); and J. M. Barbalet, *Citizenship: Rights, Struggle and Class Inequality* (Milton Keynes, England: Open University Press, 1988).

65. Charles Tilly, "Conclusion: Why Worry about Citizenship?" in *Extending Citizenship, Reconfiguring States,* ed. Michael Hanagan and Tilly (Lanham, Md.: Rowman and Littlefield, 1999), 253.

66. Tilly's view stands in stark contrast to the classic statement of T. H. Marshall, who implied that citizenship smoothly and inexorably broadened from civil to political to social rights. Tilly, "The Emergence of Citizenship in France and Elsewhere," in *Citizenship, Identity, and Social History,* ed. Tilly (New York: Cambridge University Press, 1996), 227; Marshall, *Citizenship and Social Class* (Cambridge: Cambridge University Press, 1950).

67. See Craig Calhoun, "Indirect Relationships and Imagined Communities: Large-Scale Social Integration and the Transformation of Everyday Life," in *Social Theory for a Changing Society,* ed. Pierre Bourdieu and James S. Coleman (Boulder, Colo.: Westview, 1991), 108.

68. Anne Norton, *Reflections on Political Identity* (Baltimore: Johns Hopkins University Press, 1993 [1988]), 54.

69. See Joel S. Migdal, "Mental Maps and Virtual Checkpoints: Struggles to Construct and Maintain State and Social Boundaries," in *Boundaries and Belonging,* ed. Migdal (Cambridge: Cambridge University Press, 2004).

70. See Michael Sandel, "What Money Can't Buy: The Moral Limits of Markets," Tanner Lectures on Human Values, Oxford University, May 1998; Morris Janowitz, *The Reconstruction of Patriotism: Education for Civic Consciousness* (Chicago: University of Chicago Press, 1983); and Moskos, *Call to Civic Service.* For a defense of the all-volunteer force and a general critique of the communitarian stance, see Richard A. Posner, "An Army of the Willing," *New Republic,* 19 May 2003, 27–29.

71. This contrasts to republican *theory,* which prizes freedom from domination for all. See

Philip Pettit, *Republicanism: A Theory of Freedom and Government* (Oxford: Clarendon Press, 1997).

72. Jon Elster, *The Cement of Society* (Cambridge: Cambridge University Press, 1989).

73. For the first, see, among many others, David Laitin, *Identity in Formation: The Russian-Speaking Populations in the Near Abroad* (Ithaca: Cornell University Press, 1998); Jeffrey W. Legro, "Culture and Preferences in the International Cooperation Two-Step," *American Political Science Review* 90, no. 1 (March 1996): 118–37; and Ashutosh Varshney, "Nationalism, Ethnic Conflict, and Rationality," *Perspectives on Politics* 1, no. 1 (March 2003): 85–99. For the second, see, among others, Thomas Schelling, *The Strategy of Conflict* (Cambridge: Harvard University Press, 1960), chaps. 3–4, and Barry R. Weingast, "A Rational Choice Perspective on the Role of Ideas and Shared Beliefs: State Sovereignty and International Cooperation," *Politics and Society* 23, no. 4 (1995): 449–64.

74. For related arguments, see James Johnson, "Symbol and Strategy in Comparative Political Analysis," *APSA-CP* 8, no. 2 (Summer 1997): 6–9, and Jack Snyder, "Anarchy and Culture: Insights from the Anthropology of War," *International Organization* 56, no. 1 (Winter 2002): 7–45.

75. See Consuelo Cruz, "Identity and Persuasion: How Nations Remember Their Pasts and Make Their Futures," *World Politics* 52 (April 2000): 275–312.

76. Lisa Wedeen, "Conceptualizing Culture: Possibilities for Political Science," *American Political Science Review* 96, no. 4 (December 2002): 721.

77. Swidler, "Culture in Action: Symbols and Strategies," *American Sociological Review* 51, no. 2 (April 1986): 273–86.

78. See Robert H. Bates et al., "The Politics of Interpretation: Rationality, Culture, and Transition," *Politics & Society* 26, no. 4 (December 1998): 603–42, esp. 628–29.

Chapter 2. The Power of Military Service

1. See Maury Feld, *The Structure of Violence: Armed Forces as Social Systems* (Beverly Hills, Calif.: Sage, 1977), 141–68; Morris Janowitz, "Military Institutions and Citizenship in Western Societies," *Armed Forces and Society* 2, no. 2 (February 1976): 185–204; Daniel Moran and Arthur Waldron, eds., *The People in Arms: Military Myth and National Mobilization since the French Revolution* (Cambridge: Cambridge University Press, 2003); and Peter Riesenberg, *Citizenship in the Western Tradition* (Chapel Hill: University of North Carolina Press, 1992).

2. The armed forces have often been employed to suppress popular demands for reform and been marked by discriminatory recruitment and promotion practices. They have generally not reflected national demographic patterns. See Richard H. Kohn, "The Social History of the American Soldier: A Review and Prospectus for Research," *American Historical Review* 86, no. 3 (June 1981): 553–67, and Nuria Sales de Bohigas, "Some Opinions on Exemption from Military Service in Nineteenth-Century Europe," *Comparative Studies in Society and History* 10, no. 3 (April 1968): 261–89.

3. See Chris Hedges, *War Is a Force That Gives Us Meaning* (New York: PublicAffairs, 2002), and Gerald F. Linderman, *The World within War: America's Combat Experience in World War II* (Cambridge: Harvard University Press, 1999).

4. William James, "The Moral Equivalent of War," delivered at Stanford University (1906), published in *International Conciliation* 27 (February 1910): 6, 15.

5. Anthony D. Smith, "War and Ethnicity: The Role of Warfare in the Formation, Self-Images, and Cohesion of Ethnic Communities," *Ethnic and Racial Studies* 4, no. 4 (October 1981): 375–97.

6. See George Mosse, *The Nationalization of the Masses: Political Symbolism and Mass Movements in Germany from the Napoleonic Wars through the Third Reich* (Ithaca: Cornell University Press, 1975), and Scott Hughes Myerly, *British Military Spectacle: From the Napoleonic Wars through the Crimea* (Cambridge: Harvard University Press, 1996).

204   NOTES TO PAGES 17–20

7. This link was also initially present in ancient India and Mesopotamia, though it was later suppressed. Max Weber, *General Economic History* (New York: Greenberg, 1927), 321–22. See also Antonio Santosuosso, *Soldiers, Citizens, and the Symbols of War: From Classical Greece to Republican Rome, 500–167 B.C.* (Boulder, Colo.: Westview, 1997).

8. J. G. A. Pocock, *The Machiavellian Moment: Florentine Political Thought and the Atlantic Republican Tradition* (Princeton: Princeton University Press, 1975), 194–218, 535–39.

9. April Carter, "Liberalism and the Obligation to Military Service," *Political Studies* 46 (1998): 69.

10. James Burk, "The Military Obligation of Citizens since Vietnam," *Parameters* 31, no. 2 (Summer 2001): 48–60.

11. Hintze, "Military Organization and the Organization of the State," in *The Historical Essays of Otto Hintze,* ed. Felix Gilbert (New York: Oxford University Press, 1975), 211.

12. Address, 4 July 2002, www.whitehouse.gov/news/releases/2002/07/20020704-3 .html.

13. Isser Woloch, *The French Veteran from the Revolution to the Restoration* (Chapel Hill: University of North Carolina Press, 1979), 316.

14. See Willi Paul Adams, *The First American Constitutions: Republican Ideology and the Making of the State Constitutions in the Revolutionary Era* (Chapel Hill: University of North Carolina Press, 1980), 207–17, and Chilton Williamson, *American Suffrage: From Property to Democracy* (Princeton: Princeton University Press, 1960), 79–82.

15. Eric J. Leed, *No Man's Land: Combat and Identity in World War I* (Cambridge: Cambridge University Press, 1979), 204; Stephen Garton, *The Cost of War: Australians Return* (Melbourne: Oxford University Press, 1996), 95–96.

16. Quoted in Eric Foner, *Reconstruction: America's Unfinished Revolution, 1863–1877* (New York: Harper and Row, 1988), 8–9.

17. Paul R. Brass, *The Politics of India since Independence* (Cambridge: Cambridge University Press, 1990), 171.

18. Brian Loveman, *For La Patria: Politics and the Armed Forces in Latin America* (Wilmington, Del.: SR Books, 1999), 51. See also Charles J. Kolinski, *Independence or Death! The Story of the Paraguayan War* (Gainesville: University of Florida Press, 1965), 49–51, 192–96.

19. Kevin O'Brien has identified a similar form of contention, but he does not explore systematically either the dynamics or conditions of sustainable rhetorical contestation. O'Brien, "Rightful Resistance," *World Politics* 49, no. 1 (October 1996): 31–55.

20. John Bagot Glubb, quoted in Joseph A. Massad, *Colonial Effects: The Making of National Identity in Jordan* (New York: Columbia University Press, 2001), 205.

21. On these terms, see Hugh Heclo, *Modern Social Politics in Sweden and Britain: From Relief to Income Maintenance* (New Haven: Yale University Press, 1974).

22. See the various works cited in chapter 1, note 73.

23. See Jean L. Cohen, "Strategy or Identity: New Theoretical Paradigms and Contemporary Social Movements," *Social Research* 52 (1985): 663–716, and Craig Calhoun, "The Problem of Identity in Collective Action," in *Macro-Micro Linkages in Sociology,* ed. Joan Huber (Newbury Park, Calif.: Sage, 1991).

24. See Murray Edelman, *The Symbolic Uses of Politics* (Urbana: University of Illinois Press, 1964), and Edelman, *Politics as Symbolic Action* (New York: Academic Press, 1971). On framing and collective mobilization, see David A. Snow et al., "Frame Alignment Processes, Micromobilization, and Movement Participation," *American Sociological Review* 51, no. 4 (August 1986): 464–81, and Snow and Robert D. Benford, "Ideology, Frame Resonance, and Participant Mobilization," *International Social Movement Research* 1 (1988): 197–217. Jack Snyder also focuses on elite mythmaking, but he pays little attention to rhetorical competition and its implications. See Snyder, *Myths of Empire: Domestic Politics and International Ambition* (Ithaca: Cornell University Press, 1991), and Snyder, *From Voting to Violence: Democratization and Nationalist Conflict* (New York: W. W. Norton, 2000).

25. Michel Foucault, "The Order of Discourse," in *Language and Politics*, ed. Michael J. Shapiro (New York: New York University Press, 1984), 124.
26. See Robin T. Lakoff, *The Language War* (Berkeley: University of California Press, 2000).
27. William A. Gamson and Andre Modigliani, "The Changing Culture of Collective Action," in *Research in Political Sociology*, vol. 3, ed. Richard D. Braungart (Greenwich, Conn.: JAI, 1987), 143. For other definitions, see Robert D. Benford and David A. Snow, "Framing Processes and Social Movements: An Overview and Assessment," *Annual Review of Sociology* 26 (2000): 614.
28. Subcomandante Insurgente Marcos, "The Word and the Silence," in *Our Word Is Our Weapon: Selected Writings*, ed. Juana Ponce de Léon (New York: Seven Stories Press, 2001), 84.
29. See Hendrik Hartog, "The Constitution of Aspiration and 'The Rights That Belong to Us All,'" *Journal of American History* 74, no. 3 (December 1987): 1014–15.
30. Samantha Power, "To Suffer by Comparison?" *Daedalus* 128, no. 2 (Spring 1999): 31–66.
31. As even E. H. Carr, the preeminent realist, acknowledged, "The necessity, recognized by all politicians, both in domestic and in international affairs, for cloaking interests in a guise of moral principles is in itself a symptom of the inadequacy of realism." Carr, *The Twenty Years' Crisis, 1919–1939: An Introduction to the Study of International Relations*, 2nd ed. (London: Macmillan, 1951 [1939]), 92.
32. See James D. Fearon, "Domestic Political Audiences and the Escalation of International Disputes," *American Political Science Review* 88 (1994): 577–92, and Anne Sartori, "The Might of the Pen: A Reputation Theory of Communication in International Disputes," *International Organization* 56, no. 1 (Winter 2002): 123–51.
33. For the seminal work on prospect theory, see Daniel Kahneman and Amos Tversky, "Prospect Theory: An Analysis of Decision under Risk," *Econometrica* 47 (1979): 263–91.
34. James N. Druckman, "The Implications of Framing Effects for Citizen Competence," *Political Behavior* 23, no. 3 (2001): 225–56.
35. See James N. Druckman, "Political Preference Formation: Competition, Deliberation, and the (Ir)relevance of Framing Effects," *American Political Science Review* 98, no. 4 (2004): 671–86, and Paul M. Sniderman and Sean M. Theriault, "The Structure of Political Argument and the Logic of Issue Framing," in *Studies in Public Opinion*, ed. Willem E. Saris and Paul M. Sniderman (Princeton: Princeton University Press, 2004).
36. On the speaker's credibility, see Arthur Lupia, "Who Can Persuade Whom? Implications from the Nexus of Psychology and Rational Choice Theory," in *Thinking about Political Psychology*, ed. James H. Kuklinski (Cambridge: Cambridge University Press, 2002).
37. "Normative claims," Martha Finnemore avers, "become powerful and prevail by being persuasive"; Finnemore, *National Interests in International Society* (Ithaca: Cornell University Press, 1996), 141. For similar assessments, see Rodger A. Payne, "Persuasion, Frames and Norm Construction," *European Journal of International Relations* 7, no. 1 (2001): 37–61, and Alastair Iain Johnston, "Treating International Institutions as Social Environments," *International Studies Quarterly* 45, no. 3 (2001): 487–515.
38. Martha Finnemore and Kathryn Sikkink, "International Norm Dynamics and Political Change," *International Organization* 52, no. 4 (Autumn 1998): 914.
39. See, among others, Jeffrey Checkel, "Why Comply? Social Learning and European Identity Change," *International Organization* 55, no. 3 (2001): 553–88; Neta Crawford, *Argument and Change in World Politics: Ethics, Decolonization, and Humanitarian Intervention* (Cambridge: Cambridge University Press, 2001); Finnemore and Sikkink, "International Norm Dynamics"; James M. Jasper, *The Art of Moral Protest: Culture, Biography, and Creativity in Social Movements* (Chicago: University of Chicago Press, 1997), esp. chaps. 12–13; Margaret E. Keck and Kathryn Sikkink, *Activists beyond Borders: Advocacy*

Networks in International Politics (Ithaca: Cornell University Press, 1998); Thomas Risse et al., eds., *The Power of Human Rights* (Cambridge: Cambridge University Press, 1999); and Risse, "'Let's Argue!' Communicative Action in World Politics," *International Organization* 54, no. 1 (Winter 2000): 1–39.

40. See Checkel, "Why Comply?"; Checkel, "'Going Native' in Europe? Theorizing Social Interaction in European Institutions," *Comparative Political Studies* 36, nos. 1–2 (February–March 2003): 209–31; Crawford, *Argument and Change*, 26–27; and Johnston, "Treating International Institutions."

41. See Richard E. Petty and Duane T. Wegener, "Attitude Change: Multiple Roles for Persuasion Variables," in *The Handbook of Social Psychology*, 4th ed., ed. Daniel T. Gilbert et al. (Boston: McGraw-Hill, 1998), and Wendy Wood, "Attitude Change: Persuasion and Social Influence," *Annual Review of Psychology* 51 (2000): 539–70. For a critique, see Michael Billig, *Arguing and Thinking: A Rhetorical Approach to Social Psychology*, 2nd ed. (Cambridge: Cambridge University Press, 1996), 93–102.

42. See Ian Johnstone, "Security Council Deliberations: The Power of the Better Argument," *European Journal of International Law* 14, no. 3 (2003): 437–80; Jennifer Mitzen, "Reading Habermas in Anarchy: Multilateral Diplomacy and Global Public Spheres," *American Political Science Review* 99, no. 3 (August 2005): 401–17; Harald Müller, "International Relations as Communicative Action," in *Constructing International Relations: The Next Generation*, ed. Karin M. Fierke and Knud Erik Jorgensen (Armonk, N.Y.: M. E. Sharpe, 2001); and Risse, "'Let's Argue!'"

43. This all-too-brief summary of Habermasian discourse ethics may or may not be "correct," but it is how liberal constructivists read his work and is close to mainstream ways of understanding Habermas's work. See, for example, Mary Dietz, "Working in Half-Truth: Habermas, Machiavelli, and the Milieu Proper to Politics," in her *Turning Operations: Feminism, Arendt, and Politics* (London: Routledge, 1995), esp. 145–48.

44. Risse seeks to square Habermas with Foucault by suggesting that "argumentative rationality" may nonetheless be embraced *"within* those structural boundaries of a discourse" ("'Let's Argue!'" 18). Such a reconciliation is possible, however, only if one ignores the normative implications of these theorists' work. Theorists of deliberative democracy, such as Habermas, implicitly treat consensus (mutual understanding) as the ideal, but those inspired by Foucault conclude that any conception of politics that fails to recognize and even celebrate persistent contestation is unrealistic and ultimately apolitical. Habermas recognized the deep incompatibilities between their political visions; see Habermas, "The Critique of Reason as an Unmasking of the Human Sciences: Michel Foucault," in *Critique and Power: Recasting the Foucault/Habermas Debate*, ed. Michael Kelly (Cambridge: MIT Press, 1994). See also Seyla Benhabib, ed., *Democracy and Difference: Contesting the Boundaries of the Political* (Princeton: Princeton University Press, 1996), esp. the essays by Benhabib, Habermas, Mansbridge, and Mouffe; Kelly, ed., *Critique and Power*, esp. the essays by Fraser, McCarthy, and Kelly; and Nancy S. Love, "Foucault and Habermas on Discourse and Democracy," *Polity* 22, no. 2 (Winter 1989): 279–85.

45. Dietz, "Working in Half-Truth," 152.

46. Alice H. Eagly and Shelly Chaiken, *The Psychology of Attitudes* (Fort Worth, Texas: Harcourt Brace Jovanovich, 1993), 559–625.

47. See Susan E. Fiske and Shelley E. Taylor, *Social Cognition* (Reading, Mass.: Addison-Wesley, 1984), 171–78, and Richard E. Nisbett and Lee Ross, *Human Inference: Strategies and Shortcomings of Social Judgment* (Englewood Cliffs, N.J.: Prentice-Hall, 1980).

48. Plato, *The Republic*, 487b, as cited in Billig, *Arguing and Thinking*, 40.

49. Definitions of coercion typically focus on the use of force and the manipulation of material costs and benefits, but they too tightly link the instrument of influence with the nature of influence. The defining feature of coercion is nonconsensual compliance: "The basic intuitive notion of coercion refers to a high degree of constraint on the alternative

courses of action available to . . . the target of an influence attempt." David Baldwin, *Economic Statecraft* (Princeton: Princeton University Press, 1985), 38.

50. Crawford, *Argument and Change,* 28–33, 104; Richard M. Price, "Reversing the Gun Sights: Transnational Civil Society Targets Land Mines," *International Organization* 52, no. 3 (1998): 613–44; Price, "Transnational Civil Society and Advocacy in World Politics," *World Politics* 55 (July 2003): 579–606, at 590; and Thomas Risse and Kathryn Sikkink, "The Socialization of International Human Rights Norms into Domestic Practices: Introduction," in *Power of Human Rights,* ed. Risse et al., 1–38.

51. Risse suggests that this is consistent with Habermasian communicative action ("'Let's Argue!'" 23), but rhetorical coercion does not depend on actors' openness to new ideas or on their having been persuaded by the "force of the better argument." The result of such entrapment would not be "reasoned agreement" in the Habermasian sense, but rather "a conformity that is at once rather shallow and normatively suspect," as James Johnson puts it. Johnson, "Arguing for Deliberation: Some Skeptical Considerations," in *Deliberative Democracy,* ed. Jon Elster (Cambridge: Cambridge University Press, 1998), 172–73.

52. See William Riker, *The Art of Political Manipulation* (New Haven: Yale University Press, 1986), and Riker, *The Strategy of Rhetoric: Campaigning for the American Constitution* (New Haven: Yale University Press, 1996).

53. See Frank Schimmelfenig, "The Community Trap: Liberal Norms, Rhetorical Action, and the Eastern Enlargement of the European Union," *International Organization* 55, no. 1 (Winter 2001): 47–80, and Schimmelfenig, *The EU, NATO and the Integration of Europe: Rules and Rhetoric* (Cambridge: Cambridge University Press, 2004).

54. See, respectively, Michael N. Barnett, *Dialogues in Arab Politics: Negotiations in Regional Order* (New York: Columbia University Press, 1998), esp. 43–49; Stacie E. Goddard, "Uncommon Ground: Indivisible Territory and the Politics of Legitimacy," *International Organization* 60, no. 1 (January 2006: 35–68); Janice Bially Mattern, *Ordering International Politics: Identity, Crisis, and Representational Force* (New York: Routledge, 2005); and K. M. Fierke and Antje Wiener, "Constructing Institutional Interests: EU and NATO Enlargement," *Journal of European Public Policy* 6, no. 5 (1999): 721–42.

55. Chaim Perelman, *The Realm of Rhetoric* (Notre Dame, Ind.: University of Notre Dame Press, 1982).

56. Doug McAdam, "The Framing Function of Movement Tactics: Strategic Dramaturgy in the American Civil Rights Movement," in *Comparative Perspectives on Social Movements,* ed. McAdam et al. (Cambridge: Cambridge University Press, 1996).

57. Jon Elster, "Strategic Uses of Argument," in *Barriers to Conflict Resolution,* ed. Kenneth J. Arrow et al. (New York: W. W. Norton, 1995), 244–52, at 250.

58. John Shotter calls these forms *topoi,* or rhetorical commonplaces. See Shotter, *Cultural Politics of Everyday Life: Social Construction, Rhetoric, and Knowing of the Third Kind* (Toronto: University of Toronto Press, 1993). See also Patrick T. Jackson, *Civilizing the Enemy: German Reconstruction and the Invention of the West* (Ann Arbor: University of Michigan Press, 2006).

59. J. David Greenstone, *The Lincoln Persuasion: Remaking American Liberalism* (Princeton: Princeton University Press, 1993); Lyn Spillman, "Culture, Social Structures, and Discursive Fields," *Current Perspectives in Social Theory* 15 (1995): 129–54, at 140. See also Marc W. Steinberg, *Fighting Words: Working-Class Formation, Collective Action, and Discourse in Early Nineteenth-Century England* (Ithaca: Cornell University Press, 1999), esp. 19–20, 236–37.

60. See David I. Kertzer, *Ritual, Politics, and Power* (New Haven: Yale University Press, 1981), and James C. Scott, *Weapons of the Weak: Everyday Forms of Peasant Resistance* (New Haven: Yale University Press, 1985).

61. See Murray Edelman, *Constructing the Political Spectacle* (Chicago: University of Chicago Press, 1988), and W. Lance Bennett, "The Paradox of Public Discourse: A

Framework for the Analysis of Political Accounts," *Journal of Politics* 42, no. 3 (August 1980): 792–817.

62. Bernard Bailyn, *The Ideological Origins of the American Revolution* (Cambridge: Harvard University Press, 1967), 351.

63. On "grafting," see Price, "Reversing the Gun Sights," 627–31. On "fit" and "resonance," see Benford and Snow, "Framing Processes," 623–25, 629; Crawford, *Argument and Change*, 36–37, 113–15; Price, "Transnational Civil Society," 584, 596; and Sidney Tarrow, *Power in Movement: Social Movements and Contentious Politics*, 2nd ed. (New York: Cambridge University Press, 1998), 108–22.

64. Lisa Wedeen, *Ambiguities of Domination: Politics, Rhetoric, and Symbols in Contemporary Syria* (Chicago: University of Chicago Press, 1999).

65. K. M. Fierke, *Changing Games, Changing Strategies: Critical Investigations in Security* (Manchester: Manchester University Press, 1998).

66. Billig, *Arguing and Thinking*, 246.

67. This was Wittgenstein's position in the *Philosophical Investigations*. See Hans Sluga, "Ludwig Wittgenstein: Life and Work: An Introduction," in *The Cambridge Companion to Wittgenstein*, ed. Sluga and David G. Stern (Cambridge: Cambridge University Press, 1996).

68. Talk among political contestants is more diverse and less disciplined than that among attorneys, but Stanley Fish's concept of an "interpretive community" is nonetheless relevant—as long as the political community shares some norms regarding the boundaries of legitimate speech. Fish's emphasis on *social sustainability* contrasts with Ronald Dworkin's focus on the *fit* between interpretation and principles. See Fish, *Doing What Comes Naturally: Change, Rhetoric, and the Practice of Theory in Literary and Legal Studies* (Durham: Duke University Press, 1989), and Dworkin, *Law's Empire* (Cambridge: Harvard University Press, 1986).

69. Perelman, *Realm of Rhetoric*, 16. On the importance of audiences, see also R. Keith Sawyer, *Creating Conversations: Improvisation in Everyday Discourse* (Cresskill, N.J.: Hampton Press, 2001), chap. 3.

70. Stanley Fish, "Working on the Chain Gang: Interpretation in Law and Literature," *Texas Law Review* 60 (1982): 562.

71. This choice may be conscious, but it is equally possible that it is not. As Wittgenstein put it, "'To follow a rule' is a practice. And to *think* one is following a rule is not the same as following it." Frames conceivable to an outside observer may never even occur to actors embedded within a particular context. Unfortunately, it is often difficult to know, given available data, whether an actor failed to advance a given frame because it never occurred to him or because he deemed it too costly. Quoted in Joachim Schulte, *Wittgenstein: An Introduction* (Albany: SUNY Press, 1992), 119, and generally 115–19.

72. Speakers are, therefore, subject to what Jon Elster calls a "consistency constraint." Naturally, leaders prefer vague rhetorical formulations with which few subsequent statements could be judged inconsistent. But vague assurances will often fail to satisfy tenacious claimants, and leaders may eventually feel compelled to issue commitments that are more firm than they would otherwise like. Thanks to David Edelstein for discussion on this point. See Elster, "Deliberation and Constitution Making," in *Deliberative Democracy*, ed. Elster, 104.

73. Billig, *Arguing and Thinking*, 137. See also Fierke, *Changing Games*, 115, and Anatol Rapaport, *Fights, Games, and Debates* (Ann Arbor: University of Michigan Press, 1960), 291. For examples, see, among others, Matthew Evangelista, "Norms, Heresthetics, and the End of the Cold War," *Journal of Cold War Studies* 3, no. 1 (winter 2001): 17–21; Price, "Reversing the Gun Sights," 631–37; and Riker, *Art of Political Manipulation*, 40–42.

74. Stephen Majeski and David Sylvan, "How Foreign Policy Recommendations Are Put Together: A Computational Model with Empirical Applications," *International Interactions* 25, no. 4 (1999): 306.

75. Stephen Toulmin, *The Uses of Argument* (Cambridge: Cambridge University Press, 1958).
76. These four do not exhaust the possibilities, but they appear to be the most widely accepted and fundamental. See Kathleen M. McGraw, "Managing Blame: An Experimental Test of the Effects of Political Accounts," *American Political Science Review* 85, no. 4 (December 1991): 1135–36, 1153–54.
77. The social movement literature reflects the difficulty of generalizing about when frames "resonate." Such efforts have either proved circular (we know a frame resonated because it "worked"), begged the question (resonant frames are "empirically credible" or display "narrative fidelity"), or invoked characteristics of the speaker (credibility). Thus I focus on the rhetorical possibilities available in concrete cases of contestation.
78. I am indebted to Bob Jervis for suggesting this point.
79. As William Gamson puts it, "There is no theme without a countertheme." See Gamson, "Political Discourse and Collective Action," *International Social Movement Research* 1 (1988): 221. See also Billig, *Arguing and Thinking,* 123–24, and J. G. A. Pocock, *Politics, Language, and Time: Essays on Political Thought and History* (New York: Atheneum, 1971), chap. 1.
80. Christopher Caldwell, "With Gay Marriage, La Belle France Turns Conservative," *New York Times,* 13 June 2004.
81. Richard A. Primus, *The American Language of Rights* (Cambridge: Cambridge University Press, 1999), 2.
82. Hartog, "Constitution of Aspiration," 1027–28.
83. R. Keith Sawyer, *Improvised Dialogues: Emergence and Creativity in Conversation* (Westport, Conn.: Ablex, 2003).
84. Albert O. Hirschman, *The Rhetoric of Reaction: Perversity, Futility, Jeopardy* (Cambridge: Harvard University Press, 1991), x.
85. See Billig, *Arguing and Thinking;* John J. Gumperz, *Discourse Strategies* (Cambridge: Cambridge University Press, 1982); Perelman, *Realm of Rhetoric;* Sawyer, *Creating Conversations;* Shotter, *Cultural Politics of Everyday Life;* and Toulmin, *Uses of Argument.*
86. For the classic statement, see Isaiah Berlin, *Two Concepts of Liberty* (Oxford: Oxford University Press, 1958).
87. See Michael J. Sandel, "The Procedural Republic and the Unencumbered Self," *Political Theory* 12, no. 1 (February 1984): 81–96; Quentin Skinner, "The Republican Ideal of Political Liberty," in *Machiavelli and Republicanism,* ed. Gisela Bock et al. (Cambridge: Cambridge University Press, 1997), 296; and Maurizio Viroli, *Republicanism* (New York: Hill and Wang, 2002), 35–43.
88. For example, as Charles Taylor puts it, "From the liberal democratic point of view, a person has a right to claim equal recognition first and foremost on the basis of his or her universal human identity and potential": *Multiculturalism and "The Politics of Recognition"* (Princeton: Princeton University Press, 1992), 88.
89. Keck and Sikkink, *Activists beyond Borders,* 205.
90. Notwithstanding the dominance of a liberal citizenship *discourse,* individuals may still cling to racist *beliefs.* However, those who *openly* call on racist or ethno-national ideals invite punishment.
91. Philip Pettit, *Republicanism: A Theory of Freedom and Government* (Oxford: Clarendon Press, 1997), 148.
92. Communitarians stress that communities have deep historical roots and are more discovered than created. Republicans, in contrast, are dedicated to civic ideals and thus remain open to the expansion of the civic community. For a seminal communitarian statement, see Michael Sandel, *Democracy's Discontent: America in Search of a Public Philosophy* (Cambridge: Harvard University Press, 1996).
93. For this understanding of republicanism, see Pettit, *Republicanism;* Quentin Skinner, "The Idea of Negative Liberty," in *Philosophy in History,* ed. Richard Rorty et al. (Cambridge: Cambridge University Press, 1984); Skinner, "Republican Ideal"; and Viroli, *Republicanism.*

94. Adrian Oldfield, *Citizenship and Community: Civic Republicanism and the Modern World* (London: Routledge, 1990), 5–8, at 5.

95. See, among others, Feld, *Structure of Violence,* and Pocock, *Machiavellian Moment.*

96. See Charles Tilly, *From Mobilization to Revolution* (Reading, Mass.: Addison-Wesley, 1978). To the extent, however, that the behavior is truly self-sacrificing, it poses a challenge to my argument, which is premised on a minimal rationality assumption. See Tilly, "Do Unto Others," in *Political Altruism?,* ed. Marco Giugni and Florence Passy (Lanham, Md.: Rowman and Littlefield, 2001).

97. Doug McAdam, *Freedom Summer* (New York: Oxford University Press, 1988), 70–71. The example is invoked, but interpreted quite differently, in Tilly, "Do Unto Others."

98. Horowitz, *The Deadly Ethnic Riot* (Berkeley: University of California Press, 2001), 525, 528.

99. This discussion of the trust game draws freely on Andrew Kydd, "Trust, Reassurance, and Cooperation," *International Organization* 54, no. 2 (Spring 2000): 325–57.

100. The language of cooperation and defection is awkward in this case. How one characterizes mobilization presumably depends on one's preferences. This suggests again how inappropriate these terms are for many social scenarios. See Robert Jervis, "Realism, Game Theory, and Cooperation," *World Politics* 40, no. 3 (April 1988): 329–32.

101. Military manpower policy may naturally respond to *minority* signaling as well: a minority that, through its behavior, indicates its willingness to serve and, more important, its loyalty will prove more attractive than a minority that shows little inclination to sacrifice for the polity. This dynamic is worth exploring, but the focus here is on explaining the consequences of military participation policy, not its origins.

102. That such fears of betrayal have typically been unfounded is irrelevant here, since what matters is the policy's *expected* cost, which is a function of the perceived likelihood of betrayal.

103. The size of the minority may also factor into the signal's cost. However, the expected strategic costs of inclusion do not correlate perfectly with size, since the treason of even a handful may prove disastrous.

104. Scholars disagree as to whether military organizations are capable of independent innovation or require civilian intervention. For the traditional view, see Barry R. Posen, *The Sources of Military Doctrine: France, Britain, and Germany between the World Wars* (Ithaca: Cornell University Press, 1984), and Jack Snyder, *The Ideology of the Offensive: Military Decision-Making and the Disasters of 1914* (Ithaca: Cornell University Press, 1984). Even critics, however, generally presume that militaries are biased against fundamental change. See Stephen P. Rosen, *Winning the Next War: Innovation and the Modern Military* (Ithaca: Cornell University Press, 1991), and Kimberly Marten Zisk, *Engaging the Enemy: Organization Theory and Soviet Military Innovation, 1955–1991* (Princeton: Princeton University Press, 1993). Deborah Avant has suggested that armed forces often change of their own accord, but only in ways consistent with their organizational culture; see her *Political Institutions and Military Change: Lessons from Peripheral Wars* (Ithaca: Cornell University Press, 1994).

105. On the primacy of autonomy, see Morton Halperin, with Priscilla Clapp and Arnold Kanter, *Bureaucratic Politics and Foreign Policy* (Washington: Brookings Institution, 1974).

106. Even civilian-led policy reforms may vary in cost. The political costs are relatively low when the military is firmly subject to civilian control, relatively alienated from political life, or not respected. Conversely, when civilian leaders are unusually credible authorities on military matters, imposing reform is easier. The lower these costs, the weaker the corresponding manpower-policy signal.

107. See Charles Tilly, *Coercion, Capital, and European States, AD 990–1992* (Cambridge: Blackwell, 1992), and Michael C. Desch, "War and Strong States, Peace and Weak States?" *International Organization* 50, no. 2 (Spring 1996): 237–68.

108. On the fragility of wartime institutions, see Daniel Kryder, *Divided Arsenal: Race and the American State during World War II* (Cambridge: Cambridge University Press, 2000), 89. On state capacity after war, see Desch, "War and Strong States."

109. This is similar to what Douglas Arnold has called "visibility." See Arnold, *The Logic of Congressional Action* (New Haven: Yale University Press, 1990).

110. James Johnson terms this the problem of "comprehensibility" and argues that game theorists typically assume it away. Johnson, "Is Talk Really Cheap? Prompting Conversation between Critical Theory and Rational Choice," *American Political Science Review* 87, no. 1 (March 1993): 81.

111. Jervis, "Signaling and Perception: Drawing Inferences and Projecting Images," in *Political Psychology*, ed. Kristen R. Monroe (Mahwah, N.J.: Lawrence Erlbaum, 2002), 298, 302.

112. Schelling, *Arms and Influence* (New Haven: Yale University Press, 1966), 148.

113. Baruch Kimmerling, "Patterns of Militarism in Israel," *Archives Européenes de Sociologie* 34 (1993): 196–223. See also Michael Mann, "Roots and Contradictions of Modern Militarism," in his *States, War and Capitalism: Studies in Political Sociology* (Oxford: Basil Blackwell, 1988), 180–83.

114. The essence of militarism does *not* lie in civilian masses and elites aping military dress or in officers maintaining a vise on government and industry. Although the term militarism has frequently been relegated to the social scientific dustbin, it does capture an important sociopolitical condition. See Volker R. Berghahn, *Militarism: The History of an International Debate, 1861–1879* (Leamington Spa, England: Berg, 1981); Asbjorn Eide and Marek Thee, eds., *Problems of Contemporary Militarism* (London: Croom Helm, 1980); and Alfred Vagts, *A History of Militarism: Civilian and Military*, rev. ed. (New York: Free Press, 1959 [1937]).

115. Major war thus may serve as a "focusing event" that heightens the prominence of certain social and political connections. See Paul Pierson, "When Effect Becomes Cause: Policy Feedback and Political Change," *World Politics* 45, no. 4 (July 1993): 619–21.

116. My understanding of "political mobilization" builds on McAdam, Tarrow, and Tilly's definition of "contentious politics" as "episodic, public collective interaction among makers of claims and their objects when (a) at least one government is a claimant, an object of claims, or a party to the claims and (b) the claims would, if realized, affect the interests of at least one of the claimants." I would add that such interaction, to qualify as mobilization, (a) must be sustained in the face of the authorities' or broader societal opposition and (b) must involve not only elites but some broader segment of the mass public in some fashion. Purely elite-centered political activity, even if sustained, or short-lived political activity, even if engaging mass publics, is not treated here as "mobilization." *Dynamics of Contention* (Cambridge: Cambridge University Press, 2001), 5.

117. I have borrowed the term "voice" from Albert Hirschman's classic work. Quiescence is similar to "loyalty" but avoids the implication of allegiance. See Hirschman, *Exit, Voice, and Loyalty* (Cambridge: Harvard University Press, 1970).

118. On the political opportunity structure, see Doug McAdam, *Political Process and the Development of Black Insurgency* (Chicago: University of Chicago Press, 1982).

119. My understanding of "contentious politics" is, therefore, narrower than that of McAdam, Tarrow, and Tilly, who include all claims-making with the exception of regular activities such as voting and associational meetings and of nonpublic claims-making. Nor does my distinction between "conventional" and "contentious" politics map easily onto their distinction between "contained" and "transgressive" contention—insofar as strikes, boycotts, and even violent demonstrations may still be "contained" in their sense of "previously established actors employing well established means of claims making." Yet, despite the value of identifying generalizable mechanisms across all forms of collective public struggle, there is a clear difference between, say, a cam-

paign run through the media and one waged in the streets. See McAdam, Tarrow, and Tilly, *Dynamics of Contention*, 4–9.

120. Peter K. Eisinger, "The Conditions of Protest Behavior in American Cities," *American Political Science Review* 67 (March 1973): 11–28.

121. See James D. Fearon and David D. Laitin, "Explaining Interethnic Cooperation," *American Political Science Review* 90, no. 4 (December 1996): 715–35. On states' multiethnic character, see Walker Connor, "Ethnonationalism in the First World: The Present in Historical Perspective," in *Ethnic Conflict in the Western World*, ed. Milton J. Esman (Ithaca: Cornell University Press, 1977). Thanks to Arman Grigorian for discussion on this point.

122. Suzanne Berger, "Bretons, Basques, Scots, and Other European Nations," *Journal of Interdisciplinary History* 3, no. 1 (Summer 1972): 167–75.

123. See Chaim Kaufmann, "Possible and Impossible Solutions to Ethnic Civil Wars," *International Security* 20, no. 4 (Spring 1996): 136–75.

124. The standard regime distinctions—e.g., democracy vs. autocracy, parliamentary vs. presidential democracy—are not relevant here.

125. Not all "empires" have imposed rigid boundaries between metropole and periphery, however. See Ian Lustick, *Unsettled States, Disputed Lands: Britain and Ireland, France and Algeria, Israel and the West Bank* (Ithaca: Cornell University Press, 1993).

126. See Michael N. Barnett, ed., *Israel in Comparative Perspective: Challenging the Conventional Wisdom* (Albany: SUNY Press, 1996); Rebecca B. Kook, *The Logic of Democratic Exclusion: African Americans in the United States and Palestinian Citizens in Israel* (Lanham, Md.: Rowman and Littlefield, 2003); and Zeev Rosenhek, "New Developments in the Sociology of Palestinian Citizens of Israel: An Analytical Review," *Ethnic and Racial Studies* 21, no. 3 (May 1998): 570–72.

127. Alexander L. George, "Case Studies and Theory Development: The Method of Structured, Focused Comparison," in *Diplomacy: New Approaches in History, Theory, and Policy*, ed. Paul G. Lauren (New York: Free Press, 1979).

128. Charles Tilly, "To Explain Political Processes," *American Journal of Sociology* 100, no. 6 (May 1995): 1602. See also Tilly, "Mechanisms in Political Processes," *Annual Review of Political Science* 4 (2001): 21–41, and Timothy J. McKeown, "Case Studies and the Statistical Worldview," *International Organization* 53, no. 1 (Winter 1999): 184–86.

129. Many thanks to Stacie Goddard for pressing me on this point.

130. McAdam, Tarrow, and Tilly, *Dynamics of Contention*, 23.

131. Quoted in R. A. Schermerhorn, *Comparative Ethnic Relations: A Framework for Theory and Research* (Chicago: University of Chicago Press, 1978 [1970]), 22.

132. See Jon Elster, "Rational Choice History: A Case of Excessive Ambition," *American Political Science Review* 94, no. 3 (September 2000): 685–95.

Part I. Introduction

1. The following case study draws on both primary and secondary sources. Nearly all the cited archival documents and most newspaper articles were written in Hebrew and have been translated by the author. Interviews were conducted in both Hebrew and English, and were transcribed and translated by the author. Transliterations of Hebrew words and names have generally followed the American Library Association–Library of Congress transliteration scheme, except when other spellings are more commonly in use (e.g. Chaim vs. Ḥayyim or Ḥaim [Weizmann], menorah vs. menora). Article, book, and document titles have been translated into English, rather than transliterated, on the assumption that most readers do not know Hebrew. Readers who desire a transliterated title may contact the author.

2. For this reason, Sammy Smooha has referred to Israel as an "ethnic democracy." See

Smooha, "Minority Status in an Ethnic Democracy: The Status of the Arab Minority in Israel," *Ethnic and Racial Studies* 13, no. 3 (July 1990): 389–413, and Smooha, "Ethnic Democracy: Israel as an Archetype," *Israel Studies* 2, no. 2 (Fall 1997): 198–241. For critiques, see As'ad Ghanem et al., "Questioning 'Ethnic Democracy': A Response to Sammy Smooha," *Israel Studies* 3, no. 2 (Fall 1998): 253–67, and Alan Dowty, "Is Israel Democratic? Substance and Semantics in the 'Ethnic Democracy' Debate," *Israel Studies* 4, no. 2 (Fall 1999): 1–15.

3. There is no accepted name for this population group, referred to variously as Arab Israelis, Israeli Arabs, Arab citizens of Israel, Palestinian citizens of Israel, and Palestinians who reside in Israel. These terms are highly charged. Rather than wade into this morass, I employ a range of labels in the following chapters, avoiding those that no longer enjoy any or much currency among the population itself.

4. For the latest figures, see *Statistical Abstract of Israel 2004*, table 2.1, www1.cbs.gov.il/shnaton55/st02_01.pdf.

5. See Nissim Dana, *The Druze in the Middle East: Their Faith, Leadership, Identity and Status* (Brighton, England: Sussex Academic Press, 2003), and Robert Brenton Betts, *The Druse* (New Haven: Yale University Press, 1988).

6. This view is now the consensus in Israel, conservatives' protests notwithstanding. See Peter Berkowitz, "Israel's House Divided," *Weekly Standard*, 12–19 April 2004. For a recent catalog of discrimination, see International Crisis Group, "Identity Crisis: Israel and Its Arab Citizens," ICG Middle East Report No. 25, 4 March 2004.

7. For excellent discussions, see Baruch Kimmerling, *The Invention and Decline of Israeliness: State, Society, and the Military* (Berkeley: University of California Press, 2001), chap. 6, and Gershon Shafir and Yoav Peled, *Being Israeli: The Dynamics of Multiple Citizenship* (Cambridge: Cambridge University Press, 2002).

8. Dan Horowitz and Moshe Lissak, *Trouble in Utopia: The Overburdened Polity of Israel* (Albany: SUNY Press, 1989), 50.

9. For a related observation, see Zeev Rosenhek and Michael Shalev, "The Contradictions of Palestinian Citizenship in Israel: Inclusion and Exclusion in the Israeli Welfare State," in *Citizenship and the State in the Middle East: Approaches and Applications*, ed. Nils A. Butenschon et al. (Syracuse, N.Y.: Syracuse University Press, 2000), 289–90.

10. Ian Lustick, *Arabs in the Jewish State: Israel's Control of a National Minority* (Austin: University of Texas Press, 1980).

11. The many possible counterarguments will be addressed throughout the empirical discussions and then more systematically in the conclusion to part 1.

12. For the sake of simplicity of analysis and exposition, I focus on the three largest Arabic-speaking groups. Other Arab minorities have developed different relationships with the IDF and the state. The tiny Circassian community, for example, has been subject to the draft since 1958. Members of certain Bedouin tribes have regularly been accepted into the IDF as volunteers.

13. For arguments against the presence of militarism in Israel, see Moshe Lissak, "A Militaristic Society, or a Nation in Uniform," in *Security Concerns: Insights from the Israeli Experience*, ed. Daniel Bar-Tal et al. (Stamford, Conn.: JAI Press, 1998), and Yoram Peri, "The Radical Social Scientists and Israeli Militarism," *Israel Studies* 1, no. 2 (Fall 1996): 230–66. For arguments to the contrary, see Eyal Ben-Ari and Edna Lomsky-Feder, eds., *The Military and Militarism in Israeli Society* (Albany: SUNY Press, 1999).

14. Dan Horowitz, "The Israel Defense Forces: A Civilianized Military in a Partially Militarized Society," in *Soldiers, Peasants, and Bureaucrats: Civil-Military Relations in Communist and Modernizing Societies*, ed. Roman Kolkowicz and Andrzej Korbonski (London: Allen and Unwin, 1982), 83.

15. Edna Lomsky-Feder and Eyal Ben-Ari, "From 'The People in Uniform' to 'Different Uniforms for the People': Professionalism, Diversity and the Israel Defence Forces," in *Managing Diversity in the Armed Forces: Experiences from Nine Countries*, ed. Joseph

Soeters and Jan van der Meulen (Tilburg, Netherlands: Tilburg University Press, 1999), 162. See also Baruch Kimmerling, "Patterns of Militarism in Israel," *Archives Européenes de Sociologie* 34 (1993): 196–223; Yagil Levy, *Trial and Error: Israel's Route from War to De-escalation* (Albany: SUNY Press, 1997), 39–48; and Eyal Ben-Ari et al., "Military Socio-logical Research in Israel," in *Military Sociology: The Richness of a Discipline,* ed. Gerhard Kummel and Andreas D. Prufert (Baden-Baden: Nomos, 2000).

16. See the annual reports issued by Sikkuy, the Association for the Advancement of Civic Equality in Israel (www.sikkuy.org.il/English/reports.html).

17. Dominguez, *People as Subject, People as Object: Selfhood and Peoplehood in Contemporary Israel* (Madison: University of Wisconsin Press, 1989), 184–85.

18. However, according to one expert, further declassification may not reveal much, since state operatives in the "Arab sector" preferred to communicate their information ver-bally rather than in written reports. Interview with Gabriel Ben-Dor, University of Ḥaifa (14 June 2000, Ḥaifa).

19. These, however, are suspect sources: memory is often selective, and manipulation of the historical record to preserve one's reputation is quite easy when few documents are available.

Chapter 3. Confronting a Land with People

1. In Hebrew, Sherut Bitaḥon Kelali, and widely known by the acronyms ShaBaK or Shin Bet.

2. Labor Zionism's socialism was subordinate to its nationalist ends. See Anita Shapira, "Socialist Means and Nationalist Aims," *Jerusalem Quarterly* 38 (1986): 14–27, and Zeev Sternhell, *The Founding Myths of Israel: Nationalism, Socialism, and the Making of the Jew-ish State* (Princeton: Princeton University Press, 1998).

3. This description, made famous by Israel Zangwill, meant that Palestine was not as-sociated with any *particular* nation—not that the territory was literally empty. But that is not the way Palestine was popularly imagined by potential Jewish immigrants. See Adam M. Garfinkle, "On the Origin, Meaning, Use, and Abuse of a Phrase," *Middle East Studies* 27 (October 1991): 539–50.

4. Quoted in Benny Morris, *Righteous Victims: A History of the Zionist-Arab Conflict, 1881–1999* (New York: Knopf, 1999), 91, 108. This theme crops up repeatedly in *Righteous Vic-tims,* chaps. 2–4.

5. Quoted in Shabtai Teveth, *Ben-Gurion and the Palestinian Arabs: From Peace to War* (Ox-ford: Oxford University Press, 1985), 70.

6. See Benny Morris, *The Birth of the Palestinian Refugee Problem Revisited* (Cambridge: Cambridge University Press, 2004), 39–64.

7. Quote of David Remez in Teveth, *Ben-Gurion and the Palestinian Arabs,* 70.

8. On Lavon's ideas, see Tom Segev, *1949: The First Israelis* (New York: Henry Holt, 1986), 44–46, and Eyal Kafkafi, *Pinḥas Lavon—Anti-Messiah: A Biography* (in Hebrew) (Tel Aviv: Am Oved, 1998), 88–93. See also Benny Morris, *1948 and After: Israel and the Pales-tinians* (Oxford: Clarendon Press, 1990), 259.

9. The preceding discussion has drawn on Yosef Gorny, *Zionism and the Arabs* (Oxford: Clarendon Press, 1987); Charles S. Liebman and Eliezer Don Yihya, *Civil Religion in Is-rael: Traditional Religion and Political Culture in the Jewish State* (Berkeley: University of California Press, 1983), chap. 2; Ian Lustick, *Arabs in the Jewish State: Israel's Control of a National Minority* (Austin: University of Texas Press, 1980), chap. 2; Morris, *Righteous Victims;* Elie Rekhess, "Initial Israeli Policy Guidelines Towards the Arab Minority, 1948–1949," in *New Perspectives on Israeli History: The Early Years of the State,* ed. Lau-rence J. Silberstein (New York: New York University Press, 1991); and Teveth, *Ben-Gu-rion and the Palestinian Arabs.*

10. Howard Morley Sachar, *A History of Israel: From the Rise of Zionism to Our Time*, 2nd ed. (New York: Knopf, 1996 [1976]), 532.

11. See Zeidan Atashe, *Druze and Jews in Israel—a Shared Destiny?* (Brighton, England: Sussex Academic Press, 1995); Shimon Avivi, "Policy Toward the Druze in Israel and Its Implementation: Consistency and Lapses, 1948–1967" (in Hebrew), PhD diss., University of Ḥaifa, 2002; Gabriel Ben-Dor, *The Druzes in Israel* (Jerusalem: Magnes Press, 1979); Kais Firro, *A History of the Druzes* (Leiden: Brill, 1992), 314–49; Yoav Gelber, "Antecedents of the Jewish-Druze Alliance in Palestine," *Middle Eastern Studies* 28, no. 2 (April 1992): 352–73; Gelber, "Druze and Jews in the War of 1948," *Middle Eastern Studies* 31, no. 2 (April 1995): 229–52; David Koren, *Steadfast Alliance: The Druze Community in Palestine and the Haganah* (in Hebrew) (Tel Aviv: Ministry of Defense, 1991); and Yehoshua Porath, *The Palestinian Arab National Movement*, vol. 2, *From Riots to Rebellion, 1929–1939* (London: Frank Cass, 1977), 271–73.

12. See esp. Kais M. Firro, *The Druzes in the Jewish State* (Leiden: Brill, 1999), and Laila Parsons, *The Druze between Palestine and Israel, 1947–1949* (New York: St. Martin's, 2000).

13. Rafiq Ḥalabi, "Israel's Minority in the Middle," *New York Times Magazine*, 27 December 1981, and Nissim Dana, *The Druze in the Middle East: Their Faith, Leadership, Identity and Status* (Brighton, England: Sussex Academic Press, 2003), 186 n. 13.

14. Naḥmani letter reprinted in Yehuda Azrieli and Jabber Abu Rukun, *A Brotherhood That Passed the Test* (in Hebrew) (New York: World Zionist Federation Publishing House, 1989), 31.

15. Atashe, *Druze and Jews in Israel*, 97–98; Avivi, "Policy Toward the Druze," 73; Firro, *Druzes in the Jewish State*, 45–46; Parsons, *Druze between Palestine and Israel*, 62–68.

16. Avivi, "Policy Toward the Druze," 76–77.

17. See Atashe, *Druze and Jews in Israel*, 100–101, and generally chaps. 3–6, and Jonathan Oppenheimer, "The Druze in Israel as Arabs and Non-Arabs: Manipulation of Categories of Identity in a Non-Civil State," in *Studies in Israeli Ethnicity: After the Ingathering*, ed. Alex Weingrod (New York: Gordon and Breach, 1985), 264–67.

18. Firro, *Druzes in the Jewish State*, chap. 2; Dana, *Druze in the Middle East*, 186 n. 13.

19. Quoted in Gelber, "Druze and Jews," 240, and Firro, *Druzes in the Jewish State*, 67.

20. For Zionist-Druze mythologizing, see Koren, *Steadfast Alliance*.

21. The following draws freely on Gelber, "Antecedents," and Gelber, "Druze and Jews."

22. Morris, *Birth*, 418, 473–79, 484, 508.

23. Quoted in Gelber, "Druze and Jews," 237.

24. The Peel Commission, charged by the British Crown with investigating the roots of Arab-Jewish conflict in Palestine and with proposing solutions, in 1937 recommended ending the mandate and imposing a two-state solution (partition). It called for extensive land exchanges and population transfers to create better defined Jewish and Arab states. Ḥushi's efforts must be understood in this context. The commission's controversial proposals were accepted by the British government but not by many on the ground and ultimately came to naught.

25. On the "transfer plan," see Atashe, *Druze and Jews*, chap. 5; Firro, *History of the Druzes*, 337–49; Gelber, "Antecedents," 360–66; and Parsons, *Druze between Palestine and Israel*, 32–38, 44–49.

26. Morris, *Righteous Victims*, 146–54.

27. Morris, *Birth*, 19, 26, and, generally, 17–28.

28. Ibid., 90–98, quote at 99.

29. Ibid., 415–23, 473–92, and Morris, *1948 and After*, 175.

30. Morris, *Birth*, chap. 8.

31. For the authoritative account to date, see Morris, ibid.

32. Morris, *1948 and After*, 187.

33. Avivi, "Policy Toward the Druze," 172–78.

34. Israel's Declaration of Independence, reprinted in Bernard Reich, ed., *Arab-Israeli Conflict and Conciliation: A Documentary History* (Westport, Conn.: Praeger, 1995), 76–78.

35. Like Britain, Israel does not have a written constitution. Deadlock on a constitution in the first Knesset led to the passage over time of a series of "Basic Laws" whose legal status is not entirely clear. Although the Knesset did approve Basic Law: Human Dignity and Liberty in 1992, three other human-rights related Basic Laws have been stalled in committee since 1994. On the Basic Laws, see http://www.knesset.gov.il/description/eng/eng_mimshal_yesod1.htm. See also Philippa Strum, "The Road Not Taken: Constitutional Non-Decision Making in 1948–1950 and Its Impact on Civil Liberties in the Israeli Political Culture," in *Israel: The First Decade of Independence*, ed. S. Ilan Troen and Noah Lucas (Albany: SUNY Press, 1995).

36. Rekhess, "Initial Israeli Policy Guidelines," 103–23, and Ilan Pappé, "An Uneasy Coexistence: Arabs and Jews in the First Decade of Statehood," in *Israel: The First Decade of Independence*, ed. Troen and Lucas.

37. Quoted in Eyal Kafkafi, "Segregation or Integration of the Israeli Arabs: Two Concepts in Mapai," *International Journal of Middle East Studies* 30 (1998): 353.

38. For examples of such ambivalence, see Department of Minorities, "Report of the Department, March 1955," 17 April 1955, SA IM C2213/12; Reuven Barakat to Yoḥanan Ratner, 17 January 1956, SA FM 2401/20; and transcript, Meeting of the Committee on Arab Affairs, Mapai, 17 March 1960, AHA 1/5/7.

39. Even today, some conservatives point to such advances as evidence that Israel's Arab citizens do not suffer discrimination. See Efraim Karsh, "Israel's Arabs v. Israel," *Commentary* 116, no. 5 (December 2003): 21–27.

40. For critical reviews of Israel's education policy, see Sami Khalil Mar'i, *Arab Education in Israel* (Syracuse, N.Y.: Syracuse University Press, 1978), and Majid al-Haj, *Education, Empowerment, and Control: The Case of the Arabs in Israel* (Albany: SUNY Press, 1995).

41. For a well-drawn critique, however, of Israeli policy toward Arab agriculture, see Simḥa Flapan, "Integrating the Arab Village," *New Outlook* 5, no. 3 (1962): 22–30; Flapan, "Planning for the Arab Village," *New Outlook* 6, no. 8 (1963): 23–31; and Flapan, "Planning Arab Agriculture," *New Outlook* 6, no. 10 (1963): 65–73.

42. See Tamar Eshel, "Statement under the Right of Reply," Third Committee, United Nations, 11 October 1960, SA FM 3759/8; State of Israel, *The Arabs in Israel* (Tel Aviv: Government of Israel, 1955); and Rekhess, "Initial Israeli Policy Guidelines," 106–8.

43. Jacob M. Landau, *The Arabs in Israel: A Political Study* (London: Oxford University Press, 1969), chap. 5.

44. These Hebrew acronyms will be employed throughout the rest of the book:

Mapai—Mifleget Po'alei Yisrael (the Workers' Party of Israel)· the forerunner of today's Labor Party.

Mapam—Mifleget Po'alim Me'uḥedet (United Workers' Party): often in Mapai's ruling coalition; an ideological (and to some extent, organizational) ancestor of today's Meretz-Yaḥad party.

Maki—Mifleget Kommunistit Yisraelit (Communist Party of Israel): had a largely Jewish leadership but a mostly Arab electoral base; was considered beyond the pale by Mapai; fractured in 1965, with the mantle of Arab nationalism falling to the more heavily Arab Rakaḥ (Reshima Kommunistit Ḥadasha—New Communist List).

45. On the mechanisms by which Arabs came to be construed as a "dangerous population," see Adriana Kemp's essay of that title in *Boundaries and Belonging*, ed. Joel S. Migdal (Cambridge: Cambridge University Press, 2004).

46. Ben-Gurion to Yizhar, 12 February 1962, SA PM C 6304/1086.

47. Quoted in Yair Baumel, "The Military Administration and the Process of Its Dissolution, 1958–1968" (in Hebrew), *Mizraḥ He-Ḥadash* 43 (2002): 147; quoted in David Grossman, *Sleeping on a Wire: Conversations with Palestinians in Israel* (New York: Farrar, Straus

and Giroux, 1993), 307. For other examples, see Don Peretz, *Israel and the Palestine Arabs* (Washington, D.C.: Middle East Institute, 1958), and Segev, *1949*, 46–47.

48. *Haaretz*, 4 April 1961, quoted in Sabri Jiryis, *The Arabs in Israel* (New York: Monthly Review Press, 1976), 139.

49. During the 1956 war, Israel apparently considered diverting valuable military personnel to Arab-populated areas and relocating Arab citizens from sensitive regions. Interview with Uri Lubrani, adviser to the prime minister for Arab affairs, 1957–61 (20 June 2000, Tel Aviv).

50. See Decision 611, 4 August 1959, SA PM C 5434/1402; "Principal Points That Require the Maintenance of the Military Administration," undated, AHA 1/5/9, and Ben-Gurion to Cabinet, 25 March 1953, SA PM C 5434/1402.

51. On the obsession with Maki, see "Recommendations for Dealing with the Arab Minority in Israel," undated [1962?], pp. 6–10, AHA 1/5/9; on interventions in the politics of Kfar Yasif, whose local council had a Communist majority, see SA C2213/11 and 2213/12, SA FM 2401/19B, SA PM C5592/4669, SA MI 2214/4. On GSS activities targeted at *all* rivals to Mapai, see Ian Black and Benny Morris, *Israel's Secret Wars: The Untold History of Israeli Intelligence* (London: Hamish Hamilton, 1991), 149–53.

52. See "The Future of Arab Policy," 2 July 1962, SA FM 3413/3, and Yisrael Gefen, "The Future of the Arab Minority—An Invitation for Discussion," 19 July 1962, SA FM 3413/3.

53. D. Carmon, "Exploitation of the Arab Minority in Israel by the Arab States for Military Operations," 4 April 1962, SA FM 3413/3. However, in 1956 a government-appointed panel reported that "there is no doubt that the Arab states [will] count on local support from Israel Arabs when the proper time comes. . . . Even today part of the Arab population in Israel maintains contact with the enemy, though this contact seldom takes the form of obvious sabotage." See Yohanan Ratner, Daniel Auster, and Ya'akov Solomon, "Report of the Committee for Examination of the Affairs of the Military Administration," 24 February 1956, SA FM 2401/20, and "Supplement: Military Government in Israel," undated (presumably same date), SA PM C 5434/1402.

54. See "Discussion on the MA," undated [1962], SA PM C 6337; "The Military Administration—Points That Require Its Continuation," undated [after 1959], SA PM C 6304/1086; "Recommendations for Dealing with the Arab Minority in Israel," undated [1962?], pp. 17–18, AHA 1/5/9. See also Baumel, "Military Administration."

55. For a good review, see Sara Osatsky-Lazar, "The Military Administration as a Control Mechanism over the Arab Citizens: The First Decade, 1948–1958" (in Hebrew), *Mizrah He-Hadash* 43 (2002): 103–32. On penetration by the GSS, see al-Haj, *Education, Empowerment, and Control,* 161–68; interviews with Amos Yanai, former GSS operative, 1949–80 (29 June 2000, Haifa), and Tsvi Inbar, former MA official (20 June 2000, Jerusalem).

56. Ben-Gurion also regularly argued that the MA was essential for deterring hostile Arab regimes; dissolving the MA, he maintained, would signal weakness to Israel's enemies and could occur only after larger changes in the Arab-Israeli conflict. See Baumel, "Military Administration."

57. Israel Press Comment, "A New Approach to Arabs in Israel," *New Outlook* 1, no. 12 (July–August 1958): 46–47, and Nissim Tokatli to Abba Hushi, "Issues That Demand Explanation in Order of Importance," undated [1960?], AHA 1/5/9.

58. See Zeev Schiff, "The Military Administration on the Scales," *New Outlook* 2, no. 9 (June 1959): 21; Seth S. King, "Arabs in Israel Still a Problem," *New York Times,* 20 June 1957; and Ratner, Auster, and Solomon, "Report of the Committee," 11.

59. Quoted in Gabriel Sheffer, *Moshe Sharett: Biography of a Political Moderate* (Oxford: Clarendon Press, 1996), 937. On criticism of the MA, see Baumel, "Military Administration."

60. Quoted in Schiff, "Military Administration," 24.

61. Interview with Shmuel Toledano, adviser to the prime minister for Arab affairs, 1965–77 (26 May 2000, Jerusalem).
62. This was the typical, and correct, charge launched against Mapai by other parties. See "Security Restrictions Relaxed," *New Outlook* 1, no. 2 (August 1957): 35–38; "A New Approach to Arabs in Israel," *New Outlook* 1, no. 12 (July–August 1958): 45–48.
63. Maki and even Mapam Knesset members regularly complained that they had been denied entry to MA areas. SA PM C5434/1402.
64. For such dissent, including from within Mapai, see Osatsky-Lazar, "Military Administration," 115–19.
65. For overviews, see Yitzḥak Oded, "Land Losses among Israel's Arab Villagers," *New Outlook* 7, no. 7 (September 1964): 10–25, and David Kretzmer, *The Legal Status of Arabs in Israel* (Boulder, Colo.: Westview, 1988). For more fine-grained analysis, see Geremy Forman and Alexandre (Sandy) Kedar, "From Arab Lands to 'Israel Lands': The Legal Dispossession of the Palestinians Displaced by Israel in the Wake of 1948," *Society and Space* 22, no. 6 (December 2004): 809–30, and Kedar, "The Jewish State and the Arab Possessor: 1948–1967," in *The History of Law in a Multicultural Society: Israel, 1917–1967*, ed. Ron Harris et al. (Aldershot, England: Ashgate/Dartmouth, 2002).
66. There is no agreement on precisely how much land Arabs/Palestinians owned before the outbreak of war in 1948: figures range from over seven million to over twenty-two million dunams. See Sami Halawi, *Palestinian Rights and Losses in 1948: A Comprehensive Study* (London: Saqi Books, 1988), 89–114, and Alexandre (Sandy) Kedar, "The Legal Transformation of Ethnic Geography: Israeli Law and the Palestinian Landholder, 1948–1967," *New York University Journal of International Law and Politics* 33, no. 4 (September 2001), 945–49.
67. An ignored recommendation from an Interior Ministry official clarifies the existing policy: "It seems to me that we must change our policy toward the Druze and Christians and convert them into trustworthy partners. In this manner, we can fill the gap in Jewish settlement and establish a counterweight to the Muslim majority." O. Kreen to Y. Shani, "Judaization of the Galilee," 19 December 1954, IDFA 70/72/649.
68. On land seizures among the Druze, see H. Levital to Director, Village Division, Guardian for Absentee Properties, 25 June 1951, "Abandoned Lands in Kfar Kisra," IDFA 66/263/324; 1952 correspondence between the residents of Kisra and the military governor, IDFA 66/263/197, 66/263/656; a public appeal by the residents of Peki'in, AHA 6/102A; and 1961 correspondence on a conflict with Bet Jan, SA PM C 6405. For similar conclusions, see Firro, *Druzes in the Jewish State*, 128–41, and Avivi, "Policy Toward the Druze," 181–222.
69. See Ghazi Falaḥ, "Israeli 'Judaization' Policy in Galilee and Its Impact on Local Arab Urbanization," *Political Geography Quarterly* 8, no. 3 (July 1989): 229–53, and Arnon Soffer, "The Changing Situation of Majority and Minority and Its Spatial Expression: The Case of the Arab Minority in Israel," in *Pluralism and Political Geography: People, Territory, and State*, ed. Nurit Kliot and Stanley Waterman (New York: St. Martin's, 1983).
70. Yuval Ne'eman, "The Problem of the Development of the Galilee," 24 December 1954, IDFA 70/72/649. See also A. Harsina to Shmuel Divon, "Judaization of the Galilee," 2 December 1955, IDFA 70/72/649.
71. Kreen to Shani, "Judaization of the Galilee."
72. Address to World Zionist Congress, quoted in Don Peretz, "Early State Policy Towards the Arab Population, 1948–1955," in *New Perspectives on Israeli History*, ed. Silberstein, 86.
73. Charles S. Kamen, "After the Catastrophe I: The Arabs in Israel, 1948–51," *Middle Eastern Studies* 23, no. 4 (October 1987): 482–94.
74. Sharett to Ben-Gurion, 30 August 1951; Ben-Gurion to Sharett, 30 August 1951; Yosef Weitz, "Report: 'Operation Yoḥanan,'" 19 March 1952; Sharett to Ben-Gurion, 21 October 1952—all in SA PM C 5592/4669B.
75. Although Pinḥas Lavon was skeptical as to whether mass Arab emigration could be

achieved at acceptable cost, even he argued that it was "worthy of encouragement and complete assistance by all the relevant institutions." Lavon to Ben-Gurion, "Problems of the Military Administration in the Arab Territories," 12 November 1952, SA FM 2401/19A; Dayan quoted in Sheffer, *Moshe Sharett*, 544.

76. Meeting of the Committee on Arab Affairs, Mapai, 5 May 1961, AHA 1/5/13.

77. Unsigned (probably Ḥushi), early 1960s, "The Military Administration," AHA 1/5/9.

78. See Baruch Kimmerling and Joel S. Migdal, *Palestinians: The Making of a People* (Cambridge: Harvard University Press, 1994), 161–72, and Kretzmer, *Legal Status*, esp. chap. 6.

79. Y. Shimoni to Ya'akov Hertsog, 30 April 1953, SA FM 2402/29B (emphasis added).

80. On development and local councils, see Avivi, "Policy Toward the Druze," 225–67. Avivi does purport to show (234–36) that state aid to towns with no or smaller Druze populations was correspondingly lower, but he fails to recognize that such aid compensated for lower levels of tax collection in Druze villages (and thus less local spending); moreover, the statistics look far less impressive if one excludes the two Druze villages on the Carmel that had long cultivated relations with the Zionist and later Israeli authorities.

81. Interview with Nissim Tokatli, former head, Northern Office, Office of the Adviser to the Prime Minister for Arab Affairs (13 June 2000, Ḥaifa).

82. Israeli officials who worked in the Arab sector in the 1950s and 1960s repeatedly told the author in interviews that the Druze were treated better than other Arabs, but when pressed for details they could not give many concrete examples. Until the documents of the MA, the Minorities Department of the Interior Ministry, and the Office of the Adviser to the Prime Minister for Arab Affairs are more fully declassified, any conclusion must be tentative. Interviews with Shmuel Toledano (26 May 2000, Jerusalem); Aharon Layish (7 June 2000, Jerusalem); Amnon Lin, who headed the Arab departments of the Histadrut, Mapai, and the Labor Party for some thirty years (15 June 2000, Ḥaifa); Nissim Tokatli (13 June 2000, Ḥaifa); and Tsvi Inbar (20 June 2000, Jerusalem). However, Uri Lubrani admitted in an interview (20 June 2000, Tel Aviv) that at best minor perks were bestowed on the Druze; in general, he averred, the state's policy toward the Druze and other Arabs was identical.

83. Avivi, "Policy Toward the Druze," 399.

84. Josh Palmon quoted in Lustick, *Arabs in the Jewish State*, 48. On population figures, see Kamen, "After the Catastrophe I," 457–59.

85. After the Israeli victory in 1956, the military governor of the north noted that many Arabs, disappointed that the war had not led to their liberation, were resentful that their vehicles had been mobilized for the war effort and that a special "security tax" had been imposed. Yet he observed that Arab mukhtars and other prominent figures almost uniformly expressed joy at Israel's triumph. See Monthly Security Report, November 1956, IDFA 65/1034/946.

86. Landau, *Arabs in Israel*, 184–219.

87. *Moslems, Christians and Druzes in Israel: Data from State 'A' and 'B' of the Census*, Population and Housing Census 1961, No. 17 (Jerusalem: Central Bureau of Statistics, 1964), tables 13–14.

88. Y. L. Ben-Or, "Some Problems of Arab Education," *New Outlook* 1, no. 4 (October 1957): 24; Asher Goren to Y. Shimoni, 23 February 1954, SA FM 2402/29B.

89. Firro, *Druzes in the Jewish State*, 154–56, 169–77.

90. In 1948 an official in the Ministry of Minorities suggested drafting the Arabs, but there is no evidence that this recommendation got any attention outside the ministry, whose detractors had branded the ministry the "defender of Islam" and the "slanderer of the army." See Alon Peled, *A Question of Loyalty: Military Manpower Policy in Multiethnic States* (Ithaca: Cornell University Press, 1998), 135, and Rekhess, "Initial Israeli Policy Guidelines," 112–16.

91. K. Kadish, "Report on the Progress of the Registration of Minorities for Mobilization into the IDF," 4 October 1954, IDFA 56/642/160.

92. Kafkafi, "Segregation or Integration," 357; Kafkafi, *Pinḥas Lavon*, 271.

93. A. S. Mu'i'el to the Director-General, Ministry of Defense, "Reactions to and Repercussions of the Order for the Registration of Arabs," December 1954, SA IM C 2215/29.

94. In an interview (14 May 2004, by telephone), Amnon Lin claimed that Arab radicals encouraged draft registration so that they could learn Israel's military secrets, acquire training, and ultimately betray Israel. It is hard to square this, however, with the widespread enthusiasm with which the registration order appears to have been greeted. Nor does this allegation appear anywhere in the declassified documentation.

95. With little evidence, Ilan Pappé asserts that most Arab citizens of Israel demanded recruitment to the army. See Pappé, "Uneasy Coexistence," 624–25.

96. The above has drawn on Yehuda Ariel, "The Registration of Minorities," 24 August 1954, *Haaretz*, SA IM C 2215/29; Yosef Suma to Department of Minorities, "The Registration of the Minorities in Ḥaifa to the IDF," SA IM C 2215/29; K. Kadish, "Report on the Progress of the Registration of Minorities," 4 October 1954, IDFA 56/642/160; Department of Minorities, "Report on the Activities of the Department, October 1954," 11 November 1954, SA IM C 2215/29.

97. Amnon Yanai to Operations Branch, 24 June 1954, and Yosef Eytan to several recipients, 6 July 1954, IDFA 56/8/27; Ya'akov to Hafez Mahmad Kassem Adu'i, 24 October 1955, IDFA 57/222/4.

98. Dayan to Lavon, 13 September 1954, IDFA 56/636/46.

99. The affair also had political overtones, as Lavon was a rival of both Dayan and Shimon Peres, at the time the Defense Ministry's director-general. See Yoram Peri, *Between Battles and Ballots: Israeli Military in Politics* (Cambridge: Cambridge University Press, 1983), 232–39.

100. Firro, *Druzes in the Jewish State*, 114.

101. See Amnon Yanai to Head of Operations, "Report on the Situation in the Unit," 9 January 1953, IDFA 54/79/71; Yanai, "Mobilization of Druze for IDF," 15 October 1953, SA FM 2402/28B; Ya'akov to Military Governor, Northern Region, "Weapons Permits," 23 February 1955, IDFA 57/222/1; Ya'akov to Military Governor, Northern Region, 24 February 1955, IDFA 57/222/1; and Shmuel Divon, "The Treatment of Minority Veterans of the IDF," 18 May 1955, IDFA 56/637/67.

102. Avivi, "Policy Toward the Druze," 96–100.

103. Avivi (ibid., 132, 265, 382, and passim) argues that the Druze continued to be viewed as a security threat well into the 1960s.

104. Koren, *Steadfast Alliance*, 68.

105. Yanai to Head of Operations, "Report on the Situation in the Unit," 9 January 1953, IDFA 54/79/71; Ya'akov to IDF General Staff, "Druze in Mixed Units," 23 February 1955, IDFA 57/222/1.

106. Quoted in Peled, *A Question of Loyalty*, 158. See Jack Katzenell, "Minorities in the IDF," *IDF Journal* 4, no. 3 (Fall 1987): 41, and Peled, *A Question of Loyalty*, chap. 4.

107. *Israel Government Yearbook 1957* (Jerusalem: Government Printer), 47.

108. See various letters in IDFA 57/222/5 and AHA 6/102B. See also Avivi, "Policy Toward the Druze," 102–3.

109. See Ya'akov to IDF General Staff, "Druze in Mixed Units," 23 February 1955, IDFA 57/222/1; Meir Amit to Commander, Minorities Unit, "Summary of the Visit," 27 June 1955, IDFA 56/637/67; Ya'akov, "Meeting to Discuss Mandatory Conscription for the Druze Community," 31 July 1955, IDFA 57/222/3; A. Pereg, "Druze—Mandatory Conscription," 6 October 1955, IDFA 56/637/67; Ya'akov to General Staff Branch, "Supplements to the Report of the Committee on the Application of Mandatory Conscription to the Druze Community," 3 November 1955, IDFA 56/637/67; Ya'akov to [illegible], 23 November 1955, IDFA 57/222/5.

110. Ascertaining the authorities' motives is hampered by continued classification of relevant documents, but even full declassification may not completely clarify matters be-

cause divining motives is always difficult and because such sensitive issues may have been dealt with verbally.

111. Lustick, *Arabs in the Jewish State;* Firro, *Druzes in the Jewish State.*

112. "Recommendations for Dealing with the Arab Minority in Israel," undated [1962?], AHA 1/5/9. This was also confirmed by officials then active in the Office of the Adviser to the Prime Minister for Arab Affairs: Shmuel Toledano (26 May 2000, Jerusalem), Aharon Layish (7 June 2000, Jerusalem), and Nissim Tokatli (13 June 2000, Ḥaifa).

113. Quoted in Firro, *Druzes in the Jewish State,* 101–2; also interview with Amos Yanai (29 June 2000, Ḥaifa). See also Avivi, "Policy Toward the Druze," 91–96.

114. Officer of the North, Tiberias, to Director, Department of Minorities, "Report on Minorities—March–April 1956," 1 May 1956, SA IM C 2214/3.

115. Farhud Qasim Farhud and Salaḥ Nasib Haber to various ministries, 22 March 1957, SA FM 3751/21; Petition from Abu Snan, 28 March 1957, SA IM C 2214/125; S. Landman to U.S. Department, Foreign Ministry, "Druze Demonstrations in Front of the American Consulate in Ḥaifa," 3 April 1957, SA FM 3107/4A. See also Firro, *Druzes in the Jewish State,* 158–59; Atashe, *Druzes and Jews,* 106–7; and Eli El'ad, "Young Druze Complain," *Haaretz,* 13 November 1966.

116. In several instances, archival documents refer to Druze petitioners denying their involvement, alleging that their signatures had been forged. For examples, see Avivi, "Policy Toward the Druze," 104.

117. In general, see ibid., 102–13.

118. See Firro, *Druzes in the Jewish State,* 94–97, 99–100; Oppenheimer, "Druze in Israel."

Chapter 4. Two Roads to Jerusalem

1. Moshe Lissak, "A Militaristic Society, or a Nation in Uniform," in *Security Concerns: Insights from the Israeli Experience,* ed. Daniel Bar-Tal et al. (Stamford, Conn.: JAI Press, 1998); Yoram Peri, "The Radical Social Scientists and Israeli Militarism," *Israel Studies* 1, no. 2 (Fall 1996): 230–66; and Daniel Shimshoni, *Israeli Democracy: The Middle of the Journey* (New York: Free Press, 1982), 215–16.

2. Baruch Kimmerling, "Patterns of Militarism in Israel," *Archives Européenes de Sociologie* 34 (1993): 196–223.

3. Eyal Ben-Ari and Edna Lomsky-Feder, eds., *The Military and Militarism in Israeli Society* (Albany: SUNY Press, 1999); Dan Horowitz and Baruch Kimmerling, "Some Social Implications of Military Service and the Reserves System in Israel," *Archives Européenes de Sociologie* 15 (1974): 265–68.

4. Myron J. Aronoff, "Wars as Catalysts of Political and Cultural Change," in *The Military and Militarism in Israeli Society,* ed. Eyal Ben-Ari and Edna Lomsky-Feder.

5. Peter Y. Medding, *The Founding of Israeli Democracy, 1948–1967* (New York: Oxford University Press, 1990).

6. A. R. Luckham, "A Comparative Typology of Civil-Military Relations," *Government and Opposition* 6, no. 1 (Winter 1971): 5–35; Uri Ben-Eliezer, "Rethinking the Civil-Military Relations Paradigm: The Inverse Relation between Militarism and Praetorianism through the Israeli Case," *Comparative Political Studies* 30, no. 3 (1997): 356–74.

7. See Moshe Lissak, "Boundaries and Institutional Linkages between Elites: Some Illustrations from Civil-Military Relations in Israel," *Research in Politics and Society* 1 (1985): 129–48; Yoram Peri and Moshe Lissak, "Retired Officers in Israel and the Emergence of a New Elite," in *The Military and the Problem of Legitimacy,* ed. Gwyn Harries-Jenkins and Jacques van Doorn (Beverly Hills, Calif.: Sage, 1976).

8. Reuven Gal, *A Portrait of the Israeli Soldier* (Westport, Conn.: Greenwood, 1986), 45. See also Dan Horowitz, "The Israel Defense Forces: A Civilianized Military in a Partially Militarized Society," in *Soldiers, Peasants, and Bureaucrats: Civil-Military Relations*

in *Communist and Modernizing Societies,* ed. Roman Kolkowicz and Andrzej Korbonski (London: Allen and Unwin, 1982).

9. Gal, *Portrait.* For an update, see Stuart Cohen, *Towards a New Portrait of a (New) Israeli Soldier* (Ramat Gan: Bar Ilan University, Begin-Sadat Center for Strategic Studies, 1997).

10. Quoted in Eli El'ad, "A Policy of Honor Him and Suspect Him," *Haaretz,* 14 November 1966, GH (9)8D:323.1.

11. Quoted in Tom Segev, *1949: The First Israelis* (New York: Henry Holt, 1986), 45–46.

12. SA FM 2401/20.

13. Eli El'ad, "Intrigues and Divisions Due to Patrons," *Haaretz,* 11 November 1966.

14. Even today, the ḥamula still dominates *local* politics, but since the late 1970s it has had little influence on voting patterns in *national* campaigns. See Majid al-Haj, "Kinship and Local Politics among the Arabs in Israel," *Asian and African Studies* 27 (1993): 47–60.

15. Gabriel Ben-Dor, *The Druzes in Israel* (Jerusalem: Magnes Press, 1979), 138–47 and passim.

16. On veterans and travel restrictions, see Appeal to Military Governor, Tarshiḥa, 26 March 1958, IDFA 66/263/777, and others in that same file. On continuing discrimination, see Eli El'ad, "Young Druze Complain," *Haaretz,* 13 November 1966, and El'ad, "Policy of Honor"—both in GH (9)8D:323.1.

17. Nissim Dana, *The Druze in the Middle East: Their Faith, Leadership, Identity and Status* (Brighton, England: Sussex Academic Press, 2003), 80–84, 92–96; Kais M. Firro, *The Druzes in the Jewish State* (Leiden: Brill, 1999), 161–66; interview with Aharon Layish (7 June 2000, Jerusalem).

18. "Druzes in Israel Gain New Rights," *New York Times,* 8 April 1957; Joseph Vaschitz, "Toward Minority Integration," *New Outlook* 1, no. 1 (July 1957): 58–60.

19. "The Druze Youth on the Term 'Druze'," *Al-Ittihad,* 27 July 1962, in "The Minorities in Israel: Selections from the Press," 13 August 1962, SA FM 3413/5B; for protests, see SA PM C6337/1653.

20. "Discussion on the MA," undated [1962?], SA PM C 6337.

21. See Shimon Avivi, "Policy Toward the Druze in Israel and Its Implementation: Consistency and Lapses, 1948–1967" (in Hebrew), PhD diss., University of Ḥaifa, 2002, 238–42.

22. Interview with Nissim Tokatli, former head, Ḥaifa office, Office of the Adviser to the Prime Minister for Arab Affairs (13 June 2000, Ḥaifa).

23. "The Future of Arab Policy," 2 July 1962, SA FM 3413/3, and "Political, Communal, and Social Organizations in the Arab Minority in Israel," 7 May 1962, SA FM 3413/3.

24. See, for example, correspondence between the Organization of Released Soldiers in Ussafiya and Abba Ḥushi, July–August 1957, AHA 6/102C. On Druze political activity in this period, see Firro, *Druzes in the Jewish State,* 154–56, 168–79, and Avivi, "Policy Toward the Druze," 278–98.

25. Interview with Zeidan Atashe, former member, Druze League; former MK (13 June 2000, Ussafiya).

26. Interview with Uri Thon, also former adviser to Deputy Prime Minister and Minister of Education and Culture Yigal Allon (14 June 2000, Ḥaifa).

27. Interview with Ramzi Ḥalabi, mayor, Daliyat-al-Carmel (30 June 2000, Daliyat-al-Carmel). In interviews, Druze activists Fadil Mansour (14 June 2000, Ussafiya) and Fayz Azzam (29 June 2000, Ussafiya) also expressed this idea.

28. Interview with Fayz Azzam (29 June 2000, Ussafiya).

29. In substance and style, the Druze have epitomized what As'ad Ghanem has identified as the "Israeli-Arab stream." Ghanem, *The Palestinian-Arab Minority in Israel, 1948–2000* (Albany: SUNY Press, 2001), chap. 3.

30. Interview with Salman Falaḥ, longtime Druze official, Ministry of Education (15 June 2000, Ḥaifa).

31. This account draws freely on Firro, *Druzes in the Jewish State,* 184–97, and Avivi, "Pol-

icy Toward the Druze," 289–98. If not otherwise noted, data on Druze mobilization from the mid-1960s through the mid-1970s is derived from these sources.

32. Avivi, "Policy Toward the Druze," 290–91.

33. Amnon Lin, "Guidelines for the Discussions of the Committee on Arab Affairs," 15 October 1968.

34. However, in an interview (12 June 2000, Tel Aviv), Aharon Shlush, who represented the police on key government committees charged with designing and coordinating policy for the Arab sector, said that while such protest "was not always comfortable for us . . . [,] overall, when we sat and spoke about this matter, we saw it . . . as a positive development." For differing conclusions, see Zeidan Atashe, *Druze and Jews in Israel— A Shared Destiny?* (Brighton: Sussex Academic Press, 1995) 119–20; Ben-Dor, *Druzes in Israel,* 235–38.

35. Interview with Zeidan Atashe (13 June 2000, Ussafiya).

36. Interview with Amnon Lin (15 June 2000, Ḥaifa).

37. "Prime Minister Informs Druze Delegation: The Affairs of the Druze Community— For Direct Care by Government Ministries," *Davar,* 11 October 1967; "The End of the 'Druze Minority,'" *Maariv,* 11 October 1967—both in GH (9)8D:323.1.

38. For contemporaneous accounts of political mobilization among young Druze, often stressing the role military service had played in prompting their assertiveness, see Barukh Nadel, "What Pains the Druze?" *Yediot Ahronot,* 26 April 1970, GH (9)8D:323.1; Yaacov Ardon, "Young Druse Charge Discrimination," *Jerusalem Post,* 8 February 1971, GH (9)8D/J; Reuven Ben-Tsvi, "A Community without Land Is Not a Community," *Maariv,* 3 March 1971, GH (9)8D:333; and Atallah Mansour, "Radicals' Voice Gets a Rest," *Haaretz,* 20 August 1974, GH (9)8D/J.

39. See Ron Linberg, "The Young Druze Turn to Rakaḥ," *Pi Ha-Aton,* 24 February 1970, GH (9)8D/J.

40. "The Arab Committee in 'Labor' Discussed Accepting the Druze," *Yediot Ahronot,* 19 May 1969; Amnon Lin, "The Druze in Israel–at the Edge of a New Period," *Yediot Ahronot,* 12 June 1970.

41. These examples come from Ben-Dor, *Druzes in Israel,* 111, and Firro, *Druzes in the Jewish State,* 202, 207.

42. Muhammad Ramel, "The Druze and the Labor Party," *Ot,* 15 July 1971, GH (9)8D:329. See also Tsvi Tal, "Young Druze Demand That Labor Accept Them," *Yediot Ahronot,* 12 June 1969, GH (9)8D/J.

43. Atashe, *Druze and Jews in Israel,* chap. 7; Ben-Dor, *Druzes in Israel,* 111–17; Uzi Benziman and Atallah Mansour, *Subtenants: The Arabs of Israel, Their Status, and the Policies Toward Them* (in Hebrew) (Jerusalem: Keter, 1992), 75; Raja Khalidi, *The Arab Economy in Israel: The Dynamics of a Region's Development* (London: Croom Helm, 1988), 161; and Ian Lustick, *Arabs in the Jewish State: Israel's Control of a National Minority* (Austin: University of Texas Press, 1980), 209–11.

44. Interview with Gabriel Ben-Dor (14 June 2000, Ḥaifa); Mansour, "Radicals' Voice."

45. For the Ben-Dor report, see Gabriel Ben-Dor, Fayz Azzam, and Salman Faraj, "Report of the Committee to Investigate the Problems of the Druze in Israel," November 1974, CDG. For the Schechterman report, see State of Israel, Knesset, "To Strengthen the Druze Community of Israel" (Jerusalem: Office of Information, June 1975). For a trenchant critique, from the center-left, see Dani Rubinstein, "Reward and Punishment for Minorities," *Davar,* 4 June 1975, GH (9)8D:323.1.

46. Interview with Gabriel Ben-Dor (14 June 2000, Ḥaifa).

47. See undated pamphlet, "A Voice Calling to the Government of Israel," Druze-Zionist Movement in Israel, in author's possession; Yusuf Nassr-al-Din, "The Israeli Zionist-Druze Movement," 13 May 1987, in "The Druze-Zionist Group," DA. See also Firro, *Druzes in the Jewish State,* 209–11.

48. Quoted in Arnold Sherman, *The Druse* (Tel Aviv: Bazak, 1975), 110.

49. Dana, *Druze in the Middle East,* 119–22.

50. On the DIC, see Robert Brenton Betts, *The Druse* (New Haven: Yale University Press, 1988) 104–5; Firro, *Druzes in the Jewish State,* 212–13; and Joshua Teitelbaum, "Ideology and Conflict in a Middle Eastern Minority: The Case of the Druze Initiative Committee in Israel," *Orient* 26 (1985): 341–59.

51. On the movement cycle, see Sidney Tarrow, *Power in Movement: Social Movements and Contentious Politics* (Cambridge: Cambridge University Press, 1998).

52. See, for example, Benny Tadmor to Amos Eran, "Translation of a Proclamation Distributed by the Branch of the Druze Initiative Committee in Shfar'am," 17 August 1976, CDG.

53. State co-optation and the manipulation of ḥamula politics no doubt played a role, but these were characteristic of the state's policies toward the Arab population as a whole, regardless of religion. Since Druze villages are typically composed of populations of mixed religious backgrounds, ascertaining the precise vote of Druze residents is impossible. On Druze voting patterns, see Abraham Diskin, *Elections and Voters in Israel* (Westport, Conn.: Praeger, 1991), 94–98, and Majid al-Haj and Avner Yaniv, "Uniformity or Diversity: A Reappraisal of the Voting Behavior of the Arab Minority in Israel," in *The Elections in Israel—1981,* ed. Asher Arian (Tel Aviv: Ramot, 1983).

54. Sammy Smooha, *The Orientation and Politicization of the Arab Minority in Israel* (Ḥaifa: University of Ḥaifa, Jewish-Arab Center, 1984), 38, 97–99, 118, 131, 144; Smooha, *Arabs and Jews in Israel,* vol. 1, *Conflicting and Shared Attitudes in a Divided Society* (Boulder, Colo.: Westview, 1989), 98–107; Smooha, *Arabs and Jews in Israel,* vol. 2, *Change and Continuity in Mutual Intolerance* (Boulder, Colo.: Westview, 1992), 94–108, 206.

55. This assessment of the CDG gives it far more credit for change than do many others (such as Firro, *Druzes in the Jewish State,* 216). This is largely because it is based on documentation to which others have not had access. I am deeply grateful to Salman Falaḥ—a longtime public servant in the Education Ministry and the coordinator of the CDG—for sharing his files. Because they have not been properly cataloged, the documents can be identified only by title and date; copies of all cited documents are in my personal possession.

56. In November 1975, for example, Shaykh Jabber Mu'addi, who had profited so much under the old system, appeared before the CDG to raise questions regarding contested Druze lands. "Summary of the Meeting of the CDG, 19 October 1976," CDG.

57. See hundreds of documents in the files of the CDG.

58. This account has had to be severely truncated. For more full detail and citation, see Ronald R. Krebs, "Rights and Gun Sights: Military Service and the Politics of Citizenship," PhD diss., Columbia University, 2003, 239–45.

59. "Summary of the Meeting of the CDG," 26 December 1983, CDG; Salman Falaḥ to CDG, "A Short Survey of the Druze in Israel," 29 November 1983; Atallah Mansour, "Living Off the Army," *Haaretz,* 26 November 1990. See also Hillel Frisch, "The Druze Minority in the Israeli Military: Traditionalizing an Ethnic Policing Role," *Armed Forces and Society* 20, no. 1 (Fall 1993): 51–67.

60. Moshe Arness to Prime Minister Yitzḥak Shamir, 16 January 1987, CDG; Atashe to Peres, "The Jews and the Druze: A Covenant on the Verge of Failure," 28 April 1985, CDG.

61. Quoted in Oren Yiftachel and Michaly D. Segal, "Jews and Druze in Israel: State Control and Ethnic Resistance," *Ethnic and Racial Studies* 21, no. 3 (May 1998): 487.

62. Yeraḥ Tal, "They Want to Be Blue and White," *Haaretz,* 13 May 1991; Yosef Algazi and Gidon Alon, "The Opposition Refuses Rabin's Request to Postpone the No-Confidence Vote over the Discrimination against the Druze," *Haaretz,* 8 December 1994; Algazi and Alon, "Council of Druze and Circassian Authorities Warns Against 'the Intifada That Nobody Wants,'" *Haaretz,* 11 December 1994; Algazi, "The Strike of the Druze and Circassian Councils Has Ended; The Government Will Increase Their Budgets," *Haaretz,*

12 December 1994. See also Hillel Frisch, "State Ethnicization and the Crisis of Leadership Succession among Israel's Druze," *Ethnic and Racial Studies* 20, no. 3 (July 1997): 580–93.

63. Quoted in Rafiq Halabi, "Israel's Minority in the Middle," *New York Times Magazine*, 27 December 1981. Other Arab epigrams—"Attach yourself to the sword even if it strikes you"; "If you cannot sting a hand, kiss it and secretly wish it to fracture"—have the same message. See Kassem Zaid, "Israel's Arabs after Twenty-Five Years," *New Outlook* 16, no. 6 (July–August 1973): 14.

64. See Yael Yishai, *Land of Paradoxes: Interest Politics in Israel* (Albany: SUNY Press, 1991), 247–79, esp. 276–78.

65. Quoted in Firro, *Druzes in the Jewish State*, 201.

66. Quoted in Sherman, *Druse*, 72.

67. Halabi, "Israel's Minority in the Middle."

68. Dov Zakin, "For Druze Integration into Israeli Society," *Al Ha-Mishmar*, 28 March 1976, GH (9)8D:323.1.

69. Interview with Aharon Shlush (12 June 2000, Tel Aviv).

70. Peter Grose, "Arabs in Israel: Minority Torn between Two Worlds," *New York Times*, 29 January 1971.

71. For a full catalog of the factors contributing to Arab quiescence, see Alan Dowty, *The Jewish State: A Century Later* (Berkeley: University of California Press, 1998), 193–97.

72. Sam Lehman-Wilzig, *Stiff-Necked People, Bottle-Necked System: The Evolution and Roots of Israeli Public Protest, 1949–1986* (Bloomington: Indiana University Press, 1990), 7–45.

73. The ease with which radio and television broadcasts from Cairo and Beirut could be heard in Israel contributed to this trend. In the mid-1960s half of Israel's television sets were owned by Arabs, in part because Hebrew-language television did not exist in Israel until 1968. See James Feron, "Status of Arabs in Israel Shifting," *New York Times*, 4 April 1966, and Jacob M. Landau, *The Arabs in Israel: A Political Study* (London: Oxford University Press, 1969), 31–32.

74. See a series of reports by Lawrence Fellows in the *New York Times*: "Arabs in Israel Riot against Government," 22 September 1961; "Rioting in Israel Leaves 12 Hurt," 23 September 1961; "Arab Areas Grow Quieter in Israel," 24 September 1961; "Riots Deplored by Israeli Arab," 27 September 1961. See also reports in SA FM 3319/27.

75. Shaul Bar-Haim to Uri Lubrani, 27 April 1961, SA FM 3759/8.

76. As Joel Beinin concludes, "National communism prevailed, eroding the common internationalist position on the Palestine question shared by most Arab and Jewish Marxists in the late 1940s and 1950s." Beinin, *Was the Red Flag Flying There? Marxist Politics and the Arab-Israeli Conflict in Egypt and Israel, 1946–1965* (Berkeley: University of California Press, 1990), 248.

77. "The Future of Arab Policy," 2 July 1962, SA FM 3413/3.

78. "Political, Communal, and Social Organizations in the Arab Minority in Israel," 7 May 1962, SA FM 3413/3.

79. The most notable case was that of al-Ard (literally, "the land"), which was outlawed in 1964. When its leaders appeared on the Arab Socialist List's slate of candidates the following year, the Central Elections Commission, supported by the Israeli Supreme Court, refused to register the party. See Sabri Jiryis, *The Arabs in Israel* (New York: Monthly Review Press, 1976), 185–96; David Kretzmer, *The Legal Status of Arabs in Israel* (Boulder, Colo.: Westview, 1988), 22–31; Pnina Lahav, *Judgment in Jerusalem: Chief Justice Simon Agranat and the Zionist Century* (Berkeley: University of California Press, 1997), 181–95; and Landau, *Arabs in Israel*, 92–107.

80. See, for example, Ya'akov Hertsog to Foreign Minister, "Report (on the Arab Minority)," 27 April 1953, SA FM 2402/29B. See also Ori Stendel and Emanuel Ha-Reuveni, *The Minorities in Israel* (in Hebrew) (Jerusalem: Office of the Adviser to the Prime Minister for Arabs and Druze, 1973).

81. Yohanan Peres, "Ethnic Relations in Israel," *American Journal of Sociology* 76, no. 6 (May 1971): 1038–41.

82. Landau, *Arabs in Israel*, 49–68.

83. Peres, "Ethnic Relations in Israel," 1041–45; Peres, "Modernization and Nationalism in the Identity of the Israeli Arab," *Middle East Journal* (Fall 1970).

84. Elie Rekhess, "Israeli Arabs and the Arabs of the West Bank and Gaza: Political Affinity and National Solidarity," *Asian and African Studies* 23 (1989): 121–32.

85. Ikrit and Berem even received substantial international attention. See the reports in the *New York Times*, largely by Peter Grose and Henry Kamm, on 24 July, 7 August, 8 August, 9 August, 24 August, and 31 August 1972. See also Amos Elon, "Two Arab Towns That Plumb Israel's Conscience," *New York Times Magazine*, 22 October 1972; Sara Osatsky-Lazar, *Ikrit and Berem: The Complete Story* (in Hebrew) (Givat Haviva: Center for Arab Studies, 1993); and Baruch Kimmerling, "Sovereignty, Ownership and Presence in the Jewish-Arab Territorial Conflict: The Case of Bir'm and Iqrit," *Comparative Political Studies* 10, no. 2 (1974): 155–76.

86. Sam Lehman-Wilzig, "Copying the Master? Patterns of Israeli Arab Protest, 1950–1990," *Asian and African Studies* 27 (1993): 129–47, and Lehman-Wilzig, *Stiff-Necked People*. See also Oren Yiftachel, "Minority Protest and the Emergence of Ethnic Regionalism: Palestinian-Arabs in the Israeli 'Ethnocracy,'" in *Ethnic Challenges to the Modern Nation-State*, ed. Shlomo Ben-Ami et al. (New York: St. Martin's, 2000).

87. Smooha, *Arabs and Jews in Israel*, 2:130–35.

88. Israel's Arab citizens have as a rule employed lawful tactics and have not generally abetted terrorist activity or engaged in other large-scale violence. But the limits of the law are not coextensive with the "rules of the game." Strikes and demonstrations may be legal, but they clearly constitute a very different form of activity from lobbying parliamentarians, building coalitions with other aggrieved groups, and publicizing one's grievances.

89. See Ori Stendel, *The Arabs in Israel* (Brighton: Sussex Academic Press, 1996), 92–144.

90. By the early 1980s, this phrase was in common use. See, for example, Elie Rekhess, "The Politicization of Israel's Arabs," in *Every Sixth Israeli: Relations between the Jewish Majority and the Arab Minority in Israel*, ed. Alouph Hareven (Jerusalem: Van Leer Jerusalem Foundation, 1983), 140.

91. See Majid al-Haj and Henry Rosenfeld, *Arab Local Government in Israel* (Boulder, Colo.: Westview, 1990); Jacob M. Landau, *The Arab Minority in Israel, 1967–1991: Political Aspects* (Oxford: Clarendon Press, 1993), 101–3.

92. Elias Zeidan and As'ad Ghanem, *Patterns of Giving and Volunteering of the Palestinian Arab Population in Israel* (Beersheba: Israeli Center for Third Sector Research, 2000). See also Shany Payes, "Palestinian NGOs in Israel: A Campaign for Civic Equality in a Non-Civic State," *Israel Studies* 8, no. 1 (Spring 2003): 60–90.

93. See Landau, *Arab Minority in Israel*, chap. 7; Nadim Rouhana, "The Political Transformation of the Palestinians in Israel: From Acquiescence to Challenge," *Journal of Palestine Studies* 18, no. 3 (Spring 1989): 51–52.

94. See Elie Rekhess, "Resurgent Islam in Israel," *Asian and African Studies* 27 (1993): 189–206; Reuven Paz, "The Islamic Movement and the Municipal Elections of 1989," *Jerusalem Quarterly* 53 (Winter 1990): 3–26; and David Grossman, *Sleeping on a Wire: Conversations with Palestinians in Israel* (New York: Farrar, Straus and Giroux, 1993), chap. 14.

95. As they have grown more politically active, Israel's Arab citizens have increasingly embraced Palestinian nationalism. Whether this represents politicization or radicalization is the subject of much debate within Israeli academic circles. But this debate is of little theoretical import. See Elie Rekhess, *The Arab Minority in Israel: Between Communism and Arab Nationalism, 1965–1991* (in Hebrew) (Tel Aviv: Tel Aviv University, Moshe Dayan Center, 1993), and Sammy Smooha, "The Arab Minority in Israel: Radicalization or Politicization?" in *Israel: State and Society, 1948–1988*, ed. Peter Y. Medding (Oxford: Oxford University Press, 1989).

96. See Rekhess, "Israeli Arabs," and Nadim Rouhana, *Palestinian Citizens in an Ethnic Jewish State: Identities in Conflict* (New Haven: Yale University Press, 1997), chap. 5.
97. See also Yiftachel, "Minority Protest," 168–71.
98. Note that these Arab voting figures include the votes of Druze, Circassians, and Bedouins who have generally been far more likely to support the Zionist parties and their affiliated lists. For the cited electoral statistics, see Rosenfeld and al-Haj, *Arab Local Government,* 71.
99. Quoted in Landau, *Arabs in Israel,* 84.
100. In a 1989 survey of fifty Arab political leaders, the vast majority expressed a preference for some version of a "state of all its citizens." See Rouhana, *Palestinian Citizens,* 175. On the tension between the DFPE's commitment to international Communism and the separationist agenda, see Ilana Kaufman, *Arab National Communism in the Jewish State* (Gainesville: University Press of Florida, 1997). See also Ghanem, *Palestinian-Arab Minority,* 77–83.
101. Quoted in Deborah Sontag, "Israel's Next Palestinian Problem," *New York Times Magazine,* 10 September 2000.
102. Abigail Fraser and Avi Shabat, "Between Nationalism and Liberalism: The Political Thought of Azmi Bisharah," *Israel Affairs* 9, nos. 1–2 (Autumn–Winter 2003): 16–36, at 23.
103. Quoted in Smooha, *Arabs and Jews in Israel,* 2:97–98.
104. Jewish Israelis are often accused of misunderstanding Arabs' objectives. But compare Balad's "Principles and Aims" (http://www.balad.org/display.x?cid=173&sid=394&id=1791) with Ruth Gavison's summary of that agenda (in Peter Berkowitz, "Israel's House Divided," *Weekly Standard,* 12–19 April 2004).
105. Ghanem, *Palestinian-Arab Minority,* chap. 5, quote at 108. See also Elie Rekhess, "The Arabs of Israel after Oslo: Localization of the National Struggle," *Israel Studies* 7, no. 3 (Fall 2002): 1–44.
106. Landau, *Arab Minority in Israel,* 105.
107. Zeev Rosenhek and Michael Shalev, "The Contradictions of Palestinian Citizenship in Israel: Inclusion and Exclusion in the Israeli Welfare State," in *Citizenship and the State in the Middle East: Approaches and Applications,* ed. Nils A. Butenschon et al. (Syracuse, N.Y.: Syracuse University Press, 2000), 295.
108. Paz, "Islamic Movement in Israel," 11–12, 18–19.
109. See Sammy Smooha, "Minority Status in an Ethnic Democracy: The Status of the Arab Minority in Israel," *Ethnic and Racial Studies* 13, no. 3 (July 1990): 404–6, and Smooha, *Autonomy for the Arabs in Israel?* (in Hebrew) (Ra'anana: Institute for Israeli Arab Studies, 1999). For vivid descriptions of Arab self-help, see Amina Minns and Nadia Hijab, *Citizens Apart: A Portrait of the Palestinians in Israel* (London: I. B. Tauris, 1990).
110. Majid al-Haj, "Strategies of Mobilization among the Arabs in Israel," in *Whither Israel? The Domestic Challenges,* ed. Keith Kyle and Joel Peters (London: I. B. Tauris, 1993), and Benyamin Neuberger, "The Arab Minority in Israeli Politics, 1948–1992—from Marginality to Influence," *Asian and African Studies* 27 (1993): 157. See also Ghanem, *Palestinian-Arab Minority,* and Rekhess, "Arabs of Israel after Oslo," 12–17.
111. For studies tracking this trend, see John E. Hofman and Nadim Rouhana, "Young Arabs in Israel: Some Aspects of a Conflicted Social Identity," *Journal of Social Psychology* 99, no. 1 (1976): 75–86; Mark A. Tessler, "Israel's Arabs and the Palestinian Problem," *Middle East Journal* 31, no. 3 (1977): 313–29; Smooha, *Arabs and Jews in Israel,* vols. 1 and 2; Rouhana, *Palestinian Citizens,* 120–23; and Baruch Kimmerling and Dahlia Moore, "Collective Identity as Agency and Structuration of Society: The Israeli Example," *International Review of Sociology* 7, no. 1 (1997): 25–49.
112. Eliezer Ben Rafael and Stephen Sharot, *Ethnicity, Religion and Class in Israeli Society* (Cambridge: Cambridge University Press, 1991), 239. See also Rouhana, *Palestinian Citizens,* chap. 8.
113. Quoted in Grossman, *Sleeping on a Wire,* 51. The process of Palestinization has been

accompanied by increasing absorption of Israeli cultural norms and habits, leaving Palestinian citizens "doubly marginal." See Alex Weingrod and 'Adel Manna', "Living along the Seam: Israeli Palestinians in Jerusalem," *International Journal of Middle East Studies* 30 (1998): 369–86, and Grossman, *Sleeping on a Wire.*

114. See Smooha, *Orientation and Politicization,* 36–37, 56–58; Smooha, *Arabs and Jews in Israel,* 2:88–108.

115. Arab organizations are thus rather unusual among Israeli interest groups, which have generally shied away from such direct action. The turn to demonstrations, protests, and the like has been very common, however, among "ordinary citizens"— that is, individuals and loose social movements—and the prevalence of such protest is widely perceived as a sign of the political system's sclerosis. See Yishai, *Land of Paradoxes,* 248–57; Gadi Wolfsfeld, *The Politics of Provocation: Participation and Protest in Israel* (Albany: SUNY Press, 1988); and, on Israel's Arab citizens, see Wolfsfeld, "The Politics of Provocation Revisited: Participation and Protest in Israel," in *Israeli Democracy under Stress,* ed. Ehud Sprinzak and Larry Diamond (Boulder, Colo.: Lynne Rienner, 1993), 211–13.

116. See K. Kadish, "Report on the Progress of the Registration of Minorities," 4 October 1954, IDFA 56/642/160. This list of Arab complaints appears repeatedly in Israeli declassified documents, and also in contemporary newspaper reports.

117. See M. Assaf, S. Salmon, and J. Palmon to David Ben-Gurion, undated (before 1953?), SA FM 2402/23B.

Chapter 5. Military Rites, Citizenship Rights, and Republican Rhetoric

1. In their otherwise sensitive analysis of Israel's multiple discourses of citizenship, Gershon Shafir and Yoav Peled fail to explore the tensions within and among these various discourses. These tensions, the Druze discovered, create space for change. Shafir and Peled, *Being Israeli: The Dynamics of Multiple Citizenship* (Cambridge: Cambridge University Press, 2002).

2. For examples, see appeals for assistance from Druze to Abba Ḥushi in AHA 6/102B, 6/102C, 6/102D; the "Druze Students" to Levi Eshkol, 3 June 1968, SA FM 4199/18; numerous letters from Druze local councils to government ministries, CDG; and the many clippings at the Givat Haviva library, (9)8D. This frame is so prevalent that countless instances could be adduced.

3. Quoted in Eli El'ad, "A Policy of Honor and Suspect Him," *Haaretz,* 14 November 1966, GH (9)8D:323.1.

4. Interview with Fayz Azzam (29 June 2000, Ussafiya).

5. Quoted in Kais M. Firro, *The Druzes in the Jewish State* (Leiden: Brill, 1999), 187 (slightly edited); quoted in "Equality of Obligations Obligates Equality of Rights," *La-Merḥav,* 28 July 1970, GH (9)8D/J.

6. Mansour, "The Druze in the Party: To Where?" *Ot,* 22 July 1972, GH (9)8D:329.

7. Menaḥem Michaelson, "Death Comes to Bet Jan," *Yediot Ahronot,* 19 November 1982, GH (9)8D:355.

8. Gabriel Ben-Dor, *The Druzes in Israel* (Jerusalem: Magnes Press, 1979), 134–35.

9. Oren Yiftachel and Michaly D. Segal, "Jews and Druze in Israel: State Control and Ethnic Resistance," *Ethnic and Racial Studies* 21, no. 3 (May 1998): 487.

10. See Yosef Algazi and Gidon Alon, "Council of Druze and Circassian Authorities Warns against 'the Intifada That Nobody Wants,'" *Haaretz,* 11 December 1994; Yeraḥ Tal, "They Want to Be Blue and White," *Haaretz,* 13 May 1991.

11. Quoted in Gabi Zohar, "A One-Sided Alliance," *Haaretz,* 21 October 1991.

12. Reuven Barakat quoted in "Druzes in Israel Gain New Rights," *New York Times,* 8 April 1957.

13. Quoted in Salman Falaḥ, "Druze Communal Organization in Israel," *New Outlook* 10, no. 3 (March–April 1967): 43–44 (slightly edited).

14. "Prime Minister Informs Druze Delegation," *Davar*, 11 October 1967, GH (9)8D:323.1.

15. Quoted in Musabaḥ Ḥalabi, *A Covenant of Blood: Tales of the Lives and Deaths of the Druze Who Fell in the Battles of Israel* (in Hebrew) (Tel Aviv: Otpaz, 1970), 14.

16. Shafir and Peled, *Being Israeli*.

17. Zeev Rosenhek and Michael Shalev, "The Contradictions of Palestinian Citizenship in Israel: Inclusion and Exclusion in the Israeli Welfare State," in *Citizenship and the State in the Middle East: Approaches and Applications*, ed. Nils A. Butenschon et al. (Syracuse, N.Y.: Syracuse University Press, 2000), 297; Pnina Lahav, "Rights and Democracy: The Court's Performance," in *Israeli Democracy under Stress*, ed. Ehud Sprinzak and Larry Diamond (Boulder, Colo.: Lynne Rienner, 1993).

18. Yoav Peled, "Ethnic Democracy and the Legal Construction of Citizenship: Arab Citizens of the Jewish State," *American Political Science Review* 86, no. 2 (June 1992): 432–43.

19. Alan Dowty suggests that the roots of much Israeli political practice lie in older Jewish traditions. See his *The Jewish State: A Century Later* (Berkeley: University of California Press, 1998), 31–32, and in general chap. 2.

20. See Dan Horowitz and Moshe Lissak, *Origins of the Israeli Polity: Palestine under the Mandate* (Chicago: University of Chicago Press, 1978), and Charles S. Liebman and Eliezer Don Yihya, *Civil Religion in Israel: Traditional Religion and Political Culture in the Jewish State* (Berkeley: University of California Press, 1983).

21. Nathan Yanai, "The Citizen as Pioneer: Ben-Gurion's Concept of Citizenship," *Israel Studies* 1, no. 1 (Spring 1996): 127–43. On mamlakhtiyut, see Peter Y. Medding, *The Founding of Israeli Democracy, 1948–1967* (New York: Oxford University Press, 1990), chap. 7; and Liebman and Don-Yihya, *Civil Religion in Israel*, chap. 4.

22. *Divre Ha-Knesset*, 16 January 1950, 3:537.

23. Quoted in Lahav, "Rights and Democracy," 130–31.

24. Yagil Levy persuasively argues that the republican citizenship discourse and the centrality of the military served the interests of the Ashkenazi middle class in maintaining its preeminence. See Levy, *Trial and Error: Israel's Route from War to De-Escalation* (Albany: SUNY Press, 1997), chap. 2.

25. Yael Yishai, *Land of Paradoxes: Interest Politics in Israel* (Albany: SUNY Press, 1991), 318.

26. Quoted in Sara Helman, "Rights and Duties, Citizens and Soldiers: Conscientious Objection and the Redefinition of Citizenship in Israel," in *Citizenship and the State in the Middle East*, ed. Nils A. Butenschon et al., 324.

27. Peled, "Ethnic Democracy," 435. See also, among many other works, Baruch Kimmerling, "Between the Primordial and the Civil Definitions of the Collective Identity: Eretz Israel or the State of Israel?" in *Comparative Social Dynamics: Essays in Honor of S. N. Eisenstadt*, ed. Erik Cohen et al. (Boulder, Colo.: Westview, 1985).

28. Helman, "Rights and Duties," 320.

29. See Uri Ben-Eliezer, *The Making of Israeli Militarism* (Bloomington: Indiana University Press, 1998), and Zeev Drori, "Utopia in Uniform," in *Israel: The First Decade of Independence*, ed. S. Ilan Troen and Noah Lucas (Albany: SUNY Press, 1995). See also Maurice M. Roumani, *From Immigrant to Citizen: The Contribution of the Army to National Integration in Israel* (The Hague: Foundation for the Study of Plural Societies, 1979).

30. Quoted in Ian Lustick, *Arabs in the Jewish State: Israel's Control of a National Minority* (Austin: University of Texas Press, 1980), 40–41.

31. Myron J. Aronoff, *Israeli Visions and Divisions: Cultural Change and Political Conflict* (New Brunswick, N.J.: Transaction, 1989), 132. See also Avishai Margalit, *Views in Review: Politics and Culture in the State of the Jews* (New York: Farrar, Straus and Giroux, 1998), 64–66.

32. Baruch Kimmerling, "Patterns of Militarism in Israel," *Archives Européenes de Sociolo-*

gie 34 (1993): 196–223. On conscientious objection, see Ruth Linn, "Conscientious Objection in Israel during the War in Lebanon," *Armed Forces and Society* 12, no. 4 (Summer 1986): 489–511, and Linn, "When the Individual Soldier Says 'No' to War: A Look at Selective Refusal during the Intifada," *Journal of Peace Research* 33, no. 4 (November 1996): 421–31.

33. Daniel Maman et al., "Military, State, and Society in Israel: An Introductory Essay," in *Military, State, and Society in Israel*, ed. Maman et al. (New Brunswick, N.J.: Transaction, 2001), 4–5.

34. See Dowty, *Jewish State*, chap. 5, and Baruch Kimmerling, *The Invention and Decline of Israeliness: State, Society, and the Military* (Berkeley: University of California Press, 2001), chap. 7.

35. Rebecca L. Schiff, "Civil-Military Relations Reconsidered: Israel as an 'Uncivil State,'" *Security Studies* 1, no. 4 (1992): 636–58.

36. See Terence Smith, "Former Generals Are the Elite Corps of Israeli Society," *New York Times*, 25 August 1973; Daniel Friedman, "Connections as Qualifications," *Haaretz*, 14 June 1973; Eliyahu Salpeter, "Retired Senior Officers," *Haaretz*, 15 June 1973. See also Yoram Peri, *Between Battles and Ballots: Israeli Military in Politics* (Cambridge: Cambridge University Press, 1983).

37. Zeev Schiff, "The Military Administration on the Scales," *New Outlook* 2, no. 9 (June 1959): 22. See also Dowty, *Jewish State*, 91–102, on security and democracy.

38. Gad Barzilai, "The Argument of 'National Security' in Politics and Jurisprudence," in *Security Concerns: Insights from the Israeli Experience*, ed. Daniel Bar-Tal et al. (Stamford, Conn.: JAI, 1998).

39. Maoz Azaryahu, "The Independence Day Military Parade: A Political History of a Patriotic Ritual," in *The Military and Militarism in Israeli Society*, ed. Eyal Ben-Ari and Edna Lomsky-Feder (Albany: SUNY Press, 1999), chap. 2; Eliezer Don-Yehiya, "Festivals and Political Culture: Independence Day Celebrations," *Jerusalem Quarterly* 45 (1988): 61–84.

40. See Don Handelman and Elihu Katz, "State Ceremonies of Israel—Remembrance Day and Independence Day," in Handelman, *Models and Mirrors: Towards an Anthropology of Public Events* (Cambridge: Cambridge University Press, 1990), chap. 9, at 192–93.

41. Interview with Shmuel Toledano, former adviser to the prime minister for Arab affairs (26 May 2000, Jerusalem); interview with Amos Eran, former director-general, Prime Minister's Office (7 June 2000, by telephone).

42. Rosenhek and Shalev have noted similar dynamics in a different context. Since Israel's child allowances were framed in terms of universal (liberal) citizenship, denying them outright to Arabs "might have required steps that were irreconcilable with either the constitutional-legal fabric of the state or its all-important standing in the international community." Fully excluding Palestinian citizens was consequently impossible. See their "Contradictions of Palestinian Citizenship," 312–13.

43. In interviews, Israeli decision makers—notably Shmuel Toledano (26 May 2000, Jerusalem) and his former deputy Yossi Ginat (21 May 2000, by telephone)—argued that it was the Druze's own fault that administrative integration was slow in coming, for they continued to turn to the Office of the Adviser to the Prime Minister for Arab Affairs for help. Yet contemporaneous news accounts make clear that the existing Druze leadership opposed such integration because it threatened to undercut their power. Integration was favored only by the younger generation. Israeli decision makers were only too happy to exploit this rift, alienating the younger generation and leading to calls for Toledano's dismissal. See Eli El'ad, "They Wish to Be Like the Jews," *Haaretz*, 30 August 1970, GH (9)8D:323.1; Yo'el Dar, "Debate in the Druze Community over the Integration Problem," *Davar*, 27 November 1970, GH (9)8D/J; Yaacov Friedler, "Druze Affairs Returned to Arab Affairs Adviser," *Jerusalem Post*, 13 March 1972, GH (9)8D:323.1; and Yo'el Dar, "Young Druze against the Adviser," *Davar*, 16 August 1972, GH (9)8D/J.

44. Yitzḥak White, "'There Will Be No More Clouds between Us,'" *Yediot Ahronot*, 6 May 1970, GH (9)8D:323.1.

45. Garnering any, and especially favorable, news coverage is a problem for all minorities. See Andrew Jakubowicz et al., eds., *Racism, Ethnicity, and the Media* (St. Leonards, Australia: Allen and Unwin, 1994). On coverage of Arabs in Israel, see Eli Avraham, "Press, Politics, and the Coverage of Minorities in Divided Societies: The Case of Arab Citizens in Israel," *Harvard International Journal of Press/Politics* 8, no. 4 (September 2003): 7–26, and Gadi Wolfsfeld, *Media and Political Conflict: News from the Middle East* (Cambridge: Cambridge University Press, 1997).

46. Interview with Fayz Azzam (29 June 2000, Ussafiya).

47. Interview with Asa'ad Asa'ad, former MK (20 June 2000, Tel Aviv); interview with Shmuel Toledano (21 May 2004, by telephone).

48. One might cite countless examples. See, among many others, Eli El'ad, "Intrigues and Divisions Due to Patrons," *Haaretz*, 11 November 1966; El'ad, "Policy of Honor Him"; Gideon Weigert, "They Are Partners in Arms—But What about Their Rights?" *Al HaMishmar*, 10 July 1969; Barukh Nadel, "What Pains the Druze?" *Yediot Ahronot*, 26 April 1970; El'ad, "They Wish to Be Like the Jews"; Shulamit Aloni, "The Druze between the Hammer and the Anvil," *Yediot Ahronot*, 31 May 1974—all in GH (9)8D:323.1. See also Yo'el Dar, "The Druze in Israel: State Relations and Internal Difficulties," *Davar*, 12 October 1967; Reuven Ben-Tsvi, "The Druze Reveal: It Is Difficult to Be an Israeli," *Maariv*, 28 February 1971; Yeḥezkel Me'iri, "Protest of the Druze," *Yediot Ahronot*, 21 April 1974; and Atallah Mansour, "Full Obligations to the State, But Only Thirty Percent of the Rights," *Haaretz*, 19 August 1974—all in GH (9)8D/J.

49. Interview with Salman Falaḥ (15 June 2000, Ḥaifa).

50. Interview with Shmuel Toledano (26 May 2000, Jerusalem).

51. Interview with Fayz Azzam (29 June 2000, Ussafiya).

52. Ben-Dor, *Druzes in Israel*, 134–36.

53. Amnon Lin, "The Druze in Israel—At the Edge of a New Period," *Yediot Ahronot*, 12 June 1970.

54. Interview with Ramzi Ḥalabi, mayor, Daliyat-al-Carmel (30 June 2000, Daliyat-al-Carmel).

55. Mansour, "Full Obligations."

56. Interview with Toledano (26 May 2000, Jerusalem); interview with Falaḥ (15 June 2000, Ḥaifa). In an interview (7 June 2000, Jerusalem), Aharon Layish, who served as deputy adviser under Toledano's predecessor, Reḥavam Amir, drew a similar distinction. Another former government official, Ori Stendel, has also asserted that "formulating policy was one thing; implementing it was another"; see his *The Arabs in Israel* (Brighton: Sussex Academic Press, 1996), 31–32.

57. This is a common refrain among Druze leaders. In an interview, former MK Zeidan Atashe (13 June 2000, Ussafiya) forcefully expressed this sentiment, as did Druze activists Fadil Mansour (14 June 2000, Ussafiya) and Fayz Azzam (29 June 2000, Ussafiya).

58. In an interview (21 May 2004, by telephone), Shmuel Toledano suggested that the problem lay at the lower levels of the bureaucracy: "The establishment was all for it [giving the Druze equality]. It was not a question of policy. But, in reality, we did not execute policy. It was impossible to convince the Jewish population and the *pakid* [clerk]."

59. Quoted in Arnold Sherman, *The Druse* (Tel Aviv: Bazak, 1975), 71.

60. Interview with Atashe (13 June 2000, Ussafiya).

61. Zeidan Atashe, *Druze and Jews in Israel—A Shared Destiny?* (Brighton: Sussex Academic Press, 1995), 142.

62. Rosenhek and Shalev, "Contradictions of Palestinian Citizenship," 292.

63. Ḥushi to Koussa, 25 March 1956, AHA 6/102C.

64. Ben-Gurion to Yizhar, 12 February 1962, SA PM C 6304/1086. See also Zaki Shalom,

"Ben-Gurion and Tewfik Toubi Finally Meet (October 28, 1966)," *Israel Studies* 8, no. 2 (Summer 2003): 60.

65. Lin, "Druze in Israel."

66. Shafi Gabbai, "Arab Israelis: 'We Will Not Serve,'" *Maariv,* 20 May 1987, GH (9)8A:355. See also Daniel Gavron, "Military Option?" *Jerusalem Post Magazine,* 7 December 1984, GH (9)8A:355.

67. Jaffar Farah, quoted in Erik Schechter, "Citizen Bane," *Jerusalem Post,* 5 September 2003.

68. See Sammy Smooha, *The Orientation and Politicization of the Arab Minority in Israel* (Ḥaifa: University of Ḥaifa, Jewish-Arab Center, 1984), 53–55; Smooha, *Arabs and Jews in Israel,* vol. 1, *Conflicting and Shared Attitudes in a Divided Society* (Boulder, Colo.: Westview, 1989), 95–97; Smooha, *Arabs and Jews in Israel,* vol. 2, *Change and Continuity in Mutual Intolerance* (Boulder, Colo.: Westview, 1992), 91–93.

69. Nonmilitary national service, many recognize, would not carry the same cachet. See Peter Berkowitz, "Israel's House Divided," *Weekly Standard,* 12–19 April 2004, and Alon Peled, *A Question of Loyalty: Military Manpower Policy in Multiethnic States* (Ithaca: Cornell University Press, 1998).

70. Daniel Shimshoni, *Israeli Democracy: The Middle of the Journey* (New York: Free Press, 1982), 147.

71. Ben-Gurion's formula was that "Palestine is assigned for the Jewish People and the Arabs living there." Quoted in Dan Horowitz and Moshe Lissak, *Trouble in Utopia: The Overburdened Polity of Israel* (Albany: SUNY Press, 1989), 279. See also Yosef Gorny, *Zionism and the Arabs* (Oxford: Clarendon Press, 1987).

72. Dan Rabinowitz, *Overlooking Nazareth: The Ethnography of Exclusion in Galilee* (Cambridge: Cambridge University Press, 1997), 10.

73. Majid al-Haj, "The Changing Strategies of Mobilization among the Arabs in Israel: Parliamentary Politics, Local Politics, and National Organizations," in *Local Communities and the Israeli Polity: Conflict of Values and Interests,* ed. Efraim Ben-Zadok (Albany: SUNY Press, 1993), 81–82.

74. This phenomenon was widely noted by Israeli observers at the time and afterward. See also Thomas L. Friedman, "Israeli Politicians Court Long-Ignored Arab Voters," *New York Times,* 9 July 1984.

75. The preceding discussion has drawn freely on Ian S. Lustick, "The Political Road to Binationalism: Arabs in Jewish Politics," in *The Emergence of a Binational Israel: The Second Republic in the Making,* ed. Ilan Peleg and Ofira Seliktar (Boulder, Colo.: Westview, 1989); Benyamin Neuberger, "The Arab Minority in Israeli Politics, 1948–1992—From Marginality to Influence," *Asian and African Studies* 27, nos. 1–2 (July 1993): 149–69; and Lustick, "The Changing Political Role of Israeli Arabs," in *The Elections in Israel—1988,* ed. Asher Arian and Michal Shamir (Boulder, Colo.: Westview, 1990).

76. Shafir and Peled, *Being Israeli.* See also Eliot A. Cohen, "Israel after Heroism," *Foreign Affairs* 77, no. 6 (November–December 1998): 112–28, and Tom Segev, *Elvis in Jerusalem: Post-Zionism and the Americanization of Israel* (New York: Metropolitan Books, 2002).

77. Yoram Hazony, *The Jewish State: The Struggle for Israel's Soul* (New York: Basic Books, 2000).

78. Such accounts, and the traditionalist rebuttals, are too numerous to cite here. On these debates, see the special issue of *History and Memory* 7, no. 1 (Spring/Summer 1995); Laurence J. Silberstein, *The Postzionism Debates: Knowledge and Power in Israeli Culture* (New York: Routledge, 1999); Anita Shapira and Derek J. Penslar, eds., *Israeli Historical Revisionism: From Left to Right* (London: Frank Cass, 2003); and Deborah L. Wheeler, "Does Post-Zionism Have a Future?" in *Traditions and Transitions in Israel Studies,* ed. Laura Z. Eisenberg et al. (Albany: SUNY Press, 2003).

79. Stuart Cohen, *Towards a New Portrait of a (New) Israeli Soldier* (Ramat Gan: Bar Ilan University, Begin-Sadat Center for Strategic Studies, 1997), 105–9; see also Reuven Gal and

Stuart A. Cohen, "Israel: Still Waiting in the Wings," in *The Postmodern Military: Armed Forces after the Cold War*, ed. Charles C. Moskos et al. (New York: Oxford University Press, 2000).

80. See Yaron Ezrahi, "Democratic Politics and Culture in Modern Israel: Recent Trends," in *Israeli Democracy under Stress*, ed. Ehud Sprinzak and Larry Diamond, and Gabriel Sheffer, "Individualism vs. National Coherence: The Current Discourse on Sovereignty, Citizenship, and Loyalty," *Israel Studies* 2, no. 2 (Fall 1997): 118–45.

81. When he became IDF chief of staff in 1991, Ehud Barak famously (in the eyes of some, notoriously) said that he wanted the army to become "smaller and smarter," implying that it was at present too large and too dumb.

82. Interview with Salman Falaḥ (15 June 2000, Ḥaifa); interview with Gabriel Ben-Dor (14 June 2000, Ḥaifa).

83. Asher Arian, *Israeli Public Opinion on National Security 2002*, Memorandum No. 61 (Tel Aviv: Tel Aviv University, Jaffe Center for Strategic Studies, 2002).

84. Ya'alon quoted in Sharmila Devi, "Arrests Fuel Debate on Israeli Arab Loyalty," *Financial Times*, 28 August 2002; see also Serge Schmemann, "7 More Israeli Arabs Jailed," *New York Times*, 27 August 2002.

85. Arian, *Israeli Public Opinion on National Security 2002*, 27–29, 36–37.

86. Asher Arian, *Israeli Public Opinion on National Security 2003*, Memorandum No. 67 (Tel Aviv: Tel Aviv University, Jaffe Center for Strategic Studies, 2003); Arian, *Security Opinion 2004*, unpublished ms., Jaffe Center for Strategic Studies.

Part I. Conclusion

1. Baruch Kimmerling, *The Invention and Decline of Israeliness: State, Society, and the Military* (Berkeley: University of California Press, 2001), esp. chap. 6.

2. Jack Bell, "Arabs Become Israel's Heroes," *New York Times*, 5 April 2005; Steven Erlanger, "A National Hero One Day, an Enemy to Some the Next," *New York Times*, 22 April 2005. See also Matthew Gutman, "'We'd Rather Lose Than Have an Arab Score,'" *Jerusalem Post*, 5 April 2005.

3. As'ad Ghanem, *The Palestinian-Arab Minority in Israel, 1948–2000* (Albany: SUNY Press, 2001), 160–63.

4. As'ad Ghanem and Anton Shalaḥat, "Attitudes of Jewish Israelis on Various Subjects Related to the Israeli-Palestinian Conflict and to the Palestinian Citizens of Israel" (in Hebrew), April 2005, Madar—The Palestinian Center for Israel Studies, Ramallah.

5. See, among others, Jacob M. Landau, *The Arab Minority in Israel, 1967–1991: Political Aspects* (Oxford: Clarendon Press, 1993), and Elie Rekhess, "The Arabs in Israel: In a Tangle of Identities," in *The Arabs in Israeli Politics: Dilemmas of Identity*, ed. Elie Rekhess (in Hebrew) (Tel Aviv: Dayan Center for Middle Eastern and African Studies, 1998). Alan Dowty includes this argument as well; see his *The Jewish State: A Century Later* (Berkeley: University of California Press, 1998), 193–97, 200–207.

6. Ian Lustick, *Arabs in the Jewish State: Israel's Control of a National Minority* (Austin: University of Texas Press, 1980). See also Shimon Avivi, "Policy Towards the Druze in Israel and Its Implementation: Consistency and Lapses, 1948–1967" (in Hebrew), PhD diss., University of Ḥaifa, 2002; Zeev Rosenhek, "New Developments in the Sociology of Palestinian Citizens of Israel: An Analytical Review," *Ethnic and Racial Studies* 21, no. 3 (May 1998): 558–78; and Shmuel Sandler, "Israeli Arabs and the Jewish State: The Activation of a Community in Suspended Animation," *Middle Eastern Studies* 31, no. 4 (October 1995): 932–52.

7. Moreover, Lustick seems to offer a stronger explanation for quiescence than for mobilization, since the central thrust of policy did not change in the mid-1970s. The MA was dissolved in 1966, but only the formal mechanism of surveillance and control had

changed. Many of the MA's functions had been transferred earlier to civilian authorities (i.e., police), and the GSS continued to monitor "hostile elements." Those who had opposed the MA generally did not call for an end to the "supervision" of the Arab population. See Yair Baumel, "The Military Administration and the Process of Its Dissolution, 1958–1968" (in Hebrew), *Mizraḥ He-Ḥadash* 43 (2002): 133–56.

8. See Lustick, *Arabs in the Jewish State.*

9. Aharon Layish, "Taqiyya among the Druzes," *Asian and African Studies* 19, no. 3 (1985): 245–81. See also Ḥaim Blanc, "Druze Particularism: Modern Aspects of an Old Problem," *Middle Eastern Affairs* 3 (November 1952): 315–21.

10. Eliezer Tauber, *The Emergence of the Arab Movements* (London: Frank Cass, 1993), 71–72, 149, 223, 233, 280, and Tauber, *The Arab Movements in World War I* (London: Frank Cass, 1993), 64, 78–79, 114, 132–33. On tribal motivations during the Great Arab Revolt, see Tariq Tell, "Guns, Gold, and Grain: War and Food Supply in the Making of Transjordan," in *War, Institutions, and Social Change in the Middle East,* ed. Steven Heydemann (Berkeley: University of California Press, 2000).

11. Nissim Dana, *The Druze in the Middle East: Their Faith, Leadership, Identity and Status* (Brighton: Sussex Academic Press, 2003), 9–11.

12. For other critiques of the taqiyya argument, see Kais Firro, "The Druze in and between Syria, Lebanon, and Israel," in *Ethnicity, Pluralism, and the State in the Middle East,* ed. Milton J. Esman and Itamar Rabinovich (Ithaca: Cornell University Press, 1988), 186–87, and Laila Parsons, "The Druze and the Birth of Israel," in *The War for Palestine: Rewriting the History of 1948,* ed. Eugene L. Rogan and Avi Shlaim (Cambridge: Cambridge University Press, 2001), 73–76.

13. Quoted in Arnold Sherman, *The Druse* (Tel Aviv: Bazak, 1975), 47. See also Avivi, "Policy Toward the Druze," 340–49, and Yitzhak Ben-Tsvi, *The Land of Israel under Ottoman Rule: Four Centuries of History* (in Hebrew) (Jerusalem: Bialik Institute, 1955) (Ben-Tsvi later served as Israel's second president).

14. See Parsons, "Druze and the Birth of Israel," 70–76, and Parsons, "The Druze, the Jews, and the Creation of a Shared History," in *Muslim-Jewish Encounters: Intellectual Traditions and Modern Politics,* ed. Ronald L. Nettler and Suha Taji-Farouki (Amsterdam: Harwood Academic, 1998), esp. 138–43.

15. Dana, *Druze,* 43–51.

16. I am indebted to Michael Barnett, Arman Grigorian, Ben Judkins, and Ken Waltz for discussion on these points.

17. Baruch Kimmerling, *Zionism and Territory: The Socio-Territorial Dimensions of Zionist Politics* (Berkeley: University of California, Institute of International Studies, 1983).

18. Quoted in Zaki Shalom, "Ben-Gurion and Tewfik Toubi Finally Meet (October 28, 1966)," *Israel Studies* 8, no. 2 (Summer 2003): 54–56, at 55.

19. Efraim Karsh, "Israel's Arabs v. Israel," *Commentary* 116, no. 5 (December 2003): 21–27, and former Defense Minister Moshe Arens, quoted in Peter Berkowitz, "Israel's House Divided," *Weekly Standard,* 12–19 April 2004.

20. Salaḥ Tarif (MK, Labor), quoted in Lee Hockstader, "First Arab in Israeli Cabinet Has Delicate Balancing Act," *Washington Post,* 1 April 2001.

21. For a contrary view, see International Crisis Group, "Identity Crisis: Israel and Its Arab Citizens," ICG Middle East Report No. 25, 4 March 2004.

Part II. Introduction

1. Quoted in Eric Foner, "Rights and the Constitution in Black Life during the Civil War and Reconstruction," in *The Constitution and American Life,* ed. David Thelen (Ithaca: Cornell University Press, 1988), 204–5. See also Joseph T. Glatthaar, *Forged in Battle: The*

Civil War Alliance of Black Soldiers and White Officers (Baton Rouge: Louisiana State University Press, 1990), 249–61.

2. White, *A Rising Wind* (Garden City, N.Y.: Doubleday, Doran, 1945), 48.

3. Klinkner with Smith, *The Unsteady March: The Rise and Decline of Racial Equality in America* (Chicago: University of Chicago Press, 1999). See also John Higham, "Coda: Three Reconstructions," in *Civil Rights and Social Wrongs: Black-White Relations since World War II,* ed. Higham (University Park: Pennsylvania State University Press, 1997).

Chapter 6. Great War, Great Hopes, and the Perils of Closing Ranks

1. Arthur S. Link, "Woodrow Wilson: The American as Southerner," *Journal of Southern History* 36, no. 1 (February 1970): 3–17.

2. Arthur S. Link, *Wilson: The Road to the White House* (Princeton: Princeton University Press, 1968 [1947]), 501–5; and Henry Blumenthal, "Woodrow Wilson and the Race Question," *Journal of Negro History* 48, no. 1 (January 1963): 2–5.

3. George Sinkler, *The Racial Attitudes of American Presidents: From Abraham Lincoln to Theodore Roosevelt* (Garden City, N.Y.: Doubleday, 1971), 376. See also Kenneth O'Reilly, *Nixon's Piano: Presidents and Racial Politics from Washington to Clinton* (New York: Free Press, 1995), and Russell L. Riley, *The Presidency and the Politics of Racial Inequality: Nation-Keeping from 1831 to 1965* (New York: Columbia University Press, 1999).

4. On racial segregation in the federal government before Wilson, see August Meier and Elliot Rudwick, "The Rise of Segregation in the Federal Bureaucracy, 1900–1930," *Phylon* 28 (Summer 1967): 178–84. On segregation under Wilson, see Nancy J. Weiss, "The Negro and the New Freedom: Fighting Wilsonian Segregation," *Political Science Quarterly* 84, no. 1 (March 1969): 61–79, and Kathleen L. Wolgemuth, "Woodrow Wilson and Federal Segregation," *Journal of Negro History* 44, no. 2 (April 1959): 158–73.

5. Jane Lang Scheiber and Harry N. Scheiber, "The Wilson Administration and the Wartime Mobilization of Black Americans, 1917–1918," *Labor History* 10 (Summer 1969): 433–58.

6. Quoted in Christine A. Lunardini, "Standing Firm: William Monroe Trotter's Meetings with Woodrow Wilson, 1913–1914," *Journal of Negro History* 64, no. 3 (Summer 1979): 244–64, at 249. See also Stephen R. Fox, *The Guardian of Boston, William Monroe Trotter* (New York: Atheneum, 1970), 163–86.

7. Gary Gerstle, "Liberty, Coercion, and the Making of Americans," *Journal of American History* 84, no. 2 (September 1997): 524–58.

8. Quoted in Blumenthal, "Woodrow Wilson," 8.

9. Quoted in Weiss, "Negro and the New Freedom," 62.

10. Anthony W. Marx, *Making Race and Nation: A Comparison of South Africa, the United States, and Brazil* (Cambridge: Cambridge University Press, 1998).

11. See William G. Jordan, "'The Damnable Dilemma': African American Accommodation and Protest during World War I," *Journal of American History* 81, no. 4 (March 1995): 1562–83, and David Levering Lewis, *W. E. B. Du Bois: Biography of a Race, 1868–1919* (New York: Henry Holt, 1993), 528–34.

12. Others have argued that black leaders who preached loyalty were motivated equally by fear of the expected consequences of encouraging their followers to do otherwise. See Jordan, "'The Damnable Dilemma.'"

13. Quoted in Cecilia E. O'Leary, *To Die For: The Paradox of American Patriotism* (Princeton: Princeton University Press, 1999), 211; Johnson, *Along This Way* (New York: Viking, 1961 [1933]), 337. On Johnson, see also Eugene Levy, *James Weldon Johnson: Black Leader, Black Voice* (Chicago: University of Chicago Press, 1973). For other examples, see Jonathan Rosenberg, "For Democracy, Not Hypocrisy: World War and Race Relations in the

United States, 1914–1919," *International History Review* 21, no. 3 (September 1999): 592–625.

14. Minutes of the Meeting of the Board of Directors [hereafter, Board Meeting], 9 April 1917, NAACP Papers, pt. 1, reel 1. On Ovington, see Carolyn Wedin, *Inheritors of the Spirit: Mary White Ovington and the Founding of the NAACP* (New York: John Wiley, 1998).

15. Pickens address, 1919 Annual Conference, NAACP Papers, pt. 1, reel 8.

16. Quoted in Lawrence W. Levine, "Marcus Garvey and the Politics of Revitalization," in *Black Leaders of the Twentieth Century,* ed. John Hope Franklin and August Meier (Urbana: University of Illinois Press, 1982), 112.

17. David M. Kennedy, *Over Here: The First World War and American Society* (Oxford: Oxford University Press, 1980), 39–40, and Sidney Kaplan, "Social Engineers as Saviors: Effects of World War I on Some American Liberals," *Journal of the History of Ideas* 17 (1956): 347–69.

18. *Afro-American* quoted in Jordan, "'The Damnable Dilemma,'" 1575; *Defender* quoted in Claude A. Barnett, "The Role of the Press, Radio, and Motion Picture and Negro Morale," *Journal of Negro Education* 12, no. 3 (Summer 1943): 479–80.

19. Board Meeting, 8 October 1917, NAACP Papers, pt. 1, reel 1.

20. Gunner's letter came in response to DuBois's infamous "Close Ranks" editorial. Gunner to DuBois, 25 July 1918, in *The Correspondence of W. E. B. Du Bois,* vol. 1, *Selections, 1877–1934,* ed. Herbert Aptheker (Amherst: University of Massachusetts Press, 1973), 228.

21. Robert S. Abbott, quoted in Lester M. Jones, "The Editorial Policy of Negro Newspapers of 1917–18 as Compared with That of 1941–42," *Journal of Negro History* 29, no. 1 (January 1944): 26; "Close Ranks," *Crisis* 16 (July 1918): 111.

22. DuBois denied the charge, but he did eventually come to regret his stance. See Mark Ellis, "'Closing Ranks' and 'Seeking Honors': W. E. B. Du Bois in World War I," *Journal of American History* 79, no. 1 (June 1992): 96–124; Jordan, "'The Damnable Dilemma'"; Ellis, "W. E. B. Du Bois and the Formation of Black Opinion in World War I: A Commentary on 'The Damnable Dilemma,'" *Journal of American History* 81, no. 4 (March 1995): 1584–90; and Lewis, *Du Bois: Biography of a Race,* 553–60. See also W. E. B. DuBois, *The Autobiography of W. E. B. DuBois* (New York: International Publishers, 1968), 274.

23. Horace Clayton, quoted in Theodore Kornweibel Jr., "Apathy and Dissent: Black America's Negative Responses to World War I," *South Atlantic Quarterly* 80, no. 3 (1981): 324–28, at 325.

24. Ibid., 328–38; Jordan, "'The Damnable Dilemma,'" 1574–75.

25. Randolph quoted in Elliott Rudwick, "W. E. B. Du Bois: Protagonist of the Afro-American Protest," in *Black Leaders of the Twentieth Century,* ed. John Hope Franklin and August Meier, 76; Owen, "The Failure of Negro Leadership," January 1918, in *The Messenger Reader,* ed. Sondra Kathryn Wilson (New York: Modern Library, 2000), 314–15.

26. Quoted in Scheiber and Scheiber, "Wilson Administration," 441.

27. Arthur E. Barbeau and Florette Henri, *Unknown Soldiers: Black American Troops in World War I* (Philadelphia: Temple University Press, 1974), 34–35. On Southern fears of arming blacks, see also Maj. Gen. Tasker H. Bliss to Gen. Robert K. Evans, 4 April 1917, *BUSAF* 4:3–5, and Robert B. Edgerton, *Hidden Heroism: Black Soldiers in America's Wars* (Boulder, Colo.: Westview, 2001), 72.

28. Board Meeting Minutes, 9 April 1917, 11 March 1918, NAACP Papers, pt. 1, reel 1; Baker to Rep. Edwin Webb, 21 December 1917, NAACP Papers, pt. 1, reel 15. See also Jennifer D. Keene, *Doughboys, the Great War, and the Remaking of America* (Baltimore: Johns Hopkins University Press, 2001), 82–91.

29. Jack D. Foner, *Blacks and the Military in American History: A New Perspective* (New York: Praeger, 1974), 109–32; Bernard C. Nalty, *Strength for the Fight: A History of Black Americans in the Military* (New York: Free Press, 1986), 112; Bernard C. Nalty and Morris J. MacGregor, eds., *Blacks in the Military: Essential Documents* (Wilmington, Del.: Scholarly Resources, 1981), 73–74, 82–83, 91.

30. "Documents of the War," *Crisis* 18 (May 1919), in *Writings in Periodicals Edited by W. E. B. Du Bois: Selections from the* Crisis, ed. Herbert Aptheker (Millwood, N.Y.: Kraus-Thomson, 1983), 198–205.

31. Memorandum for the Commandant, Army War College, 30 August 1924; War Department Circular No. 365, 22 July 1919; Memorandum, J. A. Hull for Deputy Chief of Staff, 15 March 1922; F. B. Payne to Walter White, 11 August 1931; *BUSAF* 4:353–54, 368–69, 374–78, 423–24. See also Nalty, *Strength for the Fight,* 128–30, and Gerald W. Patton, *War and Race: The Black Officer in the American Military, 1915–1941* (Westport, Conn.: Greenwood, 1981), chap. 7.

32. "Universal Military Training," *Crisis* 19, no. 6 (April 1920): 298, and Nell Irvin Painter, *Standing at Armageddon: The United States, 1877–1919* (New York: W. W. Norton, 1987), 330.

33. Villard and Spingarn addresses, 1919 Annual Conference, NAACP Papers, pt. 1, reel 8. On Spingarn, see B. Joyce Ross, *J. E. Spingarn and the Rise of the NAACP, 1911–1939* (New York: Atheneum, 1972).

34. Emmett J. Scott, *Scott's Official History of the American Negro in the World War* (Chicago: Homewood Press, 1919), 411, 415, 413, and generally 411–25. See also Kelly Miller, *Kelly Miller's History of the World War for Human Rights* (Washington, D.C.: Austin Jenkins, 1919), and W. Allison Sweeney, *History of the American Negro in the Great World War* (Chicago: Cuneo-Henneberry, 1919).

35. Quoted in Rosenberg, "For Democracy, Not Hypocrisy," 613.

36. Board Meeting Minutes, 10 March 1919, NAACP Papers, pt. 1, reel 1. On DuBois's never-finished history, see Chad L. Williams, "Torchbearers of Democracy: The First World War and the Figure of the African American Soldier," PhD diss., Princeton University, 2004, chap. 9.

37. Similar debates occurred after the U.S. Civil War. See Joseph T. Glatthaar, *Forged in Battle: The Civil War Alliance of Black Soldiers and White Officers* (Baton Rouge: Louisiana State University Press, 1990), 249–61.

38. Gen. Robert Bullard, who had commanded the Ninety-second Infantry Division during the war, published a damning memoir, which the NAACP sought, to no avail, to have suppressed. See Bullard, *Personalities and Reminiscences of the War* (Garden City, N.Y.: Doubleday, Page, 1925), 291–98, and articles and letters published in the *New York Herald Tribune* and elsewhere, June 1925, clippings in NAACP Papers, pt. 9, reel 3.

39. Quoted in W. E. B. DuBois, "The Negro Soldier in Service Abroad during the First World War," *Journal of Negro Education* 12, no. 3 (Summer 1943): 324–25.

40. Resolutions, 1919 Annual Conference, NAACP Papers, pt. 1, reel 8.

41. Scott address, 1919 Annual Conference, and Storey address, 1921 Annual Conference, NAACP Papers, pt. 1, reel 8; Johnson, "The Faith of the American Negro," *Crisis,* August 1922, in *The* Crisis *Reader: Stories, Poetry, and Essays from the N.A.A.C.P.'s* Crisis *Magazine,* ed. Sondra Kathryn Wilson (New York: Modern Library, 1999), 369; Resolutions, 1919 Annual Conference, NAACP Papers, pt. 1, reel 8. See also, from the 1919 annual meeting, the addresses of Leo N. Farrot, B. Harrison Fisher, William Pickens, and Charles Edward Russell; from the 1920 annual meeting, that of Moorfield Storey; and from the 1922 meeting, the addresses of James Baker and Moorfield Storey—all in NAACP Papers, pt. 1, reel 8.

42. Soldier (unsigned), Camp Grant, to NAACP [edited for punctuation], 17 November 1918, NAACP Papers, pt. 9, reel 1; Floyd P. Gibson, "Illinois Troops Are Training in France," *New York Age,* 15 June 1918, and "Our Black Troops," *Chicago Post,* 19 November 1918, both clippings in NAACP Papers, pt. 9, reel 3. For other examples, see William G. Jordan, *Black Newspapers and America's War for Democracy, 1914-1920* (Chapel Hill: University of North Carolina Press, 2001).

43. Moton, "Negro Soldiers Win Lasting Fame Despite the 'Whispering Gallery,'" n.d., clipping in NAACP Papers, pt. 9, reel 1; Trotter quoted in Rosenberg, "For Democracy,

Not Hypocrisy," 608, 593. For other examples, see Williams, "Torchbearers of Democracy," 203–7.

44. Resolutions, 1919 Annual Conference; address by Storey, 1922 Annual Conference; address by Storey, 1920 Annual Conference—all in NAACP Papers, pt. 1, reel 8.

45. On American political discourse, see Merle Curti, *The Roots of American Loyalty* (New York: Russell and Russell, 1967 [1946]), and John Bodnar, "The Attractions of Patriotism," in *Bonds of Affection: Americans Define Their Patriotism,* ed. Bodnar (Princeton: Princeton University Press, 1996), chap. 1.

46. Quoted in Rosenberg, "For Democracy, Not Hypocrisy," 599. See also Jonathan Rosenberg, *How Far the Promised Land?: World Affairs and the American Civil Rights Movement from the First World War to Vietnam* (Princeton: Princeton University Press, 2005).

47. See Paul L. Murphy, *World War I and the Origin of Civil Liberties in the United States* (New York: W. W. Norton, 1979), and Frederick Luebke, *Bonds of Loyalty: German Americans and World War One* (DeKalb: Northern Illinois University Press, 1974).

48. Kimberly Jensen, "Women, Citizenship, and Civic Sacrifice," in *Bonds of Affection,* ed. Bodnar, 141.

49. Robert D. Cuff, "Herbert Hoover, the Ideology of Voluntarism, and War Organization during the Great War," *Journal of American History* 64, no. 2 (September 1977): 358–72; Christopher Capozzola, "The Only Badge Needed Is Your Patriotic Fervor: Vigilance, Coercion, and the Law in World War I America," *Journal of American History* 88, no. 4 (March 2002): 1354–82; and Capozzola, "Uncle Sam Wants You: Political Obligations in World War I America," PhD diss., Columbia University, 2002.

50. "Proclamation of the Selective Draft Act, May 18, 1917," *Presidential Messages and State Papers,* vol. 10, *Wilson,* 397–98.

51. Gary Gerstle, *American Crucible: Race and Nation in the Twentieth Century* (Princeton: Princeton University Press, 2001), 117–18.

52. Storey address, 1921 Annual Conference, NAACP Papers, pt. 1, reel 8; Harding to Harry Davis, 24 June 1919, NAACP Papers, pt. 11, ser. B, reel 18.

53. For an overview, see Mark Robert Schneider, *We Return Fighting: The Civil Rights Movement in the Jazz Age* (Boston: Northeastern University Press, 2002).

54. Board Meeting Minutes, 9 February 1920, NAACP Papers, pt. 1, reel 1; Report of the Secretary for March 1920 Board Meeting, NAACP Papers, pt. 1, reel 4.

55. Board Meeting Minutes, 13 September 1920, NAACP Papers, pt. 1, reel 1; Report of the Field Secretary on Interview with Senator Warren G. Harding, 9 August 1920, NAACP Papers, pt. 1, reel 16; Johnson to Harding, 28 August 1920, NAACP Papers, pt. 1, reel 16; George B. Christian Jr. (Harding's secretary) to Johnson, 22 September 1920, NAACP Papers, pt. 11, ser. B, reel 19. See also Johnson, *Along This Way,* 358–60.

56. Johnson to Harding, 20 April 1921, NAACP Papers, pt. 1, reel 16; Harding, Address to Congress, 12 April 1921, *Supplement to the Messages and Papers of the Presidents* (New York: Bureau of National Literature, 1925), 8946.

57. Johnson address, 1922 Annual Conference, NAACP Papers, pt. 1, reel 8; Johnson, *Along This Way,* 364. See also Johnson's memos to Walter White, NAACP Papers, pt. 1, reel 18.

58. Annual Message of the President, 1923; Annual Message of the President, 1926; George B. Christian Jr. to James Weldon Johnson, 8 December 1922—all in NAACP Papers, pt. 1, reel 16.

59. On Harding and Coolidge's neglect of blacks, see Donald R. McCoy, *Calvin Coolidge: The Quiet President* (Lawrence: University Press of Kansas, 1988 [1967]), 328–29; Robert K. Murray, *The Harding Era: Warren G. Harding and His Administration* (Minneapolis: University of Minnesota Press, 1969), 397–403; and Andrew Sinclair, *The Available Man: The Life behind the Masks of Warren Gamaliel Harding* (New York: Macmillan, 1965), 230–35, 240.

60. Address by Leo Farrot, 1919 Annual Conference; addresses by James Weldon Johnson and Charles W. Ervin, 1922 Annual Conference—all in NAACP Papers, pt. 1, reel 8.

61. See Lee D. Baker, *From Savage to Negro: Anthropology and the Construction of Race, 1896–1954* (Berkeley: University of California Press, 1998); Desmond King, *Making Americans: Immigration, Race, and the Origins of the Diverse Democracy* (Cambridge: Harvard University Press, 2000); and Rogers M. Smith, *Civic Ideals: Conflicting Visions of Citizenship in U.S. History* (New Haven: Yale University Press, 1997).

62. James P. Shenton, "Imperialism and Racism," in *Essays in American Historiography: Papers Presented in Honor of Allan Nevins,* ed. Donald Sheehan and Harold C. Syrett (New York: Columbia University Press, 1960). See also Michael Hunt, *Ideology and U.S. Foreign Policy* (New Haven: Yale University Press, 1987), 46–91.

63. Adam Fairclough, *Better Day Coming: Blacks and Equality, 1890–2000* (New York: Vintage, 2001), 11.

64. Higham, "Coda: Three Reconstructions," in *Civil Rights and Social Wrongs: Black-White Relations since World War II,* ed. John Higham (University Park: Pennsylvania State University Press, 1997), 182.

65. Quoted in Andrew Neather, "Labor Republicanism, Race, and Popular Patriotism in the Era of Empire, 1890–1914," in *Bonds of Affection,* ed. Bodnar, 88. See also Eric Arnesen, "'Like Banquo's Ghost, It Will Not Down': The Race Question and the American Railroad Brotherhoods, 1889–1920," *American Historical Review* 99, no. 5 (December 1994): 1601–33.

66. Paul H. Buck, *The Road to Reunion, 1865–1900* (Boston: Little, Brown, 1947 [1937]); O'Leary, *To Die For;* and Nina Silber, *The Romance of Reunion: Northerners and the South, 1865–1900* (Chapel Hill: University of North Carolina Press, 1993).

67. See, on this theme, Edgerton, *Hidden Heroism.*

68. See Margaret Vining and Barton C. Hacker, "From Camp Follower to Lady in Uniform: Women, Social Class, and Military Institutions," *Contemporary European History* 10, no. 3 (2001): 353–73.

69. Linda K. Kerber, *No Constitutional Right to Be Ladies: Women and the Obligations of Citizenship* (New York: Hill and Wang, 1998), 240.

70. Quoted in Alexander Keyssar, *The Right to Vote: The Contested History of Democracy in the United States* (New York: Basic Books, 2000), 192–93. For similar arguments, in the British context, see Brian H. Harrison, *Separate Spheres: The Opposition to Women's Suffrage in Britain* (London: Croom Helm, 1978), 73–78.

71. As Joan Scott points out, feminism has often been marked by a deep tension in that feminists have sought to deny the difference between men and women while at the same time laboring on behalf of women (as a social category). Scott argues that this unavoidable paradox consigned French feminism to the margins. See Scott, *Only Paradoxes to Offer: French Feminists and the Rights of Man* (Cambridge: Harvard University Press, 1996).

72. For overviews, see Sara M. Evans, *Born for Liberty: A History of Women in America* (New York: Free Press, 1989), esp. 152–56, and Sara Hunter Graham, *Woman Suffrage and the New Democracy* (New Haven: Yale University Press, 1996), 25–32.

73. World War I also may have helped the suffrage movement by discrediting German-Americans and weakening anti-Prohibition ("wet") interests—two of suffrage's major prewar opponents. See Eileen L. McDonagh and H. Douglas Price, "Woman Suffrage in the Progressive Era: Patterns of Opposition and Support in Referenda Voting, 1910–1918," *American Political Science Review* 79, no. 2 (June 1985): 431.

74. "Proclamation of the Selective Draft Act, May 18, 1917," *Presidential Messages and State Papers,* vol. 10, *Wilson,* 397. On women's roles during the war, see Graham, *Woman Suffrage,* 99–127, and Kimberly Jensen, "Minerva on the Field of Mars: American Women, Citizenship, and Military Service in the First World War," PhD diss., University of Iowa, 1992.

75. Christine A. Lunardini and Thomas J. Knock, "Woodrow Wilson and Woman Suffrage: A New Look," *Political Science Quarterly* 95, no. 4 (December 1980): 655–71.

76. Quoted in Eleanor Flexner and Ellen Fitzpatrick, *Century of Struggle: The Woman's Rights Movement in the United States* (Cambridge: Harvard University Press, Belknap Press, 1996 [1959]), 302–3. For similar framings, see Maud Wood Park's memoir, *Front Door Lobby* (Boston: Beacon Press, 1960); Park also relates how suffragists' opponents sought to use the war to counter suffrage (140–41, 146–47). Many historians agree that the war made possible the victory of the suffrage movement; see Evans, *Born for Liberty*, 170–72; Flexner and Fitzpatrick, *Century of Struggle*, 278–319; and Keyssar, *Right to Vote*, 215–21. For quantitative support, see Eileen L. McDonagh, "Issues and Constituencies in the Progressive Era: House Roll Call Voting on the Nineteenth Amendment, 1913–1919," *Journal of Politics* 51, no. 1 (February 1989): 119–36. For a more skeptical view, see Ellen Carol DuBois, *Woman Suffrage and Women's Rights* (New York: New York University Press, 1998), 272.

77. Graham, *Woman Suffrage*, 105, 146; Harrison, *Separate Spheres*, 203–5.

78. Kennedy, *Over Here*, 284.

79. Lee Ann Banaszak, *Why Movements Succeed or Fail: Opportunity, Culture, and the Struggle for Woman Suffrage* (Princeton: Princeton University Press, 1996); Graham, *Woman Suffrage*; and Park, *Front Door Lobby*. For the debate over the Progressives' impact, see William H. Chafe, *The American Woman: Her Changing Social, Economic, and Political Roles, 1920–1970* (New York: Oxford University Press, 1972), 15–18, and McDonagh, "Issues and Constituencies."

80. Eileen McDonagh argues that women's political inclusion as voters and officeholders, in the United States and elsewhere, has been in part the product of a paradoxical combination of arguments premised on sameness and difference. Although she does not believe that women's war work played much role in winning suffrage in the United States, she does affirm the causal role of discourse in democratization. See her "Political Citizenship and Democratization: The Gender Paradox," *American Political Science Review* 96, no. 3 (September 2002): 535–52, at 536; and McDonagh, personal communication, 12 March 2004.

81. Women were not, however, granted the same rights and benefits as men during and after either world war, for what had emerged was a new gendered hierarchy that narrowly circumscribed women's citizenship. See Gretchen Ritter, "Of War and Virtue: Gender, Citizenship, and Veterans' Benefits after World War II," *Comparative Social Research* 20 (2002): 201–26.

82. Kenneth B. Clark, "Morale of the Negro on the Home Front: World Wars I and II," *Journal of Negro Education* 12, no. 3 (Summer 1943): 420.

83. Scott address, 1919 Annual Conference, NAACP Papers, pt. 1, reel 8.

84. Resolutions, 1919 Annual Conference, NAACP Papers, pt. 1, reel 8; Johnson, "The Faith of the American Negro," *Crisis*, August 1922, in *The Crisis Reader*, ed. Wilson, 368.

85. See Kenneth R. Janken, *Rayford W. Logan and the Dilemma of the African American Intellectual* (Amherst: University of Massachusetts Press, 1993), 37–43.

86. These leaders often endorsed an explicitly elitist politics. Delany, for instance, blithely assumed that the interests of black elites and masses necessarily converged. By the late 1850s, he no longer envisioned a popular emigration to Africa, advocating rather a "select" migration to lead the revitalization of the African continent. Over the course of Reconstruction, he became "increasingly estranged from Republican Reconstruction and its constituency of poor blacks." See Nell Irvin Painter, "Martin R. Delany: Elitism and Black Nationalism," in *Black Leaders of the Nineteenth Century*, ed. Leon Litwack and August Meier (Urbana: University of Illinois Press, 1988), quote at 166.

87. Dean E. Robinson, *Black Nationalism in American Politics and Thought* (Cambridge: Cambridge University Press, 2001), 24.

88. W. E. B. DuBois, "Back to Africa," *Century* 105, no. 4 (February 1923): 539–48.

89. James R. Grossman, "A Chance to Make Good: 1900–1929," in *To Make Our World Anew: A History of African Americans,* ed. Robin D. G. Kelley and Earl Lewis (Oxford: Oxford University Press, 2000), 406–8; Winston James, *Holding Aloft the Banner of Ethiopia: Caribbean Radicalism in Early Twentieth-Century America* (London: Verso, 1998), 134–36, 193–94. For a rare local study, see Emory J. Tolbert, *The UNIA and Black Los Angeles* (Los Angeles: UCLA, Center for Afro-American Studies, 1980), on the visit to Los Angeles, 70–74; on the L.A. branch, 87–108.

90. James, *Holding Aloft,* 193. See also DuBois, "Back to Africa," 546; Levine, "Marcus Garvey," esp. 112–14; and David Levering Lewis, *W. E. B. Du Bois: The Fight for Equality and the American Century, 1919–1963* (New York: Henry Holt, 2000), 62.

91. DuBois, "Back to Africa," 539, 541; "The Demagog," *Crisis* 23, no. 6 (April 1922): 252.

92. Levine, "Marcus Garvey," 105–38, quote at 133–34.

93. The following does not focus on the back-to-Africa movement for which Garvey is best known. Although Garvey's rhetoric often created the impression that he advocated a mass return to Africa, he saw such migration and the emergence of a great black empire on the African continent as gradual, long-term processes.

94. Quoted in Tony Martin, *Race First: The Ideological and Organizational Struggles of Marcus Garvey and the Universal Negro Improvement Association* (Westport, Conn.: Greenwood, 1976), 33.

95. Michael C. Dawson, *Black Visions: The Roots of Contemporary African American Political Ideologies* (Chicago: University of Chicago Press, 2001).

96. Randolph, "Reply to Marcus Garvey," *Messenger,* August 1922, in *The* Messenger *Reader,* ed. Wilson, 350; Garvey quoted in Martin, *Race First,* 355. On Garvey, see Edmund David Cronon, *Black Moses: The Story of Marcus Garvey and the Universal Negro Improvement Association* (Madison: University of Wisconsin Press, 1964); Martin, *Race First;* and Theodore G. Vincent, *Black Power and the Garvey Movement* (Berkeley: Ramparts Press, 1971).

97. "Marcus Garvey," *Crisis* 21, no. 3 (January 1921): 114–15; "Back to Africa," 542.

98. Lewis, *Du Bois: The Fight for Equality,* 37–84, 148–52, quote at 152.

99. DuBois, *Autobiography,* 274; DuBois, "The Field and Function of the American Negro College," June 1933, in *A W. E. B. Du Bois Reader,* ed. Andrew G. Paschal (New York: Macmillan, 1971), 51–69, at 67–68.

100. "Segregation," *Crisis* 41 (January 1934): 20, in *Selections from the* Crisis, ed. Aptheker, 727–28; "Field and Function," 67–68; "A Negro Nation within the Nation," *Current History* (June 1935), in *W. E. B. Du Bois Reader,* ed. Paschal, 69–78.

101. Mark Tushnet, "The Politics of Equality in Constitutional Law: The Equal Protection Clause, Dr. Du Bois, and Charles Hamilton Houston," in *The Constitution and American Life,* ed. David Thelen (Ithaca: Cornell University Press, 1988), 230–36, at 236. See also Lewis, *Du Bois: The Fight for Equality,* 330–43.

102. Chairman of the Board to White, 10 January 1934, Papers of the NAACP, pt. 11, ser. A, reel 30.

103. Kenneth R. Janken, *White: The Biography of Walter White, Mr. NAACP* (New York: New Press, 2003), 179–84, 192–96.

104. Spingarn address, 1919 Annual Conference, NAACP Papers, pt. 1, reel 8.

105. Spingarn to White, 12 January 1934; White to Spingarn, 15 January 1934; White, "On Segregation," n.d.; Spingarn to White, 25 April 1934—all in NAACP Papers, pt. 11, ser. A, reel 30.

106. Pickens article, no title, *Negro World,* December 1921; Pickens to Garvey, July 1922—both in NAACP Papers, pt. 11, ser. A, reel 35. See also Sheldon Avery, *Up from Washington: William Pickens and the Negro Struggle for Equality* (Newark: University of Delaware Press, 1989), 51–74, and Martin, *Race First,* 311–14.

107. "Returning Soldiers," *Crisis* 18 (May 1919), in *Selections from the* Crisis, ed. Aptheker, 196–97, at 197.
108. W. A. Domingo, "If We Must Die," *Messenger*, September 1919, in *The* Messenger *Reader*, ed. Wilson, 336; Harry H. Pace, address to 1921 Annual Conference, NAACP Papers, pt. 1, reel 8. See also Alain Locke, ed., *The New Negro: An Interpretation* (New York: A. and C. Boni, 1925).
109. Storey to Shillady, 21 May 1920, NAACP Papers, pt. 1, reel 24.
110. However, Steven Reich, in his study of postwar black Texas, argues that only violence snuffed out intense black political activity. Reich, "Soldiers of Democracy: Black Texans and the Fight for Citizenship, 1917–1921," *Journal of American History* 82, no. 4 (March 1996): 1478–1504.
111. DuBois ignored the most obvious conclusion and instead attributed the *Crisis*'s declining circulation to, among other things, technical difficulties, strikes, the rising costs of production, and the increased subscription price. See Board Meeting Minutes, 14 October 1918, 11 July 1919, 12 July 1920, NAACP Papers, pt. 1, reel 1. For circulation figures, see NAACP Twelfth Annual Report, *Crisis* 23, no. 5 (March 1922): 214.
112. NAACP Eleventh Annual Report (abridged), *Crisis* 20, no. 5 (March 1921): 203.
113. Even when politically quiescent, however, the black masses have often engaged in other forms of resistance. See Robin D. G. Kelley, "'We Are Not What We Seem': Rethinking Black Working-Class Opposition in the Jim Crow South," *Journal of American History* 80, no. 1 (June 1993): 75–112.
114. Jordan, "'The Damnable Dilemma,'" 1565.
115. See Fairclough, *Better Day Coming*, 102–6; Reich, "Soldiers of Democracy"; Rosenberg, "For Democracy, Not Hypocrisy," 618–20; and Williams, "Torchbearers of Democracy," chap. 7.
116. Scott quoted in Scheiber and Scheiber, "Wilson Administration," 458; Nalty, *Strength for the Fight*, 123.
117. Houston to FDR, 8 October 1937, *BUSAF* 4:469–70. On Houston, see Genna Rae McNeil, *Groundwork: Charles Hamilton Houston and the Struggle for Civil Rights* (Philadelphia: University of Pennsylvania Press, 1983).

Chapter 7. Good War, Cold War, and the Limits of Liberalism

1. E. H. Carr, *The Twenty Years' Crisis, 1919–1939: An Introduction to the Study of International Relations* (London: Macmillan, 1981 [1939]).
2. Statement of Rayford W. Logan, before U.S. House Committee on Military Affairs, *BUSAF* 4:525–27.
3. Report on Conference at the White House, 27 September 1940, and Assistant Secretary of War Robert P. Patterson to President, 8 October 1940, *BUSAF* 5:26–27, 29–30. See also "White House Conference," Secretary's Report, 14 October 1940, NAACP Papers, pt. 1, reel 6.
4. Army Chief of Staff to Secretary of War, 1 December 1941, *BUSAF* 5:114–15.
5. McCloy to Hastie, 2 July 1942, *BUSAF* 5:167.
6. Civilian Aide to the Secretary of War for Secretary of War, 22 September 1941, *BUSAF* 5:76–101, quotes at 80–81, 100–101. See also Gilbert Ware, *William Hastie: Grace under Pressure* (New York: Oxford University Press, 1984).
7. For analyses of this violence, see Daniel Kryder, *Divided Arsenal: Race and the American State during World War II* (Cambridge: Cambridge University Press, 2000), 66–74, 133–207; Stanley Sandler, "Homefront Battlefront: Military Racial Disturbances in the Zone of the Interior," *War & Society* 11, no. 2 (October 1993): 101–15; and Harvard Sitkoff, "Racial Militancy and Interracial Violence in the Second World War," *Journal of American History* 58, no. 3 (December 1971): 661–81.

8. See Richard M. Dalfiume, *Desegregation of the U.S. Armed Forces* (Columbia: University of Missouri Press, 1969), 1–131; Jack D. Foner, *Blacks and the Military in American History: A New Perspective* (New York: Praeger, 1974), 133–75; Ulysses Grant Lee, *The United States Army in World War II—the Employment of Negro Troops* (Washington, D.C.: Office of the Chief of Military History, Department of the Army, 1966); Morris J. MacGregor Jr., *Integration of the Armed Forces, 1940–1965* (Washington, D.C.: Center of Military History, U.S. Army, 1981), 17–122; and Bernard C. Nalty, *Strength for the Fight: A History of Black Americans in the Military* (New York: Free Press, 1986), 143–203.

9. Except where otherwise cited, the following discussion draws on Dalfiume, *Desegregation*, 132–47; Foner, *Blacks and the Military*, 176–200; MacGregor, *Integration*, 123–205; and Nalty, *Strength for the Fight*, 204–34.

10. Army Service Forces Study, 1 October 1945; Col. E. F. Olsen to U.S. Army Chief of Staff, 28 November 1945; Gillem Board Report, War Department Circular No. 124—all in Bernard C. Nalty and Morris J. MacGregor, eds., *Blacks in the Military: Essential Documents* (Wilmington, Del.: Scholarly Resources, 1981), 174–82 (quote at 180), 188–202.

11. See Secretary of War Robert P. Patterson to Deputy Chief of Staff, 7 January 1947; Maj. J. F. Lieblich et al. to Gen. Paul, 29 April 1948—both in *BUSAF* 7:63–71, 176–79.

12. Quoted in Donald R. McCoy and Richard T. Ruetten, *Quest and Response: Minority Rights and the Truman Administration* (Lawrence: University Press of Kansas, 1973), 37. See also Nalty, *Strength for the Fight*, 216.

13. Various Board Meeting Minutes, 1945–1949, NAACP Papers, pt. 1, reels 2–3.

14. Roy Wilkins, with Tom Mathews, *Standing Fast: The Autobiography of Roy Wilkins* (New York: Viking Press, 1982), 190; see also Board Meeting Minutes, 12 December 1949, NAACP Papers, pt. 1, reel 3.

15. See, among others, Martha Biondi, *To Stand and Fight: The Civil Rights Movement in Postwar New York City* (Cambridge: Harvard University Press, 2003); Adam Fairclough, *Race and Democracy: The Civil Rights Struggle in Louisiana* (Athens: University of Georgia Press, 1995); Gail Williams O'Brien, *The Color of the Law: Race, Violence, and Justice in the Post–World War II South* (Chapel Hill: University of North Carolina Press, 1999); and Charles M. Payne, *I've Got the Light of Freedom: The Organizing Tradition and the Mississippi Freedom Struggle* (Berkeley: University of California Press, 1995).

16. Quoted in Vincent Harding et al., "We Changed the World: 1945–1970," in *To Make Our World Anew: A History of African Americans*, ed. Robin D. G. Kelley and Earl Lewis (Oxford: Oxford University Press, 2000), 445.

17. Biondi, *To Stand and Fight*, 16.

18. W. Robert Ming Jr. address, 1941 Annual Conference, NAACP Papers, pt. 1, reel 10; Weaver quoted in Kryder, *Divided Arsenal*, 149; Walter White to Henry Stimson, in Report of Secretary to Board, September 1943, NAACP Papers, pt. 1, reel 6; Margaret C. McCulloch, "What Should the American Negro Reasonably Expect as the Outcome of a Real Peace?" *Journal of Negro Education* 12, no. 3 (Summer 1943): 559.

19. *To Secure These Rights: The Report of the President's Committee on Civil Rights* (Washington, D.C.: U.S. Government Printing Office, 1947), 8; Houston statement, in "Minutes of Meetings of PCCR, 15 May 1947," Nash Files, SMOF, Truman Papers, HSTL; Hughes quoted in Arnold Rampersad, *The Life of Langston Hughes*, vol. 2, *I Dream a World* (New York: Oxford University Press, 1988), 50.

20. Blum, *V Was for Victory: Politics and American Culture during World War II* (New York: Harcourt Brace Jovanovich, 1976), 189. See also Adam Fairclough, *Better Day Coming: Blacks and Equality, 1890–2000* (New York: Vintage, 2001), 190.

21. Statement of A. Philip Randolph, 30 March 1948, Senate Committee on Armed Services, *Hearings on Universal Military Training*, 80th Congress, 2nd session; White to Sen. Wayne Morse, 1 April 1948, NAACP Papers, pt. 9, reel 7. See also Dalfiume, *Desegregation*, 163–70, and McCoy and Ruetten, *Quest and Response*, 106–12.

22. See Lee Finkle, "The Conservative Aims of Militant Rhetoric: Black Protest during

World War II," *Journal of American History* 60 (December 1973): 692–713, and Harvard Sitkoff, "African American Militancy in the World War II South: Another Perspective," in *Remaking Dixie: The Impact of World War II on the American South,* ed. Neil R. McMillen (Jackson: University of Mississippi Press, 1997), 70–92.

23. Quoted in Sitkoff, "Racial Militancy," 662. On the lessons of World War I, see the addresses of William Hastie and Walter White, 1940 Annual Conference, NAACP Papers, pt. 1, reel 10.

24. McCloy to Hastie, 2 July 1942, *BUSAF* 5:167.

25. Quoted in Clayton R. Koppes and Gregory D. Black, "Blacks, Loyalty, and Motion-Picture Propaganda in World War II," *Journal of American History* 73, no. 2 (September 1986): 385–86. On black sympathy for the Japanese, see Roy Wilkins, "Improving Negro Morale—with Negroes," for Office of Facts and Figures, 3 April 1942, NAACP Papers, pt. 9, reel 7. The FBI was surprisingly dismissive of questions about black loyalty. See Robert A. Hill, ed., *The FBI's Racon: Racial Conditions in the United States during World War II* (Boston: Northeastern University Press, 1995).

26. Board Meeting Minutes, 8 May 1944, NAACP Papers, pt. 1, reel 3. See also Richard Dalfiume, "The 'Forgotten Years' of the Negro Revolution," *Journal of American History* 55, no. 1 (June 1968): 90–106.

27. At this time as well, the small, pacifist-leaning Congress of Racial Equality began to organize direct mass action. CORE remained marginal, however, until the early 1960s.

28. Board Meeting Minutes, 8 December 1941, NAACP Papers, pt. 1, reel 3; C. L. Dellums address, 1942 Annual Conference, NAACP papers, pt. 1, reel 11.

29. Finkle, "Conservative Aims."

30. Quoted in Kenneth R. Janken, *Rayford W. Logan and the Dilemma of the African-American Intellectual* (Amherst: University of Massachusetts Press, 1993), 114–44, at 120. See also Neil A. Wynn, *The Afro-American and the Second World War* (New York: Holmes and Meier, 1975).

31. Quoted in Finkle, "Conservative Aims," 703–4. See also addresses by W. Robert Ming Jr. and Roscoe Dunjee, 1941 Annual Conference; and Resolutions, 1942 Annual Conference—all in NAACP Papers, pt. 1, reel 10; and White address, 1944 Annual Conference, NAACP Papers, pt. 1, reel 11.

32. Quoted in Dalfiume, *Desegregation*, 26.

33. Sitkoff, "Racial Militancy," 680. See also Fairclough, *Better Day Coming*, 158–59. Daniel Kryder (*Divided Arsenal*, 246–47) suggests this was the product of the decline of black leverage as the war turned the Allies' way.

34. See John B. Kirby, *Black Americans in the Roosevelt Era: Liberalism and Race* (Knoxville: University of Tennessee Press, 1980); Patricia Sullivan, *Days of Hope: Race and Democracy in the New Deal Era* (Chapel Hill: University of North Carolina Press, 1996); and Nancy J. Weiss, *Farewell to the Party of Lincoln: Black Politics in the Age of FDR* (Princeton: Princeton University Press, 1983).

35. In the late 1940s, moreover, the federal courts repeatedly rebuffed efforts to circumvent the court's 1944 ruling. See V. O. Key Jr., with Alexander Heard, *Southern Politics in State and Nation* (New York: Knopf, 1949), 619–43.

36. Kenneth O'Reilly, *Nixon's Piano: Presidents and Racial Politics from Washington to Clinton* (New York: Free Press, 1995), 143.

37. Doug McAdam, *Political Process and the Development of Black Insurgency* (Chicago: University of Chicago Press, 1982). On the Great Migration, see also Nicholas Lemann, *The Promised Land: The Great Black Migration and How It Changed America* (New York: Knopf, 1991), and Stewart E. Tolnay, "The African American 'Great Migration' and Beyond," *Annual Review of Sociology* 29 (2003): 209–32.

38. Sullivan, *Days of Hope*, 158–62; Robert Korstad and Nelson Lichtenstein, "Opportunities Found and Lost: Labor, Radicals, and the Early Civil Rights Movement," *Journal of American History* 75, no. 3 (December 1988): 786–811.

39. See Myrdal, with Richard Sterner and Arnold Rose, *An American Dilemma: The Negro Problem and Modern Democracy* (New York: Harper, 1944), 997–1024.

40. See William C. Berman, *The Politics of Civil Rights in the Truman Administration* (Columbus: Ohio State University Press, 1970); Barton J. Bernstein, "The Ambiguous Legacy: The Truman Administration and Civil Rights," in his *Politics and Policies of the Truman Administration* (Chicago: Quadrangle Books, 1970), 269–314; Gary A. Donaldson, *Truman Defeats Dewey* (Lexington: University Press of Kentucky, 1998); and McCoy and Ruetten, *Quest and Response.*

41. See Thomas Borstelmann, *The Cold War and the Color Line: American Race Relations in the Global Arena* (Cambridge: Harvard University Press, 2001); Mary L. Dudziak, *Cold War Civil Rights: Race and the Image of American Democracy* (Princeton: Princeton University Press, 2000); Azza Salama Layton, *International Politics and Civil Rights Politics in the United States, 1941–1960* (Cambridge: Cambridge University Press, 2000); Jonathan Rosenberg, *How Far the Promised Land?: World Affairs and the American Civil Rights Movement from the First World War to Vietnam* (Princeton: Princeton University Press, 2005); and John David Skrentny, *The Minority Rights Revolution* (Cambridge: Harvard University Press, 2002).

42. See Berman, *Politics of Civil Rights,* 7–24; Robert H. Ferrell, *Harry S. Truman: A Life* (Columbia: University of Missouri Press, 1994), 292–93; Alonzo Hamby, *Man of the People: A Life of Harry S. Truman* (New York: Oxford University Press, 1995), 272, 364–65; and David McCullough, *Truman* (New York: Simon and Schuster, 1992), 53–54, 86, 110, 247–48, 588.

43. Maybank quoted in Robert J. Donovan, *Conflict and Crisis: The Presidency of Harry S Truman, 1945–1948* (New York: Norton, 1977), 33; *Crisis* quoted in McCoy and Ruetten, *Quest and Response,* 13.

44. For good overviews, placing civil rights in the context of the Fair Deal, see William H. Chafe, "Postwar American Society: Dissent and Social Reform," in *The Truman Presidency,* ed. Michael J. Lacey (Cambridge: Cambridge University Press, 1989), 156–73, and Alonzo L. Hamby, *Beyond the New Deal: Harry S. Truman and American Liberalism* (New York: Columbia University Press, 1973).

45. See, at the Truman Library, oral histories conducted with David E. Bell, 210; Clark M. Clifford, 261–64, 453–59; Matthew J. Connelly, 439–40; Donald S. Dawson, 20–21; and Stephen J. Spingarn, 181. See also Clark Clifford with Richard Holbrooke, *Counsel to the President: A Memoir* (New York: Random House, 1991), 206.

46. President's News Conference, 17 April 1945, in *Public Papers of the Presidents of the United States: Harry S. Truman, 1945* (Washington, D.C.: United States Government Printing Office), 10–11.

47. Truman to Rep. Adolph J. Sabath, 5 June 1945, in *Public Papers: Truman, 1945,* 104–5; reply to Southern representatives quoted in Donovan, *Conflict and Crisis,* 33; "Special Message to the Congress Presenting a 21–Point Program for the Reconversion Period," 6 September 1945, in *Public Papers: Truman, 1945,* 282.

48. Quoted in Hamby, *Beyond the New Deal,* 65. Some have suspected that Truman intentionally championed a permanent FEPC, which had no chance of passing Congress, while never pressing for increased appropriations for the current, temporary FEPC. See Louis Ruchames, *Race, Jobs, and Politics: The Story of FEPC* (New York: Columbia University Press, 1953), 126.

49. Critical of Truman are Berman, *Politics of Civil Rights,* 26–33, and Bernstein, "Ambiguous Legacy," 273–75. Close to this argument are Hamby, *Man of the People,* 365, and McCoy and Ruetten, *Quest and Response,* 20–30.

50. On the origins of the PCCR, see "PCCR—Statements, Reports and Press Releases," NAACP Papers, pt. 18, ser. C, reel 26; Bernstein, "Ambiguous Legacy," 276–82; William E. Juhnke, "President Truman's Committee on Civil Rights: The Interaction of Politics, Protest, and Presidential Advisory Commissions," *Presidential Studies Quarterly* 19, no.

3 (Summer 1989): 593–610; McCoy and Ruetten, *Quest and Response*, 44–48; and Walter White, *A Man Called White* (New York: Viking Press, 1948), 330–32.

51. Perhaps self-servingly, White at least thought so. See White to William Hastie, 26 September 1946, and White to Thurgood Marshall et al., 6 December 1946—both in NAACP Papers, pt. 18, ser. C, reel 25; and White to Maxwell Stewart, 20 February 1948, NAACP Papers, pt. 18, ser. C, reel 26.

52. Truman to Clark, 20 September 1946, in "Civil Rights and Negro Affairs, 1945–June 1947 (2)," Niles Papers, HSTL.

53. White was initially suspicious of the committee for that very reason. See White to Gov. Ellis Arnall, 21 September 1946, NAACP Papers, pt. 18, ser. C, reel 25, and White, *A Man Called White*, 331.

54. Richard Neustadt, "Congress and the Fair Deal: A Legislative Balance Sheet," in *The Shaping of Twentieth Century America*, ed. Richard Abrams and Lawrence W. Levine (Boston: Little, Brown, 1965), 574; "Remarks to Members of the President's Committee on Civil Rights," 15 January 1947, *Public Papers: Truman, 1947*, 98–99.

55. PCCR, *To Secure These Rights*.

56. "Address before NAACP," 29 June 1947, *Public Papers: Truman, 1947*, 311–13; White, *A Man Called White*, 348.

57. Berman, *Politics of Civil Rights*, 63–66, quote at 64.

58. Carr to George M. Elsey, 16 January 1948; Erving Kingsley to Clark Clifford, "Comments on 5th Draft of Civil Rights Message," n.d.—both in "President's Committee on Civil Rights," Elsey Files, SMOF, Truman Papers, HSTL.

59. Zachary Karabell, *The Last Campaign: How Harry Truman Won the 1948 Election* (New York: Knopf, 2000), 42–60, 107–15.

60. Hamby, *Man of the People*, 434–35; Clifford, *Counsel to the President*, 204–5, 209, 215.

61. Walter White to Sen. Wayne Morse, 1 April 1948, NAACP Papers, pt. 9, reel 7. See also Dalfiume, *Desegregation*, 163–70, and McCoy and Ruetten, *Quest and Response*, 106–12.

62. Benjamin Quarles, "A. Philip Randolph: Labor Leader at Large," in *Black Leaders of the Twentieth Century*, ed. John Hope Franklin and August Meier (Urbana: University of Illinois Press, 1982), 158–59. See also Desmond King, "'The Longest Road to Equality': The Politics of Institutional Desegregation under Truman," *Journal of Historical Sociology* 6, no. 2 (June 1993): 131–32.

63. See, for example, Roy Wilkins to David Niles, 20 January 1949, in "NAACP," PPF 393, Truman Papers, HSTL; Walter White to Matthew Connelly, 5 February 1949, OF 596-A, WHCF, HSTL; and White to Niles, 11 June 1951, in "Civil Rights and Negro Affairs, 1949–1952," Niles Papers, HSTL. See also Berman, *Politics of Civil Rights*, and Bernstein, "Ambiguous Legacy."

64. See memoranda in "Civil Rights Legislation," Civil Rights File, Spingarn Papers, HSTL, and in "Civil Rights," Clifford Files, SMOF, HSTL.

65. Spingarn's father, Arthur, had served the association as both president and chairman of the board of directors. His Uncle Joel succeeded his father as president in 1939 and was still serving in that capacity at the time of his appointment.

66. On congressional relations in general, see the oral histories of David Bell, 203; Joseph G. Feeney, 30–31; Martin L. Friedman, 15–16; and Stephen Spingarn, 200–204. On civil rights in particular, see the oral histories of Philleo Nash, 583–90, and Spingarn, 202–4, 220. All in HSTL.

67. Hamby, *Man of the People*, 492–94, and Robert J. Donovan, *Tumultuous Years: The Presidency of Harry S. Truman, 1949–1953* (New York: Norton, 1982), 118–19.

68. Morse to Walter White, 5 May 1948, NAACP Papers, pt. 9, reel 7; "Remarks to a Delegation from the National Emergency Civil Rights Mobilization Conference," 17 January 1950, *Public Papers: Truman, 1950*, 115.

69. Bernstein, "Ambiguous Legacy," 304.

70. McCoy and Ruetten, *Quest and Response*, 352.

71. This contrasts of course to its endorsement of the similar project of DuBois twenty-five years earlier. Memorandum to the Board from the Secretary, Board Meeting, 14 May 1945, NAACP Papers, pt. 1, reel 3.

72. For exceptions, however, see Report of Secretary, September 1945 Board Meeting; Report of Washington Bureau, February 1946 Board Meeting—both in NAACP Papers, pt. 1, reel 7. See also the addresses of O'Brien Boldt, Daniel E. Byrd, and Archibald Carey Jr., 1946 Annual Conference, NAACP Papers, pt. 1, reel 11; and that of Roy Wilkins, 1950 Annual Conference, NAACP Papers, pt. 1, reel 12.

73. White address, 30 June 1946, 1946 Annual Conference, NAACP Papers, pt. 1, reel 11.

74. Christopher Parker's coding of Chicago *Defender* editorials between 1941 and 1953 is generally in agreement with this conclusion. He finds that military service frames steadily declined in prominence throughout the period, while "justice and equality" and "democratic ideals" as well as "world opinion" grew increasingly prevalent. See Parker, *Fighting for Democracy: Race, Service to the State, and Insurgency during Jim Crow*, unpublished ms., Department of Political Science, University of California, Santa Barbara, 2005.

75. Louis T. Wright address, 1947 Annual Conference; Resolutions, 1948 Annual Conference—both in NAACP Papers, pt. 1, reel 12.

76. Robert K. Carr and Frances H. Williams to PCCR Subcommittee No. 2, 28 February 1947, in "Civil Rights and Negro Affairs, 1945–June 1947 (1)," Niles Papers, HSTL.

77. Statement of Grant Reynolds, 30 March 1948, Senate Committee on Armed Services, *Hearings on Universal Military Training*, 80th Congress, 2nd session, 678; Resolution, Board Meeting Minutes, 11 September 1950, NAACP Papers, pt. 1, reel 3.

78. White, 1952 Annual Convention Speech, in *In Search of Democracy: The NAACP Writings of James Weldon Johnson, Walter White, and Roy Wilkins, 1920–1977*, ed. Sondra Kathryn Wilson (New York: Oxford University Press, 1999), 285; White, *How Far the Promised Land?* (New York: AMS Press, 1973 [1955]). For other examples, see, among others, Dudziak, *Cold War Civil Rights*; Brenda Gayle Plummer, *Rising Wind: Black Americans and U.S. Foreign Policy, 1935–1960* (Chapel Hill: University of North Carolina Press, 1996), 83–216; and Rosenberg, *How Far the Promised Land?*

79. See Elazar Barkan, *The Retreat of Scientific Racism: Changing Concepts of Race in Britain and the United States between the World Wars* (Cambridge: Cambridge University Press, 1992).

80. David Plotke, *Building a Democratic Political Order: Reshaping American Liberalism in the 1930s and 1940s* (Cambridge: Cambridge University Press, 1996), 3. See also Bruce Ackerman, *We the People: Foundations* (Cambridge: Harvard University Press, 1991).

81. On wartime rhetoric, see Blum, *V Was for Victory*, 47–52; Gary Gerstle, *American Crucible: Race and Nation in the Twentieth Century* (Princeton: Princeton University Press, 2001), 192–201; Skrentny, *Minority Rights Revolution*, 21–57; and Allan M. Winkler, *The Politics of Propaganda: The Office of War Information, 1942–1945* (New Haven: Yale University Press, 1978), 38–72.

82. Robert B. Westbrook, "'I Want a Girl, Just Like the Girl That Married Harry James': American Women and the Problem of Political Obligation in World War II," *American Quarterly* 42, no. 4 (December 1990): 587–614; Westbrook, "Fighting for the American Family: Private Interests and Political Obligation in World War II," in *The Power of Culture: Critical Essays in American History*, ed. Richard Wightman Fox and T. J. Jackson Lears (Chicago: University of Chicago Press, 1993). See also Westbrook, *Why We Fought: Forging American Obligations in World War II* (Washington, D.C.: Smithsonian Books, 2004). On the difficulty of justifying obligation in a liberal state, see Michael Walzer, *Obligations* (Cambridge: Harvard University Press, 1970).

83. Race was central to the rhetoric of the Pacific War, but Americans nevertheless un-

derstood themselves to be at war with ideologies that divided the world into racial categories. Quoted in Robert B. Westbrook, "In the Mirror of the Enemy: Japanese Political Culture and the Peculiarities of American Patriotism in World War II," in *Bonds of
Affection: Americans Define Their Patriotism*, ed. John Bodnar (Princeton: Princeton University Press, 1996), 216. See also John Dower, *War without Mercy: Race and Power in the
Pacific War* (New York: Pantheon, 1986).

84. Hannah Arendt, *The Origins of Totalitarianism* (New York: Harcourt, Brace, 1951).
85. Richard A. Primus, *The American Language of Rights* (Cambridge: Cambridge University Press, 1999).
86. Louis Henkin, *The Age of Rights* (New York: Columbia University Press, 1990), 4–5.
87. "State of the Union Address," 7 January 1948, *Public Papers: Truman, 1948*, 3; "Address
at the Laying of the Cornerstone," 27 June 1950, *Public Papers: Truman, 1950*, 493–94.
88. White, "Fifty Years of Fighting," in *In Search of Democracy*, ed. Wilson, 274–77.
89. American Jewish Congress and NAACP, "Civil Rights in the United States in 1950:
A Balance Sheet of Group Relations," NAACP Papers, pt. 18, ser. C, reel 4.
90. PCCR, *To Secure These Rights*, 4; Hartz, *The Liberal Tradition in America* (San Diego:
Harcourt Brace Jovanovich, 1991 [1955]). The PCCR report was also, however, a political document, and liberal frames sat alongside other, often very practical, arguments
on behalf of integration and the elimination of discrimination.
91. "PCCR—Correspondence: General, November–December 1947," NAACP Papers,
pt. 18, ser. C, reel 25.
92. On popular skepticism of liberalism in the North as well, see Thomas J. Sugrue,
"Crabgrass-Roots Politics: Race, Rights, and the Reaction against Liberalism in the Urban North, 1940–1964," *Journal of American History* 82, no. 2 (September 1995): 551–78.
93. Sen. Allen J. Ellender of Louisiana, University of Chicago Roundtable, "Should We
Adopt President Truman's Civil Rights Program?" 6 February 1949, 6–7; pamphlet, no
title, State Democratic Executive Committee of Alabama—both in Nash Papers, box 36,
HSTL.
94. American Jewish Congress and NAACP, "Civil Rights in the United States in 1950."
95. Gov. William M. Tuck, radio address, n.d., in "PCCR—Correspondence: General,
January–March 1948," NAACP Papers, pt. 18, ser. C, reel 26.
96. Robert F. Burk, *The Eisenhower Administration and Black Civil Rights* (Knoxville: University of Tennessee Press, 1984); Michael S. Mayer, "The Eisenhower Administration
and the Desegregation of Washington, D.C.," *Journal of Policy History* 3 (1991): 24–41;
and Mayer, "With Much Deliberation and Some Speed: Eisenhower and the *Brown* Decision," *Journal of Southern History* 52 (February 1986): 43–76.
97. Powell, "The President and the Negro," *Reader's Digest* (October 1954), reprinted in
The Papers of Dwight David Eisenhower—The Presidency: The Middle Way, ed. Louis
Galambos and Daun Van Ee (Baltimore: Johns Hopkins University Press), 15:1342.
98. 24 July 1953 Diary Entry, Diary—Copies of DDE Personal 1953–54 (2), Box 4, DDE
Diary Series, Eisenhower Papers, DDEL; State of the Union address, *Public Papers of the
Presidents of the United States: Dwight D. Eisenhower, 1953*, 12–34. See also "Extempora-
neous Remarks by the President at the National Conference on Civil Rights," 9 June
1959, Box 829, PPF 47, WHCF, DDEL.
99. Riley, *The Presidency and the Politics of Racial Inequality: Nation-Keeping from 1831 to
1965* (New York: Columbia University Press, 1999), 10.
100. Niles to Truman, 11 April 1946, in "Civil Rights and Negro Affairs, 1945–June 1947
(2)," Niles Papers, HSTL.
101. PCCR, *To Secure These Rights*, 100–101; "Address before NAACP," 29 June 1947, *Public Papers: Truman, 1947*, 312; "Special Message to Congress on Civil Rights," 2 February 1948, *Public Papers: Truman, 1948*, 126; quoted in Jonathan Daniels, *The Man of
Independence* (Philadelphia: J. B. Lippincott, 1950), 336.

102. Ellen Schrecker, *Many Are the Crimes: McCarthyism in America* (Boston: Little, Brown, 1998). See also, among others, Skrentny, *Minority Rights Revolution*, 66–72.

103. The NAACP's own postmortem noted "a type of extra-sensitivity as to who is a 'red' or a fellow traveler." See Board Meeting Minutes, 14 February 1950, NAACP Papers, pt. 1, reel 3, and Wilkins to Clifford, 20 December 1949, in "National Emergency Civil Rights Mobilization," OF 596–B, WHCF, HSTL.

104. Wilkins, *Standing Fast*, 210. Such concerns began to be voiced regularly in NAACP board meetings as early as 1947; see NAACP Papers, pt. 1, reel 3. See also Carol Anderson, "Bleached Souls and Red Negroes: The NAACP and Black Communists in the Early Cold War, 1948–1952," in *Window on Freedom: Race, Civil Rights, and Foreign Affairs, 1948–1988,* ed. Brenda Gayle Plummer (Chapel Hill: University of North Carolina Press, 2003).

105. See A. Philip Randolph to George M. Houser, 13 July 1948, CORE Papers, 3:3, reel 8, and "Statement on the Communist Issue," Tenth Annual Convention and Action Conference, 1952, CORE Papers, 3:31, reel 10.

106. Erving Kingsley, "Comments on 5th Draft of Civil Rights Message," n.d., in "President's Committee on Civil Rights," Elsey Files, SMOF, Truman Papers, HSTL.

107. Clifford to Truman, 19 November 1947, in "Confidential Memo to the President [Clifford-Rowe memorandum of November 19, 1947 (1)]," Political File, Clifford Papers, HSTL.

108. NAACP publicist Henry Lee Moon published a book that year entitled *Balance of Power: The Negro Vote* (Garden City, N.Y.: Doubleday, 1948), and Walter White forwarded a copy to Truman; see White to Truman, 20 May 1948, PPF 93, Truman Papers, HSTL.

109. McGrath quoted in McCullough, *Truman*, 713.

110. Diary, 2 February 1948, in *Off the Record: The Private Papers of Harry S. Truman*, ed. Robert H. Ferrell (New York: Harper and Row, 1980), 122; Clifford, *Counsel to the President*, 204–5, 209; Nash Oral History, 331–32.

111. Quoted in McCullough, *Truman*, 638–40. See also Nash Oral History, 333–40.

112. Karabell, *Last Campaign*, 154.

113. Milton D. Stewart to George M. Elsey, 19 January 1948, in "President's Committee on Civil Rights," Elsey Files, SMOF, Truman Papers, HSTL.

114. Samuel Lubell, *The Future of American Politics* (New York: Harper, 1952).

115. Berman, *Politics of Civil Rights*, 129–30.

116. McCoy and Ruetten, *Quest and Response*, 352.

117. Dudziak, *Cold War Civil Rights*.

118. John Lewis Gaddis, *Strategies of Containment: A Critical Appraisal of Postwar American National Security Policy* (New York: Oxford University Press, 1982), 30–31, 41–42, 58–65; Melvyn Leffler, *A Preponderance of Power: National Security, the Truman Administration, and the Cold War* (Stanford: Stanford University Press, 1992); and Wilson D. Miscamble, *George F. Kennan and the Making of American Foreign Policy, 1947–1950* (Princeton: Princeton University Press, 1992), 349–50.

119. See Biondi, *To Stand and Fight*, chaps. 7–8; Dudziak, *Cold War Civil Rights*, 61–77; and Penny M. Von Eschen, *Race against Empire: Black Americans and Anticolonialism, 1937–1957* (Ithaca: Cornell University Press, 1997), chaps. 5–6.

120. Plotke, *Building a Democratic Political Order*, 14–22; Linda K. Kerber, "The Meanings of Citizenship," *Journal of American History* 84, no. 3 (December 1997): 835–36.

121. The bond between military service and citizenship was somewhat loosened, however, as Congress passed a law in 1943 enabling conscientious objectors to apply successfully for citizenship. Shortly after the war, the Supreme Court reversed its earlier decisions denying citizenship to applicants unwilling to serve in the armed forces. See James Burk, "The Military Obligation of Citizens since Vietnam," *Parameters* 31, no. 2 (Summer 2001): 48–60.

122. David R. B. Ross, *Preparing for Ulysses: Politics and Veterans during World War II* (New York: Columbia University Press, 1969), 105.

123. Koppes and Black, "Blacks, Loyalty, and Motion-Picture Propaganda," 390; Westbrook, "In the Mirror of the Enemy," 228–30; and Westbrook, "Fighting for the American Family," 207, 211–12, 215–21.

124. See Mark H. Leff, "The Politics of Sacrifice on the American Home Front in World War II," *Journal of American History* 77, no. 4 (March 1991): 1296–1318; and Leff, "Home-Front Mobilization in World War II: American Political Images of Civil Responsibility," in *Regional Conflicts and Conflict Resolution: Essays in Honor of Jeremiah D. Sullivan*, ed. Roger E. Kanet (Urbana-Champaign: University of Illinois, Program in Arms Control, Disarmament, and International Security, 1995).

125. Steven F. Lawson, *Black Ballots: Voting Rights in the South, 1944–1969* (New York: Columbia University Press, 1976), 66.

126. Quoted in McCullough, *Truman*, 588. See also Letter, 18 August 1948, in *Off the Record*, ed. Ferrell, 147; and Truman to Tom Clark, 20 September 1946, in "Civil Rights and Negro Affairs, 1945–June 1947 (2)," Niles Papers, HSTL.

127. Statement, 5 December 1946, reproduced as preface to PCCR, *To Secure These Rights*.

128. However, unlike other veterans' groups, the American Veterans Committee shied from exploiting its members' service records. Had it done so, perhaps it would have escaped some persecution. Second, unlike most mainstream civil rights organizations, the AVC actually was dominated by Communist Party members and fellow travelers. See Robert Francis Saxe, "'Citizens First, Veterans Second': The American Veterans Committee and the Challenge of Postwar 'Independent Progressives,'" *War & Society* 22, no. 2 (October 2004): 75–94.

129. Theodore Spaulding to Truman, 9 December 1946, in "PCCR—Correspondence: General, 1946–Oct. 1947," NAACP Papers, pt. 18, ser. C, reel 25.

130. The narrative of this brief case study draws freely, except where otherwise noted, on Roger Daniels, *Asian America: Chinese and Japanese in the United States since 1850* (Seattle: University of Washington Press, 1988); Daniels, *The Politics of Prejudice: The Anti-Japanese Movement in California and the Struggle for Japanese Exclusion* (Berkeley: University of California Press, 1978); Bill Hosokawa, *Nisei: The Quiet Americans* (New York: William Morrow, 1969); Hosokawa, *JACL: In Quest of Justice* (New York: William Morrow, 1982); and Robert A. Wilson and Bill Hosokawa, *East to America: A History of the Japanese in the United States* (New York: William Morrow, 1980).

131. See Roger Daniels, *Concentration Camps, U.S.A.: Japanese Americans and World War II* (New York: Holt, Rinehart and Winston, 1972); Peter Irons, *Justice at War: The Story of the Japanese Internment Cases* (New York: Oxford University Press, 1983); Greg Robinson, *By Order of the President: FDR and the Internment of Japanese Americans* (Cambridge: Harvard University Press, 2001); and Page Smith, *Democracy on Trial: The Japanese-American Evacuation and Relocation in World War II* (New York: Simon and Schuster, 1995).

132. Quoted in Daniels, *Asian America*, 223.

133. Quoted in Hosokawa, *Nisei*, 361; quoted in Hosokawa, *JACL*, 199.

134. Eric L. Muller, *Free to Die for Their Country: The Story of Japanese-American Draft Resisters in World War II* (Chicago: University of Chicago Press, 2001).

135. See Thomas D. Murphy, *Ambassadors in Arms: The Story of Hawaii's 100th Battalion* (Honolulu: University of Hawaii Press, 1954), and Orville C. Shirey, *Americans: The Story of the 442nd Combat Team* (Washington, D.C.: Infantry Journal Press, 1947).

136. Wilson and Hosokawa, *East to America*, 280. See Masaoka testimony before U.S. Senate, Subcommittee of the Committee on the Judiciary, *Hearings on H.R. 3999* (unpublished, microfilm), 80th Cong., 2nd sess., 21 May 1948.

137. *They Work for Victory: The Story of Japanese Americans and the War Effort* (Salt Lake City: JACL, 1945), 3.

138. Quoted in Hosokawa, *Nisei*, 410–11.

139. U.S. House of Representatives, Judiciary Committee, *Authorizing the Attorney General to Adjudicate Certain Claims Resulting from Evacuation of Certain Persons of Japanese Ancestry under Military Orders,* 80th Cong., 1st sess., 1947, report no. 732.

140. McCloy testimony before U.S. Senate, Subcommittee of the Committee on the Judiciary, *Hearings on H.R. 3999* (unpublished, microfilm), 80th Cong., 2nd sess., 21 May 1948.

141. Leslie T. Hatamiya, *Righting a Wrong: Japanese Americans and the Passage of the Civil Liberties Act of 1988* (Stanford: Stanford University Press, 1993); Robert Sadamu Shimabukuro, *Born in Seattle: The Campaign for Japanese American Redress* (Seattle: University of Washington Press, 2001).

142. Hastie address, 1949 Annual Convention, NAACP Papers, pt. 1, reel 12; Kenworthy to Eric Sevareid, quoted in Steven R. Goldzweig, "Civil Rights and the Cold War: A Rhetorical History of the Truman Administration's Desegregation of the United States Army," in *Doing Rhetorical History: Concepts and Cases,* ed. Kathleen J. Turner (Tuscaloosa: University of Alabama Press, 1998), 165; Fairclough, *Better Day Coming,* 189.

143. McCoy and Ruetten, *Quest and Response,* 129; Dalfiume, *Desegregation,* 226; Philip A. Klinkner with Rogers M. Smith, *The Unsteady March: The Rise and Decline of Racial Equality in America* (Chicago: University of Chicago Press, 1999), 233–34. See also Kenneth L. Karst, "The Pursuit of Manhood and the Desegregation of the Armed Forces," 38 *UCLA Law Review* 499 (1991): 522.

144. Even as ardent a segregationist as Secretary of the Army Kenneth Royall admitted that "I am not seriously concerned about disloyalty or subversive activities among the Negroes." However, insofar as Royall and others truly believed that racial integration would undermine military effectiveness, the move would have *some* expected strategic cost. Royall testimony, 26 April 1948, "National Defense Congress on Negro Affairs (1948)," Niles Papers, HSTL.

145. Kenneth M. Birkhead to William L. Batt Jr., 21 May 1948, in "Civil Rights and Negro Affairs, 1949–1952," Niles Papers, HSTL; clippings in "Minorities-Negro-organizations-NAACP-news clippings, 1945–1947," Nash Papers, HSTL. See also Berman, *Politics of Civil Rights,* 65–66, and McCoy and Ruetten, *Quest and Response,* 53, 73–74.

146. Erving Kingsley, "Comments on 5th Draft of Civil Rights Message," n.d., in "President's Committee on Civil Rights," Elsey Files, Truman Papers, HSTL.

147. White, news release, 3 April 1952, in "1945–49," OF 413, WHCF, HSTL; Wilkins to Truman, 12 January 1953, in "Civil Rights (July 1950–53)," OF 596, WHCF, HSTL; Wilkins to Charles P. Howard, 4 January 1949, in "Truman, Harry S., 1946–1949," NAACP Papers, pt. 18, ser. C, reel 31.

148. Rep. Vito Marcantonio, quoted in Berman, *Politics of Civil Rights,* 170.

149. Although Truman's advisers named civil rights as a key piece of his legacy, the only tangible accomplishment they have pointed to is military desegregation. See the oral histories of David Bell, Clark Clifford, Matthew Connelly, Donald Dawson, and Stephen Spingarn—all in HSTL.

150. Quoted in McCoy and Ruetten, *Quest and Response,* 105. See also Berman, *Politics of Civil Rights,* 122–23, and David Niles to Truman, "Public Interest in the President's Civil Rights Program," 16 February 1948, in "Civil Rights—Program—Public Interest," Nash Files, SMOF, HSTL.

151. Addresses of Walter White and Roy Wilkins, 1948 Annual Conference, NAACP Papers, pt. 1, reel 12; White to Clyde R. Miller, 1 March 1948, in "PCCR—Correspondence: General, January–March 1948," NAACP Papers, pt. 18, ser. C, reel 26.

152. See Donald S. Dawson to Truman, 9 September 1948, in "President's Committee on Equality and Opportunity in the Armed Forces (1948–April 1950)," OF 1285–O, WHCF, HSTL; and David Niles to Clark Clifford, 8 September 1948, in "July 1948–June 1949 (1)," OF 93–B, WHCF, HSTL.

153. For a more complete discussion, see Ronald R. Krebs, "Rights and Gun Sights: Mil-

itary Service and the Politics of Citizenship," PhD diss., Columbia University, 2003, 443–49.

154. Kenworthy, oral history interview, 22, HSTL.

155. Although one might argue that Truman's executive order was largely the product of black political pressure, one cannot make the same argument regarding the implementation of that order and the subsequent desegregation of the armed forces. Thus, as I have configured the case, it does not suffer from a potential endogeneity problem.

156. See, for example, David Niles to Truman, 5 October 1949, and Niles to Truman, 7 February 1950—both in "Civil Rights and Negro Affairs, 1949–1952," Niles Papers, HSTL; Niles to Truman, 22 May 1950, in "Correspondence," Nash Files, SMOF, HSTL.

157. Dalfiume, *Desegregation*, 178–79; "January 12, 1949, Meeting with the President," in Fahy Committee Meetings, Fahy Committee Records, RG 220, HSTL; Marx Leva, Oral History Interview, 92, HSTL.

158. See Fahy's accounts of his meetings with Truman in Fahy, Memorandum for the Files, 7 June 1949, in "Correspondence Referred to the Committee Chairman by the Executive Secretary," Fahy Papers, HSTL; and with Philleo Nash in Fahy, Memorandum for the President's Committee, 17 November 1949, in "Memoranda for the Fahy Committee," Fahy Committee Documents/Miscellaneous, Fahy Committee Records, RG 220, HSTL.

159. Dalfiume, *Desegregation*, 200. In general, on the Fahy Committee, see Dalfiume, *Desegregation*, chap. 9; Sherie Mershon and Steven Schlossman, *Foxholes and Color Lines: Desegregating the U.S. Armed Forces* (Baltimore: Johns Hopkins University Press, 1998), chap. 8; and Nalty, *Strength for the Fight*, 242–54.

160. Hastie, Oral History Interview, 77–78, HSTL; Wilkins to Truman, 12 January 1953, in "Civil Rights (July 1950–53)," OF 596, WHCF, HSTL; White to Roderick Stephens, 16 May 1952, NAACP Papers, pt. 18, ser. B, reel 14; outline of Report to Annual Meeting, 4 January 1954, NAACP Papers, supplement to pt. 1, reel 2.

161. Johnson, "Three Achievements and Their Significance," in *The Crisis Reader: Stories, Poetry, and Essays from the N.A.A.C.P.'s Crisis Magazine*, ed. Sondra Kathryn Wilson (New York: Modern Library, 1999), 392–93.

162. An important exception was Ella Baker, who served as the NAACP's director of branches in the mid-1940s and resigned from the association in part out of frustration with the leadership's lack of attention to local organization. See Joanne Grant, *Ella Baker: Freedom Bound* (New York: Wiley, 1998), and Barbara Ransby, *Ella Baker and the Black Freedom Movement: A Radical Democratic Vision* (Chapel Hill: University of North Carolina Press, 2003).

163. See Herbert Shapiro, *White Violence and Black Response: From Reconstruction to Montgomery* (Amherst: University of Massachusetts Press, 1988), and Stewart E. Tolnay and E. M. Beck, *A Festival of Violence: An Analysis of Southern Lynchings, 1882–1930* (Urbana: University of Illinois Press, 1995).

164. "Address to the Nation," n.d., NAACP Papers, pt. 1, reel 23. See also Robert W. Bagnall, "The Present South," in *The Crisis Reader*, ed. Wilson, 394–99.

165. Statement and Testimony of J. Edgar Hoover, Proceedings of the Committee, 20 March 1947, PCCR Papers, reel 5; PCCR, *To Secure These Rights*, 20–24, 26, 100, 126.

166. Summary of Minutes, 1954 CORE Convention, CORE Papers, 1:23, reel 2; Wilkins, "The War against the United States," *Crisis*, December 1955, in *In Search of Democracy*, ed. Wilson, 368.

167. Gerald Rosenberg, *The Hollow Hope: Can Courts Bring about Social Change?* (Chicago: University of Chicago Press, 1991), 134–38, at 137.

168. William H. Chafe, *Civilities and Civil Rights: Greensboro, North Carolina, and the Black Struggle for Freedom* (New York: Oxford University Press, 1980).

169. On Walter White and other black elites' discomfort with mass action and the masses,

see Kenneth R. Janken, *White: The Biography of Walter White, Mr. NAACP* (New York: New Press, 2003), xiv, 150, 153, 217–19, 371 and passim.

170. See Taylor Branch, *Parting the Waters: America in the King Years, 1954–1963* (New York: Simon and Schuster, 1988); Steven F. Lawson, *Running for Freedom: Civil Rights and Black Politics in America since 1941* (New York: McGraw-Hill, 1991); Aldon D. Morris, *The Origins of the Civil Rights Movement: Black Communities Organizing for Change* (New York: Free Press, 1984); and Robert Weisbrot, *Freedom Bound: A History of America's Civil Rights Movement* (New York: Norton, 1990).

Part II. Conclusion

1. Quoted in David W. Blight, "'For Something beyond the Battlefield': Frederick Douglass and the Struggle for the Memory of the Civil War," in *Memory and American History,* ed. David Thelen (Bloomington: Indiana University Press, 1990), 31, 43.

2. James W. Button, *Blacks and Social Change: Impact of the Civil Rights Movement in Southern Communities* (Princeton: Princeton University Press, 1989), 223–39.

Chapter 8. Unusual Duties, Usual Rights: Soldiering and Citizenship

1. See Elizabeth Kier, "Homosexuals in the U.S. Military: Open Integration and Combat Effectiveness," *International Security* 23, no. 2 (Fall 1998): 5–39; Aaron Belkin, "Don't Ask, Don't Tell: Is the Gay Ban Based on Military Necessity?" *Parameters* 33, no. 2 (Summer 2003): 108–19; and Belkin and Melissa Sheridan Embser-Herbert, "Privacy as a Flawed Rationale for the Exclusion of Gays and Lesbians from the U.S. Military," *International Security* 27, no. 2 (Fall 2002): 178–97.

2. The irony is that prior to the eruption of this debate, gay rights leaders saw other issues—most notably, AIDS treatment and research—as more pressing. For most gay activists, "the whole issue of gays and lesbians in the military seemed to come out of right field, or at least out of the conservative wing of the gay movement." Nevertheless, they swiftly embraced the powerful symbolism of military service. See Timothy Haggerty, "History Repeating Itself: A Historical Overview of Gay Men and Lesbians in the Military before 'Don't Ask, Don't Tell'," in *Don't Ask, Don't Tell: Debating the Gay Ban in the Military,* ed. Aaron Belkin and Geoffrey Bateman (Boulder, Colo.: Lynne Rienner, 2003), 10.

3. See Urvashi Vaid, *Virtual Equality: The Mainstreaming of Gay and Lesbian Liberation* (New York: Doubleday, 1995), 148–77, and Jacob Weisberg, "Torch Song Strategy," *New Republic,* 9 August 1993, 11–14.

4. For a similar interpretation, see Belkin and Bateman's introduction to *Don't Ask, Don't Tell,* 3–4, and Kenneth L. Karst, "The Pursuit of Manhood and the Desegregation of the Armed Forces," 38 *UCLA Law Review* 499 (1991): 499–581.

5. "Don't Speak Its Name," *National Review,* 9 August 1993, 13–14; Raspberry, "Threatened by Cultural Change," *Washington Post,* 3 February 1993.

6. "Cross Purposes," *Nation,* 9–16 August 1993, 1; Richard D. Mohr, "Military Disservice," *Reason,* August–September 1993, 42–44; Sullivan, "The Politics of Homosexuality," *New Republic,* 10 May 1993, 24–32.

7. In fact, the military's stop-loss order did not apply to discharge for reasons of sexual orientation. See Michelle Locke, "Prospect of War Brings Military Policy on Gays 'Into Sharper Focus,'" Associated Press, 13 October 2001, available at http://www.sldn.org/templates/press/record.html?section=5&record=423.

8. Sullivan, "Our War Too: Gay Heroes, and Gay Necessities" (PlanetOut.com, 21 September 2001), http://www.andrewsullivan.com/homosexuality.php?artnum= 20010921.

9. Hintze, "Military Organization and the Organization of the State," in *The Historical Essays of Otto Hintze*, ed. Felix Gilbert (New York: Oxford University Press, 1975), 181.

10. Maureen Swan, *Gandhi: The South Africa Experience* (Johannesburg: Ravan Press, 1985), 89.

11. Of course many groups, for various reasons, have not found this route attractive and have shown little interest in military service. See Cynthia H. Enloe, *Ethnic Soldiers: State Security in Divided Societies* (Athens: University of Georgia Press, 1980), 186–99.

12. Notable exceptions include Stanislav Andreski, *Military Organization and Society* (London: Routledge, 1968); Everett Carl Dolman, *The Warrior State: How Military Organization Structures Politics* (New York: Palgrave Macmillan, 2004); and Charles Tilly, *Coercion, Capital, and European States, A.D. 990–1992* (Oxford: Blackwell, 1992).

13. Republican theory, which prizes individual freedom from domination, provides no justification for such discrimination, and it sees civic participation as a means to this end, rather than as an end in itself. Nevertheless, I appropriate the language of republicanism to capture a citizenship discourse that is both deeply civic and deeply participatory. On republicanism, see Philip Pettit, *Republicanism: A Theory of Freedom and Government* (Oxford: Clarendon Press, 1997).

14. The strategy may, however, still be costly in two ways. First, when one seeks to create the foundation for republican claims-making by encouraging military service, one puts at risk the lives of young people (usually young men) in one's community. Second, the leaders of claimant groups may find it politically costly as they build expectations for meaningful progress that are likely to be disappointed.

15. For a similar argument, see John David Skrentny, *The Minority Rights Revolution* (Cambridge: Harvard University Press, 2002).

16. Dankwart Rustow, "Transitions to Democracy: Toward a Dynamic Model," *Comparative Politics* 2, no. 3 (1970): 350.

17. Juan Linz and Alfred Stepan, *Problems of Democratic Transition and Consolidation* (Baltimore: Johns Hopkins University Press, 1996).

18. The concern—not only among communitarians—with the decline of civil society in the United States reflects this. For the seminal work, see Robert D. Putnam, *Bowling Alone: The Collapse and Revival of American Community* (New York: Simon and Schuster, 2000).

19. For good collections, see Amitai Etzioni, ed., *The Essential Communitarian Reader* (Lanham, Md.: Rowman and Littlefield, 1998), and Daniel Bell, ed., *Communitarianism and Its Critics* (New York: Oxford University Press, 1993).

20. Communitarianism is rooted in the Aristotelian "positive liberty" tradition, which values democratic participation as the most genuine form of freedom; republicanism draws from a "negative liberty" tradition that values democratic participation as a means to the end of nondomination. Communitarianism is deeply particularistic, defining its membership narrowly in terms of a historically grounded community; republicanism is fundamentally inclusive, basing its membership on the boundaries of the political community. Finally, communitarianism, following Aristotle, presumes moral beings with determined ends; republicanism like liberalism, adopts no set view of "the good." See Pettit, *Republicanism*; Quentin Skinner, "The Republican Ideal of Political Liberty," in *Machiavelli and Republicanism*, ed. Gisela Bock et al. (Cambridge: Cambridge University Press, 1997); and Maurizio Viroli, *Republicanism* (New York: Hill and Wang, 2002).

21. See also Will Kymlicka and Wayne Norman, "Return of the Citizen: A Survey of Recent Work on Citizenship Theory," *Ethics* 104, no. 2 (January 1994): 352–81, and Morris Janowitz, "Observations on the Sociology of Citizenship: Obligations and Rights," *Social Forces* 59, no. 1 (September 1980): 1–24.

22. See Pettit, *Republicanism*, 138–46.

23. Ironically, it served as the basis for denying Jews full citizenship after the French Rev-

olution: impartiality and universality were the recognized bases for political life, and the Jews lacked a key "universal property"—that is, military service. See Jon Elster, "Strategic Uses of Argument," in *Barriers to Conflict Resolution*, ed. Kenneth J. Arrow et al. (New York: Norton, 1995), 245.

24. On national service, see E. J. Dionne Jr. et al., eds., *United We Serve: National Service and the Future of Citizenship* (Washington, D.C.: Brookings Institution Press, 2003), and Williamson M. Evers, ed., *National Service: Pro and Con* (Stanford: Hoover Institution Press, 1990).

25. See, for example, Gretchen Ritter, "Of War and Virtue: Gender, Citizenship, and Veterans' Benefits after World War II," *Comparative Social Research* 20 (2002): 201–26.

26. See, among many other texts, David Held et al., *Global Transformations: Politics, Economics, and Culture* (Stanford: Stanford University Press, 1999).

27. See Björn Hettne, "The Fate of Citizenship in Post-Westphalia," *Citizenship Studies* 4, no. 1 (2000): 35–46; Jürgen Habermas, "Citizenship and National Identity," in his *Between Facts and Norms: Contributions to a Discourse Theory of Law and Democracy* (Cambridge: MIT Press, 1996); and Andrew Linklater, "Citizenship and Sovereignty in the Post-Westphalian State," *European Journal of International Relations* 2 (1996): 77–103.

28. Hoffmann, "Obstinate or Obsolete? The Future of the Nation-State and the Case of Western Europe," *Daedalus* 95, no. 3 (1966): 862–916.

29. Paul Hirst and Grahame Thompson, *Globalization in Question: The International Economy and the Possibilities of Governance* (Cambridge: Polity Press, 1996).

30. David Scobey, "The Specter of Citizenship," *Citizenship Studies* 5, no. 1 (2001): 14.

31. Anne Norton, *Reflections on Political Identity* (Baltimore: Johns Hopkins University Press, 1993 [1988]).

32. See David Miller, "Bounded Citizenship," in *Cosmopolitan Citizenship*, ed. Kimberly Hutchings and Roland Dannreuther (New York: St. Martin's Press, 1999), and Herman R. van Gunsteren, "Admission to Citizenship," *Ethics* 98, no. 4 (July 1988): 731–41.

33. Richard Falk, "The Decline of Citizenship in an Era of Globalization," *Citizenship Studies* 4, no. 1 (2000): 6, 10.

34. See, for example, Martin Shaw, "Theses on a Post-Military Europe: Conscription, Citizenship, and Militarism after the Cold War," in *Social Change and Political Transformation*, ed. Chris Rootes and Howard Davis (London: UCL Press, 1994). See also Elliott Abrams and Andrew J. Bacevich, "A Symposium on Citizenship and Military Service," *Parameters* 31, no. 2 (Summer 2001): 18–22; Eliot A. Cohen, "Twilight of the Citizen-Soldier," *Parameters* 31, no. 2 (Summer 2001): 23–28; and Matthew J. Morgan, "The Reconstruction of Culture, Citizenship, and Military Service," *Armed Forces and Society* 29, no. 3 (Spring 2003): 373–91.

35. Press conference, 11 October 2001, http://www.whitehouse.gov/news/releases/2001/10/20011011-7.html.

36. See Charles C. Moskos et al., eds., *The Postmodern Military: Armed Forces after the Cold War* (New York: Oxford University Press, 2000), and Karl W. Haltiner, "The Decline of the European Mass Armies," in *Handbook of the Sociology of the Military*, ed. Giuseppe Caforio (New York: Kluwer Academic, 2003). See also Edward N. Luttwak, "Toward a Post-Heroic Warfare," *Foreign Affairs* 74, no. 3 (May–June 1995): 109–22, and Eliot A. Cohen, "A Revolution in Warfare," *Foreign Affairs* 75, no. 2 (March/April 1996): 37–54.

37. Robert Jervis, "Theories of War in an Era of Leading-Power Peace," *American Political Science Review* 96, no. 1 (March 2002): 1–14.

38. Francis Fukuyama, *The End of History and the Last Man* (New York: Free Press, 1992).

39. Herfried Münkler, *The New Wars* (Cambridge: Polity Press, 2005).

40. Edward Hallett Carr, *The Twenty Years' Crisis, 1919–1939: An Introduction to the Study of International Relations*, 2nd ed. (London: Macmillan, 1951), 215.

41. For a similar point, see Daniel Moran, "Introduction: The Legend of the *Levée en Masse*," in *The People in Arms: Military Myth and National Mobilization since the French*

Revolution, ed. Daniel Moran and Arthur Waldron (Cambridge: Cambridge University Press, 2003).

42. James Burk, "The Military Obligation of Citizens since Vietnam," *Parameters* 31, no. 2 (Summer 2001): 48–60.

43. See Peter D. Feaver, "Civil-Military Relations," *Annual Review of Political Science* 2 (1999): 211–41.

44. On the end of the cold war, see, among others, Stephen G. Brooks and William C. Wohlforth, "Power, Globalization, and the End of the Cold War: Reevaluating a Landmark Case for Ideas," *International Security* 25, no. 3 (Winter 2000–01): 5–53; Robert D. English, "Power, Ideas, and New Evidence on the Cold War's End: A Reply to Brooks and Wohlforth," *International Security* 26, no. 4 (Spring 2002): 70–92; Brooks and Wohlforth, "From Old Thinking to New Thinking in Qualitative Research," *International Security* 26, no. 4 (Spring 2002): 93–111; and Nina Tannenwald and William C. Wohlforth, eds., *Ideas, International Relations, and the End of the Cold War,* special issue of the *Journal of Cold War Studies* 7, no. 2 (Spring 2005). On chemical weapons, see Richard M. Price, *The Chemical Weapons Taboo* (Ithaca: Cornell University Press, 1997), and Michael C. Desch, "Culture Clash: Assessing the Importance of Ideas in Security Studies," *International Security* 23, no. 1 (Summer 1998): 141–70.

Index

Acheson, Dean, 153
Adeimantus, 23
African Americans in U.S.
  citizenship claims of, 28
  and Civil War, 18
  failure of claims-making, 132–34
  and military service, 147–49, 184
  post-WWII demographics, 153
  post-WWI mobilization strategy of, 41
  quiescence of, 142–43
  rights' struggle, 119–20
  and Truman administration, 172
all-volunteer force
  and clarity of signal, 33
  U.S. military, 13, 188
American Expeditionary Forces (AEF), 126,
  141
Americans for Democratic Action, 164
Amsterdam News, 148
Anderson, Benedict, 11
Anti-Lynching Conference (1921), 176
Arab citizens of Israel, 44–45
  Christians and Muslims, 44–45
  compared to Druze, 46–49, 53–55, 61–62,
    67–68, 91–93, 104–5, 109–13
  and contentious politics, 86–87
  defined, 215n3, 215n12
  discrimination against, 55–62
  effects of 1948 War, 55, 61
  exemption from military, 45
  framing choices of, 102
  and IDF exclusion policy, 62–64, 86–87,
    92–93
  institutionalization, 87–88
  Jewish distrust of, 72
  and late mobilization, 84–89, 228n88

as national minority, 88, 90
in new State of Israel, 69
protests, 1950s and 1960s, 84
1954 registration law, 62
rights, early 60s, 74
second intifada, 107–8
and separationist goals, 89–91, 110–13
1980s gains, 104–5
Arab Department, Likud party, 105
Arabic language, early Israel, 57
Arab Revolt, 52
Arabs of Palestine
  Mandate period, 51
  post-Arab Revolt, 54
argumentative self-entrapment, 23
Ashkenazim, 45
  at Israel's birth, 44
Atashe, Zeidan, 82, 102
availability of military manpower signal, 33.
  See also signal strength

Balad party, 90
Baltimore *Afro-American*, 124
Barak, Ehud, 98
Barakat, Reuven, 62
Ben-Dor, Gabriel, 78
Ben-Dor Committee, 80
Ben-Gurion, David, 44, 67, 69
  on Arab citizens, 57
  on Arab-free Israel, 59
  citizenship promises of, 102, 103
  preference for Druze, 60, 61
  proclamation of statehood, 55–56
  rights discourse of, 97
  on the "yishuv," 51, 52
Berem. *see* Ikrit and Berem conflict